T0181558

Dynamics AX

A Guide to Microsoft Axapta

Luis X. B. Mourão
and David Weiner

Apress®

Dynamics AX: A Guide to Microsoft Axapta

Copyright © 2006 by Luis X. B. Mourão and David Weiner

ISBN: 978-1-4842-2013-9   ISBN: 978-1-4302-0078-9 (eBook)

DOI 10.1007/978-1-4302-0078-9

Lead Editor: Tony Davis
Technical Reviewers: Richard Banham, Ramprasad Sandilya
Editorial Board: Steve Anglin, Dan Appleman, Ewan Buckingham, Gary Cornell, Tony Davis, Jason Gilmore, Jonathan Hassell, Chris Mills, Dominic Shakeshaft, Jim Sumser
Associate Publisher: Grace Wong
Project Manager: Sofia Marchant
Copy Edit Manager: Nicole LeClerc
Copy Editors: Candace English, Ami Knox
Assistant Production Director: Kari Brooks-Copony
Production Editor: Ellie Fountain
Compositor and Artist: Kinetic Publishing Services, LLC
Proofreader: Elizabeth Berry
Indexer: Brenda Miller
Interior Designer: Van Winkle Design Group
Cover Designer: Kurt Krames
Manufacturing Director: Tom Debolski

Distributed to the book trade worldwide by Springer-Verlag New York, Inc., 233 Spring Street, 6th Floor, New York, NY 10013. Phone 1-800-SPRINGER, fax 201-348-4505, e-mail orders-ny@springer-sbm.com, or visit http://www.springeronline.com.

For information on translations, please contact Apress directly at 2560 Ninth Street, Suite 219, Berkeley, CA 94710. Phone 510-549-5930, fax 510-549-5939, e-mail info@apress.com, or visit http://www.apress.com.

The source code for this book is available to readers at http://www.apress.com in the Source Code section.

Contents at a Glance

About the Authors xv

About the Technical Reviewer xvii

Acknowledgments xix

Introduction xxi

■ **CHAPTER 1**   What Is Axapta? 1

■ **CHAPTER 2**   Axapta Installation 11

■ **CHAPTER 3**   Configuration and Post-Installation 33

■ **CHAPTER 4**   Navigation and User Options 71

■ **CHAPTER 5**   Administration 89

■ **CHAPTER 6**   Human Resources 127

■ **CHAPTER 7**   Finance 137

■ **CHAPTER 8**   Inventory Management 151

■ **CHAPTER 9**   Trade 165

■ **CHAPTER 10**   Manufacturing 183

■ **CHAPTER 11**   Master Planning 193

■ **CHAPTER 12**   CRM 205

■ **CHAPTER 13**   Project 217

■ **CHAPTER 14**   Reporting and Business Analysis 227

■ **CHAPTER 15**   Integration APIs 237

■ **CHAPTER 16**   Enterprise Portal 255

■ **CHAPTER 17**   Architecture 273

■ **CHAPTER 18**   Development 309

■ **CHAPTER 19**   Data and Databases 355

■ **CHAPTER 20**   X++ 375

■ **CHAPTER 21**   Deployment 393

■ **APPENDIX A**   Documentation 423

■ **APPENDIX B**   Command-Line Parameters 429

APPENDIX C   Module Summaries 435

APPENDIX D   Keyboard Shortcuts 441

APPENDIX E   License Codes 449

APPENDIX F   Codes and Mappings 453

APPENDIX G   Database Compatibility 459

INDEX 461

Contents

About the Authors xv

About the Technical Reviewer xvii

Acknowledgments xix

Introduction xxi

CHAPTER 1   What Is Axapta? 1

Highlights 2
A Brief History 2
Technology and Architecture Overview 3
The Development Environment 4
Application Layers 4
3-Tier Architecture. 5
Modules. 5
The Base Package 6
Business Applications 6
Web Applications 8
Wrap-Up 9

CHAPTER 2   Axapta Installation 11

Meeting Axapta Hardware and Software Requirements. 11
General Recommendations 12
Minimum Requirements 12
Setting Up the Database. 15
Performing a New Axapta Installation 16
Accessing Axapta Documentation. 17
Installing Axapta 3.0 18
Modifying Axapta 28
Upgrading Axapta 29
Installing Hotfixes and Service Packs 30
Wrap-Up 31

■CHAPTER 3   **Configuration and Post-Installation** 33

Configuration Tools 34
2-Tier Configuration 34
    General Configuration 35
    Client Configuration 38
    Database Configuration 39
    SQL Server Configuration 42
    Oracle Configuration 45
    Tracing Configuration 47
    Business Connector 49
Managing Configurations 52
Post-Installation 54
    Compile Application 55
    License Information 56
    Configuration 57
    Adjust Global Types 58
    Synchronize 59
    Initializing the Help System 59
    Update Cross-Reference 60
    Authorization 62
3-Tier Configuration 63
    Server Manager 63
    3-Tier Client 66
Demo Data 69
Wrap-Up 69

■CHAPTER 4   **Navigation and User Options** 71

The Axapta Desktop 71
    The Title Bar 72
    The Menu Bar 73
    The Toolbar 76
    The Main Menu 77
    The Status Bar 78
Forms, Dialogs, and Reports 78
    Forms 79
    Dialogs 82
    Reports 83
Searching and Filtering 85
Shortcut Keys 86
Wrap-Up 87

CHAPTER 5   Administration 89

Authentication 90
    Overview 90
    Authenticating Users in an AOS 90
Codes and Keys 93
    License Codes 94
    Configuration Keys 96
    Security Keys 97
Authorization 97
    Domains 98
    Virtual Company Accounts 99
    Company Accounts 100
    User Groups 101
    Users 104
    Password Parameters 110
    Record-Level Security 111
Maintenance Tasks 112
    Online Users 112
    E-mail 112
    Log System 114
    Batch Jobs 116
    Data Maintenance 118
    Backups 120
Wrap-Up 124

CHAPTER 6   Human Resources 127

Setup 127
    The Employee Form 128
    The Network Form 130
    The Organization Form 130
    The Skill Types and Skills Forms 131
    The Loan Types and Loan Items Forms 132
    Recruitment 133
Wrap-Up 135

CHAPTER 7   Finance 137

Setup 137
    Dimensions 138
    Financial Periods 140

Currency 141
Chart of Accounts. 143
Journals. 144
Sales Tax 145
System Accounts 146
Customer and Vendor Groups 147
Customer and Vendor Records 148
Posting Profiles. 148
Processes 149
Wrap-Up 149

CHAPTER 8   Inventory Management 151

Setup 152
Item Type. 152
Item Group 153
Inventory Model Group 154
Dimension Group 155
Item Dimensions 157
Warehouses 158
Serial/Batch Number. 160
Processes 160
Inventory Closing and Adjustment 161
Inventory Journals 162
Wrap-Up 163

CHAPTER 9   Trade 165

Setup 165
Trade Agreements 165
External Item Numbers 172
Processes 173
Wrap-Up 181

CHAPTER 10   Manufacturing 183

Setup 183
Bill of Materials (BOM) 184
Work Center Groups and Work Centers 185
Operations. 186
Routes 188

Processes 189
    Production Orders 189
    Journals. 191
Wrap-Up 191

CHAPTER 11 **Master Planning**. 193

Setup. 193
    Coverage Groups 194
    Item Coverage 195
    Forecast Models. 197
    Item Allocation and Period Allocation 197
    Forecasts. 199
    Production Scheduling 200
    Forecast and Master Plans. 201
Processes 202
    Safety Stock Journals. 202
    Forecast Scheduling 203
    Master Scheduling. 203
Wrap-Up 204

CHAPTER 12 **CRM**. 205

Setup. 207
    Business Relations 207
    Contact Persons. 209
    Quotations. 211
    Activities 214
Processes 215
    Workbook 215
Wrap-Up 216

CHAPTER 13 **Project** 217

Setup. 218
    Prices. 218
    Line Property 219
    Journals. 220
    Project Groups 220
    Ledger Posting 222
    Categories and Category Groups 222

Processes 224
Wrap-Up 225

▪CHAPTER 14   **Reporting and Business Analysis** 227

Setup 228
    Business Analysis 228
Processes 231
    Business Analysis 231
    Auto-Report. 232
    Report Wizard 234
Wrap-Up 236

▪CHAPTER 15   **Integration APIs** 237

Journals 238
Module APIs 242
    General Ledger. 243
    Trade Series 243
    Warehouse Management 244
    Production. 245
    Number Sequences 245
Business Connector 246
Microsoft .NET 249
Commerce Gateway 252
Wrap-Up 253

▪CHAPTER 16   **Enterprise Portal** 255

Basics 256
    Internet Information Services. 256
    Web Users. 257
    Web Sites 258
Enterprise Portal 261
    Setup 261
    Roles 263
Content Management 264
    Parameters 264
    Categories. 264
    News Articles 265
    Polls 267
Wrap-Up 270

CHAPTER 17   Architecture 273

    Applications, Clients, and Servers 274
        2-Tier Setup 274
        3-Tier Setup 275
        Multiple-Client Setups 278
        Multiple-AOS Setups 279
        Multiple-Application Setups 281
    Folders and Files 282
        Application 283
        Client 287
        Server 289
        Log Files 290
    Application Layers 292
        Patch Layers 295
    Working Environment 296
        Development 296
        Test 298
        Production 299
    Runtime and Development Codes 300
    Internationalization 301
    Caching 304
        Record Caching 304
        Full Table Caching 305
        Record View Caching 307
        Read-Ahead Caching 307
    Wrap-Up 307

CHAPTER 18   Development 309

    IntelliMorph 311
    MorphX 315
        Labels 317
        The Project Tool 320
        The Application Object Tree 326
        Application Object Types 332
        Help System 344
    X++ 345
        The X++ Editor 345
        The Compiler 348
    Debugging 349

Web Applications 352
Best Practices 352
Wrap-Up 353

▪CHAPTER 19   **Data and Databases** 355

Flat Files 355
Data Dictionary 356
Database Connections 361
Administration 362
Programming 368
Transactions 368
Performance 368
System Variables 369
Database Limitations 370
Database Differences 370
Import and Export 371
Wrap-Up 372

▪CHAPTER 20   **X++** 375

Elements of X++ 376
Data Types 376
Operators. 378
Expressions. 378
Variables 379
Classes 379
Methods. 382
Statements 384
Macros. 390
Wrap-Up 391

▪CHAPTER 21   **Deployment**. 393

Sizing. 393
System Design. 395
Bandwidth. 396
Latency 396
Benchmarking 398

Performance 410
Distribution 415
    The Web Deployment Client 416
    Distributing Customizations 420
Wrap-Up 421

APPENDIX A **Documentation** 423

APPENDIX B **Command-Line Parameters** 429

APPENDIX C **Module Summaries** 435

APPENDIX D **Keyboard Shortcuts** 441

APPENDIX E **License Codes** 449

APPENDIX F **Codes and Mappings** 453

APPENDIX G **Database Compatibility** 459

INDEX 461

About the Authors

Until September 2004, **LUIS MOURÃO** was the Axapta Kernel Software Development Engineering Manager within Microsoft Business Solutions. He managed partnerships with HP, Oracle, Intel, and others. He also certified Axapta for the respective platforms and participated in research and development.

At Microsoft, he was the Copenhagen campus representative for Microsoft Training and Education, he led initiatives for Axapta integration with Microsoft platforms, and he received a Microsoft Gold Star Award for Engineering Excellence.

DAVID WEINER is the Axapta Practice Manager of Cole Systems Associates, a leading NYC Microsoft Gold partner. David is best known for his ability to partner with his clients to understand their business processes and gain operational efficiencies. David has consulted on and managed Axapta implementations in the US and internationally. As a Microsoft Axapta Certified Master of Application, David has in-depth knowledge of Axapta and holds six Axapta-specific certifications. In addition to Axapta, David has years of experience working with other business applications and custom development of eCommerce-related software. David is a PMP-certified project manager.

About the Technical Reviewer

RICHARD L. BANHAM JD, CPA, PhD., has served as chief accountant and Vice President of Technology for a manufacturing firm. In the early '80s, his consulting firm automated claim handling for oil overcharge accounting firms working with the Department of Energy. He has also participated in the design and development of integrated accounting and management systems for small businesses. In fall of 2002, his consulting firm associated with Great Plains, where he became a Certified Master in 2003 prior to switching his focus to Axapta. A faculty member at Tennessee State University, he teaches accounting information systems at the undergraduate and graduate levels. He has recently deployed a 100-user version of Axapta, which TSU is currently incorporating into its accounting, marketing, supply chain, and MBA curricula.

Acknowledgments

Thanks to all the folks who have contributed to making this book come together: Sofia Marchant, Tony Davis, Candace English, Ami Knox, Richard Banham, Ramprasad Sandilya, and Ellie Fountain. Thanks to all my friends and colleagues who have reviewed my work and provided feedback, especially Aura Buison and Laura Miller. Most importantly, thanks to Luis Mourão for bringing me with him on this journey, and for his brilliant work toward this project. Without this remarkable group this book would never have been possible.

I'd also like to thank the people who have inspired and influenced my career over the years: Tim Krammer, Jeff Palley, Mike Forte, Ross Riviere, and Ivan Cole. Without these people in my life I would not be where I am today.

Thanks to the best group of friends a guy could ever have (6669 team, LA crew; you know who you are), and specifically Connor, who has encouraged and put up with me through the writing of this book. Finally, my deepest appreciation goes to my family, mom and dad, Josh, Papa Max, and Nana; words cannot describe what you mean to me.

David Weiner

I would like to thank all the people at Apress that David has already mentioned, without whose exercise of patience and support the book wouldn't have been possible. A special thanks to David Weiner, my coauthor, who quietly endured my running off in all directions when I should have been writing this book, and without whose contribution the book would not be what it is.

A great thanks also goes to my manager, Henrik Danielsen, at WM-data in Aarhus, Denmark and Mike Gillis at Iteration2 in Irvine, California in the USA, who allowed me to write the book in spite of being short of people; and to the Axapta teams at both companies for everything I learned from them, in particular Nat Bui, Søren Boelt, Linda Kunze, Gert Christiansen, Chris Chase, Alan Dasca and Simon Chan. Two great companies with some amazingly nice people.

Thanks also to the Microsoft Business Solutions Axapta kernel development team in Vedbæk, Denmark, who really got me going with Axapta; and particularly my product unit manager Hans Jørgen Skovgaard and the campus VP and manager Niels Bo Theilgaard, who hired me and let me get away with my truant ways; and finally David Greenspoon and Hal Howard at Microsoft Business Solutions in Redmond, Washington for offering help with the book and great references.

Last but not least, my warmest thanks to my family, Lene, Thomas, Ana, and Miguel, for being cool and putting up with me with a smile while I was writing this book in the little free time I had, and in general for making everything a lot of fun even while working 32-hour days.

Luis X. B. Mourão

Introduction

Axapta is Microsoft's flagship ERP system and the most exciting ERP product currently on the scene. If Axapta hasn't come to a computer near you yet, it will soon.

Note This book is based on Axapta version 3.0. Shortly before this book went to press, Microsoft announced that Axapta was to be rebranded as Dynamics AX. Axapta and Dynamics AX are one and the same product, and in this book we consistently use the term Axapta because that is the term that will be commonly used in the field for the near future.

We'd like to start by offering the most valuable piece of advice we have for anyone working with Axapta (and with any complex system, for that matter): Keep it simple. Implement it in clearly defined and documented increments. For business consultants, architects, and developers we would add this: stick to standards whenever possible, develop simple solutions, and keep the code simple and well-commented.

We hope you will find learning Axapta to be a thrilling experience. As you progress through the book you'll find clear instructions for getting started with the various modules, along with numerous techniques and strategies for getting the most out of them. There is no better way to learn than to see the thing working for yourself, so whether you're a developer, architect, business decision maker, or end user, the first thing you'll want to do is get the system installed and running so you can work through the examples as you read the book. Hopefully, you will experience that great "aha!" feeling as things fall into place and you start to become productive with the technology.

We have packed a tremendous amount of value into this book and we hope it will help you be successful with Microsoft Axapta.

Why Read This Book?

The purpose of this book is to get you started with Microsoft Axapta—one of the world's leading ERP solutions. To be more precise, the purpose is to get you started quickly and without spending thousands of dollars, man weeks of training, and a lot of time and effort hunting around for and reading what is often redundant and/or useless product documentation (we've listed useful documentation where applicable).

This book covers the essentials of Axapta from A to Z, including the following:

- Installing and configuring the environment

- Navigating the application and development environments

- Setting up the applications and tools delivered in the standard package

- Customizing applications and creating your own

Last but not least, the book includes a comprehensive set of appendixes that you'll find very useful on a day-to-day basis.

After reading this book, you will have a comprehensive understanding of the product, and what it can do for you and your business or organization. You will know how it works and how to use and leverage it in practice, with a particular focus on how to adapt and extend it to fit your own business needs.

Axapta is a large business system and we can't walk you through every nook and cranny. This means that we have had to prioritize and make some tough decisions about what to include and what to leave out. We've tried to address the needs of as many people as possible by providing wide coverage and taking you as deep as you need to go to perform all of the most commonly required tasks. This book covers all the fundamental aspects of the product. After that, we provide advice as to how to proceed further on your own.

This book targets a wide audience, and various sections may be more interesting to you than others, depending on your role and on what you actually need to do with Axapta. Naturally, each function or role involved in an Axapta implementation has specific needs and a primary area of focus; however, a series of different people and skill sets are typically involved:

- Business decision makers who determine whether to use Axapta (or some other technology), and if so which business functions to automate, and how best to invest available resources.

- Business consultants who have to evaluate whether the product supports the necessary processes and, if not, what is missing and how to bridge the gaps.

- Developers who customize Axapta and fit it to the specific business needs of users and organizations. Their job is to develop new functionality, test it, distribute it, maintain it, and support it.

- System administrators who deploy Axapta systems, watch over them, upgrade them, patch them, and keep them running smoothly and uneventfully.

- End users who use Axapta as a tool to perform their jobs day in day out, who need it to work their way, to be easy and intuitive.

In other words, an Axapta system requires a cross-functional cooperative effort, so we recommend that you read even the chapters that are not of specific interest to you. An effective understanding of the system as a whole will make a real difference in the team's ability to communicate, set expectations, and ultimately implement Axapta in a way that meets the business's true needs.

Structure and Approach

This section provides an overview of how the book is organized. It will smooth your passage through the material that follows.

The book is organized sequentially into five main sections, each covering a particular area of Axapta functionality. These are followed by an extensive set of appendixes with reference information, lists, and tables.

- Chapter 1 provides a quick introduction to the strengths of Axapta, its history, its technology, and the functionality it provides out of the box.

- Chapters 2 through 5 are about getting Axapta up and running, navigating around the various tools and interfaces, and administering Axapta. Everyone should be sure to read Chapter 4; system administrators need to read all the chapters and try the stuff out; consultants and developers should read these chapters and consider trying things out for themselves.

- Chapters 6 through 14 describe how to set up the applications that comprise the standard package, and what they do. Business decision makers should read all the chapters to understand what business functionality Axapta allows them to automate out of the box; end users should read the chapters that fall within their respective functional areas and test the examples therein (they should also consider browsing chapters on functions with which they interface); consultants should follow the recommendations for end users, but also test out some of the modules in areas surrounding their core functions; developers and system administrators should acquaint themselves with all modules at the end-user level. These chapters follow a general pattern:

  - Basic setup

  - Business processes

  - Wrap-up

- Chapters 15 through 17 are about tools and technologies, and what you can do with them. Business decision makers and consultants should acquaint themselves with the possibilities these tools and technologies offer; system administrators should acquaint themselves with the tools and technologies, and in particular with their setups and the issues they raise for operations; developers need to clearly understand and experiment with the tools and technologies. These chapters have a slightly different structure than the previous ones:

  - Overview of each element of the technology and relevant tools

  - Wrap-up

- Chapters 18 through 21 are about development and various aspects of customizing the system and putting customizations into the hands of end users. Business decision makers should at least browse these and get a feeling for how to proceed when they need to go beyond what Axapta offers out of the box; consultants need to have a good understanding of these chapters to make sure they have realistic expectations and understand the costs associated with customizing Axapta one way instead of another; developers have to know this stuff in and out; system administrators and end users might browse these chapters if they are technically curious. These chapters often enumerate the capabilities with a short synopsis and examples in code where necessary and appropriate. They follow a pattern, as well:

- What you can do

- How to do it

- Wrap-up

- Appendixes A through G provide useful references in tabular format, such as command-line parameters and keyboard shortcuts.

▮**Note** All chapters aside from Chapter 1 include a list of documents provided with the Axapta product distribution, where you can read more on the topics covered. The file names on the product CD are meaningless; therefore we've included explanatory names as well so you can fire them up without having to use the rather cumbersome Axapta CD startup menu. The installation chapter describes where the documents included in the product CD are located and how to use the Axapta CD startup menu in case you decide to use it.

▮**Note** Before you can use a specific application module you must have a basic data set, without which the module is good for nothing. Naturally, because all modules have interdependencies, you also need to ensure that data is in place both for the modules you are working on and for the modules they depend on. Since interdependencies sometimes flow both ways and we must follow a sequence, you will not always be able to fully leverage a module until later, when data structures are set up in other modules. We flag such situations when they occur.

We hope this book will lower the learning curve for new Axapta practitioners and that old hands will find it a useful recap and reference.

Errata

We've made every effort to ensure that the text and the code in this book are accurate. However, to err is human, and this is a book about software after all! If you encounter any inaccuracies, please report them to us. Errata sheets are available at http://www.apress.com. If you find an error that hasn't already been reported, please let us know.

In addition, the Apress Web site includes the code from Apress books, sample chapters, previews of forthcoming titles, and articles on related topics.

CHAPTER 1

■ ■ ■

What Is Axapta?

Axapta is Microsoft's entry in the packaged business application market. It provides out-of-the-box functionality for managing your business or organization, including modules for every business area, from supply chain management (SCM) and financials to shop floor control and warehouse management.

■Note This book is based on Axapta version 3.0. Shortly before this book went to press, Microsoft announced that Axapta was to be rebranded as Dynamics AX. Axapta and Dynamics AX are one and the same product and in this book we consistently use the term Axapta, since this is the term that will be commonly used in the field for the near future.

The technology base of the Axapta system and its unique layered architecture make it the most modern within the enterprise resource planning (ERP) arena. It also confers a high degree of flexibility, allowing you to mix and match features and modules to create solutions that are finely tuned to your needs.

Axapta's integrated development and runtime environment combine technology and business applications into one highly integrated experience; the idea is to make it easy to work with across geographical regions, business sectors, businesses, and organizations, all the way down to the individual end users' preferences and needs.

This chapter covers the following topics:

- An introduction to Axapta's primary strengths

- A brief history of how the current Axapta product emerged, followed by a recap of Axapta product releases

- An overview of Axapta's development environment, unique layered architecture, and technology

- A listing of the functionality Axapta provides, what comes with the base package, and what is available to supplement the base package

Highlights

The following list summarizes Axapta's key strengths:

- *Ease of use*: Axapta relies on Microsoft standards and, for end users who are familiar with Microsoft Windows or Office, Axapta is easy to pick up.

- *Ease of customization*: Axapta is an ERP system that was designed to be customized.

- *Ease and speed of development*: Axapta combines an ERP with an open-source, object-oriented, rapid application development environment. This development environment is described in detail in Chapter 18.

- *Internationalization*: Axapta meets the legal and language requirements for 37 countries (and counting). It is therefore a good choice for companies operating in multiple countries, languages, and currencies. You can learn more about installing and configuring Axapta for multiple countries in Chapters 2 and 3, and about operating in multiple currencies in Chapter 7.

- *Integrated applications*: With many modules available and more on the way, Axapta allows you to run all of your business processes, no matter how complex. Chapters 6 through 13 cover all of the major modules available in Axapta.

- *Pricing*: Although Axapta has the power and functionality of a tier-one ERP system, it's priced well below its competitors. Software pricing alone can be half that of Axapta's competitors, and consultancy fees are significantly lower, as well, with a product-cost to consulting-cost ratio of 1: 1.5. If you consider that figures for major alternatives are in the millions of dollars, Axapta is a strong candidate for a business automation system, or for replacing or upgrading an existing system.

These points, in addition to extensive and comprehensive horizontal functionality out of the box, a rapidly growing offer of localized vertical solutions, and a significant and rapidly growing partner network, translate to low relative cost of ownership and excellent return on investment. Furthermore, to an end user, consultant, system administrator, or developer, they mean the highest productivity and the lowest learning curve of any ERP system on the market.

■**Note** Axapta's integrated development environment (IDE) and rapid application development (RAD) can seem unimpressive if you compare them with more-specialized development environments. Bear in mind, however, that in Axapta, the development environment is completely integrated into the ERP. It is this integration that makes Axapta unique and particularly powerful.

A Brief History

Danish company Damgaard A/S developed Axapta, and the first version was released in March 1998 in Denmark and the US. These days it's available in 45 languages, and its business solutions, partner, and customer base is growing quickly, making Axapta a major presence in the global ERP market. It's especially strong in the SME market and is advancing rapidly in the tier-one corporate accounts segment.

Its predecessor products, Concorde and XAL, go back to 1983, so although Axapta is a reasonably recent product by ERP standards, it is built on two decades of technology and business experience. It inherits heavily from these products and leverages their code bases, design, and functionality.

Axapta became part of the Business Solutions division of Microsoft when Microsoft acquired Navision A/S in 2002. The main steps leading to the current version of Axapta are as follows:

- March 1998: Release of version 1.0 in the US and Denmark. Version 1.0 included Finance, Trade, Inventory Management, Logistics, and Production modules, plus support for SQL Server 6.5 and Oracle 7.0.

- November 1998: Release of version 1.5, which added support for the Component Object Model (COM) calling interface, service pack technology, and support for Norway, Sweden, Germany, Britain, the Netherlands, Austria, Switzerland, Belgium, and Spain, and supported the Euro.

- July 1999: Release of version 2.0, which added, among other features, the Business Connector, ActiveX support, and an early release of Axapta Object Server (AOS). This was, consequently, the first 3-tier release.

- January 2000: Release of version 2.1. The first Windows logo–certified version of Axapta that also delivered support for interacting with Axapta from a Web client.

- December 2000: Release of version 2.5, which delivered a complete Web-development environment, the auto upgrade tool, support for online analytical processing (OLAP), and an application service provider (ASP) solution.

- October 2002: Release of version 3.0. This version represents a major technological leap and includes a new access control system. It also dropped feature keys, and delivered intercompany accounting and Enterprise Portal (EP).

- December 2002: Release of Service Pack 1 for version 3.0.

- October 2003: Release of Service Pack 2 for version 3.0.

- June 2004: Release of Service Pack 3 for version 3.0. This service pack contained over 1000 bug fixes and Dr. Watson support.

- May 2005: Release of Service Pack 4 for version 3.0. This service pack included major fixes to the inventory closing procedure, along with other functionality enhancements and performance improvements.

Axapta version 4.0 should hit the streets in the second quarter of 2006, bringing significant improvements in reliability, security, user experience, and functionality.

Technology and Architecture Overview

Being a Microsoft product, it's no surprise that Axapta is very comprehensively integrated with the Microsoft software stack. In particular, the financial management, customer relationship management, supply chain management, human resource management, project management, and analytics functionalities work seamlessly with Microsoft products such as SQL Server, BizTalk Server, Microsoft Exchange, Microsoft Office, and Microsoft Windows.

Axapta is built to be highly customized. The development environment and layered technology described later in this chapter set Axapta apart from its competition with regard to ease of customization. But although Axapta's layered architecture makes upgrades relatively easy, they can be very time-consuming if you have extensive customizations. As with other ERP systems, Axapta performs best in organizations that have relatively uniform processes and do not use extensive customizations.

Later chapters in this book will thoroughly explain Axapta's unique and cutting-edge technology and architecture; this chapter provides only a high-level look.

The Development Environment

Axapta's development environment is known as MorphX, an open-source, object-oriented (OO), integrated development environment (IDE). Its programming language is called X++ and is relatively easy to pick up if you're familiar with C#, Visual Basic, or Java. X++ uses OO principles such as inheritance, classes, objects, and methods. The environment is very intuitive and follows well-known Microsoft Windows standards (with a few exceptions), which makes it easy to learn. Axapta is customized using its development tools in exactly the same environment that end users work with; any difference between the development and run-time environments results from the features that are turned on or off and, consequently, the tools that are available. However, you must have licenses for the MorphX environment and X++ source code, and you must turn on X++ source access in your setup to develop. You can do a lot without coding, such as customizing what is displayed on forms and reports, and creating your own menus with only the functionality that you need and use. End users can make simple modifications and see the results right away.

Axapta consists of two distinct groups of functionality: the kernel (the technology base), and the application (the business logic and presentation). The kernel is written in C++ (though it contains parts written in X++) and delivered as a collection of Intel x86 machine binaries. The application is written in X++ and delivered in source and intermediate binary code forms. Since you get all the X++ source code, Axapta enables you to change anything in the application. It places approximately 1.2 million lines of source code at your fingertips that you can use and learn from.

Note The application also includes definitions for all types of objects, such as forms and reports (metadata). This metadata is not compiled to machine binaries, but instead persisted in source and intermediate binary form and used at run time to construct and render the respective object instances.

Application Layers

Axapta's eight application layers form a top-down hierarchy that enables customization or enhancements to be written at different levels. Having code at different layers in the application ensures that system modifications never interfere with application objects at a lower level. This layer technology, combined with Axapta's IDE, make Axapta the ultimate platform for customizations. The layers are described further in Chapter 17.

3-Tier Architecture

Axapta is a 3-tier product that implements the well-known Model-View-Controller architecture. The three tiers together consist of four components:

- A relational database for persisting data. It supports Microsoft SQL Server and the Oracle relational database management system (RDBMS), stand-alone or clustered, and is part of the data tier.

- The Axapta application files for persisting X++ source and intermediate binary code and metadata—generally called the Application or Application Server, and perceived as part of the data tier or the business logic tier.

- An object server where business logic is executed. This requires the installation of an AOS or a cluster of AOSs. This tier will often load and execute the Axapta application mentioned in the previous point.

- A client tier where the user interface resides and is executed. This can be the standard Axapta Windows client, a Web browser client, or any custom-developed application capable of acting as a COM client.

Within the 3-tier architecture Axapta enables both thin and fat clients. In a thin client configuration all processing occurs at the AOS, and the AOS communicates directly with the database server. This minimizes the client requirements and the traffic between client and server, making remote or WAN connections easy. Further, the thin clients can share the server's cache to improve performance. The fat client is useful when processing is client-centric; it is often used as a batch server, where large processes run on a high-power machine so as to not interfere with other clients' performance. Like a 2-tier client, the fat client communicates directly with the database server.

Axapta is not limited to 3-tier mode; it can also be deployed in a 2-tier mode where the client and application server tiers are merged, eliminating the AOS. It's an easier deployment architecture, and is necessary for your initial installation and configuration of Axapta. For scalability and security reasons, however, we don't recommend using 2-tier mode in production environments.

While the technology is very interesting, what is most useful is the business logic that lies on top and is implemented as a series of modules such as financials, human resources, etc. The business logic is contained in the application mentioned earlier in this chapter, and consists of definitions of all the objects that allow you to enter and output data, as well as the code to process it. We'll cover these topics in the next section.

Modules

Axapta has a breadth of functionality that matches many tier-one products. Do not let the short list of modules mislead you—Axapta has fewer modules then other ERP systems, but packs more functionality per module.

The application modules are made up of a base package that constitutes the foundation of the product, and three main functional groups:

1. *Financial Management (FIN)*: All modules related to the financial management of enterprises—general ledger, banking, fixed assets, etc.

2. *Supply Chain Management (SCM)*: All modules dealing with distribution, manufacturing, inventory, and logistics—trade, production, shop floor control, warehouse management, etc.

3. *Professional Services Administration (PSA)*: All modules that support service functions and organizations—project accounting, customer relationship management (CRM), human relations (HR), balanced scorecard, business process management, business analysis, etc.

The Base Package

The base package includes a required foundation that consists of the following:

- One user.

- Three company accounts, generally consisting of the following:

    - A demo account, which can be used for testing and training purposes (testing can also be performed safely by duplicating the application and database).

    - A DAT account, which is used to store non-company-specific data, such as user permissions.

    - A company data account that you create yourself, representing your specific business. The account holds all your businesses data and your users will work in it.

- Three dimensions (see Chapter 7).

- An unlimited number of virtual companies.

- One language. Additional languages can be licensed as needed, and the same system can use different languages for different users depending on their personal setups and preferences.

- A visual menu and form designer.

- One Microsoft Axapta AOS.

By acquiring additional company account licenses you can manage multiple companies from within the same system and you can share data between them by including shared tables in a "virtual company." For example, you can place a currency-exchange-rate table in a virtual company to share exchange-rate data with any number of other company accounts, or you can share customer and vendor records across multiple companies. Any changes to a virtual company table are instantly reflected in all companies with which the virtual company shares data.

Business Applications

Most users care only about out-of-the-box functionality for managing their business or organization. Table 1-1 provides an overview of the modules that Microsoft Business Solutions (MBS) includes with Axapta, and their interdependencies. Chapters 6 through 13 describe the most commonly used modules in detail. For an in-depth listing of what each module includes, however, consult your local Microsoft partner or the Microsoft Axapta Web site (www.microsoft.com/businesssolutions/axapta/default.mspx).

Table 1-1. *Axapta 3.0 Modules and Their Dependencies*

Functional Group	Module	Dependency
Finance	Financials I	N/A
	Financials II	Financials I
	Electronic Banking	Financials I
	Fixed Assets	Financials I
SCM	Trade	Financials I
	Trade Agreements	Trade
	Intercompany	Trade Agreements
	Logistics	Trade
	Product Builder I	Logistics
	Product Builder II	Product Builder I and Production II
	Product Builder III	Product Builder I
	Product Builder IV	Product Builder I and X++ Source Code
	Production I	Logistics and Master Planning
	Production II	Resources and Production I
	Production III	Production II
	Master Planning	Trade
	Resources	Production II and/or Project I
	Shop Floor Control I	Production I and/or Project I
	Shop Floor Control II	Shop Floor Control I
	Shop Floor Control III	Shop Floor Control I
	Warehouse Management I	Logistics
	Warehouse Management II	Warehouse Management I
PSA-PA (Project Accounting)	Project I	Trade, Resources, and Logistics (optional)
	Project II	Project I
CRM	Sales Force Automation	Financials I
	Sales Management	Sales Force Automation
	Marketing Automation	Sales Force Automation
	Telemarketing	Sales Force Automation
HR	HR I	Financials I
	HR II	HR I
	HR III	HR I and HR II
Others	Balanced Scorecard	Financials I
	BPM	Financials I

(Continued)

Table 1-1. (*Continued*)

Functional Group	Module	Dependency
	Questionnaire I	N/A
	Questionnaire II	N/A
	Business Analysis	N/A

Web Applications

Axapta has several modules that enable commerce and trading via the Internet. The first of these is the Enterprise Portal, which enables a large part of Axapta's out-of-the-box functionality to be executed via the Web. For standard Web functionality, EP is a cost-effective and easy to deploy Web portal for both internal (employee) and external (customers and vendors) access.

The Commerce Gateway is Axapta's link directly into the Microsoft BizTalk server (currently the Commerce Gateway works only with BizTalk 2002). BizTalk enables the electronic exchange of documents such as purchase orders and sales orders between business partners.

Note Axapta was not developed with the Web in mind; it was an afterthought. The Axapta team could not ignore the Web and its impact on the business scene, and thus extended the development environment, the tools, and a large application that exposes much of Axapta's functionality to the Web. If you are looking for more advanced functionality and don't want to stay within the boundaries of EP and the Axapta Web development environment, we recommend you get some good developers to build your Web portal in ASP.NET by using the Business Connector as a pipeline to the functionality and data in Axapta. For a more in-depth discussion, consult Chapters 15 and 16.

Table 1-2 provides an overview of the Web modules you get from MBS, and their interdependencies.

Table 1-2. *Axapta Web Modules and Their Dependencies*

Functional Group	Module	Dependency
EP	Enterprise Portal Framework	Enterprise Web users and minimum of one COM client; all modules require the Enterprise Portal Framework
	Employee Role	
	Sales Representative Role	Trade Agreements, Logistics, and Project I (optional)
	Customer Role	Logistics
	Vendor Role	Trade Agreements
	Consultant	Project I
	Questionnaire	Questionnaire I

Functional Group	Module	Dependency
	Human Resources	Employee Role, Human Resource Management I, Human Resource Management II (optional), and Human Resource Management III (optional)
	CRM	Sales Representative Role and Sales Force Automation
	Product Builder	Customer Role and Product Builder I
	Performance Management	Employee Role and Balanced Scorecard
Commerce Gateway	Commerce Gateway	Trade, Microsoft BizTalk Server 2002, Microsoft SQL Server
Developer Tools	Web MorphX Development Suite	Windows MorphX Development Suite

Wrap-Up

You now have a pretty good idea of what Axapta is and what it can do. This chapter covered the following topics:

- Axapta's strengths and advantages

- How Axapta got to where it is

- The technology behind the product

- What functionality Axapta offers out of the box

The next step is to install Axapta and figure our how to exploit all these features yourself.

CHAPTER 2

■■■

Axapta Installation

The first step in getting to know Axapta is installing it. If you are an end user or business decision maker, you might question the value of reading this chapter. In fact, often we meet consultants who work with Axapta on a daily basis but have never installed it. We even know system administrators and developers who feel uncomfortable with installing Axapta. This is no surprise—it's a complex product, with a complex installation procedure that is essential to get right.

However, we suggest that you read this chapter regardless of your relationship with Axapta. Working through the installation process is a quick and simple way to get an understanding of how the different software pieces fit together, and of their possibilities and limitations.

This chapter covers the following topics:

- An overview of the hardware and software you need to install and use Axapta

- Database setup requirements

- Axapta installation on a new or clean system

- Modifying an existing installation

- The upgrade process and issues

- Service packs and hotfixes

Ideally, you have a clean computer available so that you can actually work through this Axapta installation and all subsequent examples throughout the book. We recommend that you install, use, develop, upgrade, patch, and uninstall Axapta a few times—practice makes perfect.

Meeting Axapta Hardware and Software Requirements

Axapta itself is made up of three logical software components that are installed individually:

- Axapta client

- Axapta application

- Axapta Object Server (AOS)

These can be installed in different combinations; for example, on the same physical computer system or distributed across different physical systems. As with any software package, Axapta has minimal requirements for the underlying hardware and software infrastructure. Furthermore, Axapta needs an operating system and a relational database, which, of course, have their own requirements.

■**Note** We do not take the requirements of the operating system or database you select into consideration here. Refer to the respective product documentation for those requirements, and read Chapter 21 of this book, which covers deployment, for a comprehensive overview of what you need to consider and for sizing guidelines.

General Recommendations

If you are a developer, system administrator, or a technically minded consultant installing a demo system, we recommend the following:

- Windows XP Professional, at least for the machines on which you plan to install server components.

- A minimum of an Intel Pentium III–class 1GHz CPU or equivalent AMD; an Intel Pentium 4 is best. An Intel Pentium II–class CPU will tax your patience and take the fun out of learning Axapta.

- A minimum of 512MB RAM—more is better, particularly on the systems where you plan to install server components.

- A decent 17-inch screen. We recommend the largest screen you can get your hands on. If you are a developer, having a system with two 19-inch screens is really great when you need to debug and/or run other applications, like Visual Studio, side by side with Axapta.

- At least 10GB of hard disk space, depending on how many companies and databases you will be setting up. The more drive space, the better.

If you can afford the luxury, then we also recommend a networked sandbox with two or even three machines, where you can experiment with installing different components on different machines, and later running code on the client or server side.

■**Note** The previous recommendations do not cover the requirements for the Axapta Web-based client, Enterprise Portal. They are covered in Chapter 15.

Minimum Requirements

While we highly recommend that you get a setup that resembles the one suggested in the previous section, in real life the majority of people working with Axapta are customers—i.e., end users—who have neither the need nor the motivation to throw out their existing hardware and software for the sake of Axapta. Let's face it—they are not likely to recompile the system, resynchronize the application with the database, install new languages, and so on. Even on a production system, setting up Axapta will normally be done by a system administrator at off-peak hours.

End users not only can live with significantly less, but they must do so. And, for that matter, so can you. Therefore, it's important for you to know what issues you need to consider and the strict minimum requirements before you actually begin installing Axapta.

However, be aware that the following list is only a reference. Do not attempt to size a solution without reading Chapter 21, which covers deployment and includes sizing guidelines. And even then, we suggest that you not deploy your solution without an experienced developer or consultant to review your sizing recommendations the first couple of times.

- *Operating systems*: Windows XP, Windows NT 4.0 Service Pack (SP) 6a, Windows 2000, Windows 2003, Windows 98. The Axapta Object Server requires the ability to run a Windows service, which excludes Windows 98 for the server. Windows 98 systems can be used as clients, but Windows 98 support is, for all practical purposes, discontinued by Microsoft Business Solutions. Actually, it was discontinued and then revived because of the installed base of clients, but it is not likely to be supported in Axapta 4.0. We highly recommend not using Windows 98. For the same reasons, we highly recommend not using Windows NT 4.

- *Client hardware*: Current minimum hardware requirements for a client are officially 233MHz, 64MB RAM, 10Mbps network connection, or ISDN. Microsoft Business Solutions does not state which CPU it is referring to in the clock frequency specification. In practice, a low-end Intel Pentium II will do, but make sure you have at least 128MB RAM.

- *Database*: Stand-alone database server hardware sized according to the database of your choice—Microsoft SQL Server or Oracle—and the level of optimization desired. We also recommend the latest service pack. This system is either accessed directly by the Axapta clients or Axapta Object Servers that use it to persist data. Business applications are typically data-bound, so you need to pay particular attention to throughput, disk space scalability, network accessibility and latency, uptime, and data security. Make sure someone who understands database performance and reliability configures this server for you. It's wise to use multiple arrays and channels.

- *Axapta application server*: This is basically a file server where you can install as many Axapta application environments as you like. For example, developers typically have one for each customer, since customer-specific customizations must be maintained separately. So, you need to consider the same characteristics as those for a database: throughput, disk space scalability, network accessibility and latency, uptime, and data security. The data on this server is stored directly in the file system, so get the fastest hard disks you can afford.

- *Axapta Object Server*: This is the server that executes code on behalf of clients operating in 3-tier mode and communicates with the database system for thin clients. You can have multiple AOSs in a clustered environment. One of your AOSs will also need to run a server manager that takes care of starting up servers as required, grouping servers in clusters, and performing a simple round-robin form of load balancing. You need to keep in mind throughput, network accessibility and latency, uptime, and CPU power, as these nodes crunch through much of the interpreted X++ code and metadata definitions of your system on behalf of Axapta clients, as well as data access in the case of thin clients in 3-tier mode. Often, customers will choose to combine their application server and AOS into one server.

- *Testing or development server*: For this server, you should take into account all of the recommendations made for the preceding servers. It can also act as a redundant AOS, application, or database server in the case of a major failure.

Note In Axapta, you can install as many applications as you need on the same physical system. You can use the configuration tool and exported configuration files to manage what gets started where and when. Applications can either be loaded directly by clients running in 2-tier mode or by AOSs when running in 3-tier mode.

MICROSOFT-RECOMMENDED SYSTEM SETUP

Microsoft suggests the setup shown in the following table for an installation of the whole Axapta suite on a single machine in a light environment, which they define as the following:

- Only the Financial and Production modules are used.

- The system has between 1 and 15 concurrent users.

- Reports are requested only irregularly.

- The system processes a maximum of 500 transactions per day.

- Data import is minimal or performed at off hours.

- There is a dedicated SQL Server machine.

Hardware	Requirements
CPU	Pentium III 1.1 GHz or higher
Hard Disks	Minimum: 6–9. RAID 5 for OS, logs, and SQL data files Recommended: 8 or 9. 1GB RAID 1 for OS and logs, RAID 5 for SQL data files
RAM	Minimum: 512 MB Recommended: 1GB
CD-ROM	Any
Network Card	32-bit, 10/100 MB Ethernet full duplex

Note that you may not actually need the "required" CD-ROM and network card. The CD-ROM drive requirement assumes that you have no alternative way of get the content to the target machine, and the network card requirement assumes that Ethernet is your only option.

There you have it. The list is short and quite complete. However, because of the many possible deployment scenarios that Axapta supports, very little beyond the client is predefined. What is important is that you now understand that identifying the requirements for an Axapta installation is a complex subject and varies from installation to installation. If you want to really understand how all the pieces fit together and the many ways Axapta can be and is installed in the field, finish reading this chapter. Then read Chapter 17 to learn about the architecture, and Chapter 21 for deployment details before continuing to Chapter 3.

Setting Up the Database

Axapta requires that you have installed and have access to a version of either the Oracle or Microsoft SQL Server RDBMS that is supported by your version of Axapta. If you plan to use the Axapta Business Analysis functionality, you need to install Microsoft Analysis Services SP3a, which is typically included with the SQL Server distribution package. You can theoretically use Business Analysis with Oracle—but, good luck! In practice, Oracle's implementation of OLAP differs from Microsoft's, which Axapta is developed against, so typically, Oracle houses install SQL Server and Analysis Services to support the Business Analysis functionality of Axapta.

■**Note** Microsoft Business Solutions maintains a database-compatibility matrix at its PartnerSource portal at www.microsoft.com/BusinessSolutions/partnersource.mspx. However, you need to be a partner to consult it. For your convenience, we have included a database-compatibility matrix in Appendix F of this book.

Make a full, plain-vanilla installation of your preferred database on your playground system so that you can get started. If you will be using a separate physical machine for your database server in your test environment, remember that clients running in 2-tier or 3-tier fat mode access the database directly, and therefore circumvent the AOS. In this scenario, make sure you have installed the appropriate client drivers to communicate with your database.

Here are a few quick notes regarding a SQL Server setup:

- Make sure you are set up for mixed mode authentication, as shown in Figure 2-1. We assume this mode throughout the book. Leave Windows authentication mode for when you have become an expert.

- Install Microsoft Data Access Components (MDAC) 2.6.

- Install the latest service pack.

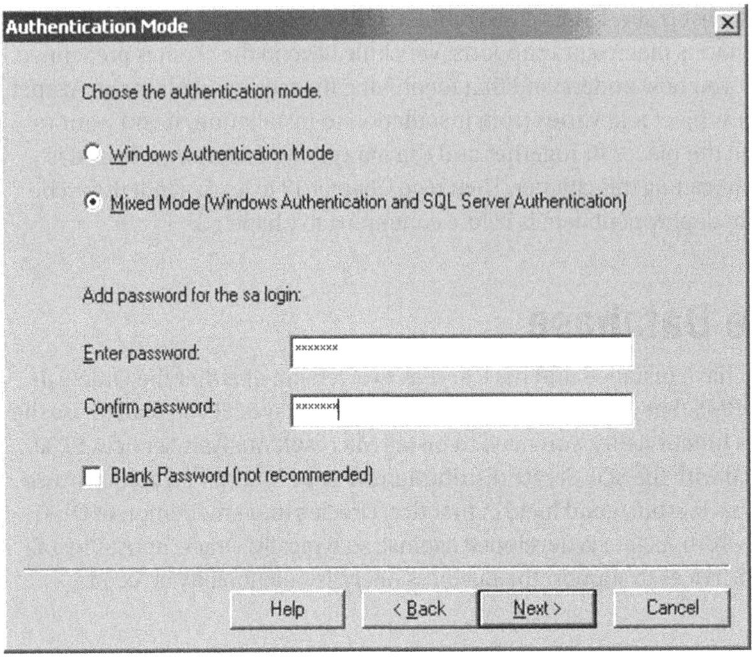

Figure 2-1. *Use mixed mode authentication for a SQL Server setup.*

▮**Note** When you use mixed mode authentication for SQL Server, you need to provide the password for the sa user (the system administrator). You can choose to leave the password blank, but this is not recommended.

That's all there is to it. Verify that the database is running and continue with your installation. Note that in the examples in this book, we use SQL Server. Chapter 19 provides an overview of the major differences between SQL Server and Oracle.

▮**Note** You can also use Microsoft SQL Server Desktop Engine (MSDE) as your database, if you're desperate. However, you can't use MSDE in a real production environment. MSDE should be used only for Axapta demo systems.

Performing a New Axapta Installation

You will normally install Axapta from the distribution CD or from an image or copy on a shared hard disk. The procedure is exactly the same either way: Insert the CD or go to the top-level folder of the Axapta copy on the hard disk, and run the program *Setup.exe*. This will bring up the Axapta installation portal, as shown in Figure 2-2. We will begin with an installation in 2-tier mode, as you must install and configure Axapta in 2-tier mode before connecting any 2-tier clients. As noted earlier, we are using SQL Server in this installation.

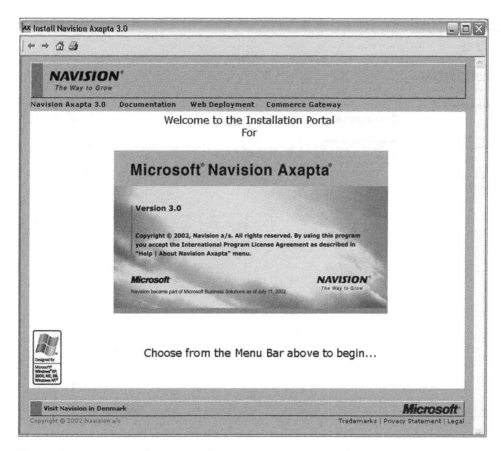

Figure 2-2. *Axapta installation portal*

The portal displays a menu bar between the Navision logo and the main work window. Clicking a menu bar option displays a submenu on the left side of the main work area, with further options and context-sensitive information to the right.

Accessing Axapta Documentation

You can access the documentation available with the standard CD distribution by choosing the Documentation option on the menu bar, as shown in Figure 2-3. We suggest that you read the Prerequisites and Installation Guide sections, and browse through the others. After installing Axapta, you will need to rely on the Guides and Technical Information sections. These are located in the respective folders under the *Documentation* folder in the root of the CD.

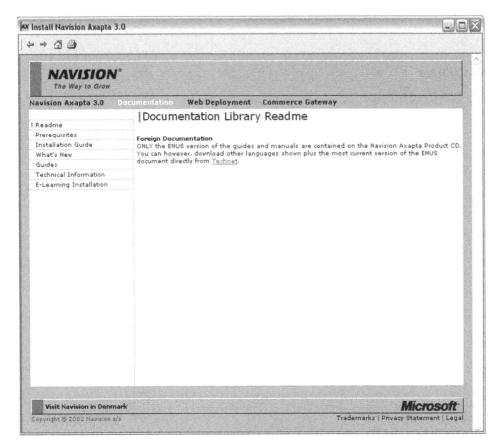

Figure 2-3. *The installation portal's Documentation section*

Note We usually copy the *Documentation* folder to the hard disk so that we can easily get to the different documents; however, the file names are, for the most part, meaningless. You can either try to figure out the file names and open the files directly, or place the *Setup.htm* file and the *Autorun* folder (that is, the installation portal), located at the root of the CD, under the same path as the *Documentation* folder. You can then fire up the installation portal and use the links it provides. (Actually, you can also place the *Setup.htm* file and *Autorun* folder anywhere you please, as long as you correct all the references to point to the correct base path.)

Installing Axapta 3.0

Let's go ahead and install Axapta. Click the Navision Axapta 3.0 menu bar option. In the submenu displayed on the upper left side of the resulting page choose Readme. You'll see the Readme information, as shown in Figure 2-4. Scan it for any issues that might be of particular interest to you.

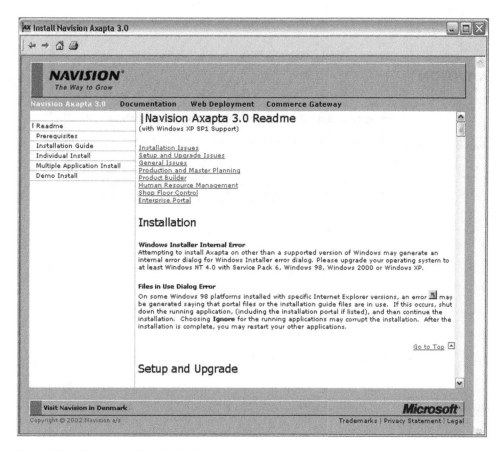

Figure 2-4. *The Axapta Readme information*

Next, choose Prerequisites from the submenu. This takes you to a section from which you can install Internet Explorer and an SQL Server client. The Internet Explorer link takes you to the Microsoft Web site, where you can download the browser, if necessary. If you are going to use a SQL Server database that is installed on a separate machine, you might be tempted to install the client provided. However, we recommend that you go to the Microsoft Web site and download the latest service pack for your SQL Server installation and the latest version of the client.

To start the installation process, choose the Individual Install menu from the submenu on the left menu pane. You'll see some brief information and three links, one for each of the Axapta software components that you need to install, as shown in Figure 2-5.

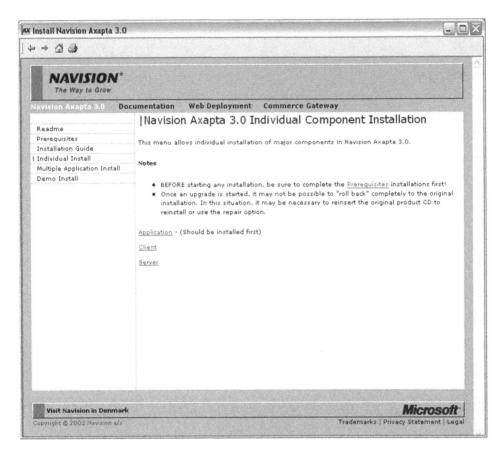

Figure 2-5. *Beginning individual component installation*

We'll follow the order indicated to install each component.

Installing the Application Component

Follow these steps to install the application component.

1. Click the Application link to start installing the Application component. A dialog box will pop up, asking if you want to run or save the file the link points to, and you might also see a security warning, depending on your operating system and security settings. Choose Run in both cases to start the installation.

2. The first page of the wizard displays some copyright information and what the wizard does. Select Next to continue.

3. The license agreement page appears next. You can use the drop-down combo box at the lower-left side to view the locale-specific version in English, and the Translate button to see the agreement in the language of the locale in which you want it displayed. Read the terms of the license and accept it if you want to proceed.

4. Fill in the customer information as you do with other software products that you are licensed for, and then continue.

5. You will now be presented with the Setup Type page, as shown in Figure 2-6. Select Custom as the installation type to perform. (If you choose Complete as the installation type, you will install stuff that you are not likely to need, and Axapta will install with a default path of \Documents and Settings\All Users\Application Data Navision\Axapta Application.) Continue by clicking Next again.

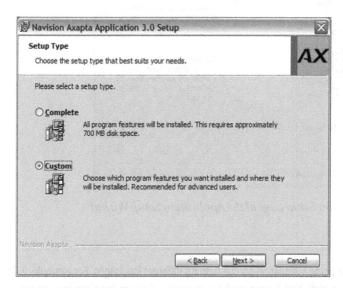

Figure 2-6. *The Setup Type page of the Application Setup Wizard*

Note Common practice in the Axapta world is to install the application, client, and server components to the following directories respectively—relative to the root of the drive you are installing to:

- \Axapta_Application
- \Axapta_Client
- \Axapta_Server

6. The Custom Setup page appears next, as shown in Figure 2-7. Notice that all the countries and interfaces (languages) that Axapta supports are marked for installation by default. This is pointless, and is the main reason why we suggest you select a custom installation. Deselect all the countries and interfaces you do not need. The easiest way to do this is by clicking the pull-down list icon for Countries and selecting the "The feature will not be available" option, repeating the procedure for each country that you do not want to install. For all countries that you do wish to install, make sure you have selected the option "This feature will be installed on the local hard drive."

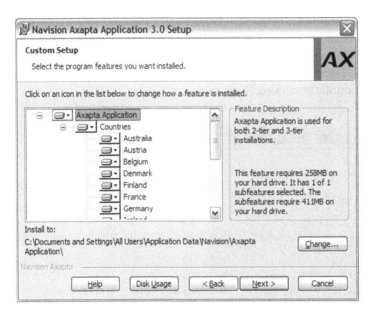

Figure 2-7. *The Custom Setup page of the Application Setup Wizard*

■**Note** Different users on the same installation can be running different languages. For example, a German employee of a French company might find it more useful to run with a German user interface, or run the user interface in French but have the online help system in German. Knowing that different languages can be installed and why gives users the ability to decide how Axapta is to be installed and tailored to fit their needs and preferences.

---

7. Click the Change button on the Custom Setup page to specify the installation path of the application component. Common practice in the Axapta world is to install the application, client, and server components to the \Axapta_Application, \Axapta_Client, and \Axapta_Server directories, respectively, relative to the root of whatever drive you are installing to. Here, change the path to \Axapta_Application, relative to the root of the drive or partition to which you are installing this component; for example, C:\Axapta_Application. When you're finished, click Next to continue.

8. The next page of the wizard simply informs you that it's your last chance to regret everything and drop Axapta altogether. But if you have read this far, it will probably take quite a bit more to break you, so be brave and click the Install button.

9. Assuming that all went as expected, the final page of the wizard informs you of exactly that. Click Finish, and the application will be installed.

Installing the Client Component

The next component to be installed is the client. Follow these steps:

1. As with the application component, launch the installation from the Individual Component Installation page (see Figure 2-5).

2. The installation process is exactly the same as for the application component, up to step 6, so follow steps 1 through 5 in the previous section.

3. At the Custom Setup page, the twist is that you will be asked to specify the path where the application component was installed. You should now select to install to \Axapta_Client (not \Axapta_Application). After you specify the path, select Next to continue.

4. The Client Type page appears, as shown in Figure 2-8. As stated earlier, you must always start Axapta in 2-tier mode, so it makes no sense to select the 3-tier installation at this point. If you were installing only Axapta clients that would eventually connect to an AOS installed elsewhere, then you could select the 3-tier mode option. The path displayed in the corresponding Axapta Application text control should match the path to which you installed the application component. If not, fix it by either typing in the correct path or using the Change button. Now accept the default suggestion of 2-tier and click Next to continue. (We will talk about 3-tier thin and fat client installation after the server installation section.)

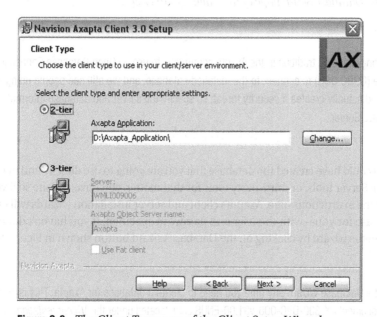

Figure 2-8. *The Client Type page of the Client Setup Wizard*

5. The next page of the wizard is the Database Setup page, where you specify information about your database, as shown in Figure 2-9. In the Database Type section on the left, select the database that you have installed.

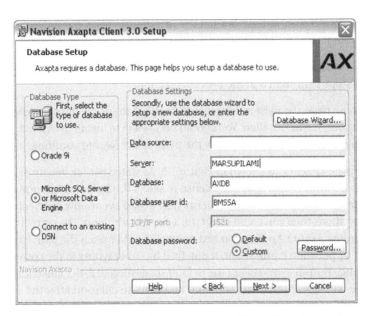

Figure 2-9. *The Database Setup page of the Client Setup Wizard*

■**Note** It has been a long-standing tradition in the Axapta community to use an Open Database Connectivity Database Source Name (ODBC DSN) to connect to the installed database, and we still see people doing it. This is not necessary and actually creates a security threat, so specify the server and database information for either Oracle 9i or SQL Server.

---

6. Although you could have created the database that you are going to use directly and manually using SQL Server tools, or third-party tools for that matter, you haven't done so if you are following the instructions here. Axapta's client and server installation wizards will create the database for you—with the user and password specified, if you haven't done so manually. Run the wizard by clicking on the Database Wizard button shown in Figure 2-9.

■**Note** You can use the Database Wizard any time you need to create a database for Axapta. This is documented very briefly in document AX-300-DVG-006-v01.00-ENUS.chm, located under the *\Documentation\guides* folder of the distribution CD.

---

7. On the next page, select your desired database type, choose Create Database, and then click Next.

8. Select your appropriate database server machine, enter the sa user ID and password, and then click Next. While we suggest going with the defaults until you are a bit more experienced, the server name specified should match the server name for the database server you will be using for your Axapta database. You can see what it is in SQL Server by looking at the SQL Server Service Manager window, as shown in Figure 2-10.

9. You now arrive at the Select Collation page. By default, Axapta selects a Danish collation. We recommend that you select the SQL_Latin1_General_CP1250_CI_AS collation. Then click Next.

10. Continue with the defaults for the database name and file locations (assuming they are correct for your database installation), and within a few blinks of the eye, Axapta will create the default database AXDB, along with the default user bmssa, with the default password of bmssa_pwd.

Figure 2-10. *SQL Server Service Manager dialog box*

■**Note** You may have noticed that one of the authors is a fan of the French comic-book series created by Rob-Vel and popularized by Jijé and by André Franquin and a series of other great comic artists at Dupuis, and that the server names do not match in Figures 2-9 and 2-10. This is because the two last screenshots were taken on different computers.

---

11. When the wizard is finished, it will display the Completing Installation page. Click the Finish button, and you will have a 2-tier installation of Axapta.

If you are only installing a 2-tier setup, you can skip ahead to the "Modifying Axapta" section. Otherwise, continue on to install the AOS, or Server, as it is called on the Individual Component Installation page. The AOS comes as part of the base package if you have purchased an Enterprise license.

■**Note** You would repeat these steps on all Axapta client machines where you need to install a native Windows client. Axapta also offers a Web Deployment feature as an alternative, which is discussed in Chapter 21.

Installing the Object Server Component

The server component installation follows the same steps as the client installation a large part of the way. Once again, remember to specify that it is installed in the appropriate directory: \Axapta_Server.

One difference in the installation process is that the Axapta Server page is followed by the Active Directory Integration page, as shown in Figure 2-11. As you can see, the possibility of integrating Axapta with Active Directory exists. However, at this point we don't care, so simply continue by clicking the Next button.

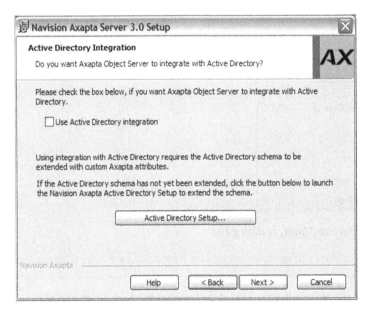

Figure 2-11. *The Axapta Active Directory Integration page of the Server Installation Wizard*

The next step is the Database Setup page, which you saw when you installed the client (Figure 2-9). If you were installing a 3-tier setup with thin clients, there would have been no reason to deal with the database while installing the clients because all database calls would go through the server, and you would do the database setup here. However, we have already performed this step while installing our 2-tier client, so just click Next to continue.

The setup of the server (AOS) finishes with the usual completion page. Click the Finish button, and there you have it—all the bits and pieces of Axapta are installed.

■**Note** With all three components installed, you can now mix and match them to suit your specific needs by using the configuration tools available, and it will help if you read the next chapter. If you need further clarification on the architecture, read Chapter 17, which provides details about the 2-tier and 3-tier setups.

Installing 3-Tier Clients

In the real world, you would select 3-tier mode to install clients that would access the application logic on the AOS or AOSs that we just installed.

Figure 2-12 shows the Client Type page of the Client Installation Wizard, which you saw earlier when we installed the 2-tier client. If you were installing a 3-tier client, you would select the 3-tier option, as in Figure 2-12, and leave the Use Fat Client check box unchecked, for the most secure and robust setup configuration. In the next chapter, we cover the actual setup of the AOS, so you need to go through that before you can successfully set up 3-tier clients. However, it is important to realize that 3-tier client setups always come last. We'll talk more about your options for setting up 3-tier clients in Chapter 3, where we actually configure the AOS and a 3-tier client.

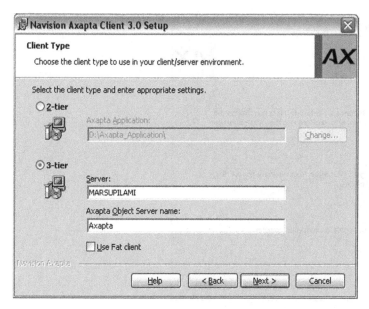

Figure 2-12. *Choosing 3-tier client setup*

■**Note** When installing 3-tier thin clients, you are not presented with the Database Setup page, because all databases calls are handled through the AOS but you will be presented with the Database Setup page if you check the Use Fat Client check box.

As we've already mentioned, in practice you always need to install at least one 2-tier client to initialize Axapta for the first time. I suggest installing all clients in 2-tier mode; then you can then produce a 3-tier configuration on one, export it, and import in all the other clients so that they all run the same configuration. This is described further in Chapter 3.

Tip Always keep a 2-tier configuration at an administrative system, just in case your 3-tier configuration fails.

Modifying Axapta

As with every software package worth its installer, Axapta can be repaired and features can be added or removed by running the installer on an existing system. To do so, simply start the Axapta installation portal, choose the Individual Installation menu option (see Figure 2-5), and click the link of the component you want to fix or modify. The page shown in Figure 2-13 will be displayed.

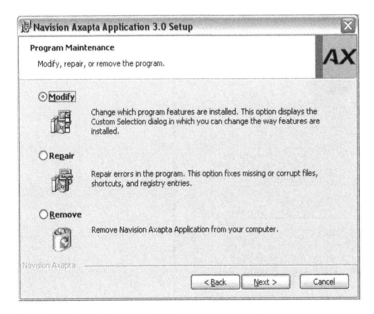

Figure 2-13. *The Program Maintenance wizard*

This page is actually a standard Windows installer dialog box, with which you are probably well-acquainted. The options work as follows:

- The Modify option allows you to add or remove options for the component in question. In practice, the only useful purpose this option serves is to allow you to add or remove countries when it displays the Custom Setup page (see Figure 2-7).

- The Repair option copies missing or corrupt files to your system and, to the best of its capabilities, restores settings. The last step usually means that your system will have settings restored to those of a newly installed system, so think before you resort to doing this.

- The Remove option will come in handy right now. Use it to uninstall the Axapta components so that you can practice reinstalling them.

■**Note** Using the standard Windows Add or Remove Software applet in the Control Panel to uninstall Axapta does not clear the Registry, and will result in any attempt to re-install Axapta leading you to the Program Maintenance wizard.

Upgrading Axapta

Upgrading is a pretty complex issue, as Microsoft does not know the customizations and changes you might have made to Axapta along the way. However, Axapta does provide an Upgrade Wizard that takes care of what Microsoft does know about, and it even throws in some tools to help you figure out what the differences are between your system and the standard system delivered by Microsoft, so that you know what pieces you must take care of yourself.

The tools not only tell you about the differences in functionality that your changes or add-ons create, but also about the differences in the metadata definitions for the different kinds of objects that exist in Axapta, such as forms, reports, and menus. The tools will even point out differences in the data dictionary.

■**Note** The Axapta Upgrade Wizard supports only the previous version of Axapta; that is, the wizard in version 3.0 can upgrade only from version 2.5. This means that if you have a version 2.1 installation and need to upgrade to 3.0, you must first upgrade to version 2.5, and then to 3.0.

As far as the as the client and server components are concerned, the upgrade simply over-writes and/or replaces the appropriate binaries. You do not have access to the source code for these, and thus couldn't have made any changes to them, so a client or server component upgrade is a no-brainer.

However, upgrading the application component is a different story. Most installations are customized to some extent, and in practice, issues can even arise with the standard application (some of these issues are documented by Microsoft, and some are not). It's not something you want to try before you are an expert and have good team to support you in the project. Also, make sure to always perform your upgrade on a test environment before attempting to upgrade your production environment.

If you start an installation wizard and it detects a previous version of the Axapta application, it will automatically bring up a dialog box asking if you wish to upgrade. Follow the wizard and read the upgrade notices for the release. That way, at least you will have an idea of the kind of trouble you are getting into.

■**Note** Even service packs for version 3.0 of Axapta provide an upgrade option.

Installing Hotfixes and Service Packs

Hotfixes are supplied by the Axapta product group at Microsoft and come in two types: private and public. The former are made when a customer with big political muscles calls a guy like Doug Burgum or Steve Ballmer with a problem—most of the readers of this book will never see one of those. The latter are issued by Microsoft for general public distribution when the product team fixes a bug that is critical and high-impact; that is, it's nasty and affects a lot of customers and users.

Hotfixes normally include a fix to a single problem, and are not cumulative. They are meant to be installed only if you experience the problem, and they are rolled into the next service pack. Hotfixes can be machine-code binaries (kernel hotfixes) or application binaries (application hotfixes). Kernel hotfixes typically consist of EXE and DLL files. Application hotfixes consist of an XPO file.

Applying hotfixes is a manual process: overwrite the old files with the new in the case of a kernel hotfix, and import the XPO into Axapta in the case of an application hotfix.

Note Importing an XPO is explained in Chapter 21 as part of the discussion of distributing your customizations. But basically, you fire up Axapta, log in, open the Application Object Tree (AOT), and use the Import menu option on the Axapta desktop main menu bar. Notice that this requires having a developer license (license codes for MorphX and X++ source code). The AOT is described later in this book, in Chapter 18, which covers the development environment.

Service packs are a very different kind of animal and resemble a normal distribution. What differentiates them from a normal release is that they generally do not include new features; they simply include bug fixes. Installing a service pack is the same as installing a normal Axapta release. Service packs come with an installation portal that follows the model described earlier in this chapter. You install the service pack for the applications, clients, and servers you have. As with an upgrade, exercise caution in applying a service pack. You will probably run into issues with your customizations.

Note Installing a service pack or hotfix to an application that you have can, and does regularly, break customizations. Therefore, many developers do not apply hotfixes or service packs unless they are necessary to fix problems. They apply only the hotfix or service pack that they consider worth the trouble of having to perform a full regression test of their customizations and of fixing anything that is broken.

Some simple differences between service packs and hotfixes are that service packs are cumulative; for example, all the fixes in SP3 are included in SP4. Therefore, if you are installing a clean version of Axapta 3.0 today, you could simply install SP4 immediately after installing the base 3.0 package.

Wrap-Up

In this chapter we have gone through the following topics:

- Meeting the minimum requirements to get you up and running

- Installing a relational database for Axapta

- Performing a new installation of all the Axapta components

- Modifying an existing installation of an Axapta component

- Understanding what's involved with upgrades

- Installing a service pack and hotfixes

As we noted in the chapter, we suggest that you try installing and uninstalling the Axapta components at least a couple of times before continuing.

In this chapter, you have acquired a sense for the components that make up Axapta and how they can be installed across different physical systems. In the next chapter, we'll talk about how these components can be configured and combined in different ways.

You can read more about the topics in this chapter in the following documents, available in the documentation folder of the product distribution package or CD:

- AX-300-ING-001-v01.01-ENUS.chm: Installation Guide

- AX-300-DVG-006-v01.00-ENUS.chm: DB Wizard

- AX-300-TIP-028-v01.00-ENUS.doc: Installing AOS on a Cluster Fail-Safe Server

CHAPTER 3

■ ■ ■

Configuration and Post-Installation

In the previous chapter you installed Axapta. Now let's dive in and start using it. We will guide you through configuring Axapta and getting it up and running. When you have it up and running you will set up a minimum of data so that you have a fictitious business to run, with which to investigate and learn the technical ins and outs of Axapta.

Get a cup of strong coffee and place yourself comfortably behind the keyboard. Axapta is a complex and extensive system, where almost anything can be done in a variety of ways. We can't cover them all here, but by the end of the chapter you will know how to work your way through the system in the most common ways, and you will learn alternatives and tips and tricks.

This chapter is essential for all Axapta users. Regardless of whether you are an end user, a system administrator, or a developer, mastering this chapter is essential because it underlies the system.

To get the best out of it, we highly recommend that you work through each explanation, example, hint, and tip in this chapter. Take whatever time you need: it is well worth it.

This chapter covers the following topics:

- Configuring Axapta

- Setting up user preferences

- Enabling access to the functionality you need

- Controlling access to the system

- Creating a basic demo data set

Configuration Tools

Before you can start Axapta you need to configure it to suit your needs. The installation procedure has already created a default configuration, but in real life you will usually work with several different configurations that fit specific needs. For example, you may need to run Axapta in different languages or access different Axapta servers from the same client. Let's therefore take a careful look at configuring Axapta for use.

When you installed Axapta you also installed a set of configuration utilities:

- *The Axapta configuration utility, AxConfig.exe*: This is installed in the client *bin* directory. This utility is used for configuring the client and the Business Connector. If you run Axapta in 2-tier mode, this is the only configuration utility you need.

Note The installation process automatically creates a shortcut to this utility named *Axapta Configuration Utility* and places it in the top level folder of your Windows Start menu when you install the Axapta Windows client.

- *The Axapta server manager utility, AxCtrl.exe*: This is installed in the server *bin* directory. This utility is used for configuring the Windows server manager service that manages Axapta Object Server (AOS) processes and clusters. It is also the entry point for configuring an individual AOS.

Tip The installation process automatically creates an *Axapta Object Server* shortcut to this utility and places it in the Windows Control Panel when you install the AOS.

All the settings that you define using these utilities can also be specified using command-line parameters if you decide to start the respective processes using a command line. However, we recommend using the utilities; they offer clues and help, and minimize your chances of getting a complex setup process wrong.

2-Tier Configuration

Let's create a configuration using the Axapta Configuration Utility to start Axapta for the first time. Remember, our first time starting Axapta on a new installation *must* be in 2-tier mode.

Note Unless stated otherwise, the following walkthrough uses Axapta's default settings and values. We will briefly explain the purpose of each parameter so that you know what possibilities Axapta offers. However, fine-tuning your configuration is outside the scope of this book.

General Configuration

Run the utility by your preferred method. For example, click on the shortcut in the Windows Start menu. The resulting window consists of seven tabs and is, at startup, set on the General tab, which contains a single control group (Settings), composed of various fields. Figure 3-1 shows our generic setup parameters.

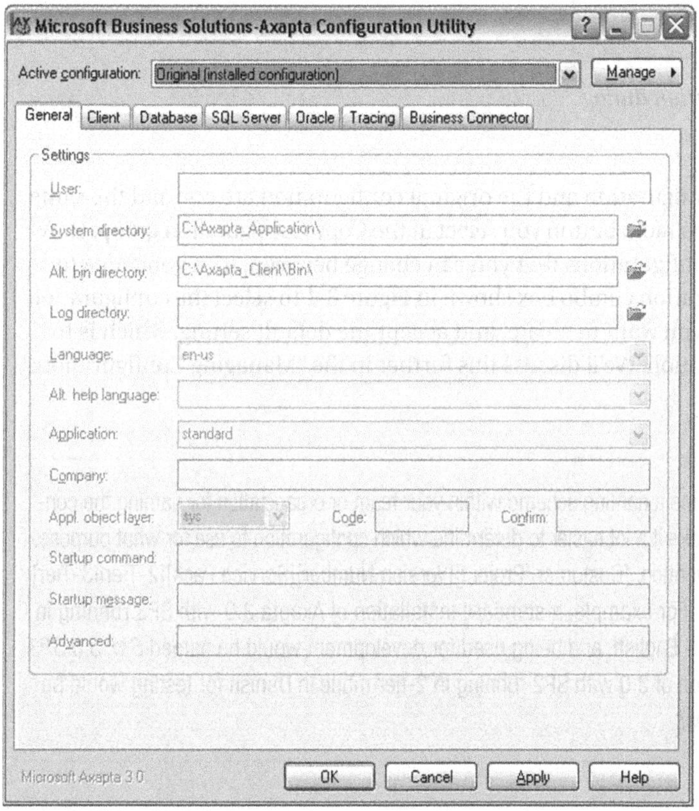

Figure 3-1. *The General tab of the Axapta Configuration Utility*

The active configuration (the only configuration at this point) is the one created by the installer. The fields are all locked—this is Axapta's way of telling you to leave this configuration alone. Unfortunately, the default configuration is not guaranteed to work. We regularly hear from people who have been unable to start Axapta the first time after installation, so we always make a new configuration that we can name descriptively and change parameters as it suits us.

To create a new configuration, click on the Manage button at the top-right corner of the window. This displays a pop-up menu. Select New Configuration. The dialog in Figure 3-2 is displayed.

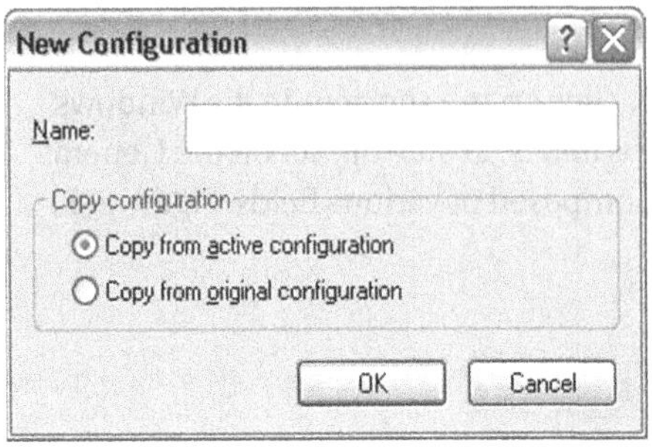

Figure 3-2. *The New Configuration dialog*

In this case, the active configuration and the original configuration are one and the same thing, so it doesn't matter which radio button you select in the Copy Configuration group. However, as you create different configurations that you can change between, it's a good idea to always use the Active Configuration combo box shown in Figure 3-1 to select the configuration that most resembles the one you want to create, and accept the default setting, which is to copy from the active configuration. We'll discuss this further in the "Managing Configurations" section of this chapter.

■**Tip** We recommend that you define a naming scheme within your team or organization for naming the configurations that you create. It will make it a lot easier to determine which configuration to use for what purpose. We use the following naming convention: [Customer‖Project][Version Number][Service Pack][2-Tier‖3-Tier] [Language Code][Dev‖Test‖Prod]. For example, a standard installation of Axapta 3.0 with SP3 running in 3-tier mode, the language set to US English, and being used for development would be named *Std. 3.0 SP3 3-Tier US Dev*, a customized version of 3.0 with SP2 running in 2-tier mode in Danish for testing would be *myCustomer 3.0 SP2 2-Tier DK Test.*

For now, let's use the naming scheme we just outlined. Enter **Std. 3.0 SP3 2-Tier US Dev** and click on the OK button. At this point, you could move on to the Post-Installation portion of this chapter. However, we recommend reading on so that you can learn about the options regarding the client and server configurations.

Now let's walk through the fields in the General tab:

- *The User field*: This provides the name of a default user, and Axapta will automatically suggest the specified user in the login credentials dialog. Since Axapta is created with an admin account, enter **admin** in the field so that you don't have to retype it when you need to log on to Axapta.

- *The System Directory field*: When creating a new configuration from the original installed configuration, this field points to the directory where the application was installed, i.e., C:\Axapta_Application\, and you don't need to change it.

- *The Alt.Bin Directory Field*: The Alt. Bin Directory field is by default the bin directory under the directory in which you installed the client; for instance, C:\Axapta_Client\Bin\.

> **■Note** Although Axapta documentation states that the standard bin directory is located in the path specified as the system directory, we have never seen the system directory contain anything other than folders, and the bin directory under it contain anything other than license and Readme files. Particularly curious is the fact that the online help states that the Alt Bin Directory parameter should be set to the path of a kernel text data (KTD) file not found in the standard bin directory. In fact, the KTD files are placed by the installer under the client bin directory and not under the supposed default path specified by the system directory. Omitting the Alt Bin Directory parameter would make Axapta look for KTD files in the wrong place, according to the documentation.

- *The Log Directory field*: By default this is not specified. We usually set it to the log directory that the installer creates under the directory where the client is installed. You can specify any directory path you like, but for now specify C:\Axapta_Client\Log. Leaving this field blank will result in the log files being written to the default path, i.e., your My Documents folder.

- *The Language field*: This is a combo box from which you can select the language to use. For now, accept the default of en-us, i.e., US English.

- *The Alt. Help Language field*: This field allows you to specify an alternative language in which to display the online help system. Typically you will use the same language as for the application, but if you prefer to have the online help in another language, go ahead and specify one.

- *The Application field*: This field is where you specify the folder containing the Axapta application to load for the configuration. You have to locate all applications under the *Appl* folder in the root of the folder where you installed the application.

- *The Company field*: This allows you to specify the ID of the company that you want to work with by default when you log in to Axapta. This is useful because the same installation of Axapta can cover multiple companies. Axapta is created with a company with the ID DAT that it uses by default if no other company is specified. For now, leave this field blank.

- *The Appl. Object Layer field*: This field allows you to select the layer to use while working with Axapta. Accept the default, sys. By default this will open Axapta to the usr layer (see Chapter 17 for more about this). If you select a layer other than sys or usr, you have to provide the code you received from MBS for the respective layer in the Code field then repeat it in the Confirm field.

> **■Note** Application developers will typically work in another application object layer, depending on the nature of their work and their partner status with Microsoft Business Solutions, who will provide special codes to make the appropriate layers available. We explain Axapta layers in Chapter 17 of this book.

- *The Startup Command field*: This is used to have Axapta execute a user-specified command at startup. For now leave it blank.

- *The Startup Message field*: This allows you to specify a message that Axapta displays in a dialog box after you have logged in. It's most practical for system administrators who need to provide a short notice to the system's users—for example, to notify users about a planned maintenance shutdown.

- *The Advanced field*: This allows you to specify startup parameters that the configuration utility does not support and that would otherwise force you to start Axapta from the command line. The syntax is the same as the command-line syntax. You can see the full list of parameters in Appendix B.

Client Configuration

The Client tab defines parameters for clients running in 3-tier mode. You'll learn how to configure a 3-tier client later in this chapter, but for now accept the defaults (shown in Figure 3-3) and move on to the Database tab.

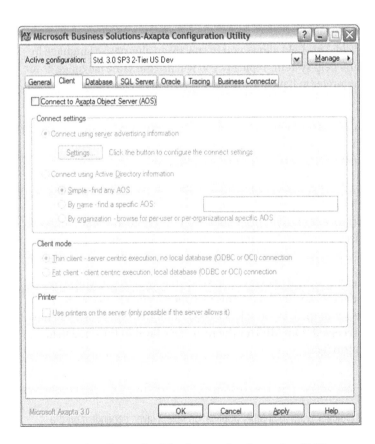

Figure 3-3. *The Client tab of the Axapta Configuration Utility*

Database Configuration

The client uses the parameters in this tab only when running in 2-tier mode or 3-tier fat mode. When running in 3-tier thin client mode, all data access goes through the AOS, so these parameters are defined in the server configuration instead.

The Database tab consists of three control groups, shown in Figure 3-4.

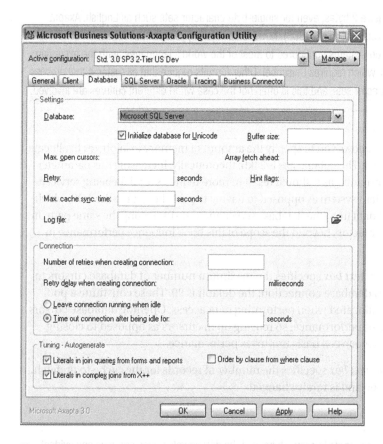

Figure 3-4. *The Database tab of the Axapta Configuration Utility*

The Settings Controls

This group allows you to set up a series of parameters that specify how Axapta deals with data, including where to log information related to database activity.

- *The Database combo box*, where you can specify one of the supported database systems: Microsoft SQL Server or Oracle. Specify the database that you are using.

■**Note** Some of the functionality described in this book might not be available or may not function exactly as described if you are using Oracle. The most important differences within the context of Axapta are covered in Chapter 19.

- *The Initialize Database for Unicode check box*, which is unchecked by default, instructs Axapta to save and retrieve string data using the database's Unicode character and string field data types, i.e., nchar, nvarchar, and ntext in Microsoft SQL Server. If this box is not checked, string data is assumed to be ANSI.

Note Unicode characters require 2 bytes, even for single-byte character sets such as English. Axapta itself is based on the Dual Byte Character Set (DBCS); however, by storing your textual data in Unicode it is guaranteed to display correctly on systems configured to most of the world's languages (with the exception of the Hindu family of languages, which requires Uniscribe). Other formats require that all systems that process your data support the same character sets, and this is often not the case when different cultures are involved.

- *The Buffer Size text box* allows you to specify the amount of memory in kilobytes to allocate to the client's data buffer. The default size is 24kb; theoretically, increasing this parameter should improve performance, as it should result in more requests for data being serviced by the cache on the client system as opposed to having to pass the data to the AOS, which in return retrieves the data from the database server and returns it along the same path. In practice, though, many factors beyond the scope of this book influence performance in Axapta.

- *The Max. Open Cursors text box* specifies the maximum number of database cursors to be kept open for each database connection; the default is 90. These constitute a pool that is managed and allocated when performing data access. Opening database cursors is expensive in terms of performance, so reusing open cursors as opposed to closing and opening them on a per-call basis improves performance.

- *The Array Fetch Ahead text box* specifies the number of records for the cache to prefetch. The default value is 100 and is rarely changed.

Note Increasing the number of records to prefetch beyond the default value does not have any evident impact on performance.

- *The Retry text box* specifies the number of seconds to wait before retrying to get hold of a lock on a resource after an attempt fails due to it being locked by another process or transaction. The default value is 30 seconds. Tuning this parameter is an art form. Setting it high means that transactions may waste a lot of time between a resource becoming available and getting a lock on it, and setting it low can result in a lot of useless attempts to get a lock on a resource that is locked by another process or transaction.

- *The Hint Flags text box* is not used.

- *The Max Cache Sync. Time text box* specifies the interval in seconds between cache refreshes. Cache synchronization pushes changes in the cache to the database, so a high value decreases database writes but increases the probability that other clients will access stale data. The default is 60 seconds.

■Note Cache synchronization is problematic up to and in Axapta 3.0 SP3, and often caches are not synchronized across AOS clusters until the AOSs are restarted. Our research into this issue leads us to conclude that this is the result of the synchronization frequency being too high and/or the atomicity of the corresponding database transaction being too large. The cache is unable to complete the synchronization transaction in the database within the time interval, so it rolls back the transaction and starts anew. This process cycles indefinitely so the cache is never updated.

- *The Log File text box* specifies a path to write SQL errors to. By default Axapta uses the system log path and the file name *SqlError.log*.

The Connection Controls

Now we move into the Connection group, which enables you to specify how Axapta manages connections to the supported relational database systems that it supports, namely Microsoft SQL Server and Oracle.

- *The Number of Retries When Creating Connection text box* specifies exactly what it says. Axapta will attempt to connect the specified number of times before giving up. We normally set this somewhere from three to five on loaded networks; however, if you need to retry often, you should review your architecture—high latency values will not only affect Axapta's ability to connect to the database, but even more importantly, will hamper its ability to maintain sessions between clients and servers while you are trying to run your everyday business.

- *The Retry Delay When Creating Connection text box* specifies an interval before re-attempting to establish a database connection if an attempt fails.

- *The Leave Connection Running When Idle radio button* specifies that database connections should be kept open even if not in use. This saves the system overhead involved in establishing a connection to the database, which is particularly heavy in the case of Oracle. However, it's uncommon for this option to be selected because it potentially consumes connections that serve no purpose.

- *The Time Out Connection After Being Idle For radio button* is most often toggled on, and you'll usually accept the default values by leaving the corresponding text box blank. Axapta defaults to a time-out value of 1 minute for SQL Server and 30 minutes for Oracle.

> ■**Note** The reason for the different default timeout values is that creating a database connection to Microsoft SQL Server is much less costly than creating one to Oracle, so the payback in freeing open connections is much more immediate with Microsoft SQL Server.

The Tuning - Autogenerate Controls

The final group in this tab is Tuning - Autogenerate, where you specify how Axapta queries are to be constructed.

- *The Literals in Join Queries from Forms and Reports check box* instructs Axapta to use literal values rather than placeholders in its queries. Literals facilitate database optimization of queries at the cost of extra load on the database server. Not selecting this check box results in Axapta using placeholders, allowing the database to reuse queries but hindering query optimization.

> ■**Note** Generally literals yield better performance for long-running queries that are not repeated, while placeholders yield better performance for queries that are repeated. Consequently, Axapta applies literals by default on join queries unless the query developer has explicitly stated otherwise.

- *The Literals in Complex Joins from X++ check box* resembles the preceding check box but applies to programmatic queries as opposed to queries in forms and reports.

- *The Order by Clause from Where Clause check box* specifies whether Axapta should generate a standard order by clause for queries, based on the data-source index of a form, or an optimal order by clause for the where clause when checked.

> ■**Note** Theoretically, enabling the Order by Clause from Where Clause option improves performance, assuming that the indexes specified by developers are suboptimal and that the overhead and algorithm behind this optimization are superior to the database optimizer. In practice, we have not experienced this and therefore we do not select it.

SQL Server Configuration

SQL Server is the next tab in the Axapta Configuration Utility window. This tab applies only when the database selected in the Database tab is Microsoft SQL Server. As with the Database tab, the client uses the parameters in this tab only when running in 2-tier mode or in 3-tier fat client mode. When running in 3-tier thin client mode, all data access goes through the AOS, so these parameters are defined in the server configuration instead.

This tab consists of the two control groups shown in Figure 3-5.

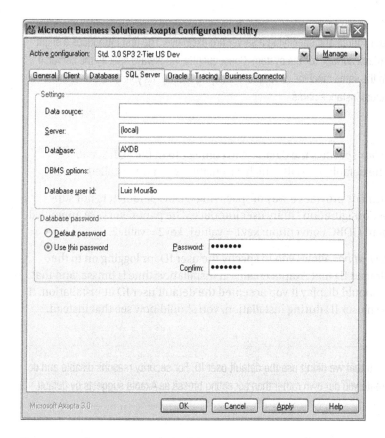

Figure 3-5. *The SQL Server tab of the Axapta Configuration Utility*

The Settings Controls

This control group specifies information about the database Axapta will use, as well as information it needs to be able to log in to it.

Note The combo boxes in this group should provide you with a list of ODBC system data sources for Microsoft SQL Server, SQL Server instances on the network, and databases for the selected data source or SQL Server instance, respectively. In practice it doesn't always work, so just type the respective names.

- *The Data Source combo box* specifies an ODBC system data source to use for connecting to Microsoft SQL Server. However, Axapta does not require a data source to work with Microsoft SQL Server even though it's common practice to create and specify one.

- *The Server combo box* lets you directly specify a Microsoft SQL Server instance, and the necessary ODBC data source will be generated automatically when needed. In the Server field enter the name of your server as specified by your SQL Server Service Manager. Simply accept the values already specified for you.

Note Specifying an ODBC data source and specifying a server are exclusive. The first introduces a slight overhead and an unnecessary attack surface for the system. Consequently, we always specify the server. If you have installed SQL Server on the same machine as Axapta, specifying "(local)" as your SQL Server instance is the same as specifying the actual instance name.

- *The Database combo box* specifies the database to connect to in the SQL Server instance specified. The default is AXDB, which we created when we installed.

- *The DBMS Options text box* provides a way of specifying ODBC parameters not supported by the Axapta Configuration Utility user interface. The parameters are appended and follow the standard ODBC convention: key1 = value1; key2 = value2.

- *The Database User ID text box* allows you to specify the user ID for logging on to the database. The default user ID that Axapta creates at installation time is bmssa, and that is what your text box should display if you accepted the default user ID at installation. If you specified your own user ID during installation, you should now see that instead.

Note You can see in Figure 3-5 that we didn't use the default user ID. For security reasons disable and do not use default users; instead create you our own rather than accepting bmssa as Axapta suggests by default.

The Database Password Controls

The Password group contains two radio buttons—Default Password and Use This Password—that allow you to specify whether to use the default Axapta password (bmssa_pwd) or a password that you specify in the Password and Confirm text boxes. Check the Default Password radio button only if you like to live dangerously.

We regularly hear from people who, either after installation or after using Axapta for some time, are unable to start Axapta, and they receive the error dialog shown in Figure 3-6.

Figure 3-6. *Axapta startup database connection error*

The cause is generally one of three things:

- The password is outright wrong and does not correspond to the user ID—this is the least common, however.

- You are using Windows authentication, wherein the user ID specified is a Windows domain user ID specially created for Axapta, and the password has expired without you noticing since it's not the account with which you log on to the network.

- SQL Server authentication is set to Windows only and the user ID does not correspond to an existing domain account. In this case the solution is to set the authentication mode to mixed, i.e., SQL Server and Windows. You do this in the SQL Server Enterprise Manager. Open the properties dialog for the SQL Server instance specified in the Server combo box, then go to the Security tab and select the correct mode, as shown in Figure 3-7. If you have chosen to use MSDE, this is a registry setting.

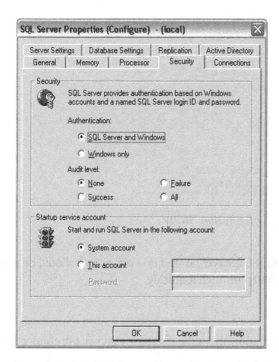

Figure 3-7. *The SQL Server Properties Security tab*

Oracle Configuration

The next tab in the Axapta Configuration Utility is the Oracle tab, whose controls are active only if you have specified Oracle as your database in the respective section of the Database tab page. The client uses it only when running in 2-tier mode or in 3-tier fat client mode, and if the database selected in the Database tab is Oracle. When running in 3-tier thin client mode, all data access goes through the AOS, so these parameters are defined in the server configuration instead, using the corresponding utility that has the exact same tab.

This tab consists of three control groups, as shown in Figure 3-8.

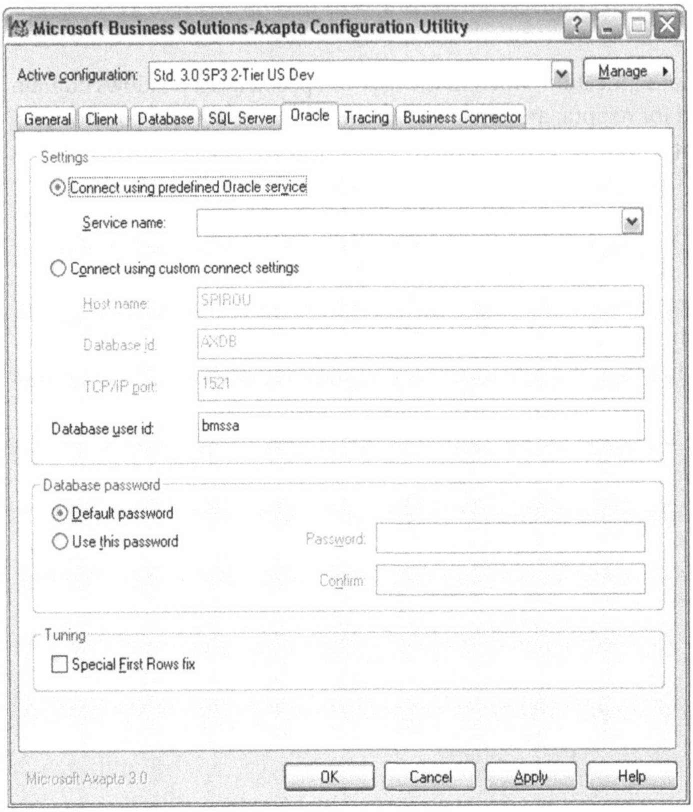

Figure 3-8. *The Oracle tab of the Axapta Configuration Utility*

This tab is the Oracle equivalent of the SQL Server tab and everything on it should be pretty evident if you are an Oracle user, so we'll step through it quickly.

The Settings Controls

The settings group is for specifying information about the database that you are connecting to, and setting connection information:

- If you have defined an Oracle service on the client workstation, you can specify it via the Connect Using Predefined Oracle Service radio button as shown in Figure 3-8. Then you can enter the name of the service in the Service Name combo box. The service contains all the connection information necessary, so that's it!

- Alternatively, you can specify the connection settings in the Axapta configuration by selecting the Connect Using Custom Connect Settings radio button and then providing the host name of the Oracle database server, the name of the database, the port on which the server listens for connections, and the user ID to use when logging on to the database specified.

The Database Password Controls

The Database Password group contains the following fields:

- *Default password*: Toggle this button for Axapta to log on with the default password for user bmssa if you are using the default installed user and have not changed the password that the Axapta database wizard creates during installation.

- *Use This Password*: Toggle this button to specify a different password for the user that you have specified.

- *Password*: If you have selected to specify the password for the user login, enter the password to use here.

- *Confirm*: Enter the password again in the Confirm field.

■**Note** For security reasons it's a good idea that you not use the bmssa user or the default password. If you do so, start straying off the default path once you know your way around Axapta.

The Tuning Control

The last group allows you to tell Axapta to tune specific database statements when using the Oracle database:

- *The Special First Rows Fix check box* is the only option and it improves sorting performance in forms. However, it's not commonly checked by default; it seems most installations do not have an issue with it.

Tracing Configuration

This tab, shown in Figure 3-9, consists of two control groups and is primarily directed at developers or technical consultants who need to trace or view different aspects of system activity to identify causes of errors or/and performance issues.

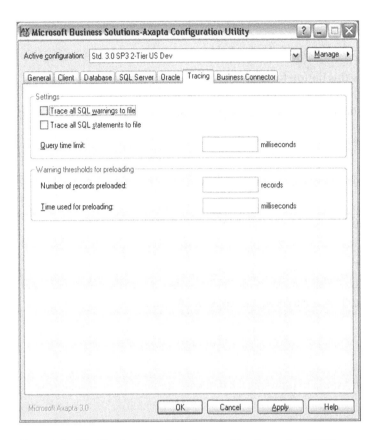

Figure 3-9. *The Tracing tab of the Axapta Configuration Utility*

The Settings Controls

This group determines which SQL statements are logged to the file indicated in the Settings group of the database tab.

- *The Trace All SQL Warnings check box* instructs Axapta to write all warnings issued by the database to a file that you can use to identify requests to the database that are not working or performing as intended. The default file name is of the form *sqlwarning_[userId].log*, where [userId] is the user ID with which you are logged on when the warning is issued (*sqlwarning_admin.log* if you are logged on as admin).

- *The Trace All SQL Statements to File check box* instructs Axapta to do exactly that; every single SQL statement that Axapta issues is logged to a file. The default file name is of the form *sqltrace_[userId].log*. This log file is written to the path specified as the log directory for the configuration.

■**Note** Checking the first check box is usually quite harmless unless you have a lot of SQL warnings. However, the second will significantly degrade performance. Neither is recommended unless you need it. Both options append logs, so when these parameters are turned on, it's a good idea to delete the log files to avoid their taking up unnecessary disk space on your system.

- The Query Time Limit text box specifies that queries whose execution time exceeds the given number of milliseconds should be logged. This is unrelated to the previous tracing parameters, and the default value is 0, in which case no SQL statements are logged based on their execution time. However, all statements will still be logged if the Trace All SQL Statements to File box is checked. The default file name for this log has the form *sqltime_[userId].log*.

The Warning Thresholds for Preloading Controls

The Number of Records Preloaded and Time Used for Preloading text boxes in the Warning Thresholds for Preloading control group allow you to instruct Axapta to preload a given number of records from tables that you specify in your user setup, and the maximum amount of time to invest in the process. Bear in mind that *preloading* in this context means that the whole table is loaded the first time it is accessed, not necessarily at startup.

■**Note** Microsoft states that preloading improves performance because it optimizes frequent access to data. However, the likelihood that all the records in a table are ever needed is questionable. This, combined with the fact that the Axapta cache must purge data to make room for newer data when it reaches its cache size limit, makes us question the benefit of fully preloading a table. Tables are preloaded the first time a user needs them, making him pay the penalty without any predetermined or evident benefit for others. We do not use preloading.

Business Connector

The Business Connector, also known as the COM Connector, is a COM interface to Axapta that enables you to call into its business logic from external processes. Within Axapta, the Business Connector is used by Microsoft Internet Information Server (IIS) to access the Enterprise Portal. It's further used by BizTalk with the Commerce Gateway, and can even be used by external applications that can act as COM clients to access Axapta's business logic and data. We'll talk much more about this in Chapter 15. For now, let's get the Business Connector up and running so that we can use it later.

This tab has three control groups and specifies various parameters for the Business Connector (the COM+ interface to Axapta), as shown in Figure 3-10.

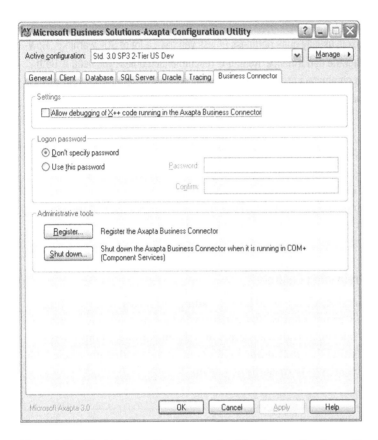

Figure 3-10. *The Business Connector tab of the Axapta Configuration Utility*

The Settings Control

The first group contains a single check box that specifies whether to permit the debugging of X++ code running in the Business Connector. This is of interest only to developers. We will explain the Business Connector in Chapter 16 but for now you should know that in practice it's the Axapta client with a COM+ interface minus the user interface. Application code executes within its context in exactly the same way as on the client whose configuration it inherits. In this example the 2-tier configuration we previously created will interact directly with the database and execute all the Axapta business logic, while in a 3-tier configuration it would, like the Windows client, function as a thin or fat client depending on the client mode settings specified in the Client tab. In short, checking the Allow Debugging of X++ Code Running in the Axapta Business Connector check box enables you as a developer to step through code running in the debugger while it executes in the Business Connector.

■**Caution** Naturally, don't enable X++ debugging in nondevelopment environments unless it's strictly needed to track down a bug. X++ debugging negatively impacts performance.

The Logon Password Controls

This group allows you to specify whether to use the password provided by the Axapta configuration for the Business Connector when logging into the database you are using, or whether to use the one specified in the COM+ object properties.

- *Don't Specify Password* instructs Axapta that the password to be used in the Business Connector when logging on is supplied programmatically by the client code. If the user specified on the General tab does not have a password assigned, this will be sufficient. We'll talk much more about passwords in Chapter 5. For now, and by default, your admin user does not have a password assigned.

- *Use This Password* instructs Axapta that the specified password is to be used by default. If you select this radio button, the Password and Confirm text boxes will be enabled and you can provide a password to use. If the user specified on the General tab does have a password assigned, it will need to be entered here.

If you specify a password programmatically, when logging on that password will always override the settings of this group.

The Administrative Tools Controls

The Administrative tools group allows you to register and shut down the Business Connector locally.

- *The Register button* brings up the dialog shown in Figure 3-11. To start using the Business Connector, you need to register it as a component service. By default, Axapta registers the Business Connector as a standard COM component server during installation. The specifics of the different options are beyond the scope of this book.

Figure 3-11. *The Register Axapta Business Connector dialog*

- • For now, select the Register COM+ (Component Services) radio button. Registering the Business Connector is required for the Business Connector to be used from IIS.

- • In the Computer text box, specify the name by which your computer is known in its domain. Alternatively, you can click on the icon to the right of the text box to bring up a dialog from which you can select the name.

- *The Shut Down button* allows you to stop the Business Connector component service. Clicking it brings up the dialog shown in Figure 3-12. This dialog is quite straightforward: in the Computer text box specify the name by which the computer is know in the domain or use the icon to the right to select it from a list of available systems, and click on the OK button to stop it.

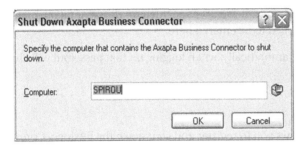

Figure 3-12. *The Shut Down Axapta Business Connector dialog*

Note Unfortunately, the Axapta Configuration Utility does not provide any way of starting the Business Connector after you have shut it down, because it's started automatically the first time you use it after a shutdown. To start, stop, disable, or configure the component service, you need to use the Windows Component Services applet in the Administrative Tools menu of your system, or the shortcut in the Control Panel. For an explanation of managing component services, see your operating system documentation or documentation on COM.

The final step when you're finished defining a configuration is to save it for use. Click on the Apply button—not the OK button, as we need to keep the dialog open a little longer.

Managing Configurations

Up to now, we have not spoken much about the Active Configuration combo box and the Manage menu button at the top of the Axapta Configuration Utility, or about the row of buttons (OK, Cancel, Apply, and Help) at the bottom. These controls and buttons allow you to manage your configurations. It's common for specific groups of Axapta users; e.g., consultants, developers, and testers, to have several configurations and move between them. Axapta makes this easy.

At this point you should have two configurations: the original that was created when you installed Axapta, and a 2-tier configuration that you created while stepping through the Axapta Configuration Utility. You can start up Axapta using either one by simply selecting it from the

Active Configuration combo box and clicking on either the OK button (which also closes the window), or the Apply button (which does not close the window). In either case, start the Axapta client using the shortcut created for you during installation.

■**Note** Later in this chapter we will configure a 3-tier setup in which the differences between using the two configuration types will be quite evident.

Let's look at the Manage button's purpose. Clicking on it will not bring up a dialog as you might expect. This is because the Manage button is a special type of Axapta button that you can recognize by a right-facing arrow on the right side of the button, and that displays a pop-up menu, as you can see in Figure 3-13.

Figure 3-13. *The Axapta Configuration Utility's Manage menu*

Suppose that we wanted to tear down the current installation or repeat it on another computer, and that instead of accepting default values we made a lot of changes. Wouldn't it be convenient if we could save the configuration and reuse it? That is exactly what you can do with the Save and Save As menu options. The Open option allows you to then read the saved configuration and consequently reuse it in other installations, either as is or as a template. The group of the first three menu options allows you to save and load individual configurations. These are saved to files with the type AXC.

■**Note** Opening or running an AXC file starts the Axapta client with the configuration parameters that you have saved in it. This allows you to save several different configurations that you can start by, for example, double-clicking on the files instead of having to start up the configuration utility, selecting a configuration, and then applying it. It is particularly useful if you place them on a network share, which allows your users to simply double-click to start a configuration.

The next group of menu items is somewhat similar; however, the Export menu option writes the configuration to a file with the extension XPO. You can't use these to start Axapta. Their purpose is instead to be imported for use at a later time. The Export All menu option exports all existing configurations to a single file instead of forcing you to create an export for each configuration.

■**Note** We use AXC files as described and XPO files for backup purposes or for sending a copy of a configuration (or all our configurations) to someone else. We suggest doing this when you place a bug report with the Microsoft Axapta sustained engineering team, to help them reproduce your configuration and bug.

The last group includes the New Configuration, which you learned about in the "General Configuration" section of this chapter. The Delete Configuration option deletes the selected configuration if you respond positively to the confirmation request, and the Rename Configuration option brings up a dialog containing the current name and a text box where you can enter a new name.

■**Note** Axapta configuration data is stored in the Windows registry and read from it. However, if you start a client with an AXC file, the configuration data is read from the file instead.

Post-Installation

We are now ready to fire up Axapta and begin the post-installation phase. Start your client now by using the shortcut that was created for you during the installation phase. You will be presented with the login dialog that will suggest admin as the user—we set this up in the 2-tier configuration we created and applied earlier, and since admin is created without a password, simply click Logon, and you're in.

■**Note** All the tasks presented in the installation checklist can be performed at any time and in different ways; you can even call up this exact same checklist at any time. However, unless you disable it for your user account, Axapta will automatically show it to you every time you log in if you have not completed all the tasks. Press the F1 key with the checklist as the active window for an explanation of what the different icons in the checklist represent.

On startup you will be presented with the installation checklist, shown in Figure 3-14. This is a list of steps that need to be performed before you can start using Axapta. Each step is detailed in the following sections of this chapter.

Compile Application

The first step is to compile the application code. This step will often require an hour or more, so muster your patience or take a lunch break once you've started it. It is important that this step be carried all the way through. If you fail to do so, you'll have to start again from scratch. You begin the process (as with all the processes in the checklist) by simply clicking on the text link—in this case, Compile Application.

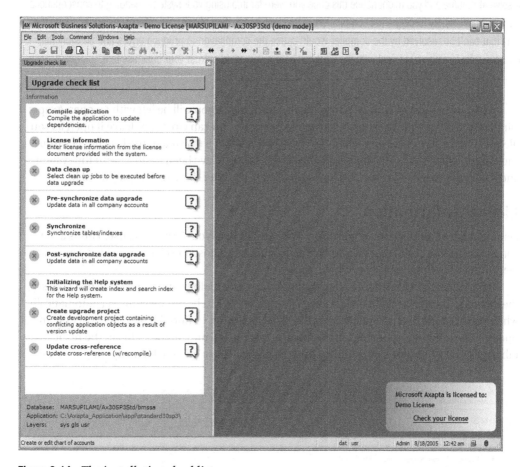

Figure 3-14. *The installation checklist*

Note For the most part Axapta executes in the main thread; consequently, the user interface will not update until a task is completed, so don't panic—the system is most likely not hanging. The task will eventually terminate and you will once again be able to interact with Axapta.

> ■**Note** People regularly ask us why Microsoft doesn't simply provide the application in binary form and save users the trouble and time of having to do a full compile of the X++ code base. The reason is twofold: First, the standard application on its way to end users is changed during localization, then by option pack providers, etc., and it's only at installation time that the exact makeup of the system is known, a sane binary can be produced, and the schema can be generated. Second, if a binary were delivered from the Microsoft product unit and contributors to the application code added their code and schema modifications and extensions, they might not resolve at runtime and you might notice this once you were far into using your system—leading to consequences for your business. By forcing a full compilation in the post-installation phase, any references added along the way that can't be resolved by the compiler would cause the compilation to produce errors and possibly fail, consequently forcing you to deal with the situation before you could entrust your business to it.

When a post-installation step from the list terminates, you will be left with an open Axapta window or dialog, typically showing progress or status. You can close it or leave it open as you please. When a step is finished, the blue circle to the left of each step in the list changes from showing an ellipsis (. . .) to showing a check mark. If you have been fiddling with the system and have not proceeded correctly from step to step, the blue circle will display a red X.

License Information

Once you have compiled the application, you need to load your Axapta license. This is a file containing license codes that your Microsoft partner or Microsoft itself has provided you, which determine what functionality you have access to.

Clicking on the License Information link brings up a dialog containing three text boxes at the top and a button labeled Load License File. Ignore the text boxes; these are set automatically when you load the license code from a file. Use the button to find the file, then select it and open it. The remaining controls, including the tab control and all the fields in the respective tab pages, will be set according to the contents of the license file (see Figure 3-15).

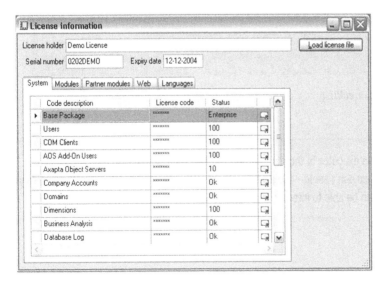

Figure 3-15. *The License Information form*

The different tabs provide information about what you are licensed for, and the tab-page labels are self-explanatory. However, there is one particularly interesting piece of information on the System tab: the Base Package status, which shows what kind of license you have. Where relevant, you can also see the number of licenses installed.

Note In many countries, only the Enterprise license is available, and it includes the use of an AOS. If you have a Professional license, you do not have AOS privileges, and thus you can only run Axapta in 2-tier mode, though you can add an AOS and AOS add-on users to go 3-tier. The Small Business license existed only in Scandinavia and is no longer available.

Load your license file and close the form.

Configuration

Next, click on the Configuration link. Now that you've told Axapta which modules or functionality you are licensed for, you can tell it which ones you want to use, as Figure 3-16 illustrates.

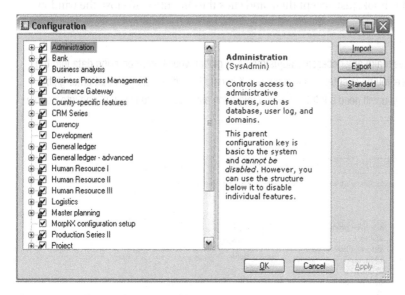

Figure 3-16. *The Configuration form*

This form presents a treeview control that displays all the licensed Axapta modules and whether they are enabled or not. Grayed nodes are totally or partially disabled, and you can't enable or disable an installed feature by checking or unchecking the top-level node. To change the state of a feature, you need to expand the top-level node and check or uncheck the child nodes to suit your needs. For now, simply check all the nodes except Country-Specific Features (it's enough that you check and enable the United States node, which we use as the reference throughout this book).

Click the Apply button to activate the changes you have made without closing the window, or OK to activate them and close the window.

The Configuration form contains three buttons on the right side. The Export button enables you to save the configuration to a file that can then be used in other installations via the Import button. The Standard button resets the configuration to its out-of-the-box state (i.e., practically all modules disabled).

Note As developers, we always enable all features and modules, and we regularly make new installations. Since the default configuration has almost everything disabled, we save time by exporting our standard configuration and then using the Import button to load it, thus avoiding having to expand all the nodes and check them repeatedly.

Adjust Global Types

Now click on the Adjust Global Types link. This step allows you to specify how to format various data types so that you can adjust them to your particular needs. We suggest that you quickly browse through the types (see Figure 3-17) to acquaint yourself with them and so you know what to expect when they are used. If necessary, adjust them when you have a real installation. But for the purpose of following along in this book, just accept them and click the OK button to close the window.

Note You should always make any necessary adjustments to global types before entering data into the system. Altering them once you have entered data may result in data loss. If you simply must enter global types after you enter data, you will need a full-blown data migration plan in place to avoid getting into trouble.

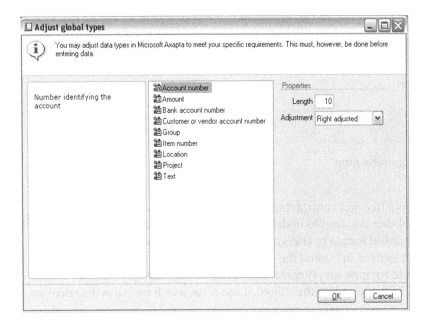

Figure 3-17. *The Adjust Global Types form*

Synchronize

The Synchronize item on your installation checklist ensures that your database schema is consistent with the metadata definitions of your application. In other words, it runs through your table object definitions and pushes their definitions to your SQL Server or Oracle database, making sure that the two are in sync. The amount of time this task takes varies depending on the number of discrepancies and your computer's power. You'll see a progress dialog that will close automatically when the application and database are fully synchronized.

■**Warning** You can't use the system without synchronizing.

Initializing the Help System

Although this is a pretty straightforward task, it's quite time-consuming, so let's save time by doing no more than is necessary. Clicking on the Initializing the Help System link will execute an Axapta wizard. As the first page of the wizard states, if an index is skipped now, it will be created the first time it is accessed by a user (see Figure 3-18).

Figure 3-18. *The Initializing the Help System wizard start page*

Click on the Next button. The next page of the wizard, shown in Figure 3-19, allows you to specify which languages the help system should be initialized for. Be sure to initialize any languages that will be used now, as this task takes time and if a user invokes it accidentally, it will hinder system performance. Depending on the speed of your system and the languages selected, this task can take several hours; we recommend running it overnight. Once you know your way around, you can skip this step when installing and run it later if you wish; just remember to not open the Help system until you've completed this step.

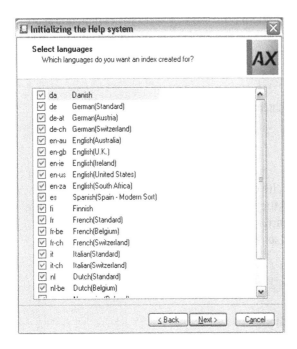

Figure 3-19. *The Initializing the Help System Select Languages page*

The next page in this wizard asks whether an index should be created. We recommend accepting the default, which places a check in the box. Help text is stored in your database, and creating an index will speed things up.

The last page of the wizard informs you that this is a time-consuming process and asks you to click Finish to confirm that you really want to embark on it. A progress dialog is displayed while the help system is initialized. When the process is complete, the bar disappears.

Update Cross-Reference

Documentation on this feature of Axapta is nonexistent. This section will help you understand what it's all about.

Axapta application objects can contain references to each other. A very common case is a table that consists of fields that are defined by extended data type objects. In practice, the table refers to the extended data types in question. The extended data types, in turn, might have relations to tables (they reference tables, and so on). Axapta provides the ability to follow and look up these cross-references at runtime. However the cross-references must first be persisted to the database.

This is quite a complex process, and we will go through it in detail. The Update Cross-Reference (w/Recompile) form consists of two tabs: General and Batch.

The General tab of the Update Cross-Reference form (shown in Figure 3-20) specifies the strategy for the cross-reference update and the types of Axapta application objects whose cross-references should be pushed to the database. The Batch tab allows you to set up the execution of this task as a batch job.

■**Note** The Batch tab is a standard batch job form. We'll cover batch jobs in detail in Chapter 5.

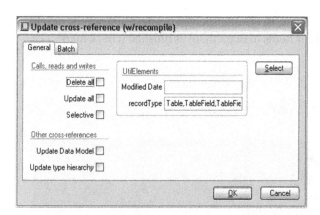

Figure 3-20. *The General tab of the Update Cross-Reference form*

The General tab page consists of three control groups. The first, Call, Reads and Writes, has three check boxes:

- *Delete All* specifies that references in code should be updated by simply deleting all existing cross-reference information in the database and generating it anew from scratch.

- *Update All* specifies that cross-references already in the database should be updated.

- *Selective* specifies that the update should only create and persist data for inexistent references and update those that are no longer in sync between the application and the database.

The second group, Other Cross-References, specifies whether the Axapta data types and the tables as defined in Axapta are to be included.

In the UtilElements group, you can specify that only references modified at a specific date should be included, and the types of objects whose cross-references should be included. You can specify these using the Select button. For now, leave this at the default.

■**Note** Some of the options on the General tab are a bit nonsensical. For example, what is the rationale of being able to specify Update All and Selective simultaneously in the Calls, Reads and Writes control group? All systems have these oddities, so simply work around them. We never select Delete All, and never check both the Update All and Selective check boxes together.

For our purposes, check the Update All, Update Data Model, and Update Type Hierarchy check boxes on the General tab of the form, as shown in Figure 3-20.

Click the OK button and take a break; this is another time-consuming task.

Authorization

There is actually no task with this designation in the installation checklist. However, Authorization is the general task that encompasses the last four items in the list: User Groups, Password Parameters, Users, and Company Accounts.

The steps in question require planning and preparation, and are used routinely as part of the normal daily administration of Axapta so we will discuss them in detail in the administration chapter of this book.

For now, and to make sure that the checklist is not displayed the next time we log on, click on the ellipsis next to each of the last four items to mark them as finished (check mark); see Figure 3-21.

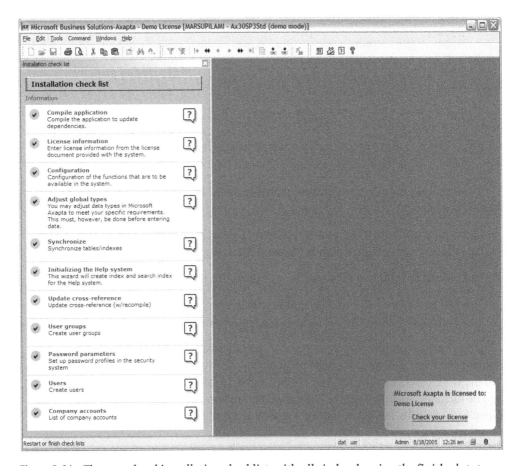

Figure 3-21. *The completed installation checklist, with all circles showing the finished state*

Now close down Axapta by selecting the Exit menu option from the File menu bar at the top of the window or by any standard method that you prefer.

■**Note** Axapta always requests confirmation about exiting.

3-Tier Configuration

To set up Axapta to run in 3-tier mode, we need to create at least one AOS and then go back to the Axapta Configuration Utility to create and configure a 3-tier client.

Server Manager

The first step is to go to the Windows Control Panel of the system where you installed the AOS and run the AOS configuration applet, named Navision-Axapta Object Server. The resulting dialog, shown in Figure 3-22, is where you will configure your AOS. This form consists of a combo box labeled Computer and two control groups, Server Manager and Object Servers.

Figure 3-22. *The Axapta Server Manager dialog*

The Computer Combo Box

The Computer combo box contains a list of computers detected on your domain. Selecting one will list the AOSs in the Object Servers grid running on the selected computer. By default the local computer is selected, and this should be the computer on which you installed the server when you installed Axapta.

Server Manager Controls

The first step in managing your AOS is to deal with the server manager. It is a Windows service that manages AOSs. When you install the server part of Axapta, it's installed and registered with the Windows services system using a configuration that is very rarely changed. You can stop and start the service using the Stop and Start buttons, and you can configure it using the Startup button. (Alternatively, you can use the services applet in the Windows Control Panel, as the startup configuration is a standard Windows service configuration dialog.)

Note The server manager not only allows you to configure your AOS, but also establishes sessions between clients and AOSs when running in 3-tier mode, and provides a "round robin" form of load balancing for AOS clusters.

Object Server Controls

As with a standard Windows server manager, you have buttons for starting and stopping the Object Server. The New and Delete buttons allow you to add AOSs to the computer that is selected. This allows you to use the same computer to run different instances or configurations, for example.

The Startup Button

The Startup button allows you to specify how the server manager is to start a particular AOS (see Figure 3-23). It is somewhat equivalent to the startup dialog of the Windows service manager.

Figure 3-23. *The Object Server Startup dialog*

This dialog consists of three control groups. In the first, Startup Type, you specify how you actually want the AOS to be started:

- Select Automatic for the server manager to run the AOS when the system boots.

- Select Manual if you want to do it yourself from the Server Manager dialog.

- Select On Demand if you want the server manager to start the AOS when a request for it is received from a client.

- Select Disable if you do not want to allow the server to be run.

The second control group, Object Server Executable, allows you to specify a binary other then the default installed. We have never heard of this being used except by the Axapta kernel development team to be able to debug the kernel, which is written in C++. The kernel team needs to use a binary that is built with debug information, and that is stripped out when the kind of kernel you are likely to have is built.

The last control group, Logon Account, allows you to specify a specific system user account to use when starting the AOS, typically to run it under the credentials of a restricted user for security reasons. On the other hand, you could just have installed Axapta under its own user account and made sure that it was allowed to have access only to the necessary resources.

The Settings Button

With this done we need to configure the server by clicking on the Settings button on the Object Servers control group of the Server Manager. The dialog for configuring AOSs is very similar to the one used to configure clients in the 2-tier setup, so we will cover only the Server tab, shown in Figure 3-24.

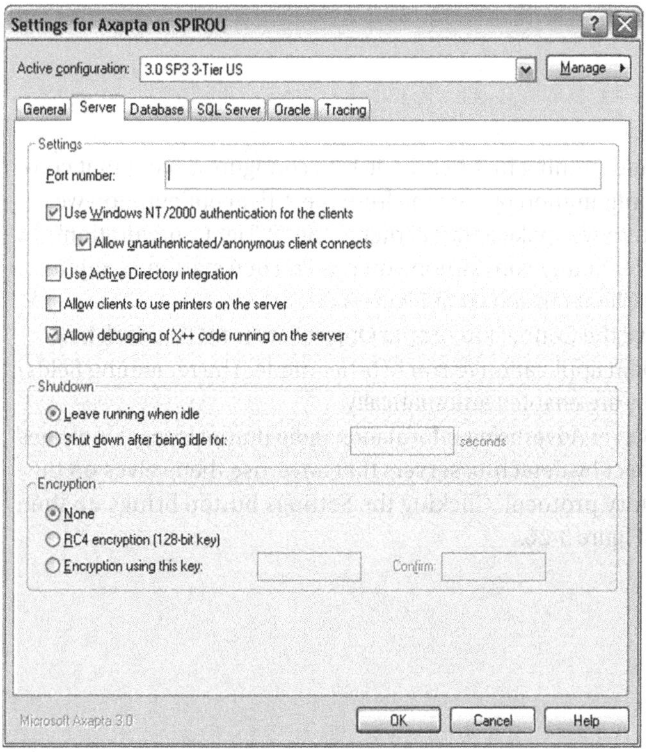

Figure 3-24. *The Object Server Startup dialog*

This tab page consists of three control groups. The first, Settings, allows you to specify the port number on which servers listen for TCP connections. The default port is 2048. However, you can change this if your security policy mandates it. The Use Windows NT/2000 Authentication for the Clients check box specifies whether to use Windows security and, in turn, to accept anonymous connections. In practice this instructs Axapta to simply accept connections from clients, to validate them against existing accounts in the domain, and to allow connections from unknown clients, but manage them as anonymous. The Allow Clients to Use Printers on the Server check box lets you enable Axapta clients to print to printers connected to the AOS; Allow Debugging of X++ Code Running on the Server permits debugging of code running in the server process.

The Shutdown control group specifies whether the AOS should run all the time or should be shut down to save resources, and the time to wait before shutting down when the AOS is idle. You should configure the AOS startup to On Demand in the Object Server Startup dialog if you specify here that it should be shut down when idle—this is so that the server manager can start it again when a request arrives for it.

The Encryption control group specifies how communication between clients and services is encrypted. Checking None means your data is transmitted in plain text. RC4 uses the famous cipher to encrypt your data. The Encryption Using This Key option uses a cipher developed by the Axapta product team.

■**Note** Axapta's home-grown encryption algorithm is easy to break, and only offers a false sense of security. If you don't care about having your data encrypted, don't bother wasting CPU cycles by checking this option; just select None.

3-Tier Client

The last step in getting Axapta up and running in 3-tier mode is to configure a client that connects to the server. Create a new configuration by copying from the 2-tier configuration we created, and name it using the pattern we spoke about earlier in the "2-Tier Configuration" section, but replace 2-tier with 3-tier or any convention you prefer. Then start the Axapta Configuration Utility and go to the Client tab shown in Figure 3-25.

At the top left of the tab we have the Connect to Axapta Object Server (AOS) check box. Checking it instructs the Axapta client application to run in 3-tier mode. The remaining fields are parameters to this mode, so they are enabled automatically.

By default the Connect Using Server Advertising Information radio button is set. It indicates that the Axapta client should connect by detecting servers that advertise themselves on the network using an Axapta proprietary protocol. Clicking the Settings button brings up the Connect Settings dialog, shown in Figure 3-26.

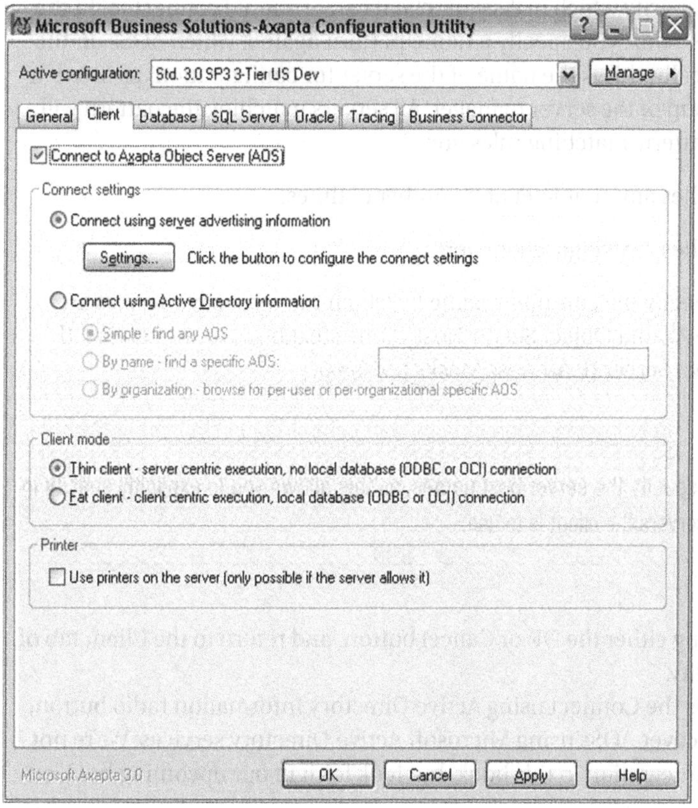

Figure 3-25. *The Axapta Configuration Utility's Client tab page*

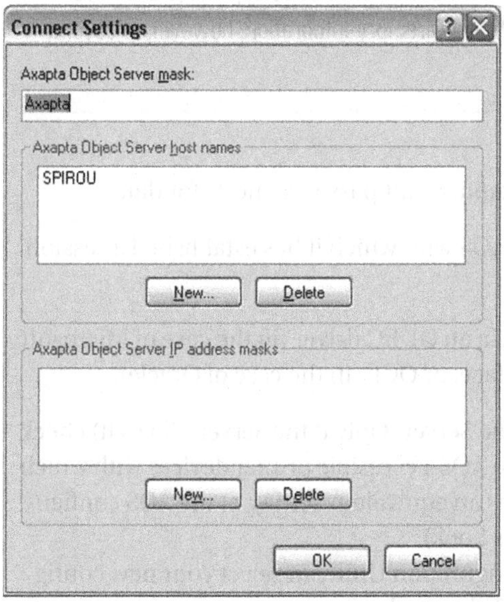

Figure 3-26. *The Axapta Configuration Utility's Connect Settings dialog*

This dialog allows you to specify which AOSs your client can or should connect to. In the Axapta Object Server Mask text box, you specify a name pattern against which AOSs on the network are matched. Specifically, this is the name of the server (or configuration) as listed in the Object Servers control group of the server manager. All servers matching the pattern will be usable by the client. The pattern-matching rules are:

- The "*" character matches any character any number of times.

- The "?" character matches any single character.

Additionally, you must specify the computer name by which the respective servers are known on the network (in the Axapta Object Server Host Names text box), or the servers' IP addresses (in the Axapta Object Server IP Address Masks text box).

■**Note** The most common is to specify the server host names, as this allows you to explicitly specify in a human-meaningful way which servers the client is to use.

Close the dialog by clicking either the OK or Cancel button, and return to the Client tab of the Axapta Configuration Utility.

The next field in the tab is the Connect using Active Directory Information radio button, which allows the client to discover AOSs using Microsoft Active Directory services. We're not getting into Active Directory integration in this book, but look for it in our upcoming book on advanced administration.

■**Note** To use this functionality, you must have access to a Windows Active Directory server and have installed the Active Directory Integration from Chapter 2. Active Directory Integration, however, is beyond the scope of this book.

The next two radio buttons specify how the Axapta client passes requests for data:

- The thin client passes requests through the AOS with which it has established a session, and thus processing is server-centric.

- The fat client accesses its database directly via an ODBC driver (in the case of Microsoft SQL Server) or through the Oracle Call Interface, or OCI, (in the case of Oracle).

The last field in this tab is the Use Printers on the Server (Only If the Server Allows It) check box. This specifies that the client prints hard copy to AOS-accessible printer devices with which it has established a session. This parameter requires an equivalent setting of the AOS configuration (AOS server setup is beyond the scope of this book).

You should now be able to use the Axapta Configuration Utility to select your new configuration and apply it so that you can run Axapta in 3-tier mode.

Demo Data

By now you have a running system, but in order for you to make any real use of it you need data. In a production environment you will, of course, want to create your own data. For demo and learning purposes, though, you can simply import one of several demo data sets that Microsoft provides for you.

The simplest data set for beginning to learn Axapta is *Light Company* (from the root of the Axapta distribution CD, choose Import ➤ Data ➤ Demonstration Data). However, this data set is specific for an installation running the Switzerland configuration. If your configuration is specific to the United States, you can download US-specific demo data from the Microsoft PartnerSource or CustomerSource Web sites, assuming you have login credentials. This data is specific to Service Pack 1 and thus it's recommended that you upgrade to SP1 before importing it.

■**Note** After you import demo data, we recommend running a consistency check (with the Module combo box set to All, the Check/Fix combo box set to Correct Error, and the From date blank, choose Basic ➤ Periodic ➤ Consistency Check) to check and fix the internal structure and integrity of your data.

Wrap-Up

This chapter has covered the following:

- Creating an Axapta 2-tier configuration as required to perform the post-installation

- Managing, saving, and reusing your startup function configurations to save yourself work in future installations

- Starting up Axapta, logging on, and performing the basic post-installation steps

- Creating an Axapta 3-tier configuration—the mode of operation that we recommend you stick to in test and production systems

- Finding and importing a basic data set to help you maneuver through the system

Although there is more to configuring Axapta than what we have walked you through here, you should now have a good understanding of which aspects of Axapta you can and need to configure, and how they fit together. You are still not a hardened expert, but there aren't many standard Axapta configuration requirements that you can't tackle.

You can read more about the topics in this chapter in the following documents, available in the documentation folder of the product distribution package or CD:

- *AX-300-DVG-004-v01.00-ENUS.chm*: Configuration Utility

- *AX-300-DVG-005-v01.00-ENUS.chm*: Server Manager

- *AX-300-TIP-041-v01.00-ENUS.doc*: Demonstration Data

CHAPTER 4

■ ■ ■

Navigation and User Options

In this chapter, we'll be walking through the Axapta integrated environment, grouping navigation into the following areas:

- *Axapta Desktop*: The main workspace/window for the development and run-time environments, and its navigation elements. Perhaps the most important element of the desktop is the main menu, from which you access the majority of the application's runtime functionality.

- *Forms, Dialogs, and Reports*: Objects in Axapta with specific navigation elements.

- *Searching and Filtering*: Functionality in Axapta with specific navigation elements.

Before you can really begin using Axapta, you need to know how to get around, and as in any Microsoft Windows–based software system, there are often several ways to do the same thing. However, because most of the applications that make up the Axapta system are Windows-compliant and support all the navigational bells and whistles you're used to, navigating Axapta should be no harder than learning how to invoke the functionality of any other Windows application. Try out the techniques in this chapter and experiment with the different ways of navigating specific areas of Axapta to figure out what works best for you. For instance, one of the authors tends to use the mouse heavily, but many people find keyboard shortcuts more effective.

■**Note** This chapter assumes that you have a basic data set in your company. Without a data set it will be difficult to follow along.

The Axapta Desktop

Figure 4-1 shows the Axapta desktop. This is the main window of Axapta's client component and contains virtually all the tools and windows that you work with in Axapta. The exceptions are the configuration utilities, the server manager, the HTML editor, and the debugger, which are described in Chapters 3 and 18, respectively. The figure indicates the areas of the Axapta desktop as they are usually designated in Microsoft documentation.

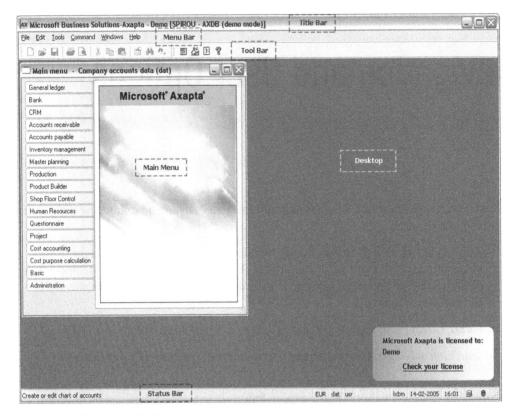

Figure 4-1. *The Axapta desktop*

Let's look at each of the areas individually.

The Title Bar

This is a standard Windows element and has a purely informative function. It is a concatenation of the following information:

- *The name*: Microsoft Business Solutions—Axapta.

- *The owner of the loaded license file*: This is Demo in Figure 4-1, which indicates that I'm running on a demo license.

- *Opening square bracket ([)*.

- *The name of the server that the client is connected to*: This is the local machine name when running in 2-tier mode, or the AOS name when running in 3-tier mode (in Figure 4-1, it's SPIROU).

- *The name of the database that's in use*: AXDB in my case.

- *The mode in which the client is running:* This applies only if it's in demo mode, enclosed in parentheses ( ).

- *The closing square bracket (])*.

The Menu Bar

This too is a standard Windows element. It provides a series of context-sensitive menus, which are enabled or disabled depending on the active child window of the desktop; i.e., the main menu, a specific form, etc.

The File Menu

The File menu contains the following menu and submenu options:

- *New* ➤ *New*: Creates a new application object. The object type is determined by the active window. So, for example, in a form it creates a new record (in the Projects form it creates a new project), and in the job's root node of the AOT it creates a job. It is used constantly, but everybody seems to use the shortcut key rather then the menu option (Ctrl-N).

- *New* ➤ *Wizard*: Creates a new Axapta wizard to automate a specific task, and is usually left to developers or technically minded consultants.

- *New* ➤ *User Menu*: Creates a new user menu. This is a great feature for end users. If in your work you use only a subset of the main menu, you can create a personalized version in which you define your own tabs, menu folders, and items by simply dragging them from the standard main menu. Figure 4-2 shows an example.

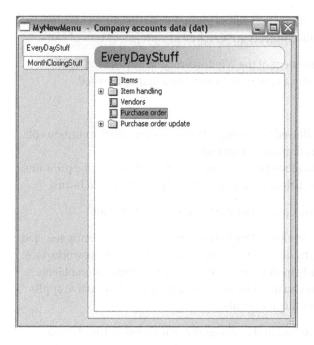

Figure 4-2. *A sample user menu*

- *Open* ➤ *Open*: Opens the last form or dialog you opened if you have since closed it; if it is open, it will do nothing. You can also use the shortcut key combination of Ctrl-O.

- *Open* ➤ *Main Menu*: Opens the main menu. This is useful if, for example, you closed the main menu because you generally use your own personalized menu, but now you need to access some functionality that your custom menu does not include.

- *Open* ➤ *Menu*: Opens a predefined application menu. These include all the installed sub-menus on the main menu, and many more. The resulting pull-down is divided into two parts with a standard Windows menu separator. The top portion lists the menus defined by the currently logged-on user, and the lower portion shows system-defined menus.

- *Open* ➤ *Company*: Displays a dialog from which you can select a company other than the current one to work with.

■**Note** Axapta allows you to manage separate companies within the same system. You can then move between them easily, and even consolidate them (though you normally can see data only for the active company).

- *Open* ➤ *Application Object Tree*: A developer tool that provides access to the application objects in the active application in a tree control.

- *Open* ➤ *Project*: Another developer tool that allows grouping of application objects. Typically used to keep track of which objects are touched in a project or unit of work.

- *Open* ➤ *AOT Recycle Bin*: The equivalent of the Windows recycle bin, but for AOT objects. This recycle bin is automatically emptied when the instance is exited.

- *Close*: Closes the active window.

The preceding menu options are followed by a group of options that save the contents of the active window—for example, application objects and data.

The following group is a standard Windows printing group, with the twist that the printouts are Axapta reports and consequently the dialogs they invoke are Axapta dialogs and forms.

- *Send*: Equivalent to the Print menu option, but the output device is e-mail.

- *Properties*: Displays the Application Object Properties window for the currently selected object in the AOT. The window is by default anchored to the right side of the workspace. This menu option is used primarily by developers to set values in application objects, system administrators and others can use it to see information about the active application object. Chapter 18 provides further details.

- *Exit*: The standard Windows menu option that closes the main window (the Axapta client desktop).

The Edit Menu

Next on the menu bar is Edit. For the most part the options on this menu perform standard functions, but they're applied to data or application objects. We will mention only the two that lack a keyboard shortcut. For the others please refer to Appendix D.

- *Duplicate*: Creates a copy of the selected application object.

- *Word Wrap*: Creates a word wrap when the active window is an internal text editor, like the X++ editor.

The Tools Menu

The third menu on the menu bar is the Tools menu, which is specific to Axapta and has the following menu options:

- *Telephone List*: Displays local and mobile phone numbers of the employees created in the employee table of the HR module for the active company account.

- *System Date*: Axapta keeps track of two dates—the computer clock date and the Axapta system date. The first is simply whatever your computer clock is set to, but you can set the system date yourself. This can be quite useful if your need to perform an operation back or ahead in time relative to the actual current date.

■**Note** If you change the date on your computer clock, the change is carried over to Axapta automatically, but the system date is not adjusted accordingly. However, the system data is reset to the computer date when you shut down and restart Axapta.

- *Calculator*: Fires up the Windows calculator.

- *Calculator for Units*: Converts between Axapta unit types based on the data setup using the forms at the main menu path *Basic* ➤ *Setup* ➤ *Units*.

- *Print Archive*: Displays a list of print jobs executed from Axapta for the user currently logged on.

- *Select Company Accounts*: This is a very important menu option and it's how you move between the different companies that you have created in the currently active application.

- *Development Tools*: Applies only to developers and technically minded consultants; please refer to Chapter 18.

- *Customize*: Brings up the form shown in Figure 4-3, which allows you to specify which groups of menu buttons to display on the desktop toolbar for the user currently logged on. It's buggy and we generally turn them all on with small buttons because the large ones do not display correctly.

Figure 4-3. *The Customize form of the Tools menu*

- *Options*: This is where you set up your general preferences for the Axapta environment.

- *Compiler*: Allows you to specify additional personal settings for the X++ compiler.

The Command Menu

The Command menu varies significantly based on the active application object and is quite extensive, so instead of covering it in depth here, we will refer to it throughout this book as appropriate. Some of the things you can do from this menu are filter records, sort, import and export object definitions. Investigate the menu by opening different types of application objects, such as forms, reports, the AOT, etc, to see what commands are available.

The last two menus on the menu bar, Windows and Help, are standard Windows menus that you can work out easily.

The Toolbar

This is a standard Windows element that provides a series of menu buttons for the most commonly used commands and activities, as shown in Figure 4-4. You will recognize the majority of the buttons from other Windows applications; for those you don't, just place the cursor on the menu button for a hint.

■**Note** The menu buttons available on the toolbar change based on the active window. For example, forms add data navigation to it, and the AOT and Project organizer add developer-related buttons. Buttons beyond the base set shown in Figure 4-4 do not have equivalent options in the menu bar. You must use either the toolbar or keyboard shortcuts.

Figure 4-4. *The basic toolbar*

The Main Menu

The main menu is a hierarchical structure consisting of tabs. These are the top levels of each module. The submenu pane appears to the right of a selected module. The pane is labeled with the name of the expanded tab, as demonstrated in Figure 4-5.

■**Note** Unfortunately, the structure of the main menu and the concept of the module in Axapta are not always consistent. Therefore, we call tabs modules rather than application modules. Some application modules span several tabs, and some have functionality that is accessible from tabs of other modules.

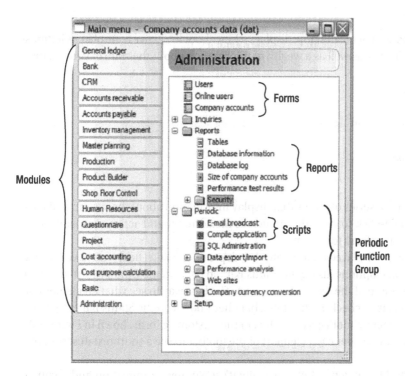

Figure 4-5. *The main menu and its options pane*

Figure 4-5 provides a good overview of how the main menu elements are structured. Each module is identified by a tab. Each tab, in turn, contains folders and forms. Folders contain subfolders, which group other elements, i.e. forms, reports, and scripts (folders may also contain reports and scripts, though this is rare). As a general rule each subfolder corresponds to a function group. The default function groups are as follows:

- *Journals*: In Axapta, journals are used for both standard accounting and to manually update data throughout the system.

- *Inquiries*: Form views of system data. These are used for reporting purposes and we prefer them over standard flat reports because inquires are much quicker and easier to filter and sort.

- *Reports*: Standard flat reports. Axapta has many built-in reports, and it's possible to create your own. Chapter 14 focuses on reporting and business analysis.

- *Periodic*: Jobs or scripts used periodically for data updates.

- *Setup*: Used to control the base setup of features and functionality for the specific tab or module.

Navigating around the main menu is pretty simple—simply position the cursor over a tab to display its contents in the submenu pane. Click once on the plus (+) or minus (-) symbol to the left of a folder to expand or collapse it, or double-click on the folder itself. Double-click on the form, report, and script icons to run them, or click once on their labels.

The Status Bar

The Status bar, at the bottom of the desktop, displays a hint about the active control in its leftmost pane, as shown in Figure 4-6, as well as a wealth of information about the state of your Axapta configuration.

Figure 4-6. *The status bar*

To the right of that is a series of panes that display information about the system and its activities. You can double-click some of these, such as the currency and active company, to bring up the corresponding form for editing.

The exact information displayed on the status bar depends on which fields you have selected to display in your personal options (using the Status Bar tab page on the Options form that you display from the Tools menu of the Axapta menu bar). The best way to see what an element of the status bar represents is to check all the status bar check boxes on the Status Bar tab page. Also be sure to check the Show Tool Tips check box in the Customize form shown in Figure 4-3. You can then place the cursor over each element of the toolbar to see a short text description of its purpose.

That covers the desktop in a nutshell. Basically it's a Windows application and it can be re-sized, maximized, closed, etc., just like all Windows applications.

Forms, Dialogs, and Reports

Data is presented to a user in Axapta via a form, dialog, or report. It's important you know what each does and what your options are when you encounter them:

- Axapta uses forms for the majority of data that is displayed in the system. Generally forms are resizable windows and contain data in fields that can be sorted.

- Axapta uses dialogs to capture specific data or alert the user for informational purposes.

- Axapta uses reports for standard flat reporting. There are many options for reporting, and you'll learn the basics here. Chapter 14 talks more about creating your own reports.

Forms

Forms are where most of the action happens in Axapta, so knowing how to get around in them is crucial. Figure 4-7 shows a sample form (access it by selecting Accounts Receivable ➤ Customers).

Note Different options are enabled and displayed depending on the form. Not all forms support all functionality.

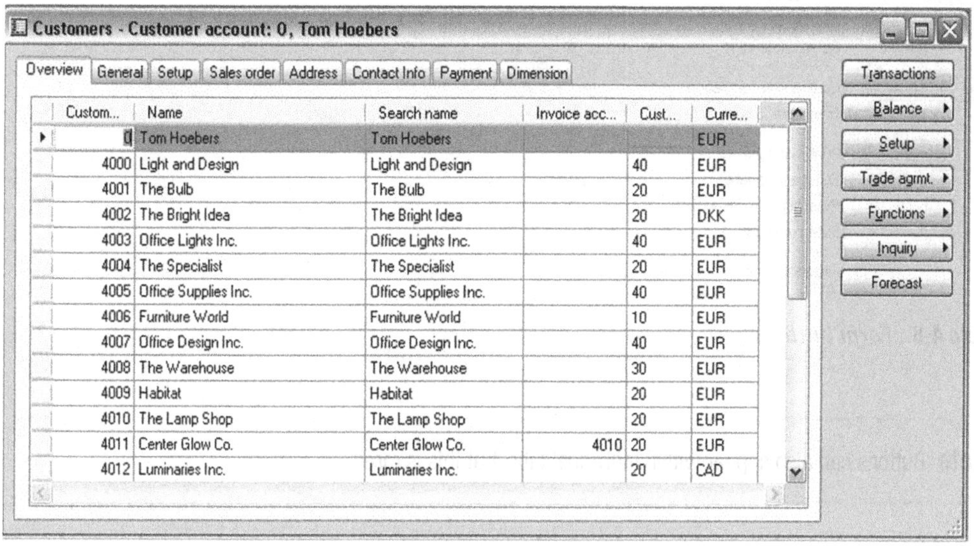
Customers - Customer account: 0, Tom Hoebers
Overview
General
Setup
Sales order
Address
Contact Info
Payment
Dimension
Custom...
Name
Search name
Invoice acc...
Cust...
Curre...
0 Tom Hoebers Tom Hoebers EUR
4000 Light and Design Light and Design 40 EUR
4001 The Bulb The Bulb 20 EUR
4002 The Bright Idea The Bright Idea 20 DKK
4003 Office Lights Inc. Office Lights Inc. 40 EUR
4004 The Specialist The Specialist 20 EUR
4005 Office Supplies Inc. Office Supplies Inc. 40 EUR
4006 Furniture World Furniture World 10 EUR
4007 Office Design Inc. Office Design Inc. 40 EUR
4008 The Warehouse The Warehouse 30 EUR
4009 Habitat Habitat 20 EUR
4010 The Lamp Shop The Lamp Shop 20 EUR
4011 Center Glow Co. Center Glow Co. 4010 20 EUR
4012 Luminaries Inc. Luminaries Inc. 20 CAD
Transactions
Balance
Setup
Trade agmt.
Functions
Inquiry
Forecast

Figure 4-7. *The Overview tab of the Customers form*

The title bar of the form displays the form name, and possibly two fields of the currently selected record.

The first tab, labeled Overview, presents core data from an underlying table or set of tables in tabular format with one record per line and one field per column.

The table uses the field names as column headings. Clicking on a column heading automatically sorts the data set by the field. An up or down arrow is displayed to indicate the order; i.e., ascending or descending.

The leftmost column of the table is unlabeled. It is used to indicate the selected row with a right-facing arrow. Additionally, the selected row's background appears gray.

Note The fields to be displayed are determined by the form's properties specified at design time in the property editor. These fields can be edited by a user with privileges to the Setup function (right-click on the form, and select Setup from the pop-up menu that is displayed).

Typically the right side of the form will display a group of buttons. These fall into two categories:

- *Menu buttons* display a pop-up menu from which you can select a menu option that executes an associated function. These have a right-pointing arrow aligned with the right side, as in Figure 4-8.

- *Command buttons* execute functions. These are standard Windows buttons and do not have an arrow.

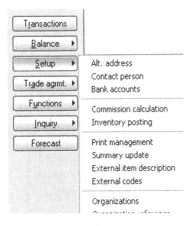

Figure 4-8. *Form buttons*

■**Note** Buttons can also appear within individual tabs, but this is rare.

Pop-Up Menus

Axapta offers a pop-up menu that you can invoke by right-clicking on any field. The menu offers options to perform common tasks based on selecting a field, plus a few options that are form-wide (see Figure 4-9; you can access this menu by selecting Accounts Receivable ➤ Customers ➤ Setup tab).

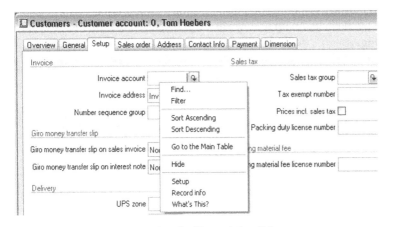

Figure 4-9. *A pop-up menu invoked by a right click*

The menu options are as follows:

- *Find* searches for records with a given pattern in the selected field.

- *Filter* blocks out all records that do not contain the value in the selected field.

- *Sort Ascending* and *Sort Descending* sort the records in the current data set by the selected field in ascending or descending order, respectively.

- *Go to the Main Table* is useful when you need to enter data in a field that is looked up in a table or is a foreign key of a parent table. You can use it to look up a valid value or even to create the necessary data, and then return to the form you are working in and enter or select the data.

- *Hide* hides the selected field or control. The form setup is saved for the currently logged-in user, and persists across sessions.

- *Show* displays fields/controls that have been hidden previously, and is displayed only if you have previously hidden a control on the form.

- *Setup* is mostly a developer-utility function that displays information about how the form is designed. Other users can, if authorized by the designer, use this to customize the form by moving controls around, adding or removing fields, etc.

- *Record Info* shows all the fields in the form on one single screen or produces an equivalent report.

- *What's This?* displays the online help text associated with the selected control.

■**Note** Right-clicking outside a field brings up a shorter version of the pop-up menu.

These menu options can also be invoked from the toolbar, from the Command menu in the menu bar, and by using keyboard shortcuts.

The Forms Toolbar

Whenever you're active within a form, you will notice an additional panel (shown in Figure 4-10) on the toolbar, and several form-specific menu options.

Figure 4-10. *The forms toolbar*

Let's look at the buttons from left to right:

- *The Filter button* filters out all records that do not contain the value in the selected field.
- *The Remove Filter button* removes the currently applied filter.
- *The arrow buttons* let you navigate back and forth through the records.
- *The Document Handling button* displays the document handling for the selected record.
- *The Previous Field and Next Field buttons* are a quick way to hop from one field group to another on tabs that use a flow layout.
- *The Delete Record button* does exactly what its name indicates.

Saving and Restoring Form Data

There are two very important data-set navigation commands that we haven't covered: saving and restoring data. The only way to explicitly save data is by using the standard Windows keyboard shortcut Ctrl-S. However, when you exit the selected record, Axapta automatically saves any data you entered.

If, *before saving*, you regret the changes you have made, you can invoke the Restore a Menu option on the Command menu of the menu bar.

Tip The record state can be restored only as long as it's not saved, and moving off a record in Axapta saves it automatically. We usually use the keyboard shortcut F5 to restore the state of the current record when we regret our changes. Alternatively, you can press Esc to get out of a form and answer No in the dialog that asks if you would like to save your changes.

Caution When working through a form and going from tab to tab, give careful consideration to whether you should save along the way. Not saving may result in your losing any data you have entered; saving, on the other hand, means you will not be able to restore the record to its initial state.

Dialogs

This brings us to a variation on forms: dialogs. In Axapta dialogs generally have purely informational purposes, with buttons for accepting or canceling an operation, and some are standard Windows dialogs or equivalents. However, this is not a requirement and developers can create dialogs with any of the controls that can be used in a form.

We distinguish forms from dialogs by classifying all non-resizing windows as dialogs. Figure 4-11 is an example of a dialog.

Figure 4-11. *A sample dialog. This dialog appears after you create a new record in a form and use the Esc button to exit the form before saving the record.*

Reports

Reports are a different kind of animal. Running a standard report displays either the Report Options dialog or the Query Definition form. If the Report Options dialog includes a Select button, it will take you to the Query Definition form.

The Report Options Dialog

Figure 4-12 shows a typical Report Options dialog:

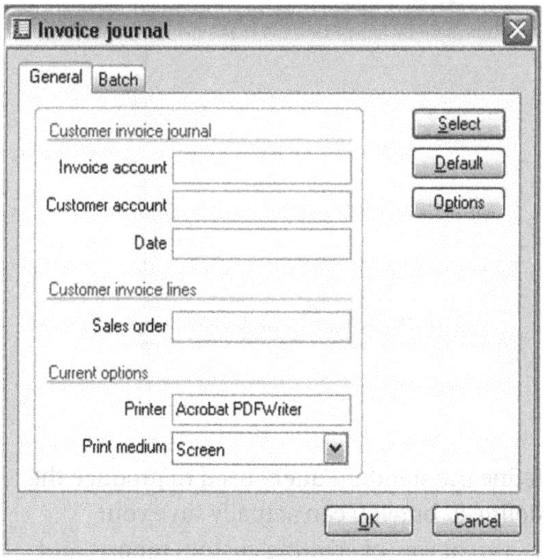

Figure 4-12. *A Report Options dialog*

The General tab of this dialog allows you to specify criteria for the report—the specific fields available depend on the report. The Current Options group is not editable. The print medium is always the screen of the Axapta client (where the report can be previewed), and the printer is the system default printer (where the report will actually be printed if you decide to print after previewing it). The Default button resets the dialog fields, and the Options button displays the Print Options dialog, where you can change the printer, printer medium, and various other print options.

The Batch tab allows you to create a batch job to handle the report and is particularly useful for large reports that you want to print in off hours, or for jobs that recur.

Note Batch jobs are described in Chapter 5 and queries are covered in Chapter 18.

The Query Definition Form

Figure 4-13 shows a typical Query Definition form.

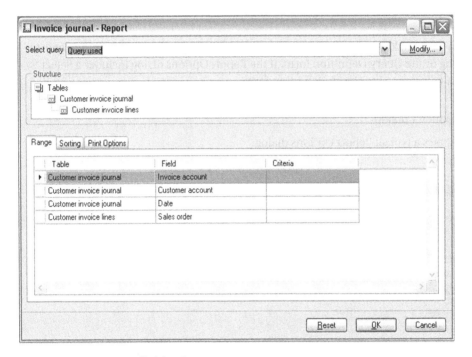

Figure 4-13. *A Query Definition form*

The Query Definition form enables you to define the standard query used to produce the report that you are running. You can not only redefine it, but you can actually save your altered query so that you can reuse it later. This is a great way of creating custom reports and queries when an available query is close to what you need but not exactly it.

Printing the Report

The final step in a report is to press OK and let the report run. If you've chosen to print your report to the screen, it will open using the preview window.

Tip Do not generate previews of reports for which you create a batch job— i.e., do not select the screen as the print medium—or the report will be displayed to your screen and then wait for you to print it to the final output device.

The preview window form provides a pop-up menu for resizing the report to the window size or to a set of fixed scalings that you can display by right-clicking anywhere within the report pane. The toolbar shown in Figure 4-14 provides buttons for printing and navigating the pages of the report.

Figure 4-14. *The report toolbar*

You use the toolbar to print the report to the printer selected in the Report Options dialog and to navigate the report preview on-screen. Place the cursor on a button to see a tooltip with a short explanation of the button's function and its keyboard shortcut.

Searching and Filtering

Axapta's searching and filtering features make it easy for you to obtain the exact information you need, organized the way you want it. They are accessible via the menu bar, the buttons on the toolbar, keyboard shortcuts, and/or the pop-up menu invoked by right-clicking on a field within a form.

Not all navigation features are available from every navigation element of Axapta; try them out now to get an idea of what is available where.

Start by opening the Item form (Inventory Management ➤ Items), position your cursor in one of the fields, then right-click. Figure 4-15 shows the result.

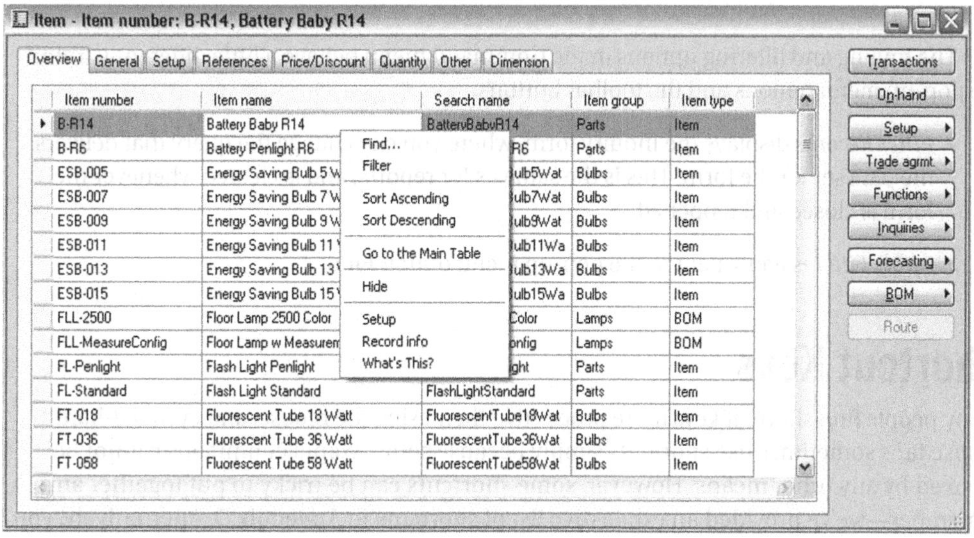

Item number	Item name		Search name	Item group	Item type
▶ B-R14	Battery Baby R14		BatteryBabyR14	Parts	Item
B-R6	Battery Penlight R6	Find...	R6	Parts	Item
ESB-005	Energy Saving Bulb 5 W	Filter	ulb5Wat	Bulbs	Item
ESB-007	Energy Saving Bulb 7 W		ulb7Wat	Bulbs	Item
ESB-009	Energy Saving Bulb 9 W	Sort Ascending	ulb9Wat	Bulbs	Item
ESB-011	Energy Saving Bulb 11 W	Sort Descending	ulb11Wa	Bulbs	Item
ESB-013	Energy Saving Bulb 13 W	Go to the Main Table	ulb13Wa	Bulbs	Item
ESB-015	Energy Saving Bulb 15 W	Hide	ulb15Wa	Bulbs	Item
FLL-2500	Floor Lamp 2500 Color	Setup	Color	Lamps	BOM
FLL-MeasureConfig	Floor Lamp w Measurem	Record info	nfig	Lamps	BOM
FL-Penlight	Flash Light Penlight	What's This?	ght	Parts	Item
FL-Standard	Flash Light Standard		FlashLightStandard	Parts	Item
FT-018	Fluorescent Tube 18 Watt		FluorescentTube18Wat	Bulbs	Item
FT-036	Fluorescent Tube 36 Watt		FluorescentTube36Wat	Bulbs	Item
FT-058	Fluorescent Tube 58 Watt		FluorescentTube58Wat	Bulbs	Item

Figure 4-15. *The pop-up menu in the Item form*

We covered the pop-up menu options in the "Pop-Up Menus" section of this chapter. Now we'll explore the menu's filtering options in more detail.

Both the Find and Filter options create a filter that constrains the displayed data set. After you find or filter, your form will display only a subset of the records you had originally. If you want to see them all again, use the Remove Filter button on the toolbar (second from the left in Figure 4-11—a funnel with a red X on it). Alternatively, you could use the Remove Filter menu option in the menu bar's Command menu—see Figure 4-16.

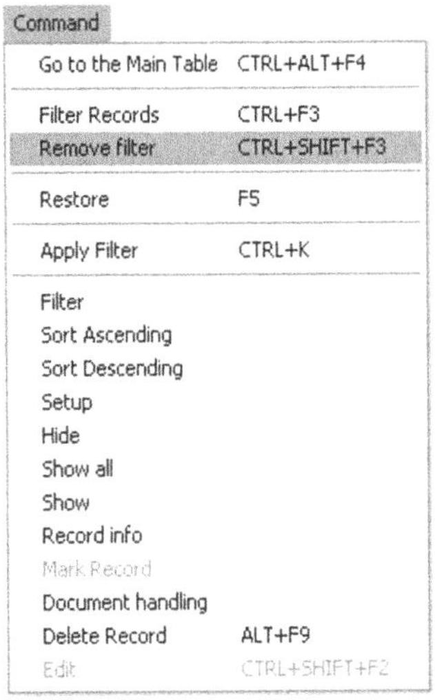

Command	
Go to the Main Table	CTRL+ALT+F4
Filter Records	CTRL+F3
Remove filter	CTRL+SHIFT+F3
Restore	F5
Apply Filter	CTRL+K
Filter	
Sort Ascending	
Sort Descending	
Setup	
Hide	
Show all	
Show	
Record info	
Mark Record	
Document handling	
Delete Record	ALT+F9
Edit	CTRL+SHIFT+F2

Figure 4-16. *The Remove Filter option in the Command menu*

The finding and filtering options in the Command menu behave a little differently from the pop-up menu options and the toolbar buttons:

- *Filter Records* displays the Inquiry form, where you can change the query that delivers the data set for the form. This is the same as for reports, and is cleared whenever the form is closed and reopened.

- *Apply Filter* is equivalent to the pop-up menu option Find.

Shortcut Keys

Many people find shortcut keys more productive then using the mouse, and even die-hard mouse fans sometimes use shortcuts simply because some Axapta commands cannot be invoked by any other means. However, some shortcuts can be tricky to put together and remember—we've provided an exhaustive list of shortcuts in Appendix D. Alternatively, you can look up the shortcuts in Axapta's online help by using the standard Windows shortcut F1.

Wrap-Up

In this chapter you learned most of what there is to know about moving around in Axapta. As you've also learned by now, Axapta is feature-rich, and there are so many ways of doing any particular thing that it's impossible to remember everything. Simply select the way that works best for you as you go.

The rest is up to you, and with a bit of experience, you will be whizzing through Axapta. Specifically, we covered the following:

- How to navigate the desktop (the main window of the client and its navigational components), the main application menu, and forms

- How to search for and filter data in your forms

- The importance of shortcut key combinations and where to look them up

You can read more about the topics in this chapter in the following documents available in the documentation folder of the product distribution package or CD:

- *AX-300-USG-011-v01.00-ENUS.pdf*—Getting Started

CHAPTER 5

■ ■ ■

Administration

The responsibilities of Axapta system administrators tend to vary significantly from one site to another; however, as with any ERP system, you need to have a system administrator who makes sure that the system is running healthily, maintains it, and where appropriate takes care of automated, routine tasks.

The majority of administrative tasks in Axapta are found under the Administration sub-menu of the main application menu. In addition, it's a good idea for Axapta administrators to know how to get an Axapta system up and running, and how to add and configure clients and servers.

A fundamental responsibility for any administrator is managing access to the system, so we will focus strongly on it here. We will cover typical administrative routines, and in order to do this, we have broken down administrative tasks into the following four categories:

- Authentication

- Codes and keys

- Authorization

- Maintenance tasks

The first three categories, covered in their own sections in this chapter, are all related to managing users and what they can and cannot do. The relevance of authentication varies depending on whether you are running Axapta in 2-tier or 3-tier mode (see Chapter 3), so make sure you read the section specific to your deployment architecture.

The fourth and last category, also discussed in its own section, covers the kind of routines that administrators typically do, or should at least be well acquainted with, such as running batch jobs, backing up the Axapta application and data, and so on.

In this chapter, you will learn how to do the following:

- Manage who to allow in and who not.

- Control the functionality that's available.

- Check on the system's state of health.

- Execute unattended routine work, for example, batch jobs.

- Get data in and out of the system.

- Prepare for disaster by backing up your system.

If you want to follow along in Axapta while you read this chapter, start your Axapta client now and log on, as you will soon need it.

Authentication

We start this section with a quick overview of what is involved in giving users access to Axapta and the functionality they need, followed by a look at authenticating users in the AOS.

Overview

To gain access to an Axapta system, users need to be authenticated as valid users and authorized to access specific areas of functionality. As an administrator, it will normally be your responsibility to select a method of authentication and set up users who can access the system.

Depending on the deployment architecture that you are using (2-tier configuration or 3-tier configuration), users need to go through the following steps to access the functionality of Axapta:

1. Start up a client application such as the native Windows application provided by MBS.

2. Log on to Axapta using the appropriate user ID and password.

In 2-tier mode, the client executes the application code and interacts directly with the database, so logging on is all that is necessary to access the Axapta application.

In 3-tier mode, users need to be authenticated by the Axapta Object Server (AOS), so you also have to manage how this works. We'll discuss this in the following section.

Authenticating Users in an AOS

Figure 5-1 shows the setting up of a 3-tier system using the AOS management utility. We covered this in Chapter 3, but let's quickly review it, expanding on the process that's concerned with how Axapta users are authenticated by AOSs. Naturally, if you have a 2-tier setup, then this does not apply, and you may want to skip ahead to the section "Codes and Keys."

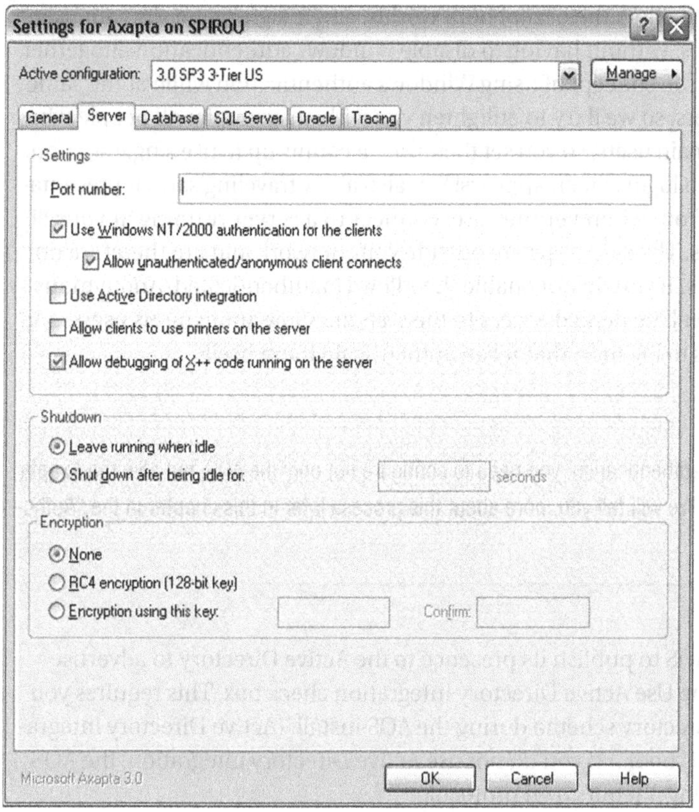

Figure 5-1. *AOS Settings form*

The important part of this utility in terms of authentication is the *Settings* control group.

■**Note** Remember, a shortcut to this utility is placed in the Windows Control Panel during installation of the server component. Refer to Chapter 3 if you need to refresh your memory as to what it does.

Enabling Windows authentication for clients instructs Axapta to use the Windows authentication system to figure out who a user is when connecting to an AOS from an Axapta client; that is, Axapta determines whether the user is a Windows domain user running the client. Disabling this option tells the AOS not to care who a user is and just ask that user to log in. It's a good idea to enable Windows authentication because it provides single sign-on—in other words, Axapta will use users' Windows logon credentials to authenticate users on the same domain as the AOS and save them the trouble of having to log on to Axapta. However, it will keep out people who are not on the domain to which the AOS belongs, so remote users will be refused access.

Allowing anonymous users offers the best of both worlds, single sign-on for domain users and the Axapta logon for others, without having to disable Windows authentication altogether. It can be tricky to understand the concept of using Windows authentication while at the same time allowing anonymous users, so we'll try to enlighten you with an example: All people who work at your company are domain users, so you set their user accounts up to use single sign-on, and when they start Axapta, no login screen appears! You also allow traveling sales representatives to fire up their laptops from wherever they are, connect to a server running at your IT center, and create sales orders. The sales reps are outside your network and are therefore not authenticated as domain users. If you do not enable the Allow Unauthenticated/Anonymous Client Connects option, they will be denied access to the system. Allow anonymous users, and Axapta will ask your sales reps to log in so that it can authenticate them itself.

Note In order to use Windows authentication, you need to configure not only the AOS, but also the Axapta system users to which they apply. We will tell you more about this process later in this chapter in the "Authorization" section.

You can also enable the AOS to publish its presence to the Active Directory to advertise itself to clients, by checking the Use Active Directory Integration check box. This requires you to have installed the Active Directory schema during the AOS install. (Active Directory integration is beyond the scope of this book.) If you do not use Active Directory integration, the AOS will broadcast its presence using Axapta's own protocol.

A practical feature of Axapta is the capability of clients printing to printers on an AOS. You can enable this feature by checking the Allow Clients to Use Printers on the Server check box and making sure that the users under which the Windows service *Axapta Object Server* runs have access to the printers you want to make available.

By default, the AOS service is installed to run as the system account, which will normally not have access to network printers. Therefore, you need to go to the Windows Services Manager utility located in the Control Panel, select the service, bring up the Properties dialog box, and specify a domain account with access to the desired printers, as shown in Figure 5-2.

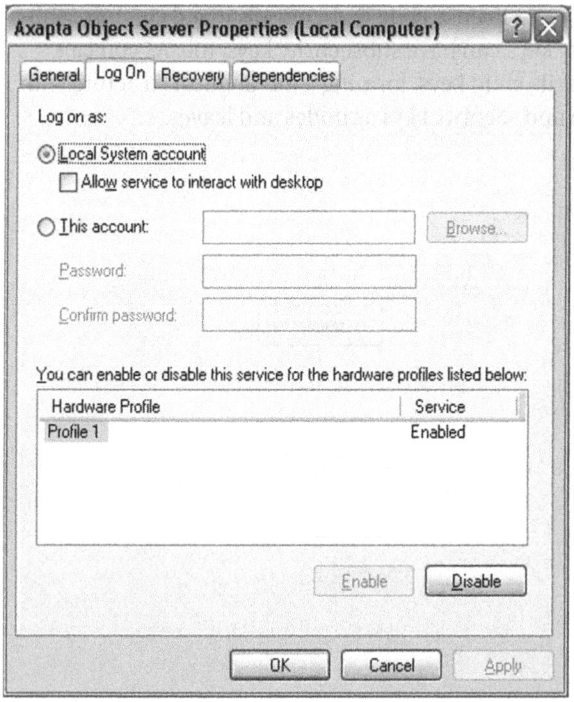

Figure 5-2. *Axapta Object Server, Windows service Log On properties*

Last but not least, you can allow or disallow the debugging of code running on the AOS. You should allow it on development and test environments, but turn off this option on production environments, as there is an associated performance penalty.

This brings you to the last step before an Axapta user is in and can get on with his or her daily business, and that is to log in to the system. Once a user's client has been recognized as legitimate by the server to which it is attempting to connect, the user will be prompted for a user name and password.

As the administrator, you need to have previously created and set up the user's permissions, which we'll examine in the "Authorization" section. But first you need to know something about codes and keys, as these determine what users can actually do, so it's a good idea to know how to use them before creating your users.

Codes and Keys

Another important administrative task in Axapta is managing what functionality is available and to whom by setting up a hierarchy of codes and keys, namely the following:

- License codes

- Configuration keys

- Security keys

Each configuration key is associated with a license code that controls it and can have subconfiguration or security keys, and security keys can have subsecurity keys, too. As you can see in Figure 5-3, each code or key controls its child keys, forming a hierarchical structure with license codes at the top and configuration and security keys as nodes and leaves.

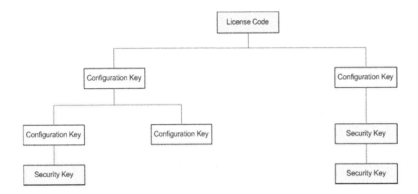

Figure 5-3. *Codes and keys structure*

Note We suggest that you read about the Application Object Tree (AOT) in Chapter 18, which discusses the development environment. Then use the AOT to browse the codes and keys in Axapta in order to get a feeling for how they fit together—this is often the only way of determining exactly what functionality gets turned on or off for each code and/or key.

Now that you have an idea of the how codes and keys relate generally, we'll take a closer look at license codes, configuration keys, and security keys in the upcoming text.

License Codes

Unlike many other systems where you only receive the binaries that you pay for, the binaries in the Axapta standard distribution package actually contain all available standard functionality. However, which areas you actually have access to depends on the modules that you have purchased and which codes you received as a result.

In Chapter 3, we showed you how to load the license codes that you received from MBS using the license file form—the file contains a series of codes that turn on the modules you have access to. This form can be accessed at any time to update your licenses, for example, if you acquire access to new modules from Microsoft Business Solutions or acquire and install third-party modules, languages, and so on. You do this by selecting Administration ➤ Setup ➤ System ➤ License Information. Take a look at the form in question, presented once more in Figure 5-4, and see what it enables you to manage.

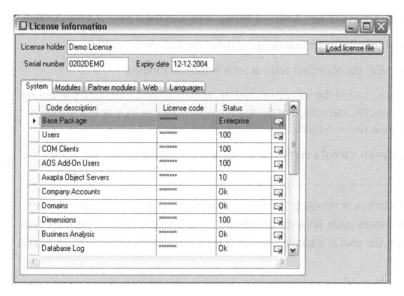

Figure 5-4. *License Information form*

The form consists of five tabs that divide Axapta into areas for which you can purchase codes. The basic principle is that you can load the codes you have from a file by using the *Load License File* button, or you can enter the values manually. When entering the codes manually, all you enter are the license code values; Axapta fills out the rest for you.

■**Caution** Any change to the license codes in this form will force a synchronization before the new codes can take effect. If you have added or removed modules, this could force tables to be created or dropped. You should always run a complete backup of your database and application before performing any changes to this form.

The license code groups are the following:

- *System*: Basic functionality, technologies, tools, and layers that you have access to

- *Modules*: Standard application modules developed by MBS and solution provider partners

- *Partner modules*: Add-on application modules provided by nonsolution provider partners

- *Web*: The Enterprise Portal module, roles related to this module, other modules integrated with this module, and the number of EP users

- *Languages*: Languages for which you are licensed

■**Note** A tab labeled "Unknown" may be present if the system encounters any codes it cannot identify.

The fields in each tab are as follows:

- *Code description*: Presents the textual designation of the feature or module

- *License code*: Specifies the code that activates the feature or module

- *Status*: Indicates the state of the feature or module, which can be a number representing a quantity of licenses; Ok, meaning that the feature is activated; or NOk or blank, indicating that the feature is not activated.

- *Certificate*: Displays an icon of a certificate for all activated features that are verified.

Note You can turn off a feature or module by deleting or mangling the respective license code, even though this may not seem to make sense, since you purchased it in the first place. However, this is the most practical way if, for example, you want to eradicate a module or feature that you have decided to discontinue within your organization.

Configuration Keys

We briefly looked at the Configuration form in Chapter 3, but we'll dig a little deeper into it now and discuss why you should care about it as a system administrator.

Every configuration key is associated with a license code that determines whether the key is active or not. If the license code for a specific configuration key is present, then the key will also be present. The key may not always be checked, and thus it's a good idea to always look at your configuration keys whenever you add modules.

You cannot deactivate features associated with configuration keys that display a small red padlock in their icon, but what you can do is disable the subkeys. In Figure 5-5, you can see we have disabled the *Giro* subconfiguration key of the *General ledger* top-level configuration key. Basically, you can't get rid of a feature or module that you have purchased and have activated in the license codes setup, but you can turn off specific subfeatures.

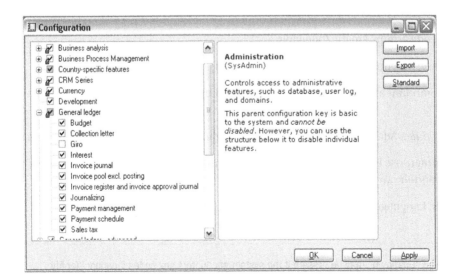

Figure 5-5. *Configuration form*

An important aspect of administering configuration keys is that when managing several installations, you can use this form to create a standard configuration key setup for your organization, export it, and reuse the export by importing it into other installations, using the respective buttons on the form, and save yourself having to set each one up manually on each system. Any change to your configuration will require synchronization before the changes take effect.

■**Note** Even if you only have one system, you should export the setup every time you change it and back it up; this way, you can restore the setup in case a problem occurs that corrupts your existing configuration key setup. Configuration key setups are exported to text files of type CFG.

Security Keys

Security keys control access to functionality for user groups, and user groups are used to control access to functionality for users, so we will keep our discussion short here and expand on it when we look at creating users and setting up their permissions later in this chapter.

What is important for a system administrator to be aware of is that developers create and specify security keys that users need to have assigned in order to access menu items, tables, and fields in the system—this controls access to the application menu and to the underlying data.

As an administrator, you dictate which security keys specific user groups have, as well as the level of access to the functionality controlled by these keys, when you set up the permissions for each user group. These groups will later be attached to users and will dictate the security settings of each user.

Authorization

User groups are the basis of authorization in Axapta; they are the elements of Axapta to which access to the different modules and parts of the system in the form of *permissions* are assigned. User groups contain individual *users* who inherit the permissions given for the groups that they belong to and who represent the actual physical users of the system. They can be combined with companies, domains, and record-level security to provide a flexible and powerful, albeit complicated, framework for controlling what users can do and where.

Fundamentally, Axapta allows you to control the following:

- What functionality members of specific user groups, companies, and domains have access to

- What data is visible to which users, using record-level security

- Which fields in forms are visible to which user groups

When setting up base data in Axapta, you can work your way through the data chain from the bottom up by right-clicking and selecting the *Go to the Main Table* menu option (as described in Chapter 4) to drill up to where you want the parent data entities and create them so that you can then select them. However, we prefer to work from the top down, that is, we define a parent entity first and then the child entities that use it.

At the start of this section, the structure of Axapta's authorization system will probably seem complicated and difficult to grasp; however, as you work your way through this section, things should clear up and make sense. So let's start with a look at domains.

Domains

Domains are groups of company accounts that, combined with user groups, allow you to define different permissions for a user group depending on the company that is active. This means, for example, that a user can have full access to the General Ledger in the context of one company and only limited access in the context of another company. You do this by assigning permissions to combinations of domains and user groups. To start, bring up the Domains form shown in Figure 5-6 by using the main application menu and selecting Administration ➤ Setup ➤ Domains.

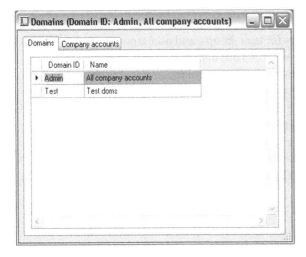

Figure 5-6. *Domains form*

You create a new domain or a record in a table/form by using the standard keyboard shortcut Ctrl-N.

■**Note** We explain how to get around in Axapta in Chapter 4, and you can find a list of Axapta keyboard shortcuts in Appendix D. For the moment, and in case you need to save a record that you have created, simply moving off the created record will do the trick; alternatively, you can use the keyboard shortcut combination Ctrl-S. You can also see if a record has been saved or not because an asterisk * is displayed in the leftmost cell of the row if you haven't saved it.

The Admin domain is always present, and cannot be deleted. This domain allows access to all company accounts, and without it you could possibly lock yourself out of a company. Go ahead and create a Test domain and enter a domain ID and name similar to what we have in Figure 5-6.

If you had already created company accounts, then you could choose a domain and go to the Company Accounts tab to select the companies associated with it. For the examples we've walked you through you haven't, so you will instead associate companies to existing domains in the Companies form and skip the second tab of the Domains form, which contains two panels and two transfer buttons that allow you to select and deselect the companies that are associated with the domain from the list of existing ones.

Virtual Company Accounts

Axapta supports what it designates as *virtual company accounts*. These allow you to create collections of data that are common to various real company accounts. This is a useful feature that allows you to share postal codes, product base data, customers, suppliers, and so on across the whole system. To work with virtual company accounts, access the Virtual Company Accounts form by selecting Administration ➤ Setup ➤ Virtual Company Accounts.

In the first tab of the form that appears, Virtual Company Accounts, you will see that you have a virtual company with an ID of *VCO*—assuming that you loaded the demo data in Chapter 3. In the second tab, *Company Accounts*, you have two panes and two transfer buttons that allow you to select which companies are associated with the virtual company. The third and last tab, Table Collections, features two panes and a couple of transfer buttons. The panes display the table collections that are associated with the virtual account selected and those available, as you see Figure 5-7. These table collections specify the tables shared by the virtual company account.

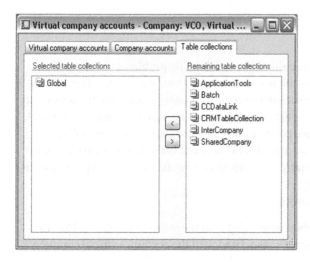

Figure 5-7. *Virtual Company Accounts form*

■**Note** *Table collections* are collections of Axapta tables that for the most part support virtual companies. They are defined by developers using the AOT. If you wish to view or edit the tables grouped by table collections, select AOT ➤ Data Dictionary ➤ Table Collections.

Company Accounts

Axapta allows you to work with several companies within the same system by supporting what it calls *company accounts*. All data in the system is associated with a company, and data for a particular company is only visible to users who have been granted access to that company.

Pull up the Company Accounts form by following the application menu path Administration ➤ Company Accounts. At this point, the form should resemble Figure 5-8.

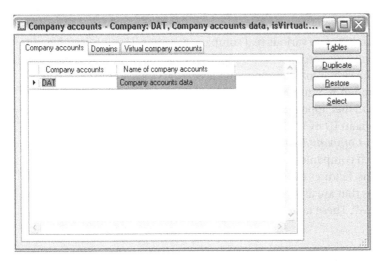

Figure 5-8. *Company Accounts form*

This form comprises three tabs, and you should by now have no problems understanding them. The first, Company Accounts, lists the accounts available on the system. The second, Domains, provides a list of the domains associated with the selected company and the remaining domains available. The third and last, Virtual Company Accounts, provides a list of the virtual companies associated with the selected real company account and a list of those available.

Go to the Domains tab and make sure that the DAT account is associated with the Admin domain, and then go to the Virtual Company Accounts tab and make sure the DAT company is associated with the VCO virtual company.

The buttons on the form do the following:

- *Tables*: Prints a report of all the tables associated with the selected company. This does not refer to the tables in the collections associated with the account's virtual company accounts.

- *Duplicate*: Creates a new company account that is a copy of the currently selected one.

- *Restore*: Restores company accounts from a backup database. This requires that you have previously created a backup using the tools available for the database system that you are using.

- *Select*: Makes the selected company the current active company and takes you automatically to the corresponding context. This can also be done by using the Tools ➤ Select Company Accounts menu option from the menu bar.

Note When working in Axapta, you are always working within a company. You can specify which one to use by default when you log on either in the client configuration or in the User Options form. The company specified in the client configuration overrides the user options setup. Also, you can move from one company to another without exiting Axapta by using the Select Company Accounts menu option of the Tools menu on the Axapta menu bar. Selecting a company in the form displayed closes it, places you in the selected account, and displays the application menu for the selected company. Closing the application menu takes you back to the company you came from.

User Groups

We could have had you start with creating your users, and then associating them with the user groups that you will create now, but we personally like creating the user groups first and then selecting the groups that our users belong to when we create the users, which is why we're walking you through tackling user groups first.

Creating User Groups

The first step is to go to the User Groups form by selecting Administration ➤ Setup ➤ User Groups—this will display the form in Figure 5-9. Installing Axapta automatically creates an Admin user group; this is the user group with which the Admin user (the user you are currently logged on as) is associated. As with the Admin domain, the Admin user and user group cannot be deleted.

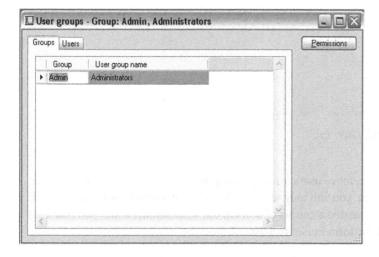

Figure 5-9. *User Groups form, Groups tab*

The first tab, Groups, does not need a lot of explanation. Note that the group name is limited to ten alphanumeric characters. Here, begin creating a user group by entering **Test** in the Group field and **Test User** in the User Group Name field.

■**Note** When you learn about development in Chapter 18, you will also learn how you can make fields longer if you need to.

Remember that in a production installation you need to define your user groups before you can associate users to them and thereby provide access to the system based on the group's permissions. Ideally, before you start creating user groups, you should have identified who in the organization needs access to what modules, functionality, forms, fields, etc., and group users accordingly; in the real world, this is of course an ongoing task. You would then define descriptive names for the groups in question and create those groups (for example, Finance, Management, Purchasing, etc.).

The second tab on the User Groups form, Users, is shown in Figure 5-10. It contains the panes Selected Users, which displays all the users associated with the group, and Remaining Users, which are those not associated with the group.

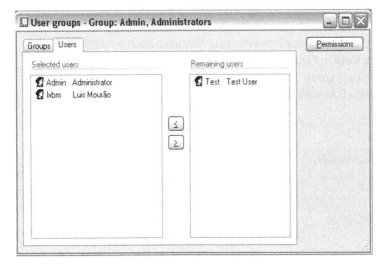

Figure 5-10. *User Groups form, Users tab*

You can add users to and remove users from the group with the two buttons between the panes of the form. At this point, you will only see the Admin user in the selected pane—we've jumped the boat and already created a couple of users in our installation so that you could see something in both panes of the form in Figure 5-10.

Specifying User Group Permissions

The Permissions button is the really interesting part of this task. Clicking it brings up the User Group Permissions form shown in Figure 5-11. It contains two tabs: Overview and Permissions.

The Overview tab consists of two panes, each containing a grid. The left pane displays all existing user groups, and the right pane the domains to which the user groups belong.

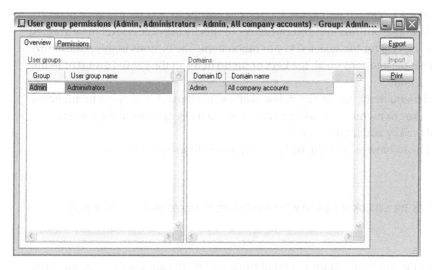

Figure 5-11. *User Group Permissions form, Overview tab*

■**Note** Remember, domains group company accounts so that by combining them with user groups, the groups can have different access rights on different companies. In practice, this means a purchaser belonging to the Purchaser group may have full access rights to the Accounts Payable module when working with company A but may have only read access for company B.

The Permissions tab, which you can see in Figure 5-12, displays a list of the security keys available on the system. This is where you specify which of the modules, features, functionality, forms, fields, and so on of Axapta the specific users group can access. You can use the Viewing pull-down menu to view the permissions for other lists of security keys as well as menu items. The two most commonly used are Security and Main Menu.

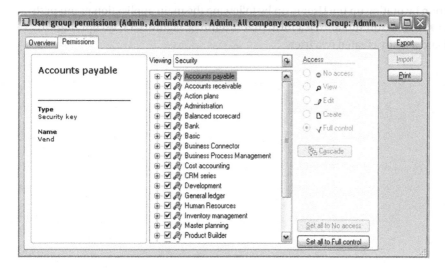

Figure 5-12. *User Group Permissions form, Permissions tab*

To the right of the key and menu items list, you can see the Access permissions pane. It displays a series of toggle buttons that you can select to specify the access level to be granted to the selected user group for the selected key or menu item. The buttons in this pane allow you to define access permissions on all the keys or menu items in the viewed group or in the tree of the selected node.

The keys and menu items can be expanded to allow selection of subkeys or menu items. When you select a key or menu item, information about that key appears in the text memo field to the left of the key and menu item list.

Take some time to browse through the keys and menu items available.

■**Note** In Chapter 18, we will look at working with security keys and menu items as AOT objects.

Setting up user group permissions is a lot of work, and it's not always the most intuitive. You should practice with a test user account associated with a test user group. It's also very important that you save your setups, both as a security measure and so you can save yourself having to create the same setup again if you are installing it on multiple systems. Use the Export and Import buttons for that. The Print button prints the settings for the viewed group, which is of limited usefulness considering that you can export and import setups.

Users

As we have mentioned before, Axapta comes out of the box with an Admin user who cannot be deleted from the system, belongs to the user group Admin, and has full access to every nook and cranny of the system. You must create the remaining users who are to have access to the system and set up their access permissions using everything that you have learned up to now. We describe this process in this section.

Creating Users

You get into action by pulling up the User form by following the main application menu path Administration ➤ Users. You should see a form that resembles Figure 5-13, except that we jumped ahead and already created two users.

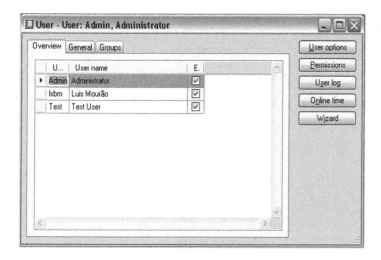

Figure 5-13. *User form, Overview tab*

This form consists of three tabs. As is common in many Axapta forms, in the Overview tab, you can see a list of users of the system and their user IDs, a short textual description (designated "User name"), and whether the account is enabled or not, which is indicated by the check box in the last row being checked or not. The Enable field is checked by default, but you can uncheck it at any time to prevent the account being used.

Go ahead and create a test user for yourself.

■**Note** The data grids that are typical in the Overview tab of Axapta forms have their columns sized automatically to the content of the respective fields and not the labels. As a result, it's not unusual for you to not be able to read what the column name is. However, you can easily do so by either enlarging the column (drag the column separator) or by placing the cursor on top of the column header, which will show the column name in a tooltip box.

The General tab shown in Figure 5-14 is the most interesting of the three on the User form, so let's take a look at each field for this tab.

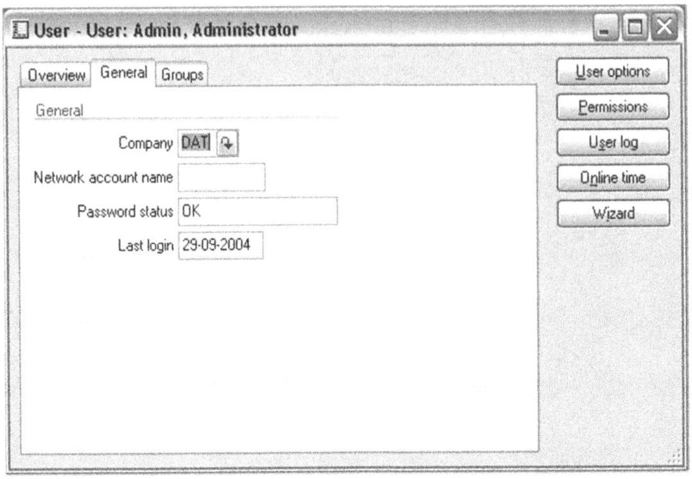

Figure 5-14. *User form, General tab*

The Company field is an Axapta custom control that you will meet in many forms. It looks and behaves somewhat like a drop-down menu, but when you click the icon beside it, it displays a table unlike the menu, which displays a simple list. This field in particular allows you to specify which company account to activate for the user when first logging on.

The *network account name* is another of those great small features of Axapta. If you specify the user's Windows domain name in the Network Account Name field, and you have configured Axapta to run in 3-tier mode using Windows authentication, then Axapta will use the respective context instead of asking the user to log on.

■**Note** If you specify a user in the General tab of the Client configuration utility, then Axapta will prompt you for a user name and password, even if you have specified the user's network account name and are running in 3-tier mode with Windows authentication.

The Password Status edit control simply indicates whether the password is OK or has expired, which is determined by the system's password settings.

The Last Login field displays the date of this user's last login.

Because the User form is an important one, let's also see what the third tab, Groups, is good for. It should resemble Figure 5-15.

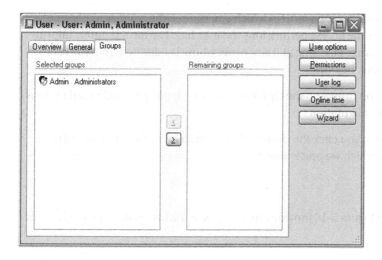

Figure 5-15. *User form, Groups tab*

Now you finally get to make some use of all the work you have done on the way here. The Groups tab has two panes and a set of transfer buttons. The pane to the right lists all remaining user groups, the one to the left the ones that this user is a member of. The buttons allow you to add the user to and remove the user from the existing groups. Every user should be a member of at least one user group. Simple, isn't it?

■**Note** If a user belongs to two groups and the permissions for a system object overlap, then the user is assigned the access level corresponding to the highest specified among the two groups.

Now for the buttons on the form, bottom up, saving the most complex of the group, User Options, for last:

- *The Wizard button* runs an Axapta wizard that prompts you for the information that you have seen on the three tabs of this form and creates a user, instead of your having to press Ctrl-N and then walking through the tabs. Either way works fine, and after you've created a few users, you'll probably find it easiest not to use the wizard.

- *The Online Time button* that prints out the record of your logins. We find it of very little use.

- *The User Log button* provides a superset of what you get in the online time report, presented in a form, and includes some very useful information about the user's logins, such as time, client name on the network, version, and so on.

- *The Permissions button* displays a form in which you can see the companies the user is associated to as well as the access permissions the user has. The form is purely informative, and you can't change anything in it since everything is inherited from the user groups to which the user belongs.

- *The User Options* button brings up the Options form, which presents additional options for fine-tuning user configuration.

The form presented when you click the User Options button is complicated enough to warrant its own discussion, which we present next.

User Options and Settings

The Options form shown in Figure 5-16 provides all the bells and whistles that you might want to hang on your users.

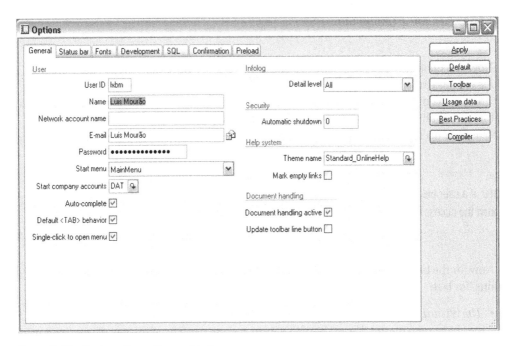

Figure 5-16. *Options form, General tab*

This is a pretty extensive form, so we will take you through only the most interesting fields; however, most of the options are fairly self-evident once you get up to speed on Axapta.

The information provided when creating the user is also displayed in this form (for example, user ID and name); while these are all that you need to create a user, there are a few more items on the Options form that are useful to specify for your users from the start, particularly the following:

- *Password*: Enter a password for the user in this field. By default, all users are created with empty passwords, and it's your job as an administrator not to allow that. Axapta will ask you to confirm the password when you explicitly save what you have entered by pressing Ctrl-S or implicitly save by moving out of the field.

- *Start menu*: This specifies the application menu that is displayed to the user when he or she logs in. (We have gone through creating and using menus other than the standard in Chapter 4.)

- *Auto-complete*: This saves users some typing by completing strings they have already entered as they continue to type. This is limited by login session and field. It is a time saver for most users, but can be a nuisance for inexperienced users.

- *Password expires*: The default for this option is never. You might want to reconsider this!

The next tab is the Status Bar, which allows you to specify what information you want Axapta to display on the status bar for the user and whether the user should be told when changing company accounts. Check it out by selecting and deselecting some of the check boxes and clicking the Apply button to see the data displayed.

The Fonts tab, as you can guess by its name, changes the fonts used in Axapta.

The Development tab presents a variety of preferences for developers, and these settings are usually left up to the developers themselves since they have no meaning for other users. We look at the options on this tab in Chapter 18, which discusses the development environment.

The next tab, SQL, is a very interesting one for you as an administrator and for developers, too. It allows you to specify the tracing of the execution of SQL statements.

■**Note** Tracing SQL statements pays a high performance penalty; you should avoid this in a production environment unless you need it for diagnostics.

In the Confirmation tab, you specify what kinds of events you would like the system to ask the user for confirmation about before going ahead and doing them—this covers data deletions and updates.

The last tab, Preload, is where you specify which tables to preload. By default, all those that can be preloaded are selected. Preloading provides faster data access statistically; however, the first time a table is accessed and preloaded, there is a performance penalty.

So now to the buttons on the Options form:

- *Apply*: Immediately applies any changes you have made. This is not a lot of fun if you are setting up another user, but it is good for seeing the results as you go when setting up your own account.

- *Default*: Resets the account to default settings. Since this form doesn't provide you with an option to export the setup and import it again later, we suggest you leave this button alone.

- *Toolbar*: Configures what buttons to display in the toolbar and whether to show tooltips or not.

- *Usage Data*: Presents a big form that provides tons of information about what you have been doing with the system. This form also allows you to reset user selections, which can be very helpful in development and testing environments.

- *Best Practices*: Axapta has a built-in set of rules about what good programming style is. This button takes you to a form where you can specify the level of validation as well as what Axapta objects it applies to.

- *Compiler*: Sets up compiler-related stuff. This is mostly for developers.

■**Note** Users have access to this form for their account and can therefore define their own settings, so you should have a word with them about what they may and may not decide themselves, particularly stuff like not turning on SQL tracing for their account.

That wraps up our discussion on creating and configuring your users, so now let's look at how you can specify password parameters to refine security in your Axapta system.

Password Parameters

The Password Parameters form contains three tabs, General, Password, and E-mail messages, respectively, and for the most part they are quite self-explanatory, so we will only show you the first tab here in Figure 5-17 and provide a quick rundown of the other two tabs. You can find the Password Parameters form by selecting Administration ➤ Setup ➤ Security.

Figure 5-17. *Password Parameters form, General tab*

In the first tab you can decide what login ID users should use and whether to disable accounts after three failed attempts—you should consider this seriously on any production system.

In the second tab, you can define the requirements for your users' passwords. It's not very fancy, but you can definitely improve on the default settings, and we urge you to do so. This tab contains a button that allows you to reset the date all passwords have last been updated—basically resetting the password expiry counter.

■**Note** Resetting the password log does not, as you would expect, reset to the current date and time; instead it resets to the date and time you logged in.

The third and last tab allows you to specify an e-mail message to be sent to the user when his or her account is created—more on this in the "Maintenance Tasks" section that follows. For now, just keep in mind that on this tab you will need to specify a standard message ID to use when issuing e-mail messages to new users, and that the variables shown in the E-mail Messages tab can be used as placeholders in the text of the message.

Record-Level Security

The last topic of this authorization discussion is record-level security, which was added to Axapta in version 3.0. It allows you to define a query for combinations of companies, user groups, and tables that restricts what records the user can see. You define record-level security by selecting Administration ➤ Setup ➤ Security ➤ Record Level Security, which will display the form shown in Figure 5-18. This form displays the currently existing restrictions and the group, company, and table that they apply to. By default, your form should be blank.

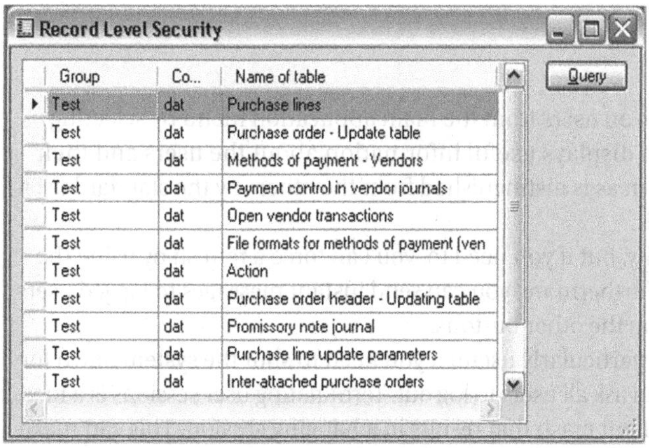

Figure 5-18. *Record Level Security form*

To create a new record-level security constraint, create a record by pressing Ctrl-N. This starts a wizard that will guide you through the process of making the necessary selections. Basically, you'll select which table(s) you wish to use in constraining a particular user group.

You can use the Query button to see the query that constrains the data set available for the selected combination of user group, company, and table—we explain queries in Chapter 18.

Note You can't constrain the Admin user group.

Maintenance Tasks

This section goes through the major periodic routines performed by system administrators within Axapta. Some of the more advanced Axapta maintenance tasks have a level of complexity beyond the scope of this book, so you will have to wait for our book on advanced administration for Axapta (currently in the works), or rely on the Axapta community.

In this section, we will look at the following common maintenance tasks:

- Determining who is online

- E-mail setup

- Log system

- Batch jobs

- Data maintenance

- Backups

Last but not least, Axapta includes a variety of reports and queries that you can use to get information on the status and general health of the system, which we do not cover here. You can find them under the main application menu path of Administration ➤ Inquiries and Administration ➤ Reports, and we strongly encourage you to explore these reports and queries on your own.

Online Users

You can see a list of currently logged-on users from the main application menu by selecting Administration ➤ Setup. This form displays useful information about the users and their logins. The user that you are logged in as is distinguished from the others by the standard user ID icon with a "C" placed on top of it.

The form refreshes automatically, but if you need to, you can force a refresh by using the corresponding button in the form. Furthermore, you can send instant messages to logged users and terminate their sessions by using the other buttons.

The ability to send messages is particularly useful if you need to shut the system down for one reason or another so that you can ask all users to log out. Terminating user sessions is a nice feature for dealing with an Axapta client crash that results in a hanging session. This can make it impossible for the affected user to log back on.

E-mail

Axapta allows you to send e-mail messages automatically to new users when their corresponding account is created, to job applicants as part of the recruitment functionality in the HR module, to owners of specific actions in the Business Process Management module, and so on.

In order to do this, you have to set up information about your outgoing e-mail server by using the form shown in Figure 5-19, which you can display from the main application menu by selecting Administration ➤ Setup ➤ E-mail Parameters. The fields in the E-mail Parameters form are self-explanatory for any system administrator. We are unsure why there is a field for the local computer name, as this does not seem to have any practical application.

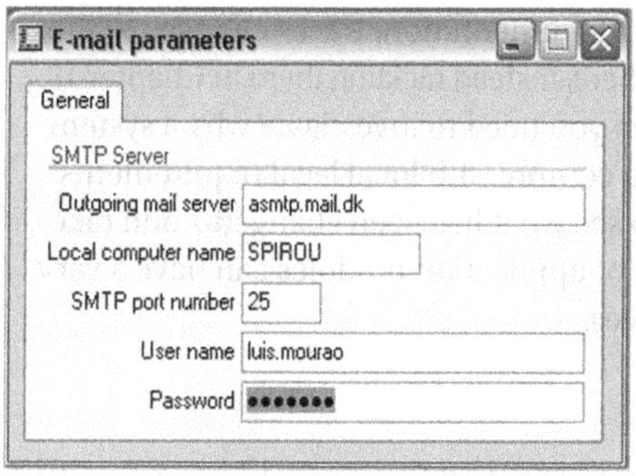

Figure 5-19. *E-mail Parameters form*

By setting up Axapta to send an e-mail message automatically when a new account is created, the system will automatically send users their account name and password, which can be quite useful. However, this requires that you have previously created a message by selecting Basic ➤ Setup ➤ E-mail Messages and filling out the form you see in Figure 5-20, and that you have specified the e-mail message as the one to be sent in the Password Parameters form that you saw in the "Password Parameters" section earlier in this chapter.

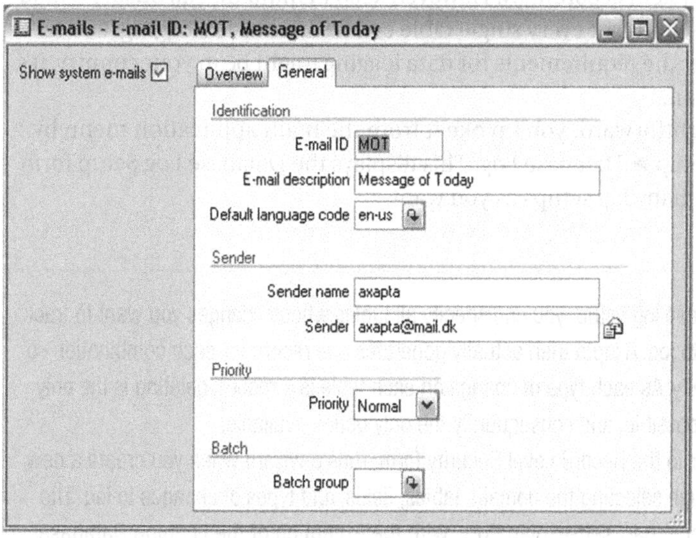

Figure 5-20. *E-mail Messages form*

The important fields here are the E-mail ID field, which you use to select this message where appropriate, the E-mail Description field, which you use to define the subject for the e-mails generated, and the Batch Group field, which you use to specify that e-mails with the given ID are to be sent as part of a batch run instead of right away.

Log System

The log system, as it is normally understood in Axapta documentation, tracks changes to the database, so we will ignore the error and execution logs here, instead tackling them in Chapter 18.

The ability to track changes to data is crucial when you need to investigate why a system suddenly begins to behave differently or if you need to comply with local legal requirements for data auditing. In both cases, you can use the log to see what has been changed—and take our word for it, changes to basic data of a system and/or application modules can have a very dramatic impact on the results that the system produces.

■**Note** Logging changes to data can generate a lot of data and add a significant processing overhead when you perform operations that you have marked for logging on the respective tables. We have seen sites that log changes to application data tables such as the inventory transaction table. In organizations that produce, buy, and/or sell products, logging is generally BIG, particularly on all possible change types (that is, insert, update, delete, and renaming of keys) and is a guaranteed performance killer and database space hog.

As a rule, we only log operations on tables that contain settings used by the system or by application modules; however, in some industries you are legally required to log changes to different types of data. If you need to log changes to anything other than settings and configuration data—which changes infrequently and represents a very small quantity of data—then make sure that you size your system accordingly. However, keep in mind that all business data in Axapta is persisted to tables, and that every single table can be marked for logging. Consequently, regardless of whatever the requirements for data logging might be in your country, it's there; you just need to turn it on.

Enabling logging is straightforward: you invoke it from the main application menu by selecting Administration ➤ Setup ➤ Database Log. This displays the Database Log Setup form from which you can create as many log setups as you want.

■**Note** When you create a database log setup, you can specify all tables whose changes you want to track and log and the types of changes to log. Axapta then actually generates one record for each combination so that you can delete them individually. As each type of change on each table is a record, deleting is the only form of editing your setups that's possible, and consequently the only option available.

The Database Log form, similar to the Record Level Security form, runs a wizard when you create a new record. The wizard steps you through selecting the domain, tables, fields, and types of changes to log. The pages of the wizard are for the most part self-explanatory, with the exception of the Logging Database Changes page shown in Figure 5-21.

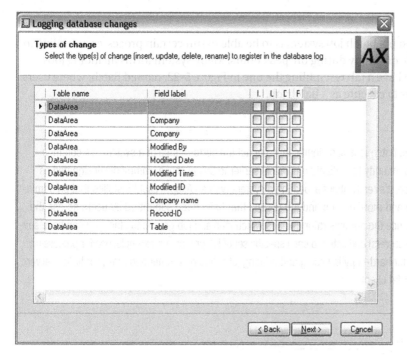

Figure 5-21. *Logging Database Changes page*

The reason for bringing you here is to call your attention to what is a perfectly sensible piece of behavior that is not always intuitive. Specifically, in the previous page of the wizard you select the tables and fields to log, and these are now shown in the form.

■**Note** Selecting a table for logging specifies that you want to log changes at the table level. If you want to log changes to particular fields such as changed time and date, you have to select the fields explicitly.

Understand that when the Field label box is empty for a particular record, that record is for the entire table listed. Otherwise, the Field label box will specify the particular field to be logged.

The four fields to the right of the grid displayed in the page contain check boxes that allow you to specify what type of changes to log: insert, update, delete, and renaming of the table key. However, since update is the only change that you can perform on a field, it's also the only check box you can mark for fields. Naturally, all the change types are valid for tables.

Clicking the Next button displays the last page in the wizard, which gives you a summary of logs that the system will maintain with the current setup. Click the Finish button, and the database log setup form will display all of the log setups defined.

You can then see a history of changes using the Database Log menu items located in the main application menu paths Administration ➤ Inquiries and Administration ➤ Reports. The first displays the logs in a form, whereas the second produces a report—as usual we always use the form instead of the report version as it allows us to sort and filter out information.

Batch Jobs

The purpose of the Axapta batch job system is to be able to run certain processes according to a predefined schedule or simply during off-peak hours. Many system forms including jobs and reports in Axapta have a tab resembling the one in Figure 5-22, named Batch, where users can set up the process to execute as a batch job.

Tip Because executing batch jobs can significantly impact the performance of a system, it's common practice in the Axapta community to dedicate a physical server to this purpose, commonly designated as a *batch server*. In practice, it's really about allocating a system with an Axapta client installed that an administrator uses to execute and monitor jobs and job groups that have been submitted by users across the organization. Naturally, since the administrator decides which jobs and job groups to start, you can have several clients (that is, batch servers) dedicated to each specific set of job groups; for example, one for processing check runs and another for hard-copy invoicing and printing jobs. It is recommended that your batch server be configured as a 3-tier fat client.

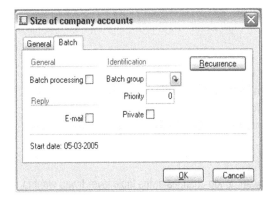

Figure 5-22. *Batch tab*

The different elements of this form serve the following purposes:

- The Recurrence button displays a dialog box in which you can specify when and how often you want to execute the job.

- The Batch Processing check box must be checked if you want to submit the current process to the batch job system—otherwise the process is simply executed immediately by your Axapta client.

- The E-mail check box specifies that an e-mail notification is to be sent when the job finishes.

- The Private check box specifies that only you, the user submitting the job, can change it. If you do not check this box, a system administrator managing the batch job queues could make changes. As a general rule, you should leave this option disabled so that administrators can change your jobs if necessary.

- The Priority text field specifies how much attention Axapta should give the job. The default is 0, meaning that you don't care, so Axapta sets it to 1 when it submits the job, which is the highest value. The lowest value is really big (in the thousands), or should we say low—and it beats us why.

In the preceding list, we did not mention the Batch Group control because that requires a little more explaining. You can submit your job to the batch job system without specifying a group, and it will be placed in a queue. However, doing so makes it very difficult for an administrator to decide where to run the job and whether to start it at all. If you want to submit the current process to the batch job system, then it's a good idea to specify a group that has been created for the grouping of jobs like the one you are submitting. Then an administrator will ensure that it's run on the appropriate batch server.

Note The batch job system requires that an administrator start the execution of batch groups manually when the Axapta client that acts as the batch server is closed and restarted. If you have only one batch server, then you will normally start all batch jobs on the client that is installed on the server. However, if you have several batch servers, then the administrator will start different groups on different servers.

Finally, we should talk about batch journals, which are set up for execution under the Batch folder by selecting Basic ➤ Setup ➤ Batch.

It's very important to understand that you can't submit normal reports and jobs using the journal system. Its purpose is to allow you to submit processes—these are pieces of code either delivered out of the box or that you create yourself. In other words, when you define a journal type, you need to specify a class name that contains the code to be executed. It's a neat feature, but you must be a developer to write the jobs or have one do it. This is beyond the scope of a system administrator's responsibilities.

If you want to research the batch system on your own, then you can find the core of it under the main application menu paths of Basic ➤ Setup ➤ Batch, Basic ➤ Periodic ➤ Batch, and Basic ➤ Inquiries ➤ Batch List.

The preceding paths will provide forms to

- Create batch groups and journals.

- Run batch jobs and journals.

- Monitor batch jobs.

Note Once you have started the processing of a batch group, a dialog box will be displayed showing what the queue in question is up to. You can use the button on the Status dialog box to stop processing the queue at any time. In the meantime, it runs and processes jobs that are in the queue and any new ones that arrive. So on a system with several batch groups, there will be several open and independent status dialog boxes.

As an administrator, it's important for you to know exactly what the status markings for jobs are when you look at the batch list form, so Table 5-1 gives the list of possible states and a short explanation.

Table 5-1. *Job Status*

Status	Explanation
Waiting	The job is ready to be run—this is the default status after submission of a job.
Withhold	The job has been temporarily suspended.
Executing	The job is being executed.
Error	An error occurred during execution of the job.
Ended	The job was executed successfully.

Data Maintenance

Managing data is a primary function of any system administrator, and Axapta provides a series of tools that you can use for this purpose.

The first is a variety of data inquiries located under the main application menu path Administration ➤ Inquiries. Tools such as the *database log* will display all logged database events that you set up in the "Log System" section of this chapter. The SQL Statement trace log under the Database folder will display any of the database logging events that you might have specified from the user Options form's SQL tab, also discussed earlier in this chapter.

The second set of tools is a series of reports located under the main application menu path of Administration ➤ Reports, that provide the following:

- *Tables*: A list of all the tables in the system.

- *Database information*: A list of your database settings, both of Axapta and of the database system you are using.

- *Database log*: All logged database events. A query is displayed, giving you the chance to modify it so you only get information about the tables you want.

- *Size of company accounts*: A list of tables with the number of records per table and the amount of bytes used; an example is shown in Figure 5-23. This is a very useful report that enables you to see which tables are taking up a lot of space in your database. However, notice that the number of bytes shown is calculated based on the field size definitions in the schema; for example, a field defined as varchar(50) counts as 50 bytes, even though in practice it may actually contain only 10.

The New Light Company

Size of company accounts - dat, Company accounts data

Name of table	Number of records	Database size (bytes)
Alt. address	2	2,474
Bank groups	2	2,600
Bank accounts	3	4,908
Bank transactions	13	4,654
Check layout	3	15,480
Check table	25	3,675
Bank transaction type	9	900
Batch transactions	19	119,396
Batch groups	2	178
Batch journal types	1	89
BOM lines	74	36,704
Configuration rules	2	320
BOM parameters	1	60
Bills of material	17	2,057
BOM versions	16	2,240
Ledger budget models	5	510
Business statistics	3	288
Cash discount	3	447
Commission rates	12	1,476
Commission customer group	2	178
Commission item group	6	534

Figure 5-23. *Size of Company Accounts report*

The next set, located at Administration ➤ Periodic, contains the menu item SQL Administration, which displays the form in Figure 5-24 and the submenu Data Export/Import.

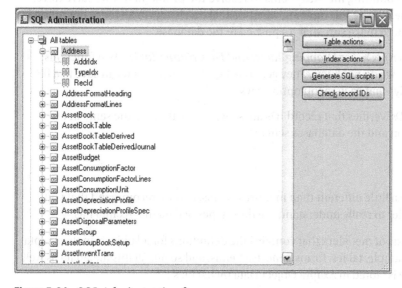

Figure 5-24. *SQL Adminstration form*

This form displays two top nodes: All tables and All indexes. Index nodes are not expandable, but tables nodes are, and they show you the respective table's indexes. You can then select a table or index node and use the buttons on the form to perform the following tasks:

- *Table Actions ➤ Synchronize*: Pushes the current Axapta definition of the table to the database schema. This is useful for developers when they make changes to a table, but can also be useful to an administrator if you suspect that the two definitions can be out of sync. This function will force the synchronization and will not alert you of changes that are made.

- *Table Actions ➤ Check/Synchronize*: Displays a dialog box that allows you to specify various things to check, what to do about anything that's found, and whether to print a report with the results. Also, here it is possible to specify a Diagnosing-only mode whereby a report is generated with changes to be made, without actually making the changes.

- *Table Actions ➤ Browse*: Opens up the Table Browser form that displays the table data in a grid.

- *Table Actions ➤ Truncate*: Deletes all the records in the table, which is useful when, as part of your regular maintenance, you want to clean up tables like the database event log. This can also be helpful when doing data conversions and imports of data that are rejected by the system.

- *Index Actions ➤ Re-index*: Drops and rebuilds all indexes if you select a table and only the selected index if you select an index. We have occasionally heard of problems with Axapta where rebuilding indexes seems to resolve the problem, but we have never experienced one. We use this function when we make a change to an index definition in Axapta and want to make sure that it's pushed to the database.

- *Generate SQL Scripts ➤ For Dropping Tables and For Creating Tables*: Two functions whose rationale we do not know. They generate SQL scripts that you can save to a file for doing exactly what each menu option says.

- *Check Record IDs*: Verifies that record IDs are sane, that is, they are the same in the Axapta definition and the databases schema.

Backups

Backups in Axapta are a little different than in most systems, and we recommend that you read Chapter 19 in order to really understand the three types of data that Axapta has:

1. The first consists of metadata that contains the definitions for all objects in the Axapta systems, for example, tables, forms, reports, menus, and so on. All this metadata as well as all X++ code is stored in Axapta Object Data (AOD) files.

2. The second consists of the text that is used in labels throughout the Axapta environment, for example, menu labels, form names, field labels, and so on, that are stored in Axapta Label Data (ALD) files.

3. The third and last consists of what most people perceive as data or business data, that is, the data you enter into forms and is produced by different processes, which is persisted to the database system that you are using.

■Note Axapta has an AOD file for each application layer and an ALD file per language. In reality, Axapta's file structure is actually a bit more complicated than this; however, the backup process we describe here will let you grab all the necessary data without having to be able to know anything about the different file types.

In order to back up the system, it's a good idea to get all users of the system to log out—use the Online Users form to see who they are and send them an instant message asking them to exit the system.

■Note You do not need to stop the system in order to back up business data, but you do to back up metadata.

Backing up your business data is straightforward, and there are two approaches you can use: exporting data using the form shown later in Figure 5-27, which you access through the main application menu path Administration ➤ Periodic ➤ Data Export/Import; or using your database tools to back up the database used by Axapta. We discuss the former method next.

■Note While you can use the Axapta export facility to back up all your data, it's most practical when you only want to back up a subset. We therefore recommend that you back up the full database using the backup facilities of your database. The same goes for restoring backups.

Export/Import Definition Groups

Using Axapta's Data Export form is straightforward. You need to specify a definition group that you have previously created using the form at the main application menu path Administration ➤ Periodic ➤ Definition Groups, which you can see in Figure 5-25.

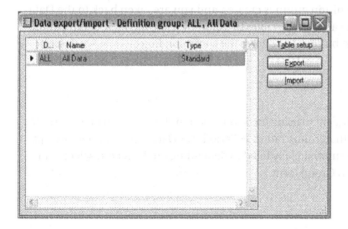

Figure 5-25. *Data Export/Import Definition Groups form*

Here you create definition groups—that is, a specification of what data is to be exported. Press Ctrl-N to create new record and display the Create Table Definition form shown in Figure 5-26.

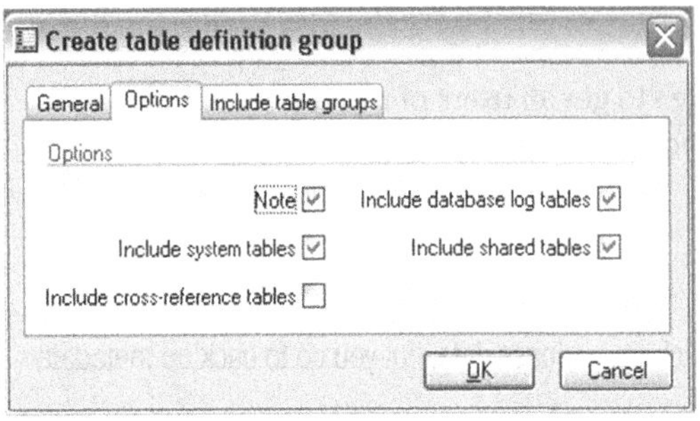

Figure 5-26. *Data Export/Import Definition Groups form*

In the General tab, specify the definition group, give it a descriptive name, and specify type standard—Custom and Excel are for importing other data types. In the Options tab, check all the options or you will miss data in your backup. Notice that we have unchecked the Include Cross-Reference Tables option. This is because these tables are really metadata used by developers to find out where different objects (for example, tables, forms, classes, and so on) are used, and you will not normally generate this data in a production environment.

■**Note** You can always regenerate the cross-reference data, so there is no point exporting it and importing it even if you are backing up a development environment.

The Include Tables Groups tab has all its check boxes checked by default. This means that all tables are marked for export, because every table belongs to one of the table groups. If you are trying to export only certain data, you can deselect some or all of these check boxes. When you click the OK button, the definition group is created and you are taken back to the Data Definitions Group form. Here you can alter the tables to export by using the Table Setup button. You can use the Export and Import buttons to perform the corresponding tasks, as we describe in the next section.

Exporting and Importing Data

Clicking the Export button is equivalent to using the Export Options form, shown in Figure 5-27, at the main application menu path Administration ➤ Periodic ➤ Data export/import, except that the Definition Group field is automatically filled in depending on the record selected in the Data Export/Import Definition Group form.

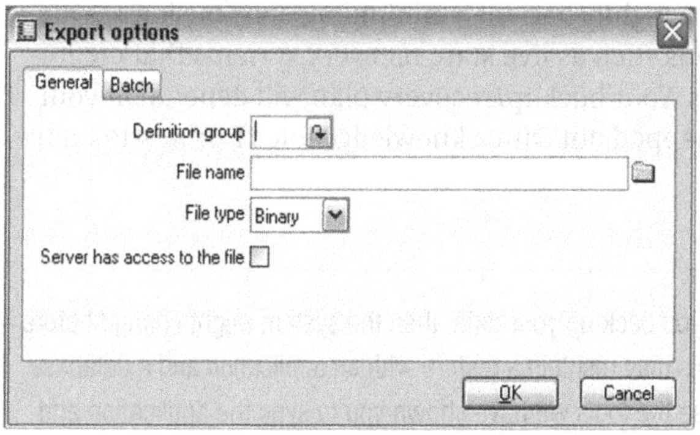

Figure 5-27. *Export Options form*

The definition group is required; if you got to the Export Options from the main application menu, then select the definition group that specifies the tables that you wish to export. The File Name field defines the file to which you want to write the backup. The File Type field allows you to specify whether the data should be exported in the default binary format or comma-separated format. Go with the default—comma-separated exports do not contain blob fields and therefore have limited usefulness.

The last control of the General tab, Server Has Access to the File, is quite important and is only available when running in 3-tier mode. It specifies whether the file should be placed on the server or on the client—always place it on the server if you are running in 3-tier mode.

The last step is to click the OK button or go to the Batch tab and submit the export to be processed by the batch job system, and the data will be written to the file specified. You can then at any time use the Import form by clicking the Import button in the Data Export/Import Definition Group form or by selecting Administration ➤ Periodic ➤ Data Export/Import ➤ Import.

What's going on in the Import form should by now be pretty obvious to you, and the only recommendation that we want to leave you with is to check the Use Record ID Reservation check box, as enabling this option makes the import process faster because it fetches IDs from the database in blocks instead of one at the time.

This brings you to the last step of your journey, where you back up the application. There is a simple way and there is a complicated way. The simple is a straightforward procedure that consists of shutting down Axapta and copying the application directory "*lock, stock, and barrel.*" Restoring is equally simple: just copy the backup back onto your system.

■Note If you followed our instructions on installing Axapta, then the application directory is *C:\Axapta_Application\Appl\Standard*—replace the drive letter with the drive letter where you actually installed Axapta.

While Axapta has this easy-to-use import/export or backup/restore functionality, it is common practice to have an enterprise-level backup system in place. This system should back up your database and application files on a nightly basis at a minimum. Many businesses are also moving to more intense backup plans such as live state recovery systems that create point-in-time snapshots of entire servers. Your backup/recovery plan will depend on your tolerance for downtime and should be mapped out with a knowledgeable IT professional to anticipate worst-case scenarios.

■**Note** If you have users on the system when you back up your data, then the system might change before you shut it down and back up the application. This may result in a restore with an application and a database that are not synchronized. You can, of course, use the tools we have shown you to sync the application and the database, but nevertheless the best way to back up is to close the system down, forget the Axapta export/import facilities, and use your database tools for the data backup. You then copy the application directory using your favorite file system utility—Windows Explorer, for example.

The last thing we want to mention and that you have probably noticed is that you can export and import data to and from Excel spreadsheets. Importing from Excel spreadsheets is commonly used to migrate data from other systems, and we will cover this process in Chapter 19; you export data to Excel primarily when you want to be able to use a spreadsheet to analyze data that you have in Axapta.

Wrap-Up

In this chapter, we have shown you how to do the following:

- Get access to the system.

- Control available functionality.

- Set up users and their permissions.

- Keep the system healthy and alive.

You can read more about the topics in this chapter in the following documents, available in the documentation folder of the product distribution package or CD:

- *AX-300-USG-009-v01.00-ENUS Admin.pdf*: User's Guide to Administration

- *AX-300-TIP-001-v01.00-ENUS.doc*: Configuration and Security

- *AX-300-TIP-025-v01.00-ENUS.doc*: Active Directory Integration

- *AX-300-TIP-030-v01.00-ENUS.doc*: Oracle Company Partitioning

If you have read through the previous chapters and tried stuff out as you have gone along, then by now you should have an overview of what it takes to get Axapta up and running and keep it running. As an administrator you might be encouraged to stop here, but don't; read the rest of this book—understanding how people with other roles use Axapta will give you valuable insights.

Once more, we recommend that you take some time to browse through the inquiries and reports submenus of the administration application menu, if you haven't already done so.

CHAPTER 6

■ ■ ■

Human Resources

In Axapta the HR module revolves around a primary set of interrelated structural and functional entities—namely, the organization and its employees.

The organization may represent structures such as companies, departments, or work groups, structured in hierarchies. Its employees could represent a variety of attributes and activities, such as education, skills, salary and benefits, presence/absence, courses, and training.

Three HR modules are available from MBS: HRM I, HRM II, and HRM III. The extent to which your business utilizes these modules will depend on the size of your business and your internal activities. You will find that the more you put into these modules, the more you get out of them. You're not required to use the majority of the functionality available here for day-to-day business, but if you do to use it, it can help your operation run smoothly. All three of these modules, in addition to Axapta's Balanced Scorecard module, are available from the Human Resources menu tab.

Our goal for this chapter is to walk you through some of the basic setup steps of the most commonly used functionalities and to describe some of the processes available. The Human Resources module's offerings are too extensive to be covered in their entirety here. But by the end of this chapter you should understand some of the benefits that the module can offer your business.

■**Note** Many customers considering this module ask if it includes any form of payroll processing. The answer is no, the current Axapta HR module does not. Although Axapta does have payroll-associated fields, such as salaries, taxes, and benefits, these fields are mainly static and used for reporting purposes only. Fortunately, many partners have created integrated payroll solutions and interfaces to external payroll processors. You should look into these solutions if you require this functionality.

Setup

Before you can use this module, you must set up a basic data infrastructure. In reality, all you need is to define your current business structure, and to create existing employees and employee data. This module contains a great many forms and tables, but you can create data as needed and add it as you go.

Unlike most other modules, the data in this module does not flow through to the financial modules. Still, it is important to think through the data that you will use in this module so you can minimize your data input and setup efforts. Try to create data that you can use repeatedly. For example, set up all the skills that your organization employs so that you can simply assign the relevant skills when you create an employee, an open position, an application for that position, etc.

As with any module in Axapta, the Parameters form (Human Resources ➤ Setup ➤ Parameters), shown in Figure 6-1, contains many of the options for how the module will function. You should be sure to take a thorough look through the options available on this form.

Tip If you have not imported demo data as described in Chapter 3, be sure to set up number sequences using the Number Sequences tab on the Parameters form. You can right-click on the Number Sequence field and choose Go to the Main Table. From the Number Sequences form, click the Wizard button.

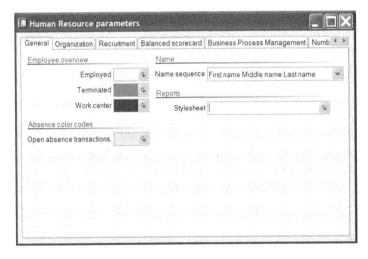

Figure 6-1. *The Human Resources Parameters form contains many of the options for how the module will function.*

The Employee Form

The Employee form (Human Resources ➤ Employee) is where you set up all of the base data regarding each of your employees (see Figure 6-2). The only required field here is the Overview tab's Employee ID, which is generally the employee's initials.

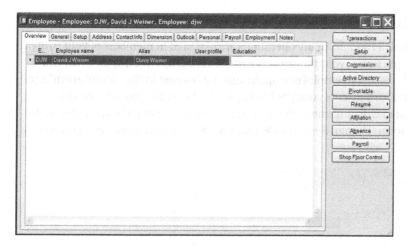

Figure 6-2. *The Employee form is used to record base data regarding each employee.*

The fields that your business will use on this form are dependent on your localization and your business practices. However, the User ID field on the General tab (see Figure 6-3) deserves special attention. It is used to link the employee record to an Axapta user login. (We set up Axapta users in Chapter 5.) This link is very important in displaying the employee name throughout Axapta on forms and reports. In addition, it is a requirement for users of the CRM module.

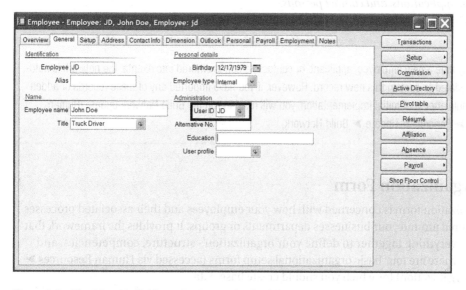

Figure 6-3. *The User ID field on the General tab of the Employee form is used to link each employee to his Axapta user ID.*

Take a look at all of the fields available on the Employee form. You can perform a wide range of reports and inquiries on this base data.

The Network Form

Throughout the Axapta HR module, many operations are assigned to members of your company's network. In Axapta terms, your network consists of your employees, applicants, and contacts. We've already discussed employees; applicants are covered in the "Recruitment" section of this chapter; and we'll discuss contacts in Chapter 12. Many functions in the HR module can be associated with any one of them. You can view your company's complete network via the Network form (Human Resources ➤ Inquiries ➤ Network) shown in Figure 6-4.

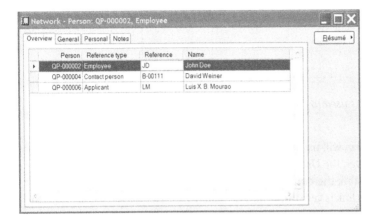

Figure 6-4. *The Network form is used throughout the Axapta HR module and includes employees, applications, and contact persons.*

▪**Note** Any time a new employee, applicant, or contact person is entered into Axapta, the network is automatically updated to contain this new record. However, if you have imported any of these records or added the HR module after your initial implementation, you will need to run the Build Network update (Human Resources ➤ Periodic ➤ Update ➤ Build Network).

The Organization Form

The Organization form is concerned with how your employees and their associated processes are structured around your businesses departments or groups. It provides the framework that connects everything together to define your organization's structure, competencies, and processes. There are four basic organizational setup forms (accessed via Human Resources ➤ Setup ➤ Organization) for which you should create base data:

- Work Tasks
- Areas of Responsibility
- Position Status
- Position Groups

Once you have thought through the essential data entities you need to assemble the structure of your organization (i.e., its units, such as companies, departments, and work groups), use the Organization form (Human Resources ➤ Organization) shown in Figure 6-5 to put it all together.

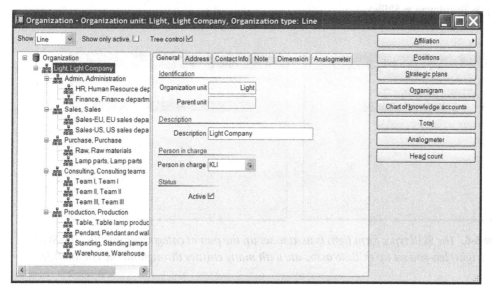

Figure 6-5. *Use the Organization form to tie your employees to their roles.*

You can work with this form using different views—specifically; Line, Matrix, and Project—which you can select in the Show combo box at the top-left corner of the form. You can also visualize the organization as a grid or as a tree by toggling the Tree Control check box.

It's important that you understand the difference between the Line, Matrix, and Project organization types:

- *Line*: The Line organizational structure is used for your company hierarchy, and contains all levels of employees and their positions within your organization. Only employees can be associated with this type. Positions in the Line organization are called Jobs.

- *Matrix*: The Matrix organizational structure is often used for long-term projects or work that spans across the Line organization. Using the Matrix type, you can associate any person from the network with the Matrix. Positions in the matrix type are called Roles.

- *Project*: The Project organizational structure is often used for short-term projects. It is similar to the Matrix type; anybody from the network can be associated with Project roles.

The buttons on the right side of the form allow you to view different types of data as it relates to your organizational units. If you are using demo data, click around to investigate. If you're inputting data as you go, there won't be anything to see yet.

The Skill Types and Skills Forms

You can create skills in Axapta and use them in a variety of situations: apply skills to employees or applications, roles or jobs, and training courses or development plans. After you've set up skills, you have the ability to run a number of reports or inquiries that compare and contrast people, positions, and goals.

Before you can set up skills, you must set up skill types. For example, the skill of being a German speaker would belong to the skill type Multi-Lingual. See Figure 6-6 for an example of the Skill Types and Skills forms. Both forms are located in the Skills folder (Human Resources ➤ Setup ➤ Employee ➤ Skills).

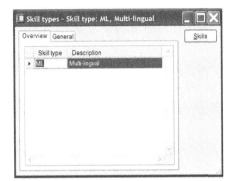

Figure 6-6. *The Skill types form (left) is used to set up the parent categories for skills. The Skills form (right) lets you set up skills to associate with many entities throughout the HR module.*

The Loan Types and Loan Items Forms

Axapta makes it very easy to control the goods (such as cell phones, computers, automobiles, etc.) that employees may have out on loan from the business. These forms are a simple way to keep control of company property.

First, set up the loan types (the categories that loan items fall into) by selecting Human Resources ➤ Setup ➤ Employee ➤ Loan ➤ Loan Types (see Figure 6-7). Loan Types also lets you specify the default grace period before the item is overdue.

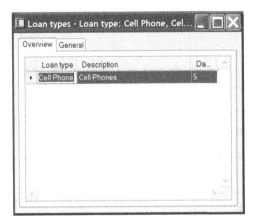

Figure 6-7. *The Loan Types form is where you set up the parent categories for loan items.*

Next, set up the actual loan items, such as Treo 600 (as shown in Figure 6-8), by selecting Human Resources ➤ Setup ➤ Employee ➤ Loan ➤ Loan Items. With Loan Item, you can specify the standard number of loan days, days of grace (if different from the default), serial number, and person who is in responsible for the item (for example, the IT manager may be responsible for all cell phones on loan). From the Loan Item screen you can also launch the Loan form that is used to loan goods to people in your network. (The Loan form is also found at Human Resources ➤ Periodic ➤ Loan.)

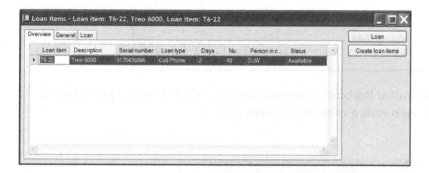

Figure 6-8. *From the Loan Item form you can create new items for loan, and check the status of items.*

Recruitment

Using the Axapta HR module, you can create recruitment projects to manage your recruitment processes. You can use this functionality to specify how you advertise your open positions and to manage incoming applications. Axapta gives you the ability to create and send template-based letters or e-mails to applicants throughout the process. Some businesses will use recruitment projects to create action plans for further structured processes.

The base setup data required to use these projects is located under the Recruitment folder in the Setup menu.

The setup of media and media types is very similar to the setup of skills and skill types, so we won't walk you through it. Figure 6-9 displays the setup for choosing the fields to use in merging templates with applicant data for creating applicant correspondence. Figure 6-10 displays how these fields (or bookmarks) are used to create an e-mail template that confirms receipt of an application.

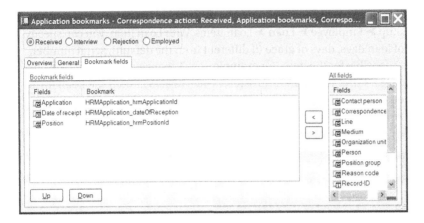

Figure 6-9. *The Application Bookmarks form lets you select which fields will be used when composing data-merge e-mails during the recruitment process.*

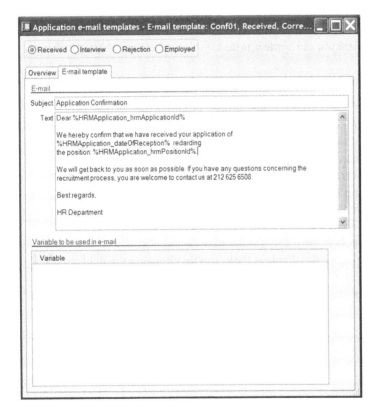

Figure 6-10. *The Application E-mail Templates form allows you to specify the text and corresponding bookmarks within the templates to be used when composing data-merge e-mails during the recruitment process.*

With this basic data setup you will be able to create Recruitment projects, add position-based lines, attach applications to these lines, and use these template e-mails to correspond easily with your applicants.

Wrap-Up

The reports and inquiries in the HR module are extensive and can provide great insight into your business if you take the time to track your organization and your employees in Axapta.

In addition, the HR module enables employee development through appraisal interviews and development plans. Furthermore it is equipped to handle absence registration, strategic plans, action plans, and the balanced scorecard Key Performance Indicator (KPI) functionality.

In this chapter we have focused on the basic setup of the most important HR functions, the organization and its employees. We've focused on some of the most commonly used functionality this module has to offer, while mentioning a few additional features in this feature-rich module.

After reading this chapter, you should have a good feeling for what consultants and end users who work with HR might request of a programmer, whether the data model supports the desired functionality or change of functionality, and where you might start looking and prototyping when you need to customize the module.

If you are interested in learning more about these processes, view the help files or the files listed in this section, which you'll find on the Axapta 3.0 CD:

- *AX-300-USG-019-v01.00-ENUS.pdf*: Getting Started Balanced Scorecard

- *AX-300-USG-020-v01.00-ENUS.pdf*: Getting Started Business Process Management

- *AX-300-USG-017-v01.00-ENUS.pdf*: Getting Started Human Resource Management

- *AX-300-USG-015-v01.00-ENUS.pdf*: User's Guide Balanced Scorecard

- *AX-300-USG-016-v01.00-ENUS.pdf*: User's Guide Business Process Management

- *AX-300-USG-013-v01.00-ENUS.pdf*: User's Guide Human Resource Management

CHAPTER 7

■■■

Finance

The Finance modules that are available from MBS include Financials I, Financials II, Electronic Banking, and Fixed Assets. In the application, the Finance activities are found in the menu tabs General Ledger, Bank, Accounts Receivable, Accounts Payable, Cost Accounting, and Cost Purpose Calculation.

To write about all the functionality available in these modules, we would need another few hundred pages. The purpose of this chapter is simply to give a high-level overview of some of the basic setup requirements, explain some of the functionality available, and to give you some tips, mainly in regards to the general ledger, customer, and vendor setup. More functionality from the Accounts Payable and Accounts Receivable tabs is discussed in Chapter 9.

No matter what your role is, it is important that you have a fundamental understanding of how financial transactions flow through Axapta. Finance is the backbone of any organization and, of course, the foundation of any ERP solution.

Setup

The setup of a business financial operation within Axapta should be preformed by someone who is well versed in the entire Axapta application, has an accounting background, and is well-educated on Generally Accepted Accounting Principles (GAAP). Finally, you want to be certain that this person has a complete understanding of your business's finance operations. Axapta's financial system is highly flexible, built to adapt to many different types of businesses. A wrong choice made during the initial setup could carry serious consequences down the road.

Before you even attempt to begin setting up the financial modules (and before you set up Axapta for that matter), you should answer some primary questions about how your business will be using Axapta:

- Will you be working with multiple companies within Axapta?

- Will you be utilizing Axapta's intercompany transactions?

- Will you be sharing information across multiple companies using the Virtual Company feature?

- Will you be consolidating using a Consolidation company?

- Will you be working with multiple currencies within Axapta?

■**Tip** If your answer to some of the questions is yes, especially when working with multiple companies and multiple currencies, we strongly recommend that you invest in the FRx product offered by MBS. Axapta handles multicompany, multicurrency, intercompany, and virtual company transactions very well. Axapta does not, however, enable the drill-down reporting often required by companies who seek these advanced features. The FRx software will allow you to easily create detailed financial reports with drill-down capability. FRx works very well across these advanced features and we consider it a must-have.

■**Note** If you will be using the Virtual Company feature, it is very important that you decide to do so before you enter data in Axapta. If you decide later to share a table using the Virtual Company feature, all records in that table will be hidden and will need to be reentered. If the records in the table have dependencies or transactions tied to them, such as the Customer or Vendor table, this could create a huge project. Virtual Company accounts are discussed in Chapter 5.

As with all modules in Axapta, the Parameters form (General Ledger ➤ Setup ➤ Parameters) contains the majority of the settings that control how the module operates. Be certain that you understand all of the fields in this form, as small changes here can have big impacts throughout Axapta.

Dimensions

Before we can talk about the chart of accounts, we need to introduce the concept of financial dimensions. Don't get confused by the word "dimensions;" there are two uses for it within Axapta. Inventory dimensions are used to specify how an item may be configured, packaged, stored, bought, sold, etc. Financial dimensions are used to simplify the chart of accounts while enabling detailed financial analysis.

The three standard financial dimensions that come with out of the box Axapta are Department, Cost Center, and Purpose. It is possible to rename these, and to add additional dimensions. But we don't recommend deleting the three dimensions. If you plan to use fewer than three, simply leave them blank, or even hide the fields to prevent user confusion.

Using dimensions, your chart of accounts can stay simple and easily manageable. For example, a typical business may have several accounts for travel expenses because businesses often want to track travel expenses by department. Without dimensions, your chart of accounts may become very lengthy and difficult to manage. The following is a classic example of an account setup for each department:

- 60140-1—Travel Expense Sales Department

- 60140-2—Travel Expense Purchasing Department

- 60140-3—Travel Expense Management Department

- 60140-4—Travel Expense R&D Department

This list could go on. Using Axapta, the different departments would each be set up in the Dimension form so only the main account would need to be set up in the chart of accounts:

- 60140—Travel Expense

Whenever a person in the accounting department books a travel expense, that person would simply record the main or natural account and analyze transactions according to department, cost center, etc., depending on the level of detail required by the company. In our example, the person would select the applicable Department Dimension to attribute an expense to the appropriate department.

■**Note** We have seen several companies get carried away with the usage of financial dimensions. While dimensions can be used for detailed analysis of your businesses financial transactions, they are not usually used for balance sheet–type reporting. It is possible to run an income statement by dimension, and it is even possible to create a balance sheet by dimension, though our experience is that the latter is very difficult, due to the high level of detail that would be necessary on every financial transaction entered into Axapta.

To set up dimensions, select Basic ➤ Dimensions to access the Dimension form, which is shown in Figure 7-1.

■**Tip** If you've taken our advice and are working with the FRx financial reporting software, you'll find that you're able to easily slice and dice your financial data by dimension. This makes for very powerful financial reporting. Further, you can use Axapta's OLAP or Business Analysis functionality to report via dimensions (see Chapter 14).

Dimension	Nu..	Description	Employee	Group
Department	Admin	Administration department	JCO	
Department	Prod	Production department	EPE	
Department	Proj	Project department	MPE	
Department	Purch	Purchase department	EWA	
Department	Sales	Sales department	TGO	
Cost center	Coun	Sales countries	TJO	
Cost center	Fina	Finance	RBA	
Cost center	Human	Human resource	JAL	
Cost center	Pend	Pendant- and wall lamps	AMO	
Cost center	Ppart	Purcase parts	MJO	
Cost center	Praw	Purcase raw material	EMA	

Figure 7-1. *Use the Dimension form to set up the financial dimensions your company will use.*

Using this form, you can specify the dimensions that are available for use throughout the system. The Number field lists the identifiers that you will use to select each dimension when assigning it. Even though this field is named Number, it is a text field and you may use letters or numbers. The Employee field is optional and is simply there for you to specify the person who is in charge of the dimension. The Group field is used to specify a mapping for the current dimension if you are consolidating with a company that uses different dimensions.

Financial Periods

Before you can record financial transactions in Axapta, you need to set up financial periods using the Periods form (General Ledger ➤ Setup ➤ Periods ➤ Periods) and pressing the Create New Fiscal Year button, shown in Figure 7-2.

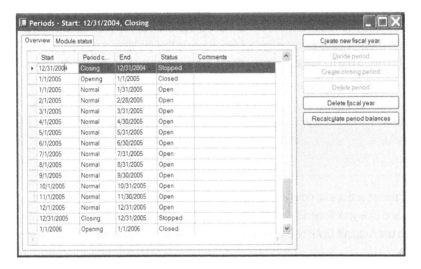

Figure 7-2. *Use the Periods form to set up Financial Periods.*

A form will open (Figure 7-3), enabling you to enter the starting and ending dates of the new fiscal year, along with the desired length of each period. Note that you can create periods of days, months, or years. Most companies will create month-long periods.

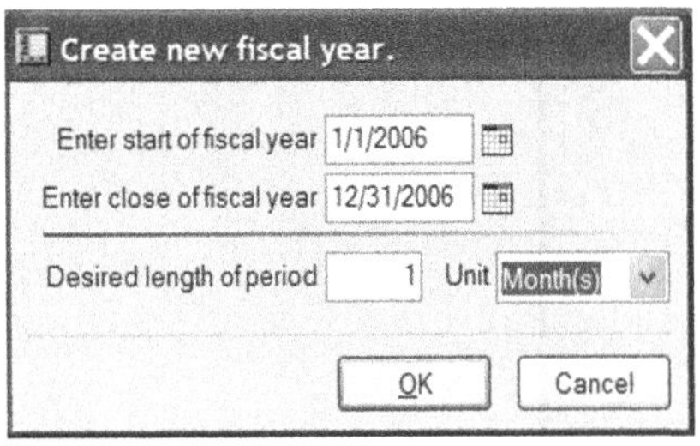

Figure 7-3. *The Create New Fiscal Year form*

In addition to creating the financial periods you specified, Axapta will create two additional periods, one with the Opening period code and one with the Closing period code. The Opening period will be used for any transactions that need to be transferred in from the previous closing, and the Closing period will be used for entering period-ending transactions. Normal periods are just that: normal periods for recording financial transactions. They are created based on the criteria you entered using the Create New Fiscal Year form.

Currency

You must have at least one currency set up to record transactions in Axapta.

Currencies are set up, along with their exchange rates, using the Currency form (General Ledger ➤ Setup ➤ Exchange Rates) shown in Figure 7-4.

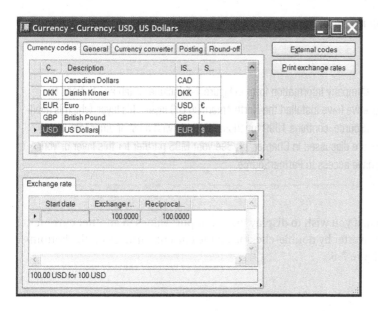

Figure 7-4. *Use the Currency form to set up all currencies you'll be using, along with their exchange rates.*

Currency exchange values are based upon the exchange rate of 100 units of the default currency. For example, 100 US dollars might be equivalent to 122.31 Canadian dollars. You must establish the exchange rate for your default currency as 100 of its own units (100 US dollars equals 100 US dollars), as shown in the Exchange Rate tab in Figure 7-4.

Note When entering multiple currencies, you can choose to enter either the exchange rate or the reciprocal value. If you enter the exchange rate, the reciprocal value will calculate automatically, and vice versa.

You can specify your default currency on the Other tab of the Company Information form (Basic ➤ Setup ➤ Company Information), shown in Figure 7-5.

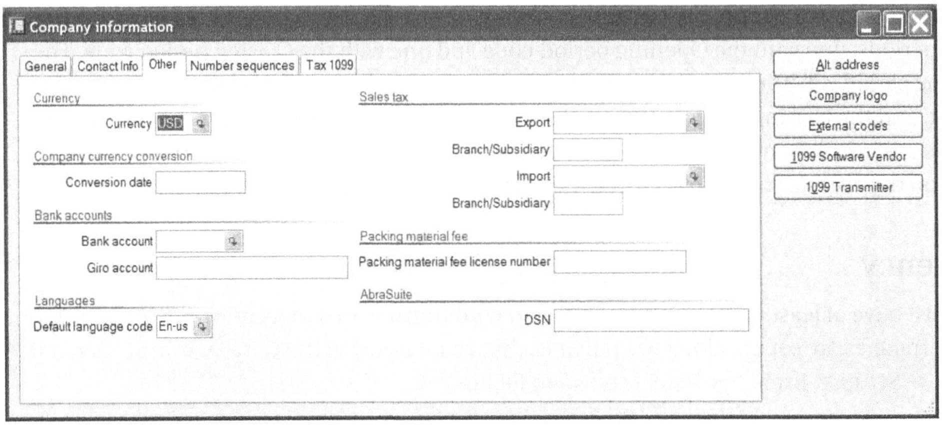

Figure 7-5. *The Company Information form*

■**Note** You may notice that the Company Information form in Figure 7-5 includes a tab and buttons for 1099 functionality. This is because we have installed the North American DIS layer. This layer, which is available for free download via PartnerSource, contains 1099 functionality along with a list of other features specific to North America. Layers are discussed in Chapter 17. See your MBS partner for this layer or your localized DIS layer if you do not have access to PartnerSource.

When working in Axapta, if you wish to display form or report values in another currency, simply open the currency converter by double-clicking on the current currency on the bottom-right status bar, shown in Figure 7-6.

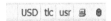

Figure 7-6. *The status bar*

Choose your new desired currency by double-clicking the house icon to the left of your desired currency, as depicted in Figure 7-7.

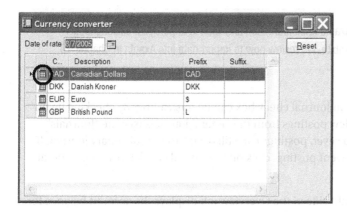

Figure 7-7. *The Currency Converter form*

Chart of Accounts

Now that we have our dimensions, financial periods, and currencies set up, we can dive into the chart of accounts. The Chart of Accounts form is located at General Ledger ➤ Chart of Accounts, and is shown in Figure 7-8.

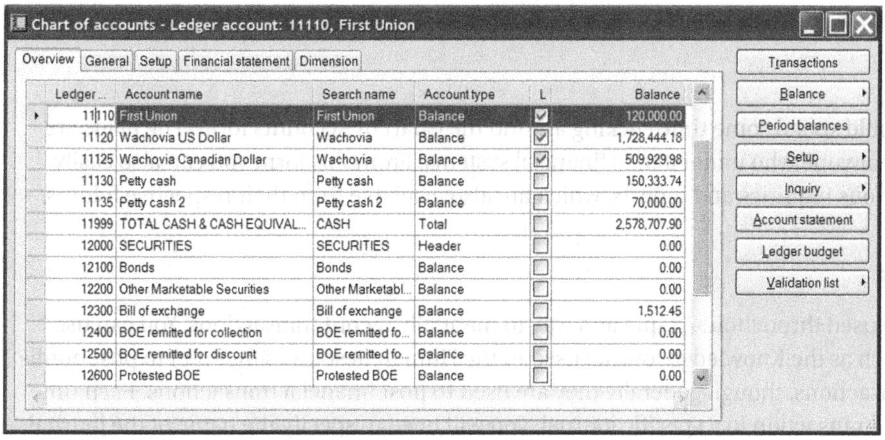

Figure 7-8. *The Chart of Accounts form*

The Chart of Accounts form is the backbone of Axapta's whole financial system. We can't go over all the fields and functionality available in this form, but we'll cover a few must-know basics:

- The Account Type field on the Overview tab is used to specify the type of account (Profit and Loss, Revenue, Cost, Balance, Asset, or Liability), and can also be used to create formatting accounts to be used in the generation of financial statements, reports, and inquiries. These formatting accounts can carry the account types of Header, Empty Header, Page Header, and Total.

Note If you are working on a new Axapta implementation and wish to import your existing ledger accounts, this table is named LedgerTable. We review how to import data into Axapta in Chapter 19.

- The Overview tab's Locked in Journal check box can be misleading. By checking it you are telling Axapta not to allow postings from the general journals (see the "Journals" section of this chapter). However, postings can still occur from a subsidiary journal. If you want to completely prevent posting, click on the Closed check box in the General tab's Administration field.

- The Balance field on the right side of the Overview tab displays the account balance for the period specified using General Ledger ➤ Chart of Accounts ➤ Balance ➤ Setup (see Figure 7-9).

Figure 7-9. *The Balance button from the Chart of Accounts form*

You should spend some time clicking around the Chart of Accounts form. The fields are intuitive for anyone who understands financial systems. From this form you can also easily perform various inquiries and reports, which are also available from their respective folders.

Journals

Journals are used throughout Axapta as a way to manually record transactions. You can use journals (such as the Knowledge Journal used in the Human Resources module) to post nonfinancial transactions, though generally they are used to post financial transactions. Each time you record a transaction in a specific journal, you will need to specify the name of the journal where you want to record your transaction; this way when viewing transactions at a later date you will be able to easily identify the transaction type.

Using the Journal Setup form (General Ledger ➤ Setup ➤ Journals ➤ Journal Names) you can set up journal names to be used for the available financial journals, as Figure 7-10 illustrates. Be certain to set these up in advance so that you have them available when recording transactions via journals.

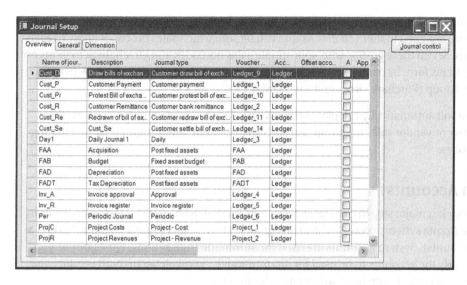

Figure 7-10. *The Journal Setup form*

Sales Tax

All of the forms needed to set up sales tax within Axapta are located in General Ledger ➤ Setup ➤ Sales Tax. We will briefly explain each of these forms and their significance, but the nature of your business will determine how much of this is relevant to you. You should set up the forms in the order they are presented in the menu:

1. *Ledger Posting Groups*: Here you specify the General Ledger accounts to be used during sales tax postings.

2. *Sales Tax Authorities*: You must set up all sales tax–payable agencies in Axapta first as vendors. Once you've done that, create records in the Sales Tax Authorities form to designate the vendor as a sales tax authority.

3. *Sales Tax Settlement Periods*: Use this form to specify the date intervals in which you will be reporting and paying your collected sales tax to the appropriate agency.

4. *Sales Tax Codes*: Use this form to calculate the different sales taxes that you will be paying or collecting. For example, if you need to charge sales tax in New York City, you would set up one record for New York State, 4.0%; one record for New York County, 4.0%; and one record for the Metropolitan Commuter Transportation District (MCTD), 0.375%; for a combined rate of 8.375%. If you need to charge sales tax in other counties in New York, you would want to set up those county-specific rates, as well.

5. *Sales Tax Groups*: Since taxes are determined by the geographic locations of the customers or vendors, it is a good idea to group them in sales tax groups. Use this form to join the New York State, New York County, and MCTD taxes mentioned in number 4 into a single group. You will attach this group to each taxable customer who resides in New York County (select the appropriate sales tax group on the Customers form by choosing Accounts Receivable ➤ Customers ➤ Setup ➤ Sales Tax). You would also want to attach this sales tax group to any vendor to whom you might be paying this same tax (Accounts Payable ➤ Vendors ➤ Setup ➤ Sales Tax).

6. *Item Sales Tax Groups*: Similar to customers and vendors, items need to have a sales tax group assigned to them so that Axapta can be sure which sales tax codes apply to each item. Set up these groups with appropriate sales tax codes and attach them to items on the Items form by choosing Inventory Management ➤ Items ➤ References ➤ Item Sales Tax Group (Purchase Order and Sales Order).

Axapta will automatically calculate sales tax on sales orders and purchase orders when the customer or vendor sales tax group and each specific item sales tax group have matching sales tax codes.

System Accounts

Finally, in our last major step in General Ledger setup, it's vital to link General Ledger accounts to each of the Axapta system accounts, shown in Figure 7-11 (General Ledger ➤ Setup ➤ Posting ➤ System Accounts). System accounts are used for automatic transactions. For example, you need to specify the accounts to be used for discounts given at invoicing (to both vendors and customers, and on both purchase orders and sales orders).

Posting type	Ledger acc...	Name
Penny difference in secondary currency	90000	Error Account
Error account	90000	Error Account
Penny difference in default currency	60815	Penny Difference
Year-end result	30160	Net Income for the Year
Cash discount	40316	Cash Discount
Consolidation differences	90000	Error Account
Customer cash discount	40316	Cash Discount
Customer invoice discount	50310	Discounts Granted
Vendor cash discount	50306	Cash Discounts Recieved
Vendor invoice discount	50305	Discount & Allowances Recieved
Order, freight	40315	Miscellaneous Charges
Order fee	40315	Miscellaneous Charges
Order invoice rounding	90000	Error Account
Purchase invoice rounding-off	90000	Error Account
Purchase, standard cost profit	50219	Standard Cost Price Inventory adj...

Figure 7-11. *The System Accounts form*

When you first arrive at this form, it will be blank. When you press the Create button, Axapta will automatically create the Posting Type records for you. You will need to enter the appropriate ledger account for each posting type.

Note Always remember to come back to this form and click the Create button after any system upgrade (new service packs, versions) to see if any new system accounts have been introduced as a result of the upgrade.

Customer and Vendor Groups

Customer Groups and Vendor Groups are the only required fields when setting up customer and vendor records, respectively. We will discuss the setup of both groups together, as they are very similar. To find the Customer Groups or Vendor Groups form, choose Accounts Receivable ➤ Setup ➤ Customer Groups or Accounts Payable ➤ Setup ➤ Vendor Groups. See Figure 7-12.

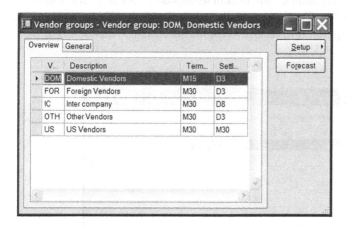

Figure 7-12. *The Vendor Groups form*

As with many of the forms in Axapta, when you create a new record you will specify a short identifier for the record that you are creating, along with a description. The field Terms of Payment specifies the time between the purchase of the goods and the actual due date of the payment. The Settle Period specifies the grace period—the time between the payment due date and the date by which the payment must be received. Right-click in either of these fields and select Go to the Main Table to bring up the appropriate forms so that you can explore further.

If you click on the Setup button, you will be directed to the Inventory Posting form, shown in Figure 7-13.

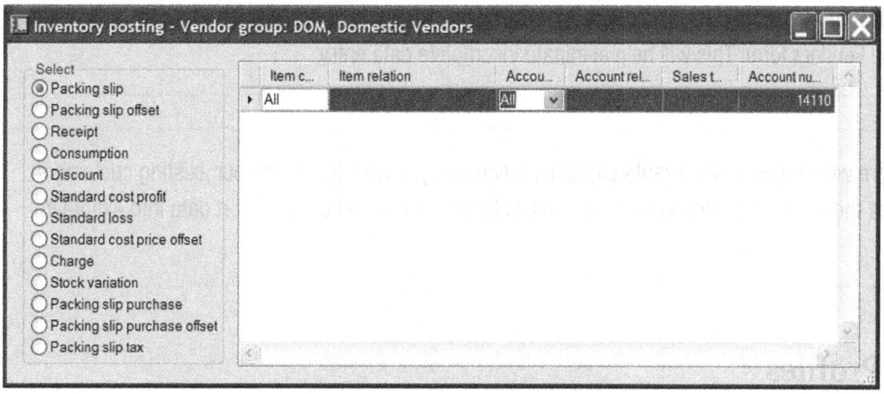

Figure 7-13. *The Inventory Posting form*

Use the Inventory Posting form to specify the general ledger accounts to be used for automatic ledger posting for each of the transactions in the Select control group. You can specify these accounts using criteria for all customers, vendors, or items; groups of customers, vendors, or items; and individual customers, vendors, or items.

Customer and Vendor Records

Customer and vendor records are very similar (but, of course, opposite—accounts receivable and accounts payable, respectively), and again we will discuss them together. To access the Customers or Vendors form (see Figure 7-14), choose Accounts Receivable ➤ Customers or Accounts Payable ➤ Vendors.

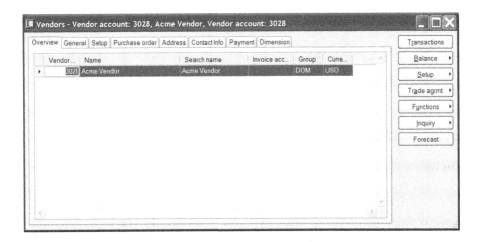

Figure 7-14. *The Vendors form*

When creating a new customer or vendor record, the only required field is Group. Without this information Axapta will be unable to post the automatic transactions that are necessary when attempting to purchase or sell goods and services.

Tip We recommend making any other fields that may be important to your business required on both the Customers and Vendors form. This will help eliminate incomplete data entry.

Tip If you are working on a new Axapta implementation and you wish to import your existing customers or vendors, use the CustTable and VendTable, respectively. We review how to import data into Axapta in Chapter 19.

Posting Profiles

You must have posting profiles set up in accounts receivable and accounts payable before you can fully process sales orders or purchase orders. At a minimum, you should have one record set up in each form to capture all accounts. The posting profile forms are located at Accounts Receivable ➤ Setup ➤ Posting Profiles, and Accounts Payable ➤ Setup ➤ Posting Profiles, respectively. Figure 7-15 shows the Vendor Posting Profiles form.

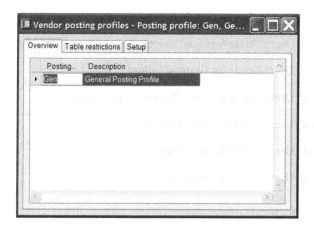

Figure 7-15. *The Vendor Posting Profiles form*

On the Overview tab you will specify a short text identifier, followed by a longer description. Using the Table Restrictions tab, you can define how and if transactions are settled, closed, and canceled. Finally, using the Setup tab you will specify the GL accounts to be used throughout the posting processes. You have the option of specifying these by all customers/vendors, by customer/vendor group, or individual customer/vendor.

Processes

As you should be able to tell by now, the setup of Axapta's General Ledger module is complex. The setup steps that we have touched on are minimal and will only get you started in being able to support the functionality available in Axapta's Finance modules. The modules in Axapta support everyday finance-department processes, such as issuing vendor payments, receiving customer payments, issuing collection letters, budgeting, creating financial statements, and managing bank reconciliation, to name a few. If you wish to become an expert in Axapta's Finance modules, you will need to take classes, read a follow-up book, and, most importantly, spend time using Axapta.

Wrap-Up

In this chapter we have focused on the basic setup necessary to begin working with Axapta's Finance modules. You have learned some tips and tricks that can help you learn about the product more quickly. Keep in mind that the setups in this chapter are extremely basic and do not cover the Parameters form in any of the Finance modules. Remember that the Parameters forms control many of the settings regarding the operation of each module.

The finance department is the backbone of any company, and most certainly it is the backbone of Axapta. Be careful when setting up these modules, and make sure you understand them completely before you attempt any modification to them.

The following is a list of the Finance-applicable guides that come on the Axapta CD. They are fairly technical and are most helpful when you need to look up specific information.

- *AX-300-USG-033-v01.00-ENUS.pdf*: Getting Started Cost Accounting

- *AX-300-USG-035-v01.00-ENUS.pdf*: Getting Started Guide for Cost Purpose Accounting

- *AX-300-USG-002-v01.00-ENUS.pdf*: User's Guide for Fixed Assets

- *AX-300-USG-001-v01.00-ENUS.pdf*: User's Guide for General Ledger

- *AX-300-USG-034-v01.00-ENUS.pdf*: User's Guide for Cost Purpose Accounting

- *AX-300-USG-005-v01.00-ENUS.pdf*: User's Guide for Accounts Payable

- *AX-300-USG-004-v01.00-ENUS.pdf*: User's Guide for Accounts Receivable

- *AX-300-USG-003-v01.00-ENUS.pdf*: User's Guide for Banking

CHAPTER 8

■ ■ ■

Inventory Management

The topic of inventory management spans across the Axapta modules Trade, Trade Agreements, Logistics, Warehouse Management I, and Warehouse Management II. In Axapta, inventory management functionality is available mainly from the Inventory Management menu tab, shown in Figure 8-1, though this information is readily available from most other menu tabs throughout the application.

Figure 8-1. *Inventory Management menu tab*

How much of this functionality you use will depend on the nature of your business. For the purpose of this chapter, we will run you through the most important and common setups and explain some of the rich functionality that is available using these modules.

Setup

The setup of your business's inventory and inventory management policies and procedures requires a great deal of initial preparation. We recommend that you read through all of the steps we present here before attempting to set up these modules.

The following setup process consists of the basic steps required to utilize the functionality in the Inventory Management modules. You should understand, though, that these steps are far from basic regarding their importance to these modules. A decision to change or modify some of these basic setup options in a live or production environment can result in incorrect or difficult inventory transactions and corresponding closings. You should establish a structure for how your inventory will be handled and managed in Axapta and be sure to thoroughly think through any postimplementation changes to this initial setup.

As with all modules in Axapta, be sure to spend some time going over all of the options available in the Parameters form, which you access by selecting Inventory Management ➤ Setup ➤ Parameters. This form contains many of the options that control the operation of these modules.

When you create a new item in Axapta's Item form, shown in Figure 8-2 (accessible by selecting Inventory Management ➤ Items), there are four required fields for which you must supply information (not including Item Number): Item Group, Item Type, Inventory Model Group, and Dimension Group. Let's take a closer look at these four fields.

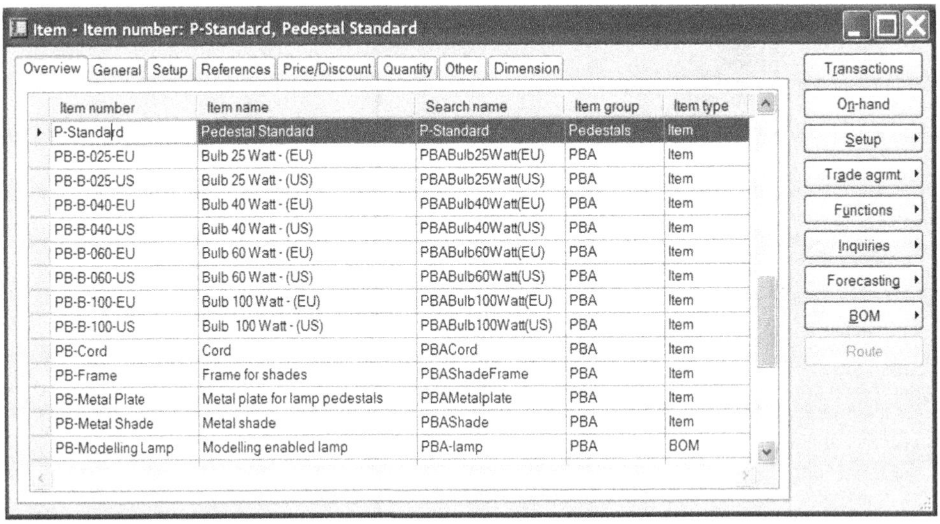

Figure 8-2. *Item form*

Item Type

The first of the four required fields on the Item form is Item Type. There are three possible item types in Axapta:

- *Item*: These are purchased items that are inventoried and either resold or used as part of a bill of materials (BOM). By default, when entering a new item in Axapta, the type is set to Item.

- *Service*: Service items are generally something that is nonphysical, such as consulting services (billed per hour), or something that is used for internal consumption, such as office supplies.

- *BOM*: Bill of material items contain other items (of type Item, Service, or BOM) in addition to a route that enables these combinations of items to be produced or packaged as another good or piece of another good. We discuss BOM items further in Chapter 10.

For the purpose of keeping it simple, we are going to concentrate on items of type Item for this chapter.

■**Note** If you wish to change an item type after an item has already been entered, use the Change Item Type form. Start by selecting Inventory Management ➤ Items ➤ Functions ➤ Change Item Type.

Item Group

The second of the four required fields on the Item form is Item Group. Axapta uses item groups to specify posting parameters. We already spoke about inventory posting briefly in the last chapter in the section "Customer and Vendor Groups."

Many businesses will also use item groups to classify or break down the items that they carry. This field is very commonly used for filtering and reporting. It can also be used for forecasting, pricing, and a number of other functions within Axapta.

The Item Group form can be accessed either from the Item form by right-clicking the Item Group field and selecting Go to Main Table from the context menu that appears or from the main application menu by selecting Inventory Management ➤ Setup ➤ Item Groups. This form is shown in Figure 8-3.

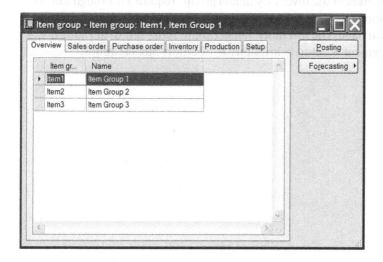

Figure 8-3. *Item Group form*

You can use this form to create new item groups and assign appropriate ledger accounts. Clicking the Posting button will bring up the Inventory Posting form (as shown previously in Chapter 7, Figure 7-13), which enables you to break down the posting selection by customers/vendors. The data presented in both of these forms is the same, whether accessed from the Inventory Management, Accounts Receivable, or Accounts Payable menu. A change in any of these forms applies to all of these forms, as they all display the same data.

Inventory Model Group

The third of the four required fields on the Item form is Inventory Model Group. Before we look at all of the settings available for inventory model groups, you should first understand the concepts of physical inventory and financial inventory, as used by Axapta:

- *Physical inventory*: This is also referred to in Axapta documentation as *floating inventory*, and describes the state of an item or transaction for which the true financial value is not yet associated. This applies to the packing slip stage of either a sales order or purchase order, where the true financial value is not yet known, since the sales or purchase order has not yet been invoiced.

- *Financial inventory*: This refers to the actual known financial or invoice value of items or transactions.

Axapta uses inventory model groups for three major purposes:

- *Inventory cost settings*: Which model to use and how costs should be tracked throughout the receipt and issue process

- *Ledger settings*: How inventory costs will appear in the ledger throughout the receipt and issue process

- *Warehouse settings*: How inventory may be reserved and picked

The setup of the parameters in the inventory model groups require a thorough understanding of inventory valuation methods, the Axapta process flow, and most importantly how these relate to the business at hand. The Inventory Model Groups form, shown in Figure 8-4, is located at Inventory Management ➤ Setup ➤ Inventory ➤ Inventory Model Groups.

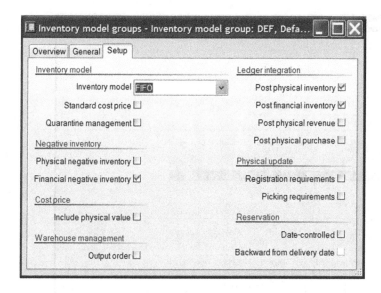

Figure 8-4. *Inventory Model Groups form, Setup tab*

Make certain that you understand the significance of each of these fields as you set up these groups. As with all modules in Axapta, use the What's This? right-click option for an explanation of these fields.

Dimension Group

The fourth and final required field on the Item form is Dimension Group. The Dimension Group form, located at Inventory Management ➤ Setup ➤ Dimensions ➤ Dimension Groups, is split into Item Dimensions and Storage Dimensions areas, as you can see in Figure 8-5. You use these areas in the Dimension Group form to specify the following:

- *Item dimensions*: Specify an item's attributes. The standard Axapta item dimensions consist of configuration, size, and color. These three can be renamed if needed. Similar to how financial dimensions are used to simplify the chart of accounts, item dimensions can be used to simplify the Items table.

- *Storage dimensions*: Specify how an item is received in inventory, stored in inventory, and issued from inventory.

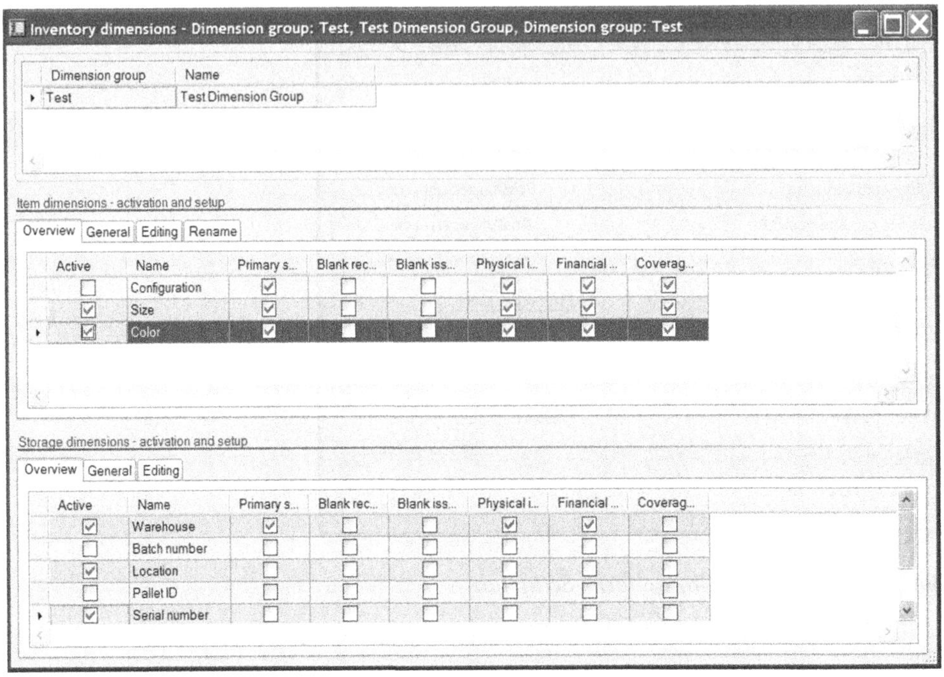

Figure 8-5. *Dimension Group form*

In order to use a particular dimension, click the Active box next to the appropriate dimension. Doing so will activate the dimension, after which you can further configure it.

Table 8-1 lists the options available on the Overview tab of the Dimension Group form.

Table 8-1. *Dimensions Overview Options*

Option	Description
Primary Stocking	By declaring a dimension Primary Stocking, you are selecting that this dimension must be specified during any update made to an item belonging to this group. All active item dimensions have the Primary Stocking option checked, as these attributes physically separate the items that use these dimensions. Primary Stocking is optional on storage dimensions.
Blank Receipt	Selecting this option tells Axapta that you will allow physical receipts with this attribute blank or not stated. This option is not available if Primary Stocking is checked.
Blank Issue	Selecting this option tells Axapta that you will allow physical issues with this attribute blank or not stated. This option is not available if Primary Stocking is checked.
Physical Inventory	Selecting this option tells Axapta to consider this dimension when checking inventory on hand. This option also tells Axapta to consider this dimension when calculating physical inventory values, if being used.

Option	Description
Financial Inventory	Selecting this option tells Axapta to consider this dimension when checking inventory on hand. This option also tells Axapta to consider this dimension when calculating financial inventory values, or actual item consumption.
Coverage Plan by Dimension	Selecting this option tells Axapta to use this dimension in coverage planning. This is used by Master Planning, which is described in further detail in Chapter 11.

■**Note** The options available on the Overview tab are just the beginning of the options that you have in defining the different inventory dimensions and how they are handled throughout Axapta. Make certain to understand all of the fields on the General and Editing tabs of this form.

Item Dimensions

For each item that uses a dimension group that has one or more item dimensions active, you will need to maintain the available item dimensions and specify any relevant combinations of the item dimensions. These can be defined under the *Item Dimensions* folder by selecting Inventory Management ➤ Setup ➤ Dimensions ➤ Item Dimensions; or, from the Item form, click the Setup button. Only the dimensions that are marked active via the item's dimension Group will be available, as you can see in Figure 8-6.

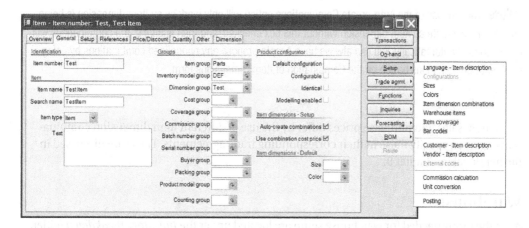

Figure 8-6. *Options available from Item form, Setup button. This item has a dimension group with size and color as active dimensions.*

Whenever you are using multiple item dimensions, it is important that you specify the combinations of different item dimensions that are available. This can be done manually by using the Item Dimension Combinations option from the Setup menu, as shown in Figure 8-6, or this can be done automatically by clicking the Auto-create Combinations check box on the General tab of the Item form, also shown in Figure 8-6.

If you have chosen to use standard costing and wish to specify cost prices by item dimension combinations, you should enable the Use combination cost price option on the General tab of the Item form (refer again to Figure 8-6), which tells Axapta to use the defined cost price for the item dimension combination as specified on the Combinations of Item Dimensions form, which appears in Figure 8-7.

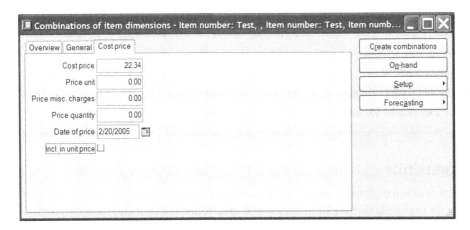

Figure 8-7. *Cost Price tab of the Item Dimension Combinations form*

■**Note** The function of the Auto-create Combinations option will only work as an item dimension is being created. If you create an item dimension without this box checked, and then enable it, the combinations will not be created automatically. You can always have Axapta propose any nondefined combinations by using the Create Combinations button on the Combination of Item Dimensions form.

If item sales and purchase prices differ by the use of different item dimension combinations, you can specify these in their corresponding trade agreements. These are discussed in further detail in Chapter 9.

Warehouses

All of the forms needed for warehouse setup are located under the *Inventory Breakdown* folder, which you access by selecting Inventory Management ➤ Setup ➤ Inventory Breakdown. We will briefly explain each of these forms and their significance. Your particular setup will be dependent on the layout and structure of your warehouses and warehouse management processes.

Some businesses may wish to have Axapta recommend and decide inventory receipt and issue locations, while others may wish to manually decide these locations. In either case, you should supply Axapta with the exact locations available in your warehouse and the goods available in these locations, so that warehouse staff can quickly and efficiently pick orders. You should set up these forms in the order that they are presented in the menu, which is as follows:

1. *Warehouses*: Use this form to create your different warehouses. Generally, businesses create a separate warehouse for each physical location where goods are stored, and/or for locations that serve a particular purpose. You can use this form to specify the level of detail that you use for stocking (aisle, rack, shelf, bin) in addition to master planning and warehouse management parameters. Additionally, you can use the Location Wizard available from the Functions button on this form to assist you in creating the data required for steps 2 through 5.

2. *Inventory Aisles*: Use this form to create the different aisles available for each warehouse specified in the preceding step. The field Aisle acts as your short identifier for the aisle, while the field Aisle Number is used for sorting locations when they are added.

3. *Store Areas*: Use this form to create groups of locations that are used to receive or pick goods. Store areas can be of type Input Area or Picking Area and will be used to further describe the locations specified in step 5.

4. *Store Zones*: Use this form to prioritize the store areas to be used for item input.

5. *Locations*: Use this form to tie together all of the data specified in steps 1 through 4 into the end warehouse locations. These end locations have the ability to be specified down to bin level, dependent on the options chosen in step 1. As you can see in Figure 8-8, the tree structure of your end locations gives a nice graphical view of your warehouse setup. Access this structure by selecting Inventory Management ➤ Setup ➤ Inventory Breakdown ➤ Locations ➤ Tree Structure.

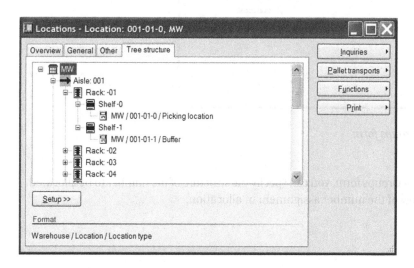

Figure 8-8. *Tree view of warehouse setup*

Note While it is possible to have Axapta recommend receipt and put away locations based upon the combination of location and item physical dimensions (sizing), it is also possible to set up default receipt and issue locations on the warehouse item records of items in inventory by selecting Inventory Management ➤ Items ➤ Setup ➤ Warehouse Items ➤ Locations. The use of either method requires a good deal of care and feeding in making sure your data is consistent.

Serial/Batch Number

The use of serial and batch numbering requires the setup of number groups. To do this, bring up the Number Groups form (shown in Figure 8-9) by selecting Inventory Management ➤ Setup ➤ Dimensions ➤ Number Groups, and select the criteria by which to base your number group. After creating one or more number groups, you can assign the number groups to the appropriate fields (Serial Number Group, Batch Number Group) on the Item form, General tab (refer back to Figure 8-6).

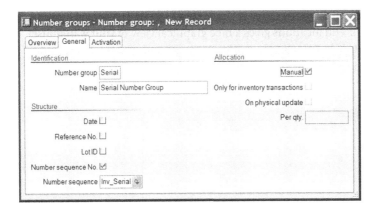

Figure 8-9. *Number Groups form*

Using the Number Groups form, you can specify the structure of the number to be allocated, and the when and how of the number assignment or allocation.

Processes

Many of the inventory processes will be described in greater detail in the next chapter, as this chapter will deal with the receipt and issue of inventory (purchase and sales orders). The processes that you will use in Axapta's inventory management will depend on the setup of your organization and your business processes. We will briefly touch on the processes of inventory closing and inventory journals, as they are vital to any business that uses inventory management.

Inventory Closing and Adjustment

You specify how Axapta should calculate the value of your inventory in the inventory model group. The inventory model selected is applied, and inventory is finally valued whenever the inventory closing procedure is run. Before this procedure is run for a given period, the true value of inventory is just an estimate, as receipts and issues have not yet been matched using the proper model. The closing and adjustment process will adjust any transactions based on the model specified and the transactions of the specific items given in the specific time period. After closing, it is no longer possible to post inventory transactions in the closed period.

Inventory closing and adjustment can be done from the Closing and Adjustment form, shown in Figure 8-10, which you access by selecting Inventory Management ➤ Periodic ➤ Closing and Adjustment.

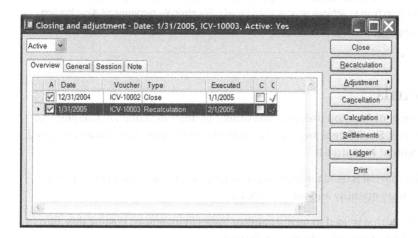

Figure 8-10. *Inventory Closing and Adjustment form*

Several functions are available from the Closing and Adjustment form:

- *Close*: The closing procedure is used to match issues and receipts in prior periods to determine the true value of inventory on hand by using the appropriate inventory model to adjust the cost prices on any issue transactions. Generally, companies will perform this process once a year.

- *Recalculation*: This process simulates the closing procedure described previously to determine item costs without actually closing the said period. Companies that need a very accurate look at their inventory value may run this process many times throughout the year.

- *Adjustment*: Use the Adjustment button to adjust the inventory value of inventory on hand or inventory transactions for a given receipt.

- *Cancellation*: This process will allow you to cancel or roll back the last closing.

- *Settlements*: The Settlements form shows any adjustments that were made and why such adjustments were made.

- *Ledger*: The Voucher Transactions button will display the voucher containing the ledger transactions related to the closing.

- *Print*: The Print button will print the settlement adjustments.

It is a good idea to have an experienced Axapta consultant available for help during a business's inventory closing procedure, as this is a complex job in Axapta and can return unexpected results if there has been inconsistent data entered in the system or if changes have been made throughout the period in the setup steps described earlier.

Tip Axapta Service Pack 4, released in May 2005, contains significant improvements and fixes to the inventory closing functionality. MBS has released a very thorough whitepaper regarding this process that is full of examples and details on how to achieve your desired results. We strongly recommend downloading the Service Pack and whitepaper from PartnerSource.

Inventory Journals

The inventory management function uses journals similar to those described in Chapter 7 to post manual transactions. Six different journals are available from the *Journals* folder (accessed via Inventory Management ➤ Journals):

- *Movement*: This journal is used for issue and receipt transactions. Posting this journal will cause inventory quantity and value to change.

- *Profit/Loss*: This journal is used to record gains or losses in inventory. Posting this journal will cause inventory quantity and value to change.

- *Transfer*: This journal is used to move an item within item or storage dimensions. Posting this journal will result in a corresponding issue and receipt between the changed dimensions. This journal is used to transfer orders between warehouses by Master Planning, which is further described in Chapter 11.

- *Bills of Material*: This journal is used to report a BOM as finished. Posting this journal will result in an issue of all BOM components and a receipt of the BOM item.

- *Item Arrival*: This journal is used to record the receipt of goods into inventory. Often, this journal is used for warehouse staff to receive purchase order goods.

- *Production Input*: This journal is used to record the receipt of a production order into inventory. This process is further described in Chapter 10.

- *Counting and Tag Counting*: These journals are used for the physical counting of inventory on hand. Posting these journals will cause inventory quantity and value to change.

Wrap-Up

In this chapter, we have gone over some of the basic setup steps required to begin working with inventory management in Axapta. These are just some of the most common setups required for most businesses, but of course, the extent of these setups will be dependent on your specific business processes and requirements. Hopefully, you've received enough groundwork to understand the flexibility offered by the Inventory Management modules.

Keep in mind that we did not cover the Parameters form, and as with all modules, this form contains many of the settings that control the operation of the Inventory Management modules.

As we cautioned earlier, carefully prepare for the setup of these modules. Post-go-live changes to these basic setups need to be carefully planned as they can have serious effects on inventory transactions and corresponding closings.

Listed here are the inventory management–specific guides that are available on the Axapta 3.0 CD that can provide further reference information into some of the topics discussed in this chapter:

- *AX-300-USG-006-v01.00-ENUS.doc*: User's Guide for Inventory Management

- *AX-300-TIP-008-v01.00-ENUS.pdf*: Inventory Dimensions Editor

- *AX-300-TIP-009-v01.00-ENUS.pdf*: Optimizing Inventory Dimension Setup

- *AX-300-TIP-007-v01.00-ENUS.pdf*: Simulated Inventory Closings

CHAPTER 9

■ ■ ■

Trade

Now that we have gone over the basic setup of Finance and Inventory Management, you should have the knowledge to enter some base data in your system, such as vendors, customers, and items. For this chapter, we are going to focus on the processes of buying and selling, and the different options for these processes in Axapta. We will begin with some of the basic setups that will make trading with vendors and customers easier, then we will show you some of the trade-related processes and features available using Axapta. It's important to keep in mind that the sales order and purchase order processes are identical, except the reverse of each other. For the purpose of keeping this chapter simple, we are going to focus on the sales order process. Once you understand the sales order process, you will find it very easy to work through the purchase order process.

Setup

With the setup you learned to do for finance and inventory management, you should be well on your way to being able to use the Trade processes. As we've mentioned already, the Parameters form in all Axapta modules contains many of the options for how the modules operate. We encourage you to explore the Accounts Receivable and Accounts Payable Parameters forms, accessible at Accounts Receivable ➤ Setup ➤ Parameters and Accounts Payable ➤ Setup ➤ Parameters, respectively.

Trade Agreements

By default, the prices used on sales orders and purchase orders are the prices listed on the Price/Discount tab of the Items form (see Figure 9-8 later in this chapter). By using trade agreements, you can set up specific pricing for any number of different situations. As we mentioned earlier, for the purpose of this chapter, we are going to focus on the sales order process, and therefore on customer trade agreements. Keep in mind that trade agreements work identically for purchase orders and vendors.

Trade agreements can be applied to all items, groups of items, or single items, in addition to all customers, groups of customers, or single customers. Furthermore, they can have date criteria. Be sure to read through the entire setup of trade agreements before attempting to perform your own setup. You will first need to understand when to use the different types of trade agreements, then you will need to know how to set up the customer or item groups to be used. Finally, you will want to make sure your trade agreements are active and being applied correctly.

First, look at the four types of trade agreements available in Axapta listed in Table 9-1, and make sure to examine their accompanying figures.

Table 9-1. *Four Types of Trade Agreements*

Type	Description
Price	A price trade agreement specifies a price for a customer, group of customers, or all customers. You can specify to and from dates for the price, and you can specify a minimum quantity to receive the price. For example, Figure 9-1 shows a price trade agreement for which all customers can purchase the test item for $9.99 during the time period 1/1/2005 through 1/31/2005, but only if they purchase in quantities of 5 or greater.
Line discount	A line discount trade agreement specifies a discount (amount and/or percent) for a customer, group of customers, or all customers. The discount can be based on to and from dates and a minimum quantity, if desired. For example, Figure 9-2 shows a line discount trade agreement for which customers who belong to the WD Customer line discount group can purchase the test item and any other items that belong to the TestL Item line discount group for 10% off up until 12/31/2005, but only if they purchase in a quantity of 10 or greater per line.
Multiline discount	A multiline discount trade agreement specifies a discount (amount and/or percent) for a customer, group of customers, or all customers. The discount can be based on to and from dates and a minimum quantity to be purchased across multiple sales order lines. For example, Figure 9-3 shows a multiline discount trade agreement for which customer 4011 can receive 10% off all goods that belong to the multiline discount group TestML if that customer purchases at least 100 pieces total among all the goods belonging to this group.
Total discount	A total discount trade agreement specifies a discount (amount and/or percent) for a customer, group of customers, or all customers. The discount can be based on to and from dates and a total amount of a given sales order. For example, Figure 9-4 shows a total discount trade agreement for which all customers receive $10 off a sales order of $1000 or more and an additional $15 off a sales order of $2000 or more.

Sales order trade agreements can be set up from the Items form by selecting Inventory Management ➤ Items and clicking the Trade Agmt button.

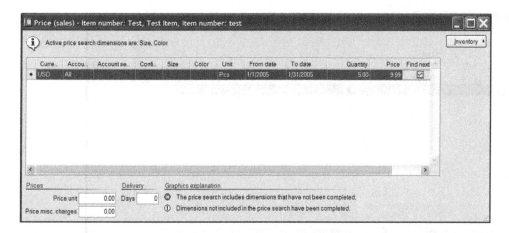

Figure 9-1. *Price trade agreement. All customers can purchase the test item for $9.99 if they purchase 5 or more on a given sales order between the dates 1/1/2005 and 1/31/2005.*

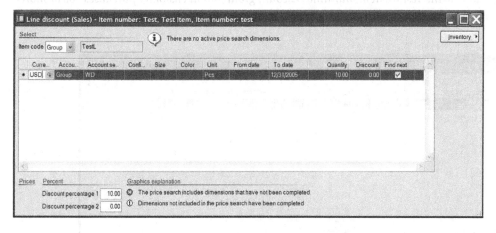

Figure 9-2. *Line discount trade agreeement. Customers belonging to the WD Customer Line Discount group can purchase the test item and any other items belonging to the TestL Item Line Discount group for 10% off if they purchase 10 or more, per line; this expires 12/31/2005.*

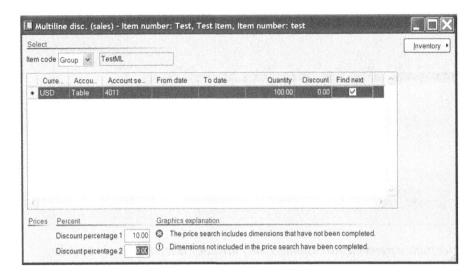

Figure 9-3. *Multiline discount trade agreement. Customer 4011 can receive 10% off any goods that belong to the TestML Item Multiline Discount group if that customer purchases 100 or more total items that belong to this group on a particular sales order.*

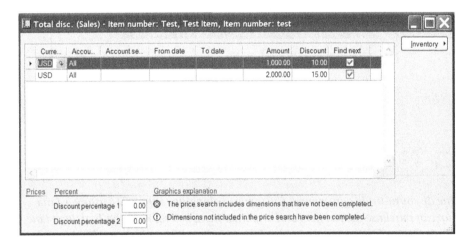

Figure 9-4. *Total discount trade agreement. All customers receive a discount of $10 off any sales order of $1000 or more, and an additional $15 off any sales order of $2000 or more, anytime. Without the Find Next check box checked on the top record, only the first discount would have been applied.*

■Note As shown in Figures 9-2, 9-3, and 9-4, fixed-value discounts are entered on the line created, while percentage discounts are entered towards the bottom of the form. Axapta allows for two discount percentages to be applied to each line, and will calculate the first discount percentage on the current net amount (price minus any fixed-value discounts) and then calculate the second discount percentage based on the net after the first discount percentage has been applied.

You have the ability to apply all trade agreements to a single customer, group of customers, or all customers. When you wish to use the group of customers feature to segment your customers, you will need to create customer price/discount groups, a process you begin by selecting Accounts Receivable ➤ Setup ➤ Price/Discount ➤ Customer Price/Discount Groups to bring up the form shown in Figure 9-5.

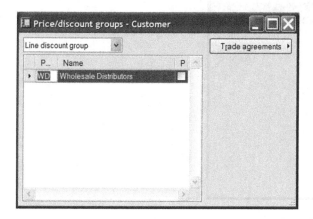

Figure 9-5. *Customer Price/Discount Groups form*

You can create these customer groups for all of the four trade agreement types. Change between the trade agreement types by clicking the pull-down menu located on the top of Figure 9-5.

Once you have created these groups, you must apply them to the records for those customers you want in the group. To do so, bring up the Customers form, as shown in Figure 9-6, by selecting Accounts Receivable ➤ Customers and clicking the Sales Order tab.

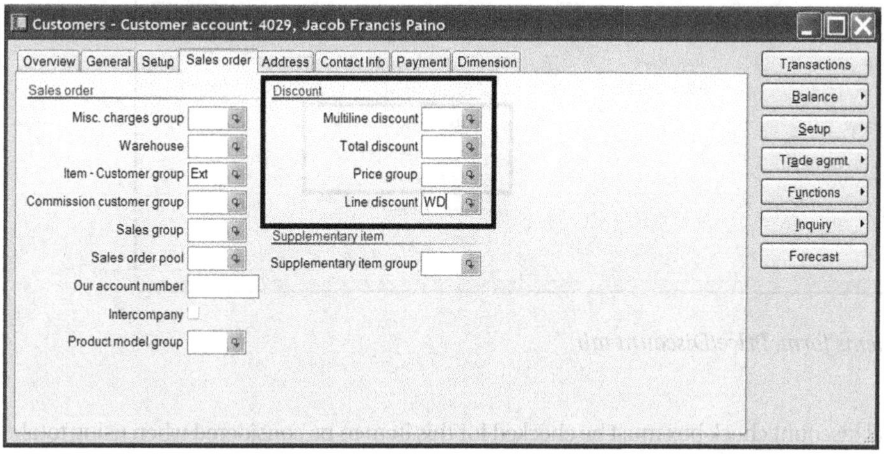

Figure 9-6. *Customers form, Sales Order tab*

For line and multiline discount trade agreements, you have the ability to use item discount groups in addition to customer price/discount groups by selecting Accounts Receivable ➤ Setup ➤ Price/Discount ➤ Item Discount Groups to bring up the Item Discount Groups form shown in Figure 9-7. By using these groups, you can create one trade agreement to be used across multiple items.

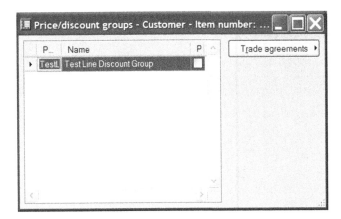

Figure 9-7. *Item Discount Groups form, line discount group TestL*

Once you have created these groups, you must apply them to the applicable item records. You do this by selecting Inventory Management ➤ Items to bring up the Items form and clicking the Price/Discount tab to access the options you see in Figure 9-8.

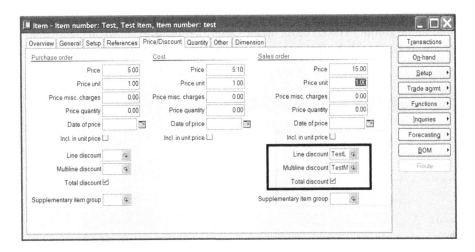

Figure 9-8. *Items form, Price/Discount tab*

The Total discount check box must be checked for this item to be considered when using total discount trade agreements. By default, this box is checked when creating a new item in Axapta.

Only active trade agreement types are usable in Axapta. You can activate trade agreements by going to the Activate Price/Discount form shown in Figure 9-9; access it by selecting

Accounts Receivable ➤ Setup ➤ Price/Discount ➤ Activate Price/Discount. Check the boxes for all types of trade agreements that should be active and the groups for which they should be active.

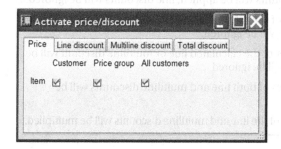

Figure 9-9. *Activate Price/Discount form*

Finally, you will want to make certain that you specify how the combination of line and multiline discounts are handled by selecting Accounts Receivable ➤ Setup ➤ Parameters to bring up the Accounts Receivable Parameters form. Click the Prices tab to bring up the options shown in Figure 9-10.

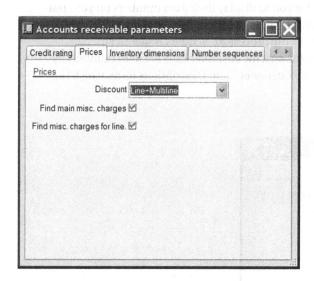

Figure 9-10. *Accounts Receivable Parameters form, Prices tab*

Table 9-2 lists the options available using the Discount pull-down menu that apply to the combination of line and multiline discounts.

Table 9-2. *Available Options on the Disount Pull-down Menu for Line and Multiline Discounts*

Discount	Description
Line	Only line discounts will be applied; multiline discounts will be ignored.
Multiline	Only multiline discounts will be applied; line discounts will be ignored.
MAX (Line, Multiline)	Whichever is larger of the calculated line or multiline discount will be applied; the smaller will be ignored.
MIN (Line, Multiline)	Whichever is smaller of the calculated line or multiline discount will be applied; the larger will be ignored.
Line+Multiline	The calculated values of both line and multiline discounts will be added together.
Line*Multiline	The calculated vales of the line and multiline discounts will be multiplied.

Note Price and line discount trade agreements are applied automatically to sales order and purchase order lines. Multiline and total discount trade agreements need to be calculated. This calculation is invoked manually and is described in the "Processes" section of this chapter.

External Item Numbers

Many customers and vendors may wish for you to display their item numbers on your purchase orders or sales orders, packing slips, and invoices. We will demonstrate how to set up these external item numbers for customers; the process for vendors is identical.

From the Items form, you can create the specific customer external item numbers by clicking the Setup button and choosing the Customer–Item Descriptions form, which is shown in Figure 9-11.

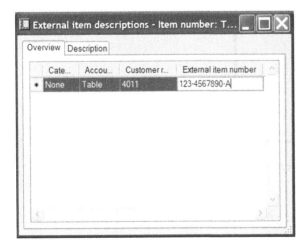

Figure 9-11. *Customer–Item Descriptions form*

Using this form, you can specify external item numbers that may be used for this item for a specific customer or for a group of customers. If you wish to use the group of customers option, you will need to create an Item–Customer Group. To do so, select Accounts Receivable ➤ Setup ➤ External Item Descriptions ➤ Item–Customer Groups, and attach this group to the Customers form, Sales Order tab (which was shown back in Figure 9-6).

You can also create these external item numbers directly from the Customers form, which you access by selecting Accounts Receivable ➤ Customers ➤ Setup ➤ External Item Descriptions.

If you wish to have these external item numbers displayed on printed sales order reports such as quotations, confirmations, packing slips, and invoices, you must specify this in the Form Setup form, shown in Figure 9-12. Access this form by selecting Accounts Receivable ➤ Setup ➤ Forms ➤ Form Setup. Use the Item Number in Forms pull-down menu to select one of the following options:

- *Our*: Your item number only is printed on the reports

- *Your*: Your customer's item number is printed on the reports if they have been set up. If they have not been set up, your internal item number will be printed.

- *Both*: Both your item number and your customer's item number are printed on the reports. Your number is always printed first, and your customer's number is always printed immediately underneath. The standard Axapta reports do not designate which number is yours and which is that of your customer.

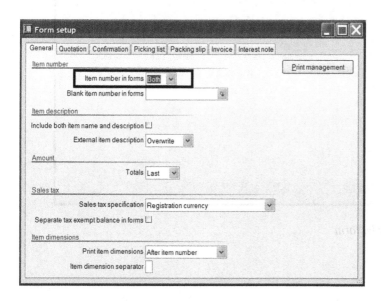

Figure 9-12. *Form Setup form*

Processes

As we mentioned in the beginning of this chapter, the sales order and purchase order processes are very similar, and for the purpose of this chapter, we are going to concentrate on sales orders. We will walk you through some sales order basics and give you information about some of the features available. Advanced features such as serial- or batch-numbered inventory, reservation, and manufacture or configure to order are outside the scope of this introductory book.

To view existing sales orders or create a new sales order, go to the Sales Orders form by selecting Accounts Receivable ➤ Sales Orders. This form will open in either Simple mode, as shown in Figure 9-13, or Advanced mode, as shown in Figure 9-14. You can toggle between each mode by clicking the button in the top right of the form. When you are in Simple mode, this button will read Advanced, and when you are in Advanced mode, this button will read Simple.

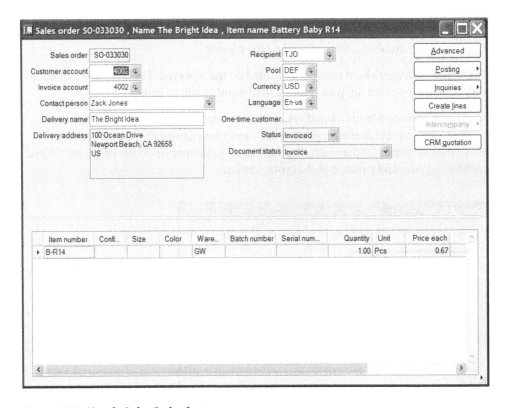

Figure 9-13. *Simple Sales Order form*

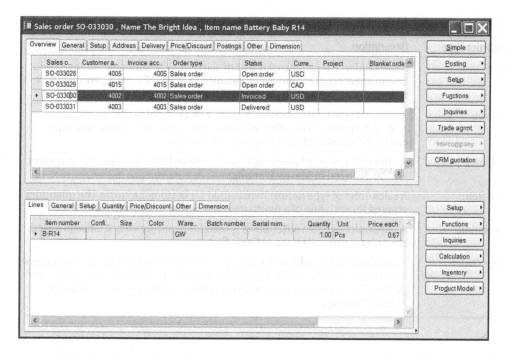

Figure 9-14. *Advanced Sales Order form*

The first major noticeable difference between these forms is that the Simple form displays a single sales order in the top half (header) of the form, while the Advanced form displays multiple sales orders in the header overview grid. Both forms display the line details for the selected sales order in the bottom half (lines) of the form. In addition, the Advanced form contains many tabs behind both the header and lines and additional functionality found via the buttons on the right side of the form.

For you to have access to all of the features and functions available for sales orders, we recommend you use the Advanced form.

■**Note** Many businesses will use a customized version of the Simple form for day-to-day use of their sales staff. This form is much easier on the eyes and leaves less room for error. For the purpose of learning Axapta, it is helpful to use the Advanced form.

Many of the fields on this form are intuitive, so we won't go into detail on all of them. Table 9-3 lists the sales order types.

Table 9-3. *Sales Order Type Options*

Sales Order Type	Description
Journal	A sales order of type Journal is a draft sales order. A sales order of this type has no effect on stock and is not included in Master Planning. We're unsure why the word "Journal" is used for this order type, as it's confusing.
Quotation	A sales order of type Quotation is similar to a journal in that it cannot reserve inventory. The major difference, though, is that a quotation order can be included in Master Planning calculations.
Sales Order	A sales order of type Sales Order is an actual order and can reserve inventory and be included in Master Planning.
Return Item	A sales order of type Return Item is used for customer returns. The quantities entered for each line of a return item sales order must be negative.
Subscription	A sales order of type Subscription is used for recurring orders. Once invoiced, the order status will return to Open Order.
Blanket Order	A sales order of type Blanket Order is used for contract orders. Release orders are created from the blanket order that deplete the blanket order until completion. The quantities remaining on a blanket order are not included in Master Planning.

■ **Note** Do not confuse the Quotation order type with a quotation created from the CRM module. While these are both named "quotation" and act very similarly, they are different. We will explore CRM quotations in Chapter 12.

■ **Note** In addition to using blanket orders for contract-style orders, they can be used when businesses need to create one order (for pricing reasons) to ship to multiple locations. This is done via the use of multiple release orders to the same customer with multiple addresses or multiple customers.

Sales orders can have the status of Open Order, Delivered, and Invoiced. Open orders are orders where one or more lines have not yet been shipped, or been packing slip posted. Delivered orders are orders where all lines have been packing slip posted, but not yet invoiced. Orders with the status of Invoiced have had all lines invoice posted.

To create a new sales order, make sure your cursor is in the header half of the Sales Order form and press Ctrl-N or click the New icon. The Create Sales Order form will appear as shown in Figure 9-15.

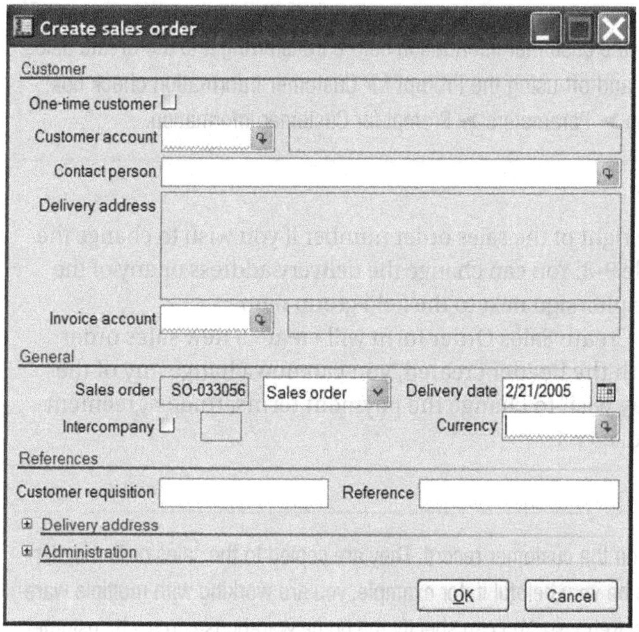

Figure 9-15. *Create Sales Order form*

Use this form to specify the customer account for which the new sales order should be created. The corresponding delivery address, invoice account, and currency will populate the form if these are set up correctly on the customer record (see Figure 9-16).

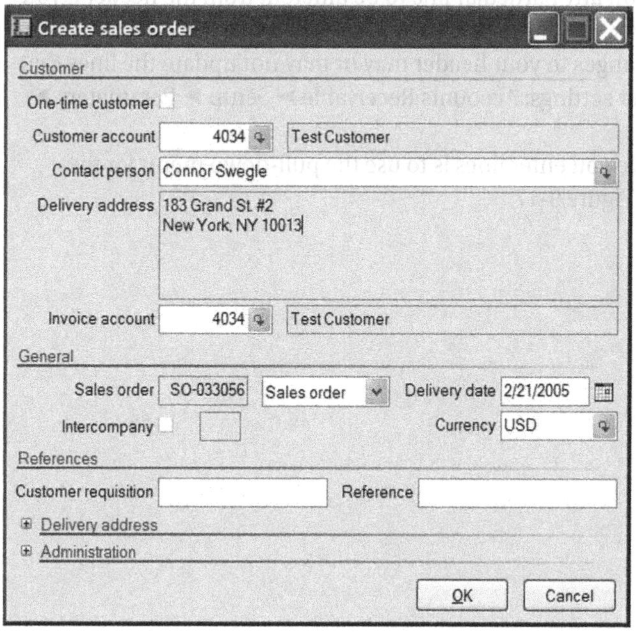

Figure 9-16. *Create Sales Order form with customer selected*

▪**Note** Axapta may prompt you to verify the customer information before transferring it to the Create Sales Order form. You can turn this feature on and off using the Prompt for Customer Information check box, available at Accounts Receivable ➤ Setup ➤ Parameters ➤ Prompt for Customer Information.

Use the pull-down menu to the right of the sales order number if you wish to change the sales order type as discussed in Table 9-3. You can change the delivery address or any of the administration fields by clicking the plus sign next to the field group name.

Clicking the OK button on the Create Sales Order form will create a new sales order header in the Sales Order form. With the header created, you can now change any of the header fields. For example, you may wish to change the payment terms, trade agreement groups, warehouse, delivery method, etc.

▪**Note** Many of these fields can be set on the customer record. They are copied to the sales order header when the sales order is created. This can be very helpful if, for example, you are working with multiple warehouses and each customer has a home warehouse. You can specify the home warehouse on each customer record so that each time a sales order is created, the header will specify the appropriate warehouse, and in turn each of the lines created will specify the home warehouse.

By clicking into the lines half of the Sales Order form, you can begin to create new lines and build the detail of your sales order. Keep in mind that the lines inherit details from the header, and that you can change the details on any particular line to be different from the header if you desire.

After you have created lines, changes to your header may or may not update the lines that follow, depending on your parameter settings; Accounts Receivable ➤ Setup ➤ Parameters ➤ Updates ➤ Update Order Lines.

An easy way to check stock while you enter lines is to use the pull-down menu for the Warehouse field, which is shown in Figure 9-17.

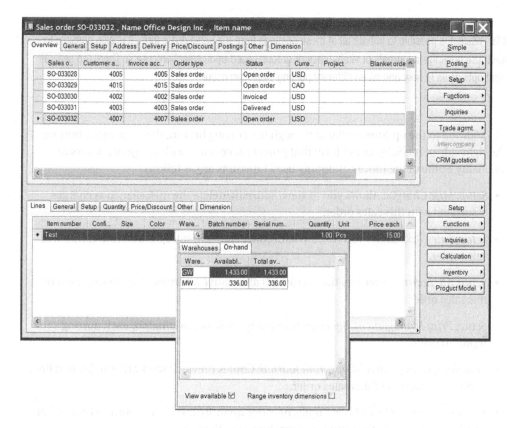

Figure 9-17. *Sales Order form with Warehouses pull-down menu showing inventory levels*

After you have entered your sales order lines, you have several posting options, available from the Postings button, described in Table 9-4. With all of the postings, you have the option to print a report containing the details.

Table 9-4. *Sales Order Posting Options*

Posting	Description
Quotation/Confirmation	Posting creates a report-style record of the sales order details. There is no ledger posting and no movement of inventory.
Picking List/Picking List Registration	Posting checks inventory for availability and can reserve physical inventory. Posting can also check credit limit availability.
Packing Slip	Posting deducts from physical inventory, corresponding GL entries are made, and delivery information is updated if entered.
Invoice	Posting deducts from financial inventory and corresponding GL entries are made.

Note While it is possible to initiate all of these postings from the sales order form, it is also possible to initiate these postings in journals or via batches or groups based upon selection criteria. There are several different options as to how and when different posting steps can occur.

In addition to the options available through the Posting button, there are many buttons on the right side of the Sales Order form that provide access to a wide range of additional functionality. Some of the more commonly used functions are as follows:

- *Setup, Misc Charges*: Allows you to view/add/edit/delete the miscellaneous charges associated with this sales order.

- *Setup, Sales Tax*: Allows you to view/add/edit/delete the sales tax associated with this sales order.

- *Setup, Alt. Address*: Specifies the customer's alternative addresses for the shipment of this sales order.

- *Setup, Print Management*: Specifies how many copies or originals of each posting report to print.

- *Functions, Copy from All/Copy from Journal*: Copies previous sales order or journal lines to the lines portion of this sales order.

- *Functions, Create Credit Note*: Copies negative quantity lines to the current order from previous invoices for the purpose of creating a credit note.

- *Functions, Create Purchase Order*: Enables the creation of a purchase order using the lines of the sales order. Commonly used for special orders and/or drop ship orders.

- *Functions, Create Release Order*: Creates a release order from a blanket order.

- *Trade Agreement*: Enables you to view/add/edit/delete any trade agreements applicable to the customer.

- *Functions, Explode BOM*: Breaks a single BOM item into its component item lines.

- *Functions, Deliver Remaining*: Updates the remaining quantity left to deliver. Helpful in underfulfillment/overfulfillment situations.

- *Inquires, Explosion*: Enables the update of pricing and availability, especially helpful in manufacturing environments.

- *Calculation, Multiline Discount/Total Discount*: Calculates and applies any discounts applicable.

- *Inventory, Reservation/Marking*: Enables the reservation of inventory.

The Sales Order form is very rich in functionality and is tightly integrated with other modules, such as Production, Master Planning, Projects, CRM, and of course all of the Finance modules. You should take some time to explore this form in detail.

Wrap-Up

In this chapter, we've gone through some of the most common trade setups and processes as related to sales orders. As we've mentioned, the sales order and purchase order functions in Axapta are very feature rich, and these processes are tightly integrated with all of the Axapta modules. Your experience using these modules will vary depending on the modules installed and line of work performed. You should have enough basic knowledge at this point to try and purchase some goods for inventory and sell them back out.

Trade is a hands-on topic in Axapta. To learn more, you should start processing purchase orders and sales orders in a demo system. The manuals that you should reference for further information are dependent on the modules you work with. For example, if you work with the Production modules, you will want to read the production guides and help files since they will guide you through what you need to know for processing trade transactions as related to manufactured goods.

The user's guides for accounts payable and receivable do a good job of explaining purchase orders and sales orders; refer to these guides for more information about these processes.

- *AX-300-USG-005-v01.00-ENUS.pdf*: User's Guide for Accounts Payable

- *AX-300-USG-004-v01.00-ENUS.pdf*: User's Guide for Accounts Receivable

CHAPTER 10

■■■

Manufacturing

In Axapta, Manufacturing is referred to as Production. There are three Production modules available: Production I, Production II, and Production III. Companies that manufacture might also be interested in the Shop Floor Control modules (which are not covered in this book) and the Master Planning module, which is described in the next chapter.

This chapter will walk you through the basic setups required to start using the Production modules in Axapta. The information here assumes that you have a basic understanding of a manufacturing environment. These modules have very advanced configurations available. The complexity of your businesses configuration will, obviously, depend on your business processes.

Setup

The setup of Axapta's Production modules should be performed by someone who fully understands your business's manufacturing processes and the information that needs to be recorded, viewed, or reported on through each step in the process. Certain businesses have stringent job-costing requirements while others need very detailed and precise scheduling and capacity requirements. Axapta supports a wide range of options in recording information about each step of the manufacturing processes and has many ways to report on scheduling, capacity, and work in progress (WIP) operations.

The setup steps presented here will give you the ability to process a very basic production order. In a basic process flow, we'll set up a BOM item with components or lines. These lines will be manufactured using a route that will specify operations to occur at work centers, and finally produce the finished BOM item. Some businesses may require BOMs without routes, while others may require very complex routes and operations.

Scheduling and planning will be covered in more detail in the next chapter, but it's important right now that you understand the difference between operations scheduling and job scheduling in Axapta.

- *Operations scheduling*: The less detailed of the scheduling methods. Schedules operations to occur by date and by work centers or work center groups.

- *Job scheduling*: The more detailed of the scheduling methods. Schedules jobs to occur by hour and by work center. Manufacturers who operate with finite capacity and detailed scheduling generally use this.

As we always recommend, you should become familiar with all of the options available in the Parameters form (Production ➤ Setup ➤ Parameters). They have significant effects on how the manufacturing modules operate.

Bill of Materials (BOM)

BOMs contain the list of component items required to make up your finished product. BOMs can be set up from the Items form or directly from the Bill of Materials form. For simplicity, it's easiest to begin from the Items form (Inventory Management ➤ Items). For an item to have a BOM attached, it must be of type BOM, as discussed in Chapter 8.

Use the BOM Line form to create a BOM from the Items form (Inventory Management ➤ Items ➤ BOM ➤ Lines); see Figure 10-1.

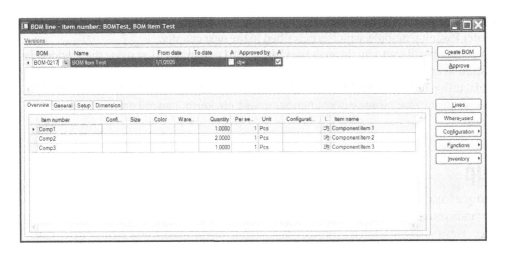

Figure 10-1. *The BOM Line form*

To create a new BOM, click the Create BOM button on the BOM Line form. After entering a description for the BOM, you will be able to add component items using the bottom half of the form. Using the Overview tab, you can specify the quantity of each component item required per series of the BOM item.

On the General tab, you can specify the line type of each BOM line:

- *Item*: Use this line type if the component is an inventoried good or a service item.

- *Phantom*: Use this line type if you have a sub-BOM that you want to keep concealed until production. During production this sub-BOM will be exploded and its attributes will be worked into the current BOM production.

- *Production*: Use this line type if you have a sub-BOM to which you would like to create an additional but linked production for the main BOM.

- *Vendor*: Use this line type to create a linked purchase order for a component line. Please note that this component line can be of type BOM and thus can contain multiple component items.

In addition to line type, the General and Setup tabs contain further setup options, such as price and consumption calculation, scrap, measurements, and positioning. Be sure to read through these; they may be applicable to your organization's manufacturing requirements.

Once you're happy with the creation of your BOM, click on the Approve button to specify that the BOM has been approved for use. Once a BOM is approved, it can be marked Active. Only BOMs that are active can be used in an actual production.

■**Note** The From and To dates for each BOM version let Axapta know which BOM version to use when automatically creating a production order, either from a sales order or from Master Planning. When creating a production order manually, it is possible to use a BOM version with a To date in the past, so long as the BOM version is marked Active.

There is no limit to the number of BOM versions you can have for each BOM item.

■**Note** The BOM designer form is also available to create, edit, and view BOMs. You can access the designer from the Items form (Inventory Management ➤ Items ➤ BOM ➤ Designer). The BOM designer is much more graphical then the BOM Line form and is drag-and-drop-friendly. Some people may prefer to use this form. Personally, we prefer the BOM Line form, which we find simpler. You should try both and see which you prefer.

Work Center Groups and Work Centers

We must set up work center groups and work centers so that we can perform the necessary operations to produce each BOM item. Work center groups are created by using the Work Center Groups form (Basic ➤ Work Center Groups), shown in Figure 10-2. Work centers can be created only from work center groups; there is a parent-child relationship in which the work center is the child of the work center group. For the use of routes and operations, it is only necessary to have one work center attached to each work center group, and for the purpose of keeping it simple that is all we will show you here. If your business requires the use of finite scheduling and detailed costing, you will likely use several work center groups and work centers.

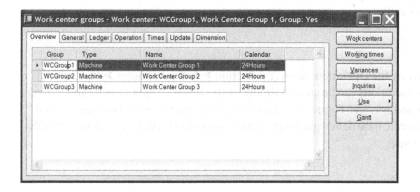

Figure 10-2. *The Work Center Groups form*

■Note Setting up a work center group requires that you have at least one calendar setup. You can set up a calendar using the Calendar form (Basic ➤ Calendar). It designates the days and hours of operation for the particular work center group. This is used for scheduling and estimation purposes.

Table 10-1 details some of the options available using the other tabs on the Work Center Groups form. (The Dimension tab is not included because it's the same everywhere in Axapta.)

Table 10-1. *The Work Center Groups Form Tabs and Their Options*

Tab	Options
General	Specify the type of work center, machine, tool, human resource, or vendor. If using the Vendor option, you should specify the vendor account. Also specify the efficiency of the work center group, its percentage to be scheduled, and its capacity details if scheduling to finite capacity.
Ledger	Specify the general ledger accounts to be used for WIP and costing as goods move into and out of this work center group.
Operation	Specify the default routing group, which controls how this work center group contributes to time and material estimation, consumption, and costing. Specify the default scrap percentage to be consumed when using this work center group in a route, along with task groups that specify how and when to use alternative work center groups. In addition, you should specify which cost categories to use for the computation of setup, process time, and quantity.
Times	Specify the time required to produce a given quantity, in addition to times required for queuing before/after, setup, run, and transit. You can also specify when overlap production may occur.
Update	Display dates created and number of work centers that belong to the work center group.

Work centers can be created for each work center group by using the Work Centers button on the Work Center Groups form shown in Figure 10-2. Each work center created will display a copy of the settings from the work center group upon creation. These settings can, of course, be changed on each work center. Changes to a work center group will not update any already created work centers—these changes must be made manually. Before you can use an operation in a route, it is important that you have set up at least one work center group with a corresponding work center.

Operations

You create operations via the Operations form (Production ➤ Setup ➤ Routes ➤ Operations); see Figure 10-3. New operations can be created simply by specifying an operation ID and name. The Operation Relation form (see Figure 10-4) launches when you press the Relations button. The form contains specific base data regarding when the operation is used in conjunction with a particular item or route.

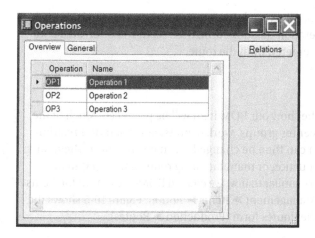

Figure 10-3. *The Operations form*

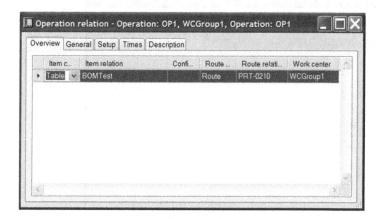

Figure 10-4. *The Operation Relation form*

You can create operation relations for a specific item, by item group, or for all items via the Item Code combo box:

- *All*: This setting means that all items use this operation relation, and thus the Item Relation field will become null and locked.

- *Group*: This setting means that a particular item group will use this operation relation and thus the Item Relation field will be used to pick your desired item group.

- *Table*: This setting means that a particular item will use this operation relation and thus the Item Relation field will be used to pick your desired item.

Operation relations are further specified by all routes or for a specific route. When you create an operation relation, you must specify the work center or work center group that should be used for the given operation relation. The base data from the work center or work center group is copied to the operation relation. This base data can then be edited if desired. When this particular relation combination is used on a route, the base data is copied to the route. In addition, if a relation of an item, route, work center, or work center group is created via a route that does not exist in the Operation Relation form, this record will be created automatically and will contain the base data entered from the route.

Routes

It is in the route that we finally tie together how our BOM item will be produced. Much of the base data that was set up in our work center groups, work centers, and operation relations will copy to the route. This information can then be changed if you desire. This is the final information that will be used in the production or manufacturing route of the BOM item.

We can create routes in a fashion very similar to how we created BOM lines. From the Items form, use the Route button (Inventory Management ➤ Items ➤ Route); Figure 10-5 shows the result. Routes can also be set up using the Routes form (Production ➤ Routes).

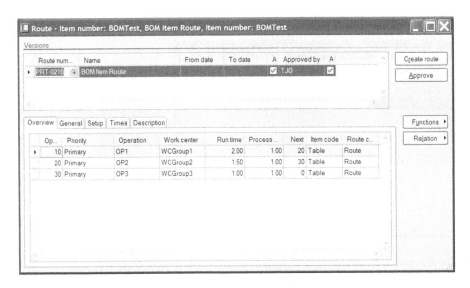

Figure 10-5. *The Route form, launched from the Items form's Route button*

Creating a route is very similar to creating a BOM, and is started by using the Create Route button. Lines are added in the bottom half of the form. During production, routes are performed in an ascending order, from the smallest operation up to the largest. Each line has an operation number that specifies the next operation. The operation with a 0 in the Next field is the final operation.

■**Note** Some businesses may require the use of simultaneous operations. By setting the Priority field to Secondary for an operation, you can specify for it to use the same operation number as its primary operation. The primary operation should always be the operation that takes the longest to complete, because this is the time Axapta will use when scheduling. Each primary operation can have up to five secondary operations.

Each line or operation specifies which operation and work center are to be used. If information regarding this combination of operation and Item/route had already been entered in the Operation Relation form, all other information would be filled in automatically. The information on the General, Setup, and Times tabs will either be filled in from the operation relation if it exists, or from the work center or work center group specified. This data is copied over when the record is created and can be changed for this particular route.

As with BOM lines, there is no limit to the number of routes that each item can have, but only one line may be active for any given date. Only approved routes can be marked Active and only active routes can be used in productions.

Processes

Now that we've gone through some of the basic steps in creating items with active BOMs and routes, we can talk about the manufacturing, or *production order*, process. This process lets us record the time and material consumption needed to make a BOM item.

We will walk you through the steps for creating a production order, and talk about the available inputs on each step. How your business processes production orders will vary depending on your unique requirements.

Production Orders

Production orders are created and maintained using the Production Orders form (Production ➤ Production Orders), which is shown in Figure 10-6. In real-world situations, most businesses have their production orders created automatically, either via a sales order or Master Planning. To create a new production order manually, press Ctrl-N or the New icon, and the Create Production Order form, depicted in Figure 10-7, will appear. Use this form to specify the BOM item, BOM number, and route number to use. You can also specify additional information such as the type of production order, quantity to be produced, general ledger posting, and inventory reservation settings.

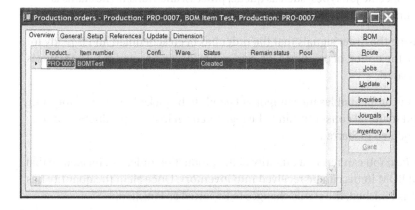

Figure 10-6. *The Production Orders form*

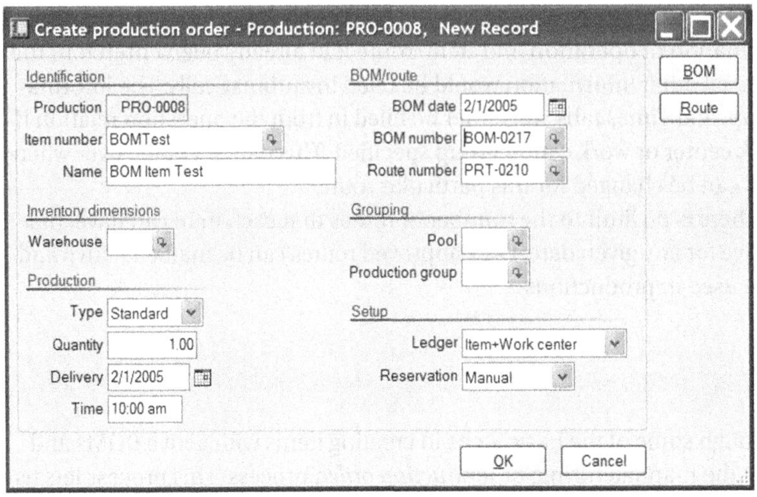

Figure 10-7. *The Create Production Order form*

Each production order must be processed through several stages. You change stages via the Update button on the Production Orders form. Take some time to review all of the options that are available for each update.

- *Estimation*: Phantom lines are exposed, subproductions and purchase orders are created. Inventory is reserved and a price is calculated. The status is updated to Estimated.

- *Operations Scheduling*: Scheduling is created based upon the scheduling direction and capacity available, if working with finite capacity. Scheduling is detailed to work center groups and days. The status is updated to Planned.

- *Job Scheduling*: Scheduling is created based upon the scheduling direction and the capacity available, if working with finite capacity. Scheduling is detailed to work centers, hours, and specific job types, such as queue, process, and transit. The status is updated to Planned.

- *Release*: Releasing the order signals that the order has been scheduled and is ready to begin. You have the option of printing a job card, route job, and route card. The status is updated to Released.

- *Start*: Starting the order enables the component goods to be picked from inventory and actual time and material consumption to be registered against the production order. The status is updated to Started.

- *Report as Finished*: You can report a quantity of the production order as Finished so that the completed BOM items can be received into inventory. Once all of the quantity has been reported as Finished, the status changes to Reported as Finished.

- *Costing*: Costing lets you calculate and post a production order's costs. If Costing is run without the End Job check box filled, the status is changed to Cost Accounted. If the End Job check box is filled, the status becomes Ended. Once a production order has the Ended status, it can no longer be modified.

It is not necessary that all of these steps be executed individually, though all of them must be executed for a production order to be completed. For example, if you create a production order, you can immediately skip all the way to the Costing process and successfully run the cost accounting for the production order. All of the prior steps—Estimation, Scheduling, Release, Start, and Report as Finished—will run automatically using the default values.

It is also possible in a production order to reset the status to any previous status via the Reset Status form (Production ➤ Production Orders ➤ Update ➤ Reset Status), as long as the production order status has not been updated to Ended. In a production environment you should be sure to limit access to this functionality.

Journals

You should remember journals from Chapters 7 and 8. In the Production module, journals are used to record actual time and material consumption on production orders:

- *Picking List*: Used to pick additional items from inventory for use in a production order

- *Route Card*: Used to record the outcome of operations, such as hours consumed, and good and error quantities produced

- *Job Card*: Used to record the outcome of jobs, such as hours consumed and good and error quantities produced

- *Report as Finished*: Used to record the outcome of the production order, in terms of total good and error quantity

Journals are used only to record consumption manually. If journals are not used, time and material consumption will be based on the amounts entered on the specific BOM and route.

Wrap-Up

You now have enough information about the production process in Axapta to begin to look around and ask more questions. We have given you a high-level overview of some of the most basic processes and setup, but we have not covered the granular features available; these will be saved for a later book. As we mentioned earlier, Axapta's Production modules contain features for advanced scheduling, estimating, and costing. If you are trying to decide if Axapta's manufacturing modules will work for your business needs, you probably will need to spend more time reviewing the additional materials and help files.

Manufacturing is a core competency of Axapta's and there are many case study implementations available in many different microverticals. If you are interested in learning how other manufacturers have increased efficiency and decreased operating costs using Axapta, you should read the case studies available at www.microsoft.com.

By now you should have an idea of some of the setup options and production order processes available in Axapta's manufacturing modules. If you plan to implement the manufacturing modules in a real-world situation, you will need to dive into all of the features and functionality. To begin with, you should review the Axapta help topics about the specific production forms. There are no specific production-related guides available on the Axapta CD. There are, however, two guides for Shop Floor Control, which is used in some manufacturing environments:

- *AX-300-USG-032-v01.00-ENUS.pdf*: Getting Started Shop Floor Control

- *AX-300-USG-028-v01.00-ENUS.pdf*: User's Guide Shop Floor Control

CHAPTER 11

■■■

Master Planning

The primary purpose of the Master Planning module in Axapta is to make sure you have what you need, where and when you need it. It is the job of Master Planning to run requirements calculations based on your inputs, and then to recommend and create purchase orders, production orders, and warehouse transfer orders.

The functionality contained in the Master Planning module revolves around the process of executing Master Scheduling, which is the end process of running requirements and scheduling calculations. There are several processes you may complete leading up to running Master Scheduling, such as running Safety Stock Journals and Forecast Scheduling.

In this chapter, we walk you through some of the basic setup options you will need to run Forecast Scheduling and Master Scheduling. We recommend you read through this chapter in it's entirety before attempting to enter or process data in Master Planning. These are complex processes, and will require trial and error to fully understand. Previous experience with material requirements planning (MRP) will certainly be helpful. Hopefully by understanding the setups of these processes, the results that you will get by running the processes will be clear. How your company uses Master Planning will depend on the nature of your business, as with any other module in Axapta. Manufacturing organizations will use this module to plan material requirements and manufacturing scheduling while distribution organizations will use it strictly for material requirements.

■**Note** You will often notice many people in the Axapta world interchanging the terms Master Planning and Master Scheduling. Technically, Master Planning is the module while Master Scheduling is the process.

Setup

As with all modules in Axapta, your setup of Master Planning will determine how the module functions. Your end goal with Master Planning is to generate and firm up planned orders (production, purchase, or warehouse transfer). How these planned orders are calculated is completely dependent on the setup. It is very important that you take time to review all of the options in the Parameters form (Master Planning ➤ Setup ➤ Parameters); it dictates much of how this module will operate.

Coverage Groups

All items (or material requirements) that are calculated using Master Planning are calculated by the settings designated in a coverage group. How you specify the coverage group depends on how unique the requirements are for your goods. You may choose to have separate coverage groups for each inventory dimension (both item and storage). We'll walk you through the different options available in the coverage groups, then we'll discuss how and where you can use them.

You can open the Coverage Groups form, shown in Figure 11-1, from Master Planning ➤ Setup ➤ Coverage ➤ Coverage Groups.

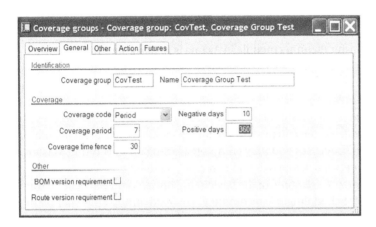

Figure 11-1. *The Coverage Groups form is used to set up the different coverage groups you will use in your Master Planning calculations.*

All of the fields on this form are important. Which fields you use will depend on how your company is using the Master Planning functionality. The fields listed in the coverage field group set the foundation for all other options in this form. Table 11-1 details the options in the Coverage Code drop-down.

Table 11-1. *Coverage Code Options*

Coverage Code	Description
Period	This coverage code is used for businesses that wish to work with ordering periods. This is the only coverage code for which the Coverage Period field is active.
Requirement	This coverage code is used to simply purchase goods as they are required, from open orders, forecasts, etc. The difference between this code and the Period code is that with Requirement each requirement of goods generates a separate order rather than the summation from a period.
Min./Max.	This coverage code is used when inventory should be filled on a minimum-to-maximum basis. This means that whenever the inventory reaches the minimum defined level, planned orders are created to bring inventory back to the maximum level.
Manual	This coverage code will not generate planned orders.

After you have decided which coverage code to use, it's important to fill in the details of all the other fields in the coverage group. Small changes in these fields can yield big changes in your planned orders.

- *Coverage Period* is active only when the coverage code is Period. This field determines how many days should be summed together when looking into the future to place orders. For example, if you place purchase orders once a week, you would set the coverage period to 7.

- *Coverage Time Fence* determines how far into the future Master Planning will look to create planned orders.

- *Negative Days* determines how may days inventory can be negative, or your tolerance for late issues. For example, if a customer has requested a product to ship in 30 days, and you have a purchase order set to be delivered in 31 days, would you want to try and purchase more of this good for receipt before the 30th day, or is it acceptable for your customer to wait an additional day before the goods are issued? A Negative Days setting of 0 in this example would tell Master Planning to create a planned order if it was possible to receive it before 30 days (via your Lead Time settings). A setting of 1 would tell Master Planning to allow inventory to be negative for the one day, and thus no order would be created.

- *Positive Day* determines how far into the future Axapta will use your positive inventory. For example, if you have inventory on hand today, and you have a customer sales order due to ship in 90 days, would you want to consider your current inventory to fulfill your customer's future demand? If your positive days are set to greater then 90 and your inventory level is sufficient (plus any expected receipts, minus any expected issues), no planned order would be created. If your positive days are set to anything less then 90, a planned order would be created based upon your other time-fence conditions, not including your current inventory levels.

Depending on your businesses needs, you should explore the other fields available on the Coverage Groups form. The Other tab allows you to define important information about when and how planned orders should and can be created. The next two tabs, Action and Futures, describe the Action Message and Futures Message functions within Master Planning. Action messages are recommendations to your existing orders, and can alert you of when you might try to advance, postpone, decrease, or increase an existing order based upon the most current Master Planning data. A Futures message can alert you of expected delays.

■Note The Action and Futures messaging system in Axapta is a very powerful tool. This information can give you great insight into your future issues and receipts, and alert you to any adjustments you want to make to them. For many businesses, this functionality might be too powerful. Be sure that you understand the basic Master Planning functions completely before you try to work with these advanced features.

Item Coverage

Now that you know how to set up coverage groups, you can apply them to your inventory items. There are three ways in which coverage groups can be assigned to items. Axapta always uses the most specific record.

- *All Items*: In the Master Planning Parameters form (Master Planning ➤ Setup ➤ Parameters) set the General coverage group to be used whenever a coverage group is not specified at the Per Item or Per Inventory Dimension level.

- *Per Item*: On the General tab of the Items form (Inventory Management ➤ Items), the coverage group can be specified in the named field.

- *Per Inventory Dimension*: Using the Item Coverage form (Inventory Management ➤ Items ➤ Setup ➤ Item Coverage), you can set up a coverage record can for each item dimension combination and for each active storage dimension that has the Coverage Planning parameter selected. Both item and storage dimensions are covered in Chapter 8.

Only one coverage group can be used per item or dimension, and thus Master Planning will first choose to take the coverage group specified on the Item Coverage record. If one does not exist, Master Planning will take the coverage group specified on the Item record. If no group is specified there, Master Planning will use the coverage group specified on the Master Planning Parameters record.

Note Many businesses will choose to use the Item Coverage records as they need to specify different Item Coverage settings for different inventory dimensions. For example, a business with multiple warehouses will often need to specify different coverage groups or coverage group settings per warehouse. This creation can be easily facilitated using the Item Setup form (Master Planning ➤ Setup ➤ Item Setup), which displays all of the items that have Item Coverage records *and* all of those that don't. It makes it easy for you to add or modify these records.

Using the Item Coverage record (Inventory Management ➤ Items ➤ Setup ➤ Item Coverage), shown in Figure 11-2, it is possible to specify additional information based upon the particular item dimensions. You can also use the wizard to create these records. This is especially helpful when you have items with multiple dimensions.

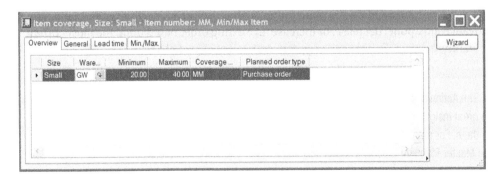

Figure 11-2. *The Item Coverage form is used to specify coverage settings by item dimensions.*

The different tabs on this form let you specify the information required to make this record unique, such as the minimum or maximum inventory levels in the case of a Min/Max coverage group, or the refilling warehouse to be used if you are allowing for transfer orders. In addition, it is possible to override the coverage group and settings that are used on the Item record, and instead specify unique settings here. Finally, you can specify the minimum and maximum keys to be used for seasonally based fulfillment, how the minimum date is calculated, and any specific lead times to be used in the Master Planning calculation.

■**Note** When using coverage codes of Period or Requirement, you are able to specify a minimum quantity to always keep in inventory, known as the *safety stock*.

Forecast Models

Before we can set up Forecasts in Axapta we must specify one or more forecast models (see Figure 11-3). These models enable you to divide your forecasts for input—for example, by region. The forecast models then enable you to create a parent-child hierarchy to bring any child forecasts together into a total, or parent, forecast. Forecast models are set up via Inventory Management ➤ Setup ➤ Forecast ➤ Forecast Models.

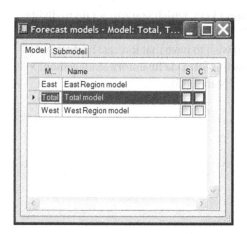

Figure 11-3. *Use the Forecast Models form to create a hierarchy for your forecasts.*

Using this form you can create the different models and the hierarchy of your forecasts. In the example in Figure 11-3, there is an East Region and a West Region forecast model. Both of these are listed on the Submodel tab of the Total model. By specifying separate forecasts by each model, you have the ability to enter forecasts by model and to then run forecast scheduling by either the parent or child model. This is a simple two-leveled hierarchy; note that any forecast model that is listed as a submodel cannot have itself a submodel.

Item Allocation and Period Allocation

Both item and period allocations are available to divide your forecasts between groups of items or time. You can use the item allocation to create a group to which you can assign a forecast.

This group can contain multiple Items or multiple item-dimension combinations. See Figure 11-4 for an example of an item allocation group, accessed via Inventory Management ➤ Setup ➤ Forecast ➤ Item Allocation Keys ➤ Lines.

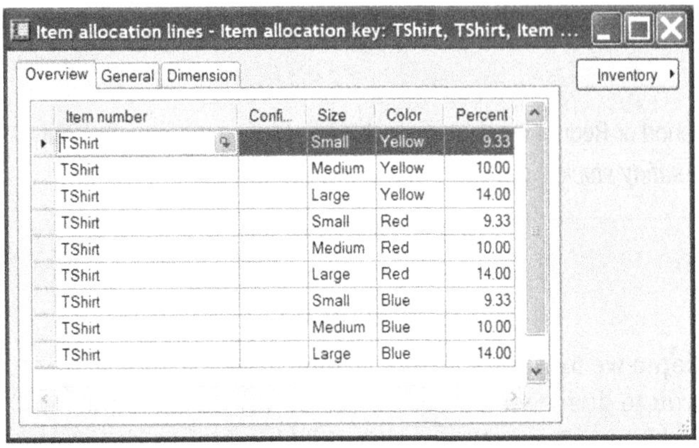

Item number	Confi...	Size	Color	Percent
TShirt		Small	Yellow	9.33
TShirt		Medium	Yellow	10.00
TShirt		Large	Yellow	14.00
TShirt		Small	Red	9.33
TShirt		Medium	Red	10.00
TShirt		Large	Red	14.00
TShirt		Small	Blue	9.33
TShirt		Medium	Blue	10.00
TShirt		Large	Blue	14.00

Figure 11-4. *Item allocation lines are used to dictate the breakdown of an item allocation group.*

Similar to item allocation keys are period allocation keys, which you can set up to divide your forecasts between particular periods in time. This is helpful when you desire to indicate a forecast for a specific duration, say one year, and you wish to have that forecast be distributed monthly according to a schedule of seasonality. Access this form via Inventory Management ➤ Setup ➤ Forecast ➤ Item Allocation Keys ➤ Lines (see Figure 11-5).

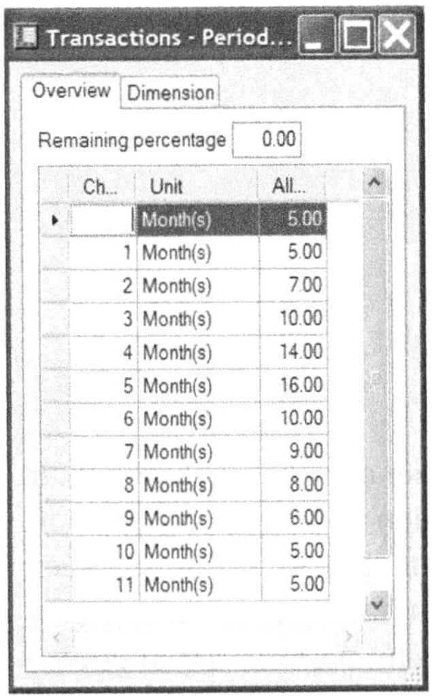

Ch...	Unit	All...
	Month(s)	5.00
1	Month(s)	5.00
2	Month(s)	7.00
3	Month(s)	10.00
4	Month(s)	14.00
5	Month(s)	16.00
6	Month(s)	10.00
7	Month(s)	9.00
8	Month(s)	8.00
9	Month(s)	6.00
10	Month(s)	5.00
11	Month(s)	5.00

Figure 11-5. *The Period Allocation key is used to distribute a forecast by percentage between multiple periods; this is a seasonality schedule.*

> **Tip** When specifying a percentage breakdown via period allocation key lines, note that the Change column indicates period changes from the starting date. For example, in Figure 11-5, the first line (which has a null Change number) would indicate the first month, or January. The last record, with the change of 11, would indicate the 11th change, into the 12th month—December.

Forecasts

In Axapta, you can specify both purchase and sales forecasts that Forecast Scheduling can use to create a forecast to be included in your Master Scheduling calculation. Most businesses forecast their anticipated sales and look to plan for purchase, production, and transfer orders based on sales. Thus they will input these sales forecasts into Axapta so that Master Planning can use these figures when computing future requirements and planned orders.

> **Note** Axapta does not offer any type of forecast-generation capabilities (besides Safety Stock Journals, which are limited to forecasting safety stock). Axapta will handle forecasts that you input and will recommend planned orders based on this input only. MBS offers the Demand Planner solution, which can take your historical sales data from Axapta and allow you to run complex algorithms to create forecasts. The Demand Planner tool is very powerful, though it is not useful in all business scenarios. If you are looking for a forecasting tool, review Demand Planner with someone who is experienced with it.

It is possible to input forecasts by many criteria in Axapta, such as item, item group, customer, customer group, vendor, or vendor group. Of course, it is also possible to specify forecasts using forecast models, item allocation, and period allocation keys.

Sales and purchase forecasts can be input from either the Forecasting button located on the Items form (Inventory Management ➤ Items ➤ Forecasting ➤ Purchase/Sales Forecasting), or from the Inquiries menu (Inventory Management ➤ Inquiries ➤ Forecast ➤ Purchase / Sales Forecast); Figure 11-6 shows the Sales Forecast form accessed via the latter method.

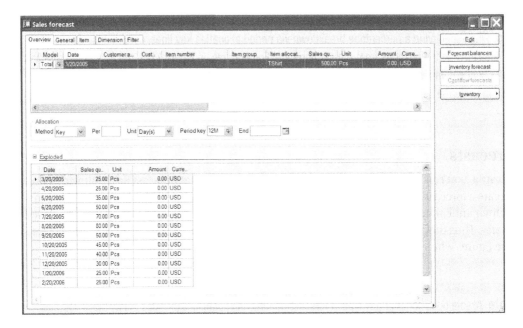

Figure 11-6. *The Sales Forecast form as accessed from the Inventory Management ➤ Inquiries menu, and using both item and period allocation*

If you click the Inventory Forecast button on the form, you'll call up the form depicted in Figure 11-7, which shows the breakdown of the forecasted lines.

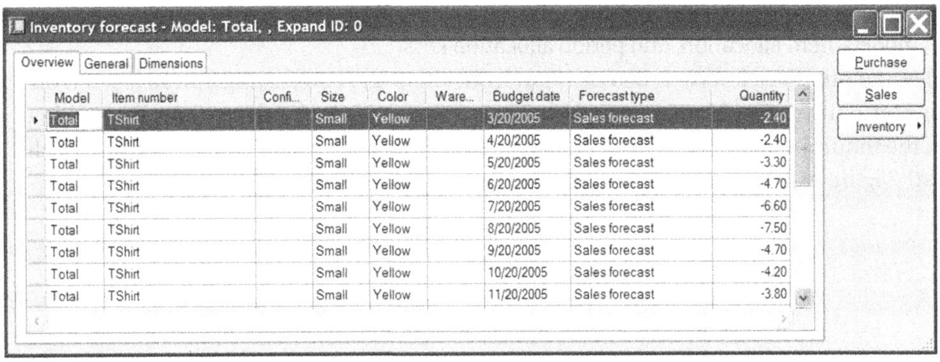

Figure 11-7. *The Inventory Forecast form displays the breakdown of the forecasted lines.*

Production Scheduling

In the previous chapter, we spoke about work center groups, work centers, and routes. Production scheduling setup is dictated by the settings on the work center groups and work centers, and the settings for each route. For the work center groups and work centers the scheduling-specific fields are listed in the Scheduling and Capacity groups (Basic ➤ Work Center Groups / Work Centers). For the routes, the scheduling-specific fields are listed on the Times tab of the Route form (Inventory Management ➤ Items ➤ Route ➤ Times, or Production ➤ Routes ➤ Route ➤ Times). In the "Processes" section of this chapter we will talk more about how the scheduling computation is made.

Forecast and Master Plans

In Axapta, forecast plans are used to enable the Master Scheduling function to use the forecast lines we spoke about earlier. You may find it helpful to create a variety of forecast plans so that you can run different what-if scenarios. Here we'll explain the settings on the Master Plans form. With this knowledge you will understand the fields on the Forecast Plans form. Forecast and master plans can be found at Master Planning ➤ Setup ➤ Plans ➤ Forecast Plans and Master Planning ➤ Setup ➤ Plans ➤ Master Plans, respectively.

The Master Plans form, depicted in Figure 11-8, is where you create your different plans or scenarios to which you will run your planning calculations. As with the forecast plans, you will find it helpful to create a number of different master plans so that you can run what-if scenarios. In addition, you will want to have more then one master plan if you will be using the two-plan (static, dynamic) strategy, which is discussed further in the "Processes" section.

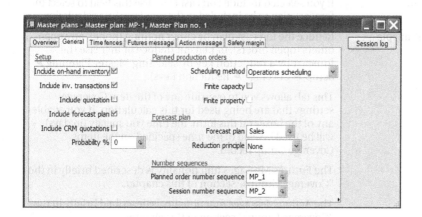

Figure 11-8. *Use different master plans to create senarios for your master planning and master scheduling calculations.*

Table 11-2 details the critical options available on the Master Plans form. With this knowledge you should be able to create forecast plans, as well.

Table 11-2. *Options Available on the Master Plans Form*

Option	Description
General—Include On-Hand Inventory	Select this option if you want your calculation to consider your on-hand inventory.
General—Include Inv. Transactions	Select this option if you want your calculation to consider any open purchase order, production order, or sales order.
General—Include Quotation	Select this option if you want your calculation to consider any purchase or sales orders of type quotation.

(continued)

Table 11-2. *(continued)*

Option	Description
General—Include Forecast Plan	Select this option if you want your calculation to consider your forecast plan, specified in the Forecast Plan field.
General—Include CRM Quotations and Probability %	Select the Include CRM Quotations option if you want your calculation to consider CRM quotations at or above the specified probability percentage.
General—Scheduling Method	Select which method you would like to have planned production orders scheduled (via operations or job scheduling). Scheduling methods were described in Chapter 10.
General—Finite Capacity	Select this option if you want your scheduling calculation to schedule via finite capacity using the times and calendars specified.
General—Finite Property	Select this option if you want your scheduling calculation to schedule via work centers with appropriate Property only. This option is used only in job scheduling and is not covered in this book.
General—Forecast Plan	If you selected Include Forecast Plan, use this field to select the forecast plan to be included in the requirements calculation.
General—Reduction Principle	Reduce the forecast plan by either nothing (none), any open orders (open orders), or percent (reduce or increase the forecast by a reduction key by selecting Master Planning ➤ Setup ➤ Coverage ➤ Reduction Keys).
Time Fences	This tab allows you to override any of the Item Coverage settings that are being used for this calculation. If you enable any of the boxes on this form, the time you specify (in days) will be used instead of the time specified on the Items Coverage Group record.
Futures Message	The Futures Messages functionality is described briefly in the "Coverage Groups" section of this chapter.
Action Message	The Action Messages functionality is described briefly in the "Coverage Groups" section of this chapter.
Safety Margin	This tab allows you to add days to the safety margins already set up on your Coverage Group records.

Processes

Now that we have gone through some of the most basic setups, we will describe the various processes that you can run in the Master Planning module. Keep in mind that there are many options available and that small changes to each option could yield big differences in the results of your calculations.

Safety Stock Journals

Axapta uses safety stock journals to make recommendations on the safety stock level (or minimum value—see the "Item Coverage" section) of each item or dimension. These journals (Master Planning ➤ Journals ➤ Safety Stock) are as close as Axapta comes to providing forecasting. Safety stock journals will evaluate your sales data and make recommendations regarding your safety stock figures based on your inputs. The Axapta 3.0 CD contains a useful guide that describes these journals; see the "Wrap-Up" section of this chapter.

Forecast Scheduling

Running the Forecast Scheduling procedure (Master Planning ➤ Periodic ➤ Forecast Scheduling) will process any of the sales or purchase forecasts that you have created for Master Planning to use. You can choose which forecast plan to employ and select your item criteria. Depending on your number of items and transactions, this process can be very time-consuming. Consider running this process on a batch server or fat client during off-peak hours.

Tip Should you wish to view the data created after running Forecast Scheduling, open the Planned Orders form (Master Planning ➤ Planned Orders) and click on the Filter icon (located on the Axapta toolbar). Change the Plan option to your desired forecast plan. In addition, you can run the Planned Order report (Master Planning ➤ Reports ➤ Planned Order) and specify your desired forecast plan to be the criteria for this report.

Master Scheduling

Running the Master Scheduling procedure will process all of the options that you have specified in the selected master plan and result in recommending planned orders or advice (such as futures and action messages). These orders could be of the Purchase, Sales, Production, or Transfer type. In addition, many of these orders may be related. For example, a sales order may prompt a production order, which could in turn create several sub–production orders and/or several purchase or transfer orders. Depending on your number of items and transactions, this process can be very time-consuming. You might consider running this process on a batch server or fat client during off-peak hours.

After running the Master Scheduling procedure, you can open the Planner Orders form (Master Planning ➤ Planned Order) to display all of the recommendations Axapta has made. Figure 11-9 demonstrates an example in which a sales order has requested the FLL-2500 to be shipped by 4/18/2005. Axapta has recommended that the FLL-2500 be produced the same day (after reviewing the days schedule and the amount of time required to produce this item). Further, Axapta has recommended purchase orders to be sent on 4/8/2005 for the materials required to produce the FLL-2500 (due to their 10-day lead time). Notice that the icon for the production-order item is different than the icon for the purchase-order items (a cascade of small white boxes, and two side-by-side yellow rectangles, respectively). Also, notice that for the four items to be purchased, there are only two vendors. With the Group by Vendor option set in Master Planning ➤ Parameters ➤ Standard Update, checking all five of these lines and firming the orders (via Master Planning ➤ Planned Orders ➤ Functions ➤ Firm) would create three orders: one production order and two purchase orders (one for each vendor).

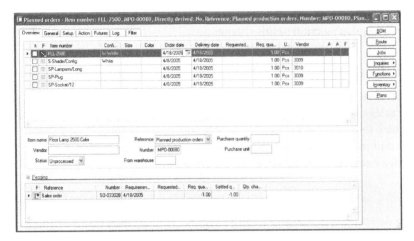

Figure 11-9. *The Planned Orders form details all of your planned production orders, purchase orders, or warehouse transfer orders.*

There are many details available from the Planned Orders form. This form can provide great insight into your future inventory and manufacturing requirements, in addition to automating your purchase, production, and transfer order process. Spend some time in this form to learn about all of the different features and functions available.

As mentioned earlier, Axapta has a feature for a two-plan master scheduling strategy. In this situation, you could periodically run Master Scheduling using a static master plan, then periodically run additional calculations using a dynamic master plan. This strategy will enable you to quickly receive planning information for a specific set of items. The Axapta 3.0 CD contains a useful guide (*AX-300-TIP-031-v01.00-ENUS.doc*) that describes this strategy.

Wrap-Up

Master Planning is a very powerful tool that can provide great insight into your business's planning and purchasing requirements. Using this module correctly can help reduce inventory-carrying costs significantly while improving customer fill rate and overall satisfaction. Armed with the information in this chapter, you can begin to poke around and learn more about the module and the different settings that can affect your results. Make sure that you spend time reviewing all of the options in the Parameters form. In addition, remember that in this module minor changes in the input settings can cause major changes to your output results. You should always perform control calculations to make certain the system is returning your desired values.

Learning Master Planning in Axapta does not happen overnight; this is a very complex subject that you do not want to get wrong. If you plan to master this topic, be prepared to spend considerable time with the online help as well as running many different options and scenarios within the module. Being APICS (American Production and Inventory Control Society)-certified or having previous experience with MRP modules will be a big help. The materials available on the Axapta 3.0 CD are specific to the Safety Stock Journals and Master Scheduling strategy:

- *AX-300-TIP-032-v01.00-ENUS.doc*: Safety Stock Journal

- *AX-300-TIP-031-v01.00-ENUS.doc*: Master Plan Strategies

CHAPTER 12

■ ■ ■

CRM

In today's customer-centric business environment it's important that system users have one place to go for all customer-relevant communication and information. In Axapta, this is done via the Customer Relationship Management (CRM) modules. There are four specific modules available for the CRM series in Axapta: Sales Force Automation, Sales Management, Marketing Automation, and Telemarketing. This chapter will focus on the first module, Sales Force Automation, as this is the most commonly used module and is required for all the additional CRM modules.

The focus of the Sales Force Automation module is around the five interrelated daily forms available from the CRM main menu (see Figure 12-1). We'll introduce four of them in the Setup section of this chapter; the fifth, the Workbook form, will be discussed in the Processes section.

- *Business Relations*: The entities in this form could be prospective or existing customers or vendors, trade organizations, or any other business with which you want to track communication and correspondence.

- *Contact Persons*: Contact Persons is a subset of Business Relations. This form is used to create and list all of the contact persons associated with the business relations.

- *Quotations*: This form is used to create quotations that can be manipulated and exchanged with customers before being converted into a sales order.

- *Activities*: This form lets users create and edit appointments, tasks, activities, and events, used in the Workbook form.

- *Workbook*: This form is used per employee to track and view to-do items such as appointments, tasks, activities, and events. Employees use this form as a daily action list.

The majority of data contained in the CRM modules is centered on the communication between your business and its business relations. In Chapter 9, we spoke about customers and vendors. These records were used to create purchase orders and sales orders, and thus were used strictly for financial transactions.

Business Relations contains the nonfinancial, customer-centric transactions. These are often the transactions or communications which lead up to the financial transactions.

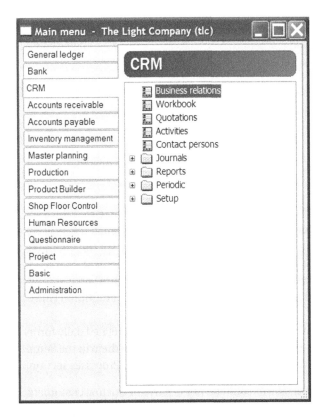

Figure 12-1. *The CRM tab on the main menu displays the five daily forms, Business Relations, Workbook, Quotations, Activities, and Contact Persons.*

The goal of this chapter will be to introduce you to the five daily forms and some of the functionality they offer. The CRM-series modules are very powerful and offer a variety of features and functionality that almost every business using Axapta can utilize.

The CRM modules are heavily integrated into other Axapta modules and functionality such as sales orders, customer statistics, document handling, and questionnaires. In addition, the CRM functionality can be linked with a Telephone Application Programming Interface (TAPI)–compliant phone system and can synchronize task and calendar information with Microsoft Outlook.

Note As you move through this module you may notice that although many forms, processes, and information are heavily integrated with other modules in Axapta, the integration doesn't appear as seamless as you may expect. Neither Damgaard, nor Navision, nor Microsoft developed these modules originally; they were created by a VAR and later purchased by Navision (prior to the Microsoft acquisition). This is not to say that these modules are not worthwhile and useful; this is just an informational note, since you may notice a disconnect within these modules. It is rumored that these modules will have much tighter integration in Axapta 4.0.

Setup

The setup of CRM is, obviously, very dependent on the modules you've purchased. By now you should know that no matter which modules you have purchased, the Parameters form is always the most important of the setup forms. In CRM, the Parameters form is located at CRM ➤ Setup ➤ CRM Parameters ➤ CRM Parameters. You will also notice an Employee Option form in this folder. The form lets you link your user IDs to your employee names. This is the same linking that was discussed in Chapter 6. In addition, the Employee Option form can be used to specify each employee's Outlook synchronization setup. The setup of Outlook synchronization can vary depending on your organization's Active Directory and Exchange setup. This topic is not discussed in this chapter.

Business Relations

Before you can open the Business Relations form and begin to create these records, you must set up some basic foundation data from the forms located under CRM ➤ Setup ➤ Contact Management ➤ Business Relations; see Figure 12-2. The setup of this data is rather self-explanatory, and you should set up the data in these forms in the order in which they are presented. Table 12-1 includes a description of each form and the data that you'll need to set up in each.

Figure 12-2. *The forms located under the Business Relations folder are used to set up the base data necessary to begin recording business relations.*

Table 12-1. *Forms Available Under the Business Relations Setup Folder*

Form	Description
Relation Types	All business relations must have a relation type. Business relations can be automatically generated from either the customer or vendor table. You should create one record for the table source of each customer table and vendor table. All other relation types should be linked to the table source, relation table. Example relation types include Prospective Customer or Competitor.
Status	This form lists all of the options available for a Business Relation status. Example Status entries include In Negotiation or Inactive.
Customer Groups	This form is another display of the Customer Groups form (Accounts Receivable ➤ Setup ➤ Customer Groups).
Vendor Groups	This form is another display of the Vendor Groups form (Accounts Payable ➤ Setup ➤ Vendor Groups).
Sales Districts	Enter your sales divisions on this form so that they may be used to classify business relations.
Segments	Enter your market segments on this form so that they may be used to classify business relations.
Subsegments	Enter any subsegments as children of the segments data. Subsegments of Retail might be Mail Order, Big Box, Small, etc.
Responsibilities	Create any of your staff's internal responsibilities pertaining to a business relation.
Business Sectors	Enter the different business sectors or classifications you might have for your business relations. This could be used to classify your business relations by SIC (Standard Industrial Classification) code.
Company Chains	Use this form to list the parent names of any chain stores or organizations. These names can be used to classify business relations belonging to these chains.

Once data is set up you can begin to enter your business relations by opening the appropriate form, shown in Figure 12-3 (CRM ➤ Business Relations). By default, when you open the form the data displayed will be filtered by the business relations where the Main Contact listed is the logged-in employee. Clicking the Show All check box on the top left will display all business relations. It is possible to further filter the displayed information by using the Employee, Type, and Name filter fields at the top of this form. These filters can be very helpful for businesses that might have many thousands of business relations. You will see similar filtering on most forms within the CRM modules.

■**Note** If you try to open the Business Relations form and you receive an error saying "No employee is mapped to the current user," this means either that you did not follow our instructions in the "Employee" section of Chapter 6, or that you don't have the Human Resources module. If the former applies to you, open the Employee form (Basic ➤ Employee) and go back to Chapter 6.

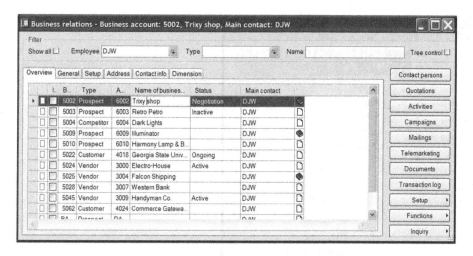

Figure 12-3. *The Business Relations form is the central place to log all activity and correspondence regarding each business relation.*

You can create records easily in this form using the New Records button or Ctrl-N. In addition, records can be created from the customer and vendor tables by using the options from the Functions menu (CRM ➤ Business Relations ➤ Functions ➤ Synchronize CustTable or VendTable). Using these synchronizations will create the appropriate business relations and display the relevant information for any customers or vendors for whom business relation records did not previously exist.

Many of the fields and buttons listed on this form are self-explanatory with knowledge of the forms described in Table 12-1 and a basic knowledge of CRM systems.

Contact Persons

You can launch the Contact Persons form from anywhere where the business relations data is visible within the CRM module. There is a parent-child relationship between the two, where contact persons are always the children of business relations. Before you can begin to set up contact persons, you must set up the base data. As with business relations, this data is relatively self-explanatory. These forms are located under the Contact Persons folder (CRM ➤ Setup ➤ Contact Management ➤ Contact Persons) shown in Figure 12-4. Table 12-2 details each form under the Contact Persons setup folder.

Figure 12-4. *The forms located under the Contact Persons folder are used to set up the base data needed to begin recording contact persons.*

Table 12-2. *Forms Available Under the Contact Persons Setup Folder*

Form	Description
Job Titles	Use this form to create a list of the job titles that may be assigned to contact persons.
Functions of Persons	Use this form to create a list of the job functions that may be assigned to contact persons.
Character	Use this form to create a list of the emotions or characters that may be assigned to contact persons.
Decision	Use this form to create a list of the applicable terms you may use in describing a contact person's influence on decision-making.
Interest	Use this form to create a list of the personal or professional interests that you may wish to assign to a contact person.
Loyalty	Use this form to create a list of loyalties that you may wish to assign to contact persons based on their loyalty to your organization or project.
Person's Title	Use this form to create a list of titles, such as Mr., Mrs., Dr., etc. This is helpful in the creation of mass mailings and e-mails.
Complimentary Close	Use this form to create a list of letter closings, such as Sincerely, Take care, etc. This is helpful in the creation of mass mailings and e-mails.
Salutation	Use this form to create a list of salutations, such as Dear, Hello, etc. This is helpful in the creation of mass mailings and e-mails.

Once you have data entered in these base forms, you can begin to add contact persons from the Contact Persons form. Given that contact persons are the children of business relations, it is easiest to launch the Contact Persons form from the Business Relations form, (CRM ➤ Business Relations ➤ Contact Persons). Launching the Contact Persons form in this way will display only contact persons belonging to the selected business relations record. Further, creating a new contact person from the form launched in this fashion will assume that the contact person belongs to the selected business relation. Figure 12-5 displays the Contact Persons form launched from the main menu.

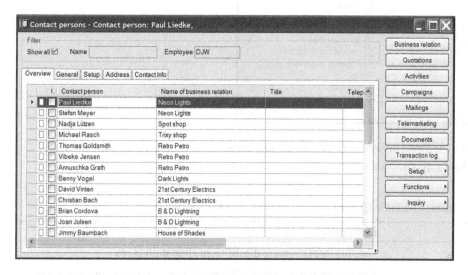

Figure 12-5. *The Contact Persons form displays all of the child contact persons from all business relations. If your form looks similar to the form shown here, you're using SP2 or later. If you have a two-part form, you're using SP1 or earlier.*

In addition to entering a contact person name, the other required field in this form is Business Account, the business relation's account number. It is generally easiest to create these contact-person records from the Business Relations form, as this will default to the appropriate business relation. All other fields on this form are either self-explanatory or mentioned in Table 12-2.

Quotations

CRM quotations are a very useful tool to handle negotiations with current customers and prospective customers. The Quotations form allows for very detailed pricing, sales analysis, and marketing information to all come together. Before you can start using the CRM quotations, you will need to set up the forms under the Quotations folder, shown in Figure 12-6 (CRM ➤ Contact Management ➤ Quotations). Table 12-3 describes the forms available and their purpose.

Figure 12-6. *The forms under the Quotations folder are used to set up the base data needed to begin recording quotations.*

Table 12-3. *Forms Available Under the Quotations Setup Folder*

Form	Description
Type	Use this form to create the different Quotation types.
Phase	Use this form to create the different phases your quotations might be in, and the appropriate order for those phases.
Prognosis	Use this form to create options for the minimum and maximum number of days from creation in which the quotation is likely to become an order. The quotation prognosis date will be the date that is the average of these numbers of days away.
Reason Won/Lost	Use this form to create reason codes for when quotations are won (and thus turned into sales orders) or lost.
Competitors	Use this form to list your business relations that may be competitors on a quotation.
Document Titles	Use this form to create the titles to which you will be creating template documents in the CRM Quotations form using the document-handling functionality.
Document Instructions	Use this form to create the verbiage or introductions to be sent to customers concerning the template documents created in the CRM quotation using the document-handling functionality.
Document Conclusions	Use this form to create the verbiage or conclusions to be sent to customers concerning the template documents created in the CRM quotation using the document-handling functionality.

Once you've set up this base data you can open the Quotations form either from the main menu or from any of the other forms that may contain business relation or contact person information (see Figure 12-7). Similar to opening the Contact Persons form from the Business Relations form, opening the Quotations form from the Business Relations form will allow you to view, edit, and create all quotations available for the selected business relation. Opening this form from the Contact Persons form will further narrow the filter to any quotations available for the selected contact person.

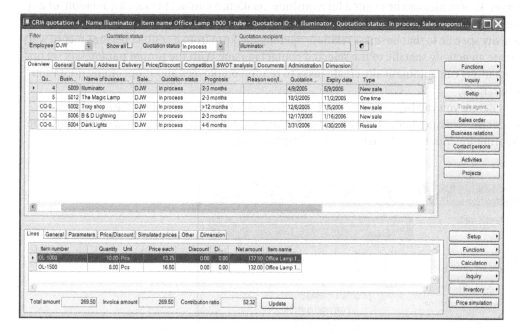

Figure 12-7. *The CRM Quotation form is used to create quotations for business relations.*

When entering new quotations, the only required field is the name of the business. This form should look very familiar if you have been through Chapter 9, as it looks very similar to the Sales Order form. The major differences lie in that the Quotations form can collect a much greater amount of information regarding all of the steps leading up to the actual sales process. You should peruse the available fields here and use the online help to understand some of the advanced features available.

■**Note** Unlike with a sales order or purchase order, in the Quotations form users are unable to directly post or print a report with the necessary information. This is because the Quotations form uses the document-handling and COM functionality to create all quotes in Microsoft Word (CRM ➤ Quotations ➤ Functions ➤ Documents). Create a new record using the New Page button on the top right, and if you've installed demo data you can select the CRM quotation. This also requires that you've linked the appropriate template to the CRM Quotations record (Basic ➤ Setup ➤ Document Management ➤ Document Types). The Axapta installer installs the CRM Quotation template, *QuotationStd.dot*, automatically to your application directory (if you've been following this book, that is *C:\Axapta_Application\Axapta Application\Share\Include\smm*). By creating CRM Quotations in Microsoft Word, employees are able to easily manipulate these quotations before sending them to business relations. Further, these Word documents are saved to the appropriate business relations record so that other Axapta users can view them later.

Activities

The CRM module contains activities that fall into four categories: actions, events, tasks, and appointments. Tasks and appointments can be synchronized directly with users' Microsoft Outlook. Activities can be created for a business relation, a contact person, a quotation, or any unrelated event. Opening the Activities form from a business relations record will create an activity specific to that business relation; opening the form from a contact persons record will create an activity specific to the selected contact person. With the proper parameters set up, quotations can automatically create tasks to remind employees about upcoming quotation expirations.

Before you can begin to work with activities, you will need to set up the forms located under the Activities folder (CRM ➤ Setup ➤ Contact Management), shown in Figure 12-8. The information input into these forms is self-explanatory.

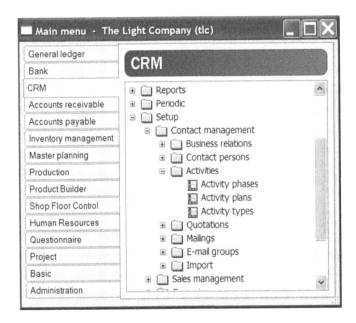

Figure 12-8. *The forms located under the Activities folder are used to set up the base data needed to begin recording activities.*

Launching the Activities form from the main menu will display all activities for the filtered employee, as in Figure 12-9. You can create a new activity easily by pressing the New icon or Ctrl-N. There are no required fields when creating a new activity since the activity start date will always default to the system date. You can change the date manually to the appropriate due date. The fields on this form are relatively self-explanatory. It is important to note that Axapta gives users the flexibility to assign activities to other employees.

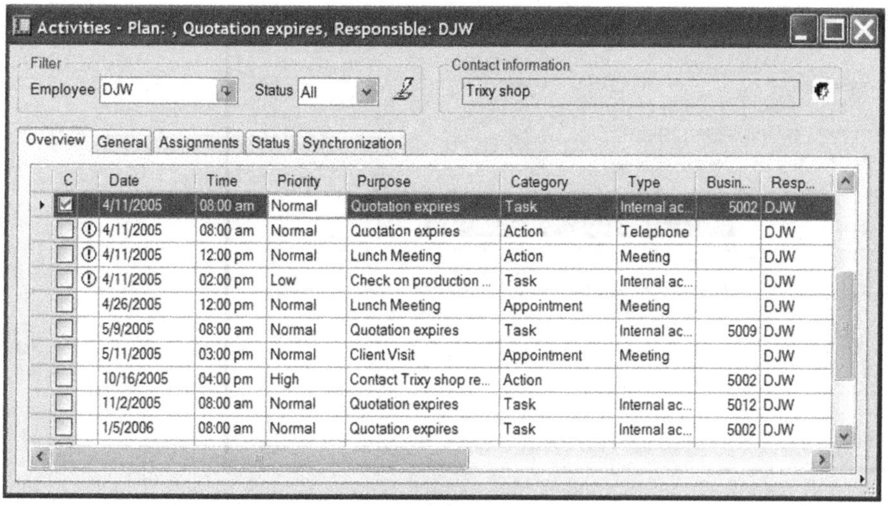

Figure 12-9. *The Activities form is used to create and edit to-dos or activities. Activities of type Task and Appointment can synchronize with Microsoft Outlook.*

Processes

After entering the base data needed to create business relations, contact persons, quotations, and activities, you should be ready to begin recording activity and correspondence with your customers and other business partners. As already stated, these forms and their data are interrelated. CRM functions often need to be carried out very quickly. Having these forms interrelated helps in the inquiry, edit, and creation of CRM activities.

Many businesses will use the document-handling functionality heavily from within the CRM modules. This functionality enables users to create and send documents to business relations and contact persons using a set of defined templates. Further, it is possible to use this functionality to record outgoing and incoming customer e-mails and any other desired files or documentation.

Workbook

We did not talk about the Workbook form in the "Setup" section of this chapter, although it is one of the five interrelated daily forms. This is because there is no real setup required to use the Workbook form. It is simply an organized display of all of the records created via the Activities form, and is used as an employee's list of to-dos and responsibilities, as Figure 12-10 illustrates. Therefore, by creating records in the Activities form you have created data to be displayed in the Workbook form. Generally, employees who serve CRM functions will either keep their Workbook open all day, or open it periodically throughout the day so that they can view and update their activities easily.

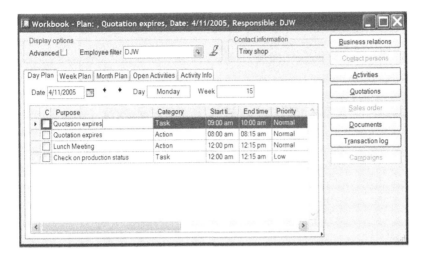

Figure 12-10. *The workbook is a daily to-do list for all employees with CRM-related responsbilities.*

Wrap-Up

As discussed at the beginning of this chapter, there are four modules available in the CRM series. The basic setup information in this chapter is limited to an introduction to the Sales Force Automation module and should give you enough information to begin recording communications with your customers. If you desire to use the Sales Management, Marketing Automation, and Telemarketing modules, you will need to consult the online help and an Axapta consultant who is trained in these modules.

Some of the features that are available from these additional modules include the following:

- Management statistics regarding tracking and analysis of sales and sales activities

- Campaigns to easily broadcast information via mail, e-mail, call lists, etc. and record the usage and success of such campaigns

- Telemarketing lists with questionnaire scripting

Your usage of these additional modules will, obviously, depend on your business needs. This chapter provided you with the powerful base functionality that you'll need no matter which modules you choose to utilize. The CRM series offers a wide range of valuable customer-centric tools and information that can help all organizations connect better with their customers and other business relations. To learn more about the features available, consult the following manuals available on the Axapta 3.0 CD:

- *AX-300-USG-022-v01.00-ENUS.pdf*: Getting Started Guide—CRM

- *AX-300-USG-021-v01.00-ENUS.pdf*: User's Guide to Sales Force Automation

CHAPTER 13

Project

Microsoft Axapta's Project module series enables businesses to track and control their projects and project accounting. The module series consists of two modules: Project I and Project II, the latter of which contains advanced calculations, advanced posting methods, and additional project types. Mainly, the Project II module enables businesses to have control over when project costs, revenue, or anticipated revenue are posted to balance sheet or P&L accounts. In this chapter, we will focus on the basic Project I module setup so that you can become familiar with the base data needed to enter projects. We will discuss the project types available for both modules in the series.

These modules are relatively straightforward for anybody who has worked with project accounting. If you have not worked with project accounting before, you might have a difficult time with this chapter. The Project modules contain four project types:

- *Time & Material*: As you would expect, this project type enables the registration of time (hours), and materials (purchased or from inventory) against the project. This project can then be invoiced to the customer throughout WIP (work in progress) or in total upon completion.

- *Fixed-Price*: This project type also enables the registration of time and materials, though in this situation the project is not invoiced based on the actual time and material consumption; rather, it is invoiced based on a predetermined amount and schedule.

- *Internal*: Internal projects are used to record time and material consumption, though in this situation the consumption is not invoiced; it is instead expensed by the business for internal purposes.

- *Summary*: Summary projects are used to create a hierarchy. No data is actually recorded on a summary project; it is simply used as the parent of which child projects can be created (of any project type).

Many businesses using Axapta may use the Project modules and not even know they are using them. In many situations these modules are used as a customization tool. Since projects can act as a form of a subledger, enabling businesses to record both revenue and expense and control the recording of such, the modules are often used to customize unique business practices that require collection of financial data. This chapter will give you some ideas on the basic setup of projects. If you are looking to customize a solution around the Project modules, we suggest that you research these modules further, as their functionality is deep.

Setup

As with any module setup in Axapta, you should have a clearly defined plan of your expected outcome before you begin. The setups given here are the basic steps needed to record basic projects in this series, and should be taken as such. As always, you should consult the Project Parameters form, Project ➤ Setup ➤ Parameters. It controls much of how the module will operate.

Many of the forms that are required for setup in this module are interrelated, and therefore there is no good order that we can recommend for you to enter your base data. We suggest you read through all of the setup steps before you attempt to enter data. We detail what we believe is the best order in which to set up these forms.

Prices

The four forms used in setting up the foundation of project pricing (Project ➤ Setup ➤ Prices) are described in this section.

First, you must specify the cost associated with your organization's time. The price for materials will either be specified via the purchase order cost for inventory items, or the journal cost for purchased noninventory items. To specify the cost of time or hours for your organization, use the Cost Price – Hour form, shown in Figure 13-1. This form allows the specification of cost prices per hour based on any combination of Valid From date, Category, Employee, and Project. The only required field in this form is the Valid From date. Your entries in this form will vary dependent on your business's time-costing variations; the cost price used on a particular project will be a valid entry (based on date) with the greatest level of detail (or with the most information present, between category, employee, and project). So far you have not set up any projects, and the category setup is explained later in this chapter.

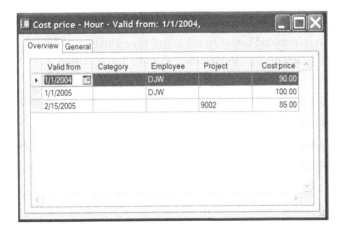

Figure 13-1. *The Cost Price – Hour form enables the definition of cost prices per hour based on any combination of date, category, employee, or project.*

Once your hour costs are set up, you need to set up your hour sales price, using the Sales Price – Hour form shown in Figure 13-2. The entries in this form dictate how sales prices will be calculated based on the criteria input. Similar to the Cost Price – Hour form, this form relies on input of a Valid From date, and possible category, employee, and project information. The difference here is the Currency field (which is of high importance in Axapta's search as to which line to use when calculating sales price). The amount in the Pricing field will vary depending on the sales price model being used. These models are described in Table 13-1.

Table 13-1. *Sales Price Models Used in Calculating Project Sales Prices*

Sales Price Model	Description
Qty.	This model simply uses the price specified in Pricing and multiplies it by the quantity of the sales unit.
Contribution Ratio	In this model the value entered in the Pricing field is the size of the contribution ratio as a percentage of the sales price.
Misc. Charges Pct.	In this model the sales price is generated by multiplying the cost price per sales unit by the value or percentage entered in the Pricing field.
Misc. Charges Amount	In this model the sales price is generated by adding the cost price per sales unit to the value entered in the Pricing field.

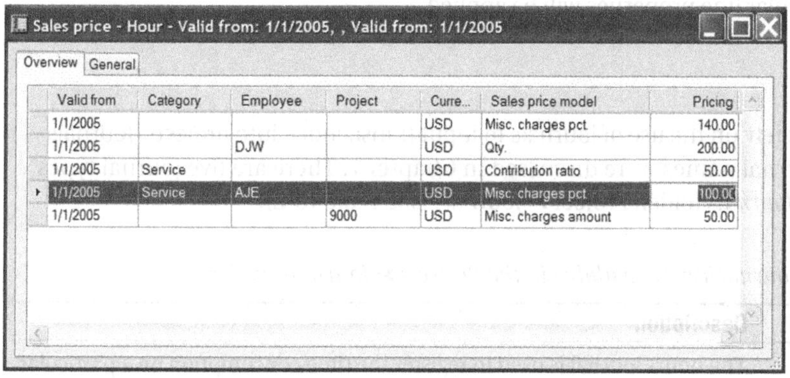

Figure 13-2. *The Sales Price – Hour form dictates how the sales price of time will be calculated.*

The remaining two forms for pricing, Sales Price – Costs and Sales Price – Revenue, can be set up easily with your knowledge of the setup of the Sales Price – Hour form. The values entered in the costs and revenue forms are used for the calculations of when costs or revenues are registered in their respective journals, as discussed later in this chapter.

Line Property

All Project transactions must specify a line property, which can dictate how each line's cost price and sales price are calculated. Of course, the calculation of sales prices is necessary only for Time & Material project types. The Line Property form can be accessed from Project ➤ Setup ➤ Line Property ➤ Line Property, and is shown in Figure 13-3. On this form you have the ability to dictate if and when an additional percentage should be added to the cost or sales price of the line, plus whether the line should be chargeable or invoiced to the customer, and whether the sales value should be accrued (the last two apply to Time & Material projects only).

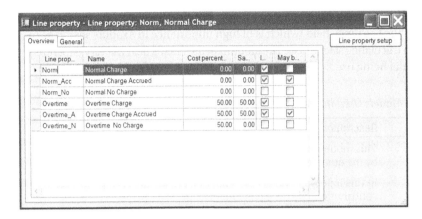

Figure 13-3. *The Line Property form dictates whether a transaction should be chargeable and accrued, and if there is any additional cost or sales percentage to be calculated.*

The Line Property Setup button opens the Line Property Setup form, which dictates when and where the particular line properties will be applied.

Journals

The Project modules rely on the use of journals to input transactions into projects. Journals and the setup of journal names were discussed in Chapter 7. There are five journal types available under the *Journals* folder, Project ➤ Journals (see Table 13-2).

Table 13-2. *The Five Journal Types Available in the Projects ➤ Journals Folder*

Journal	Description
Hours	The hours journal is used to register the time consumption on a particular project. You can set up an approval process for hours journals by using the Journal Approval form (Project ➤ Setup ➤ Journals ➤ Journal Approval).
Cost	This is simply a GL general journal. Project costs can be entered from this journal or from General Ledger ➤ Journals ➤ General Journal. The journal names for cost journals are set up via the General Ledger module.
Revenue	This journal is used to record revenue for a project.
Item Consumption	This journal is an inventory-management journal and thus the journal names are set up in the Inventory Management module. This is similar to simply using a sales order to record project item consumption.
Web	The web journal will record hours via the Enterprise Portal and place them in this journal to be transferred to another journal as specified in the Project Parameters form, Project ➤ Setup ➤ Parameters. You cannot actually post anything from a web journal. This should be considered a prejournal.

Project Groups

Project groups define how and where ledger postings are made. Project groups are set up per project type, and you must have at least one project group for every project type you plan to utilize. You can access the Project Group form (Figure 13-4) from Project ➤ Setup ➤ Posting ➤ Project Groups. Creating a new project group within this form will open the Create Project Group form (Figure 13-5), which lets you specify the project type for which the new project group will be created. In addition, depending on the project type you will have the ability to specify your preference (Balance or Profit & Loss) for ledger updates regarding the following:

- *On-account invoicing*: Upon invoicing, Time & Material project invoices will always be posted to Balance accounts. On Fixed-Price projects you have your choice to post to Balance or Profit & Loss accounts. On Internal projects there will be no invoicing, and thus no account types need to be specified.

- *Post costs*: Upon posting of cost journals, choose the account types to be used for the posting of Time & Material and Internal projects. Fixed-Price projects will always be posted to Profit & Loss accounts.

- *Post item costs*: Upon a packing slip update for inventory consumption, you can choose the account types to be used for the posting of Time & Material and Internal projects. Fixed-Price projects will always be posted to Profit & Loss accounts.

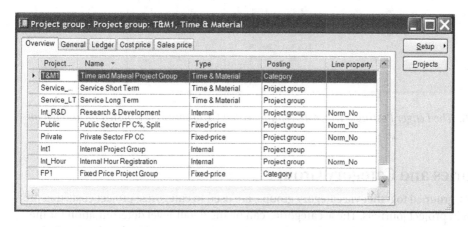

Figure 13-4. *The Project Group form is used to specify the project ledger postings.*

Figure 13-5. *The Create Project Group form is used to create new project groups.*

You should become familiar with the fields available on the General, Ledger, Cost Price, and Sales Price tabs of the Project Group form, because the data entered into this form will directly effect how the ledger posting occurs and to which ledger accounts.

Ledger Posting

With project groups, we just specified how and where ledger postings are made. In addition, Axapta gives you the ability to further define ledger postings by project and by category. This is done via the Ledger Posting form, Project ➤ Setup ➤ Posting ➤ Ledger Posting (see Figure 13-6). It is very similar to the Inventory Posting form covered in Chapter 7.

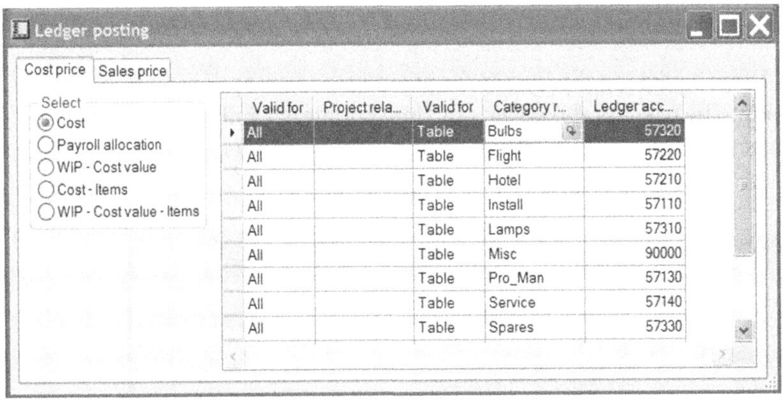

	Valid for	Project rela...	Valid for	Category r...	Ledger acc...
▶	All		Table	Bulbs	57320
	All		Table	Flight	57220
	All		Table	Hotel	57210
	All		Table	Install	57110
	All		Table	Lamps	57310
	All		Table	Misc	90000
	All		Table	Pro_Man	57130
	All		Table	Service	57140
	All		Table	Spares	57330

Figure 13-6. *The Ledger Posting settings determine which GL accounts are posted to, and when.*

Categories and Category Groups

Categories, grouped together via category groups, are used to categorize project costs that are registered in project journals. These categories can be the detail-level determination for the ledger posting and all of the sales and cost figures that we've discussed in this chapter. Before setting up categories, you must set up category groups via Projects ➤ Setup ➤ Category ➤ Category Groups (see Figure 13-7). You should set up at least one category group for each of the four transaction types (hour, cost, revenue, and item), which each relate to one of four journal types (but not to the web journal, which you'll recall is not postable and really is more like a prejournal). For example, you may set up a category group named Travel with a transaction type of Cost. Then you can attach categories of Air Travel, Hotel, and Meals to this category group. In this fashion, categories will give management an additional degree of detail for reporting purposes. Additionally, you can assign line property or GL accounts to the Cost Price and Sales Price tabs to be used for categories belonging to a certain category group.

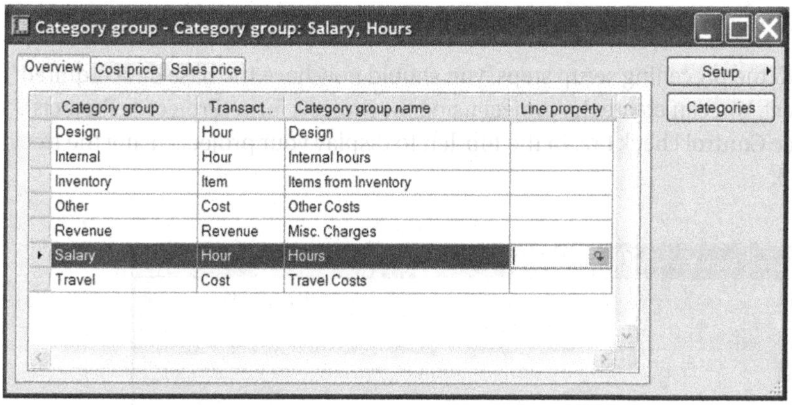

Figure 13-7. *Category groups are used to group categories together.*

Once you've set up category groups you can set up corresponding categories via Project ➤ Setup ➤ Category ➤ Categories (see Figure 13-8). In addition to entering the category (code) you must enter the category group. The corresponding transaction type will populate. The Employee field specifies whether employee IDs should be defined for the journal lines that correspond to the transaction type. Hour transaction types require that employee IDs be specified, and thus this field is set to Mandatory for these times. On the other hand, item transaction types never have employee IDs associated with them, and are thus set to Never. You can choose between Mandatory, Optional, or Never for transaction types of cost and revenue. You can also specify the line property and item sales tax group (if you have set up the Parameters form to use the item sales tax group method). You should set up at least one category for each category group, though having multiple categories per category group will enable you to differentiate ledger postings and will aid you in inquiry and reporting filtering.

The options available from the Setup button tie together many of the other forms we have discussed in this chapter.

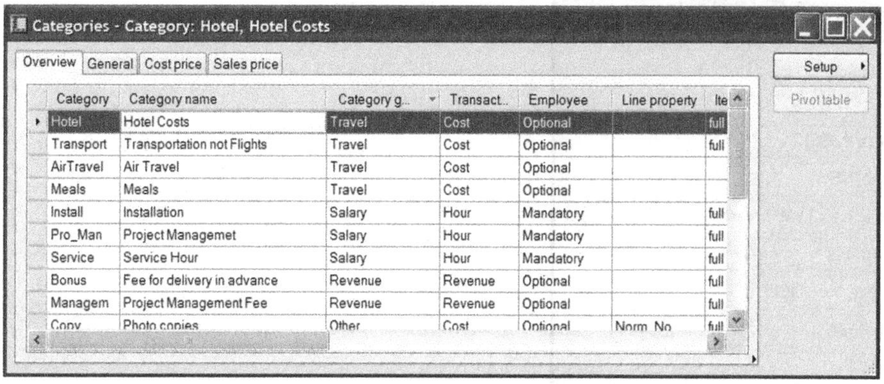

Figure 13-8. *The Categories form lets you further define ledger postings for cost and sales prices.*

Processes

If you've gone through the preceding setup steps, you should now have the base data required to create a basic project. You can create the project using the Projects form (Project ➤ Projects). You can select the Tree Control check box in the top-left to display your projects using the tree view, as in Figure 13-9.

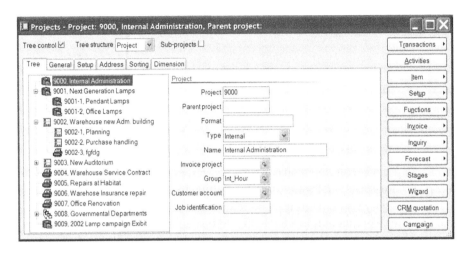

Figure 13-9. *The Project form is the central location from which you administer all projects. The clipboard icon is used for Internal projects, the form icon is for Fixed-Price projects, the printer icon is for Time & Materials projects, and the production order icon (the four small boxes) is used for Summary projects.*

Creating a new project will bring up the Create Project form shown in Figure 13-10. The fields required in this form depend on the type of project being created. All the fields should look familiar, with the exception of Invoice Project and Format.

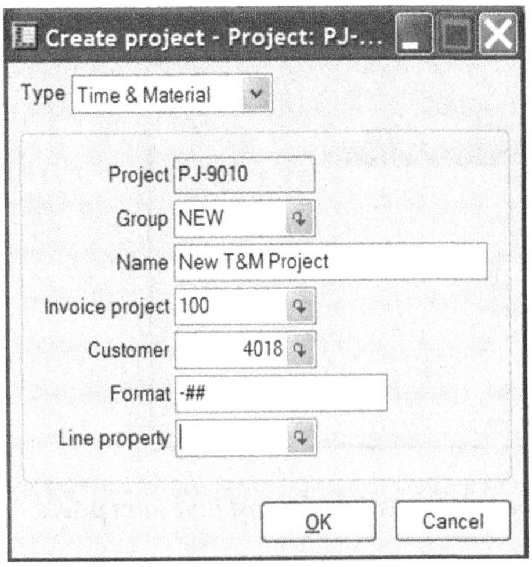

Figure 13-10. *The Create Project form, as its name indicates, is used to create new projects.*

The Format field lets you specify the numbering format of any subprojects that may be created from the initial project. You can use standard number-sequence formatting. Subprojects are useful, for example, when you wish to have a Fixed-Price project with a Time & Material subproject. This could be applicable if you have entered into a Fixed-Price project for which your customer will pay certain time and material expenses, such as transportation, hotel, meals, etc.

Specifying a line property to be used for the project will add the relation of the project and the line property to the line property setup, which will ensure that the line property defaults properly on any journals created for the particular project.

For Time & Material or Fixed-Price projects, you will need to first create an invoice project via Project ➤ Invoice Projects; the Invoice Projects form appears in Figure 13-11, and will dictate how and to whom the project is invoiced.

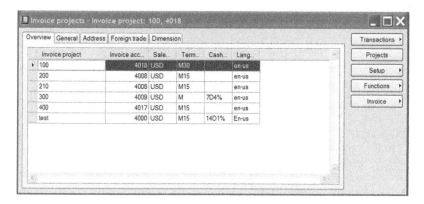

Figure 13-11. *Invoice projects must be created prior to Time & Matierals or Fixed-Price projects.*

The fields on the Invoice Projects form are very similar to those in a sales order. Additionally, similar to a sales order, once the customer account is entered, the customer information such as invoice account, currency, terms of payment, and cash discount is defaulted from the customer record. These fields can be overridden. If you need clarification on these fields, revisit Chapter 9.

There are many different ways in which businesses will use projects. The buttons on the right side of the form enable various views and inputs into the project's consumption and revenue. We strongly recommend that you explore all of the different features and functions available on this form.

Once you have created your project, you can begin to record transactions as described in the "Journals" section of this chapter. Further, you can create sales orders and purchase orders directly from the Projects form. Sales and purchase orders were described in Chapter 9. You should explore this functionality along with the registration of costs and time.

Wrap-Up

We've given you enough knowledge to get started and to try to create some projects on your own. Depending on your business needs, you may utilize many more features and functions in these modules, such as scheduling, estimating, budgeting, and other reports and inquiries that can give you insight into your project statuses, costs, and revenues, and help keep your projects on time and on budget. These are very powerful modules that are well-integrated into the Trade, Logistics, Master Planning, Production, and CRM modules, to name a few.

We have only scratched the surface of the Project modules, but hopefully we've given you enough information that you can enter data in the basic forms and start to realize the potential of these modules. Armed with your previous knowledge of journals and basic trade functionality, you will be able to create some simple projects. If this basic setup has left you wanting more, we suggest you check out the following guide, which is available on the Axapta 3.0 CD.

- *AX-300-USG-008-v01.00-ENUS.pdf*: User's Guide for Project Management

CHAPTER 14

■■■

Reporting and Business Analysis

Advanced reporting and business analysis can often be driving factors for companies looking to purchase an ERP system such as Axapta. Many businesses are trapped with several unrelated systems or systems that are simply too difficult to retrieve information from. With Axapta, reporting and overall business analysis is easy. Axapta enables users to create their own reports without relying on a developer or the IT department.

Obtaining the data you want from Axapta is very easy. Axapta's reporting and business analysis tools are not only powerful but also very straightforward. There is a variety of different ways to perform reporting and business analysis within Axapta:

- *Standard Reports*: Axapta has many standard reports as part of its out-of-the-box functionality; these reports are accessible from the *Reports* folder via any menu tab. You should take time to browse the available reports—they are not discussed in this chapter.

- *Business Analysis*: This module, available on the Axapta price list, enables OLAP (On-Line Analytical Processing) functionality from within Axapta. This functionality utilizes Microsoft SQL Analysis Services to create multidimensional cubes, or 3-D views of data, which can be sliced, disaggregated, and rearranged easily. This functionality is described in both the "Setup" and "Processes" sections of this chapter.

- *Auto-Reports*: Users can create auto-reports by simply pressing the Print button from any on-screen inquiry or form. These reports can be saved for later retrieval or retrieval by another user. This form of reporting is discussed in the "Processes" section of this chapter.

- *Report Wizard*: This advanced tool enables multitable reports to be created easily without a programmer. These reports are simple to save to the main menu so other users can employ them. The wizard is discussed in the "Processes" section of this chapter.

- *Balanced Scorecard*: This Axapta functionality is used to get a cockpit view of key performance indicators (KPIs) and requires the Balanced Scorecard module. This functionality is not discussed in this chapter.

▉Note As stressed in the preceding Standard Reports bullet, we recommend that you spend the time to go through all of Axapta's out-of-the-box reports. Users often request to have reports generated that already exist. The wide range of out-of-the-box reports can often fulfill a decent portion of a business's reporting requirements.

Setup

The only reporting tool that requires setup is the Business Analysis module, or OLAP functionality. Using Axapta it is possible to easily create OLAP cubes from a user-definable set of criteria, though we don't detail this setup in this chapter. Instead, this chapter describes the setup of the OLAP server and database settings within Axapta, and the importing of Axapta's standard cube definitions. We recommend that you perform cube creation on a fat client or 2-tier client due to the large bandwidth used between the client and the SQL Server Analysis Services and database servers.

▉Note The steps listed here assume that SQL Server 2000 Analysis Services is running with at least SP3a applied. Upgrading SQL Server 2000 to SP3a does not update Analysis Services to SP3a; this is a separate upgrade and must be performed prior to performing the steps detailed in this chapter.

Business Analysis

The first steps in setup are to input into Axapta the name of your analysis server and to create the SQL Server Analysis Services database to be used. Open the OLAP Servers form, Administration ➤ Setup ➤ Business Analysis ➤ OLAP ➤ OLAP Servers. Give your server a server ID (such as a number or short name), type the name of the physical server where Analysis Services is running, and specify a description. You can leave the OLAP server type set to Analysis Server, as we did in Figure 14-1.

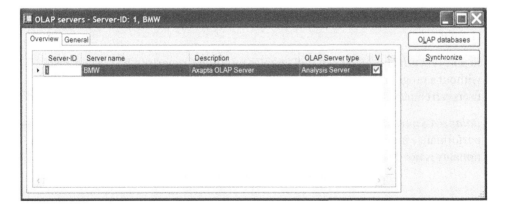

Figure 14-1. *The OLAP Servers form. Make sure you use the computer name of the Analysis Services server in the Server Name field.*

Next press the OLAP Databases button to bring up the OLAP Databases form, where you should create a new line specifying your desired database name and description. The database ID will default automatically to the next available number; see Figure 14-2.

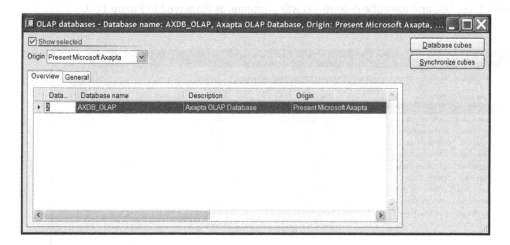

Figure 14-2. *The OLAP Databases form is used to create the new OLAP database. The user should define the database name and description.*

Close the OLAP Databases form and open the OLAP Parameters form (Basic ➤ Setup ➤ Business Analysis ➤ OLAP Parameters) to be sure your newly created database is the default database and that your time range is set up correctly, as shown in Figure 14-3.

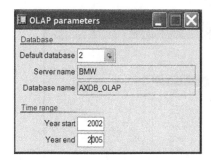

Figure 14-3. *The OLAP Parameters form is used to specify which Analysis Services database is the default Axapta database, and the time range for which to collect data.*

■**Tip** If you are using the Light Company demo database, set Year Start to 2002, as this is when the bulk of Light Company transactions took place.

Upon closing the OLAP Parameters form, open the Cube Definition Manager (Administration ➤ Setup ➤ Business Analysis ➤ OLAP ➤ Cube Definition Manager). Press the Import/Export button on the right side of the form and select the Import Cube Definitions option. Browse to find the *OLAP standard30.dat* file in the *Axapta Application\Appl\Standard\Db* folder. Press OK, and the cube definitions will populate, as displayed in Figure 14-4.

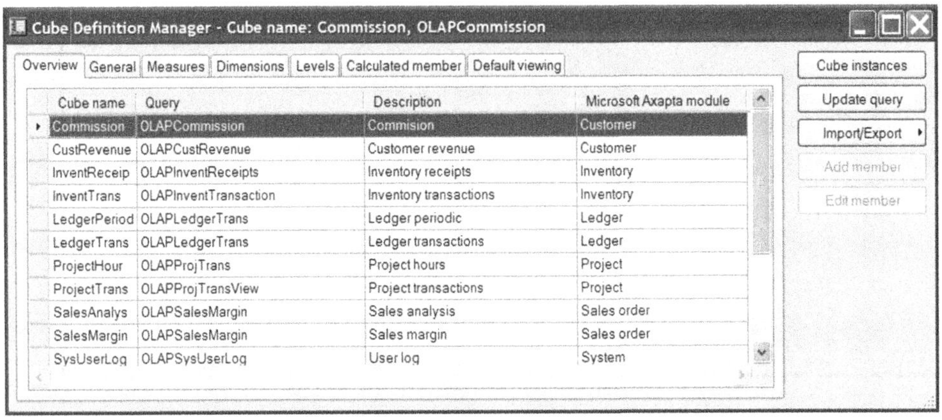

Figure 14-4. *You can use the Cube Definition Manager to import the default Axapta cube definitions.*

Once the cube definitions have been imported, close the form and open the Cube Instances form (Basic ➤ Setup ➤ Business Analysis ➤ Cube Instances). Press the Create Instances button to populate the form with all of the records from the Cube Definition Manager—see Figure 14-5.

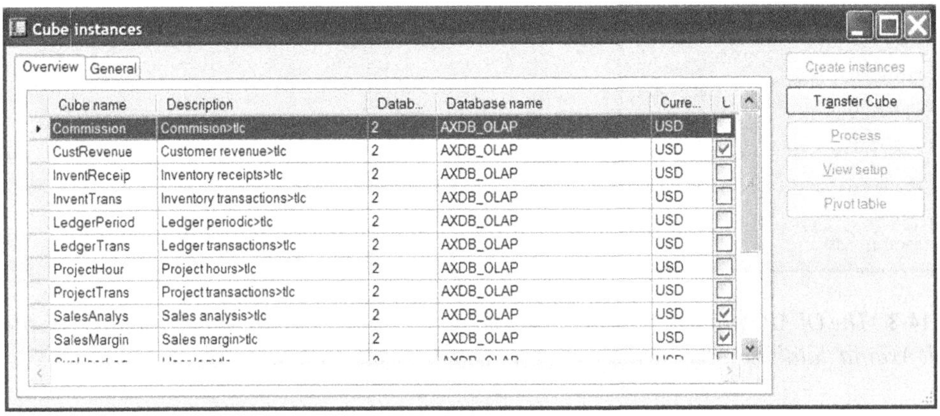

Figure 14-5. *The Cube Instances form lets you create, transfer, and process OLAP cubes.*

From the Cube Instances form, select a cube that you desire to view. Click the Transfer Cube button to run the transfer process. Upon completion of the transfer, press the Process button to process the cube. When the process is complete you will be able to press the Pivot Table button to view your cube. As stated earlier, you should run these processes on a 2-tier client or a 3-tier fat client to eliminate AOS and bandwidth issues for other system users. The time required to run these processes will depend on the number of transactions to be processed for each cube. It is also possible to transfer and process many cubes at the same time by doing a multiselect using the Ctrl key. In addition, many businesses will batch these operations to run during nonpeak hours.

Processes

Now that we have set up Axapta with the standard cube definitions we can get into viewing the cubes. Further, this section will describe using the Auto-Report and Report Wizard functionality.

Business Analysis

The easiest way to view the OLAP cubes that we set up earlier in this chapter is to simply press the Pivot Table button located on the Cube Instances form. This button is available only for cubes that have been both transferred and processed. Figure 14-6 shows a pivot table display.

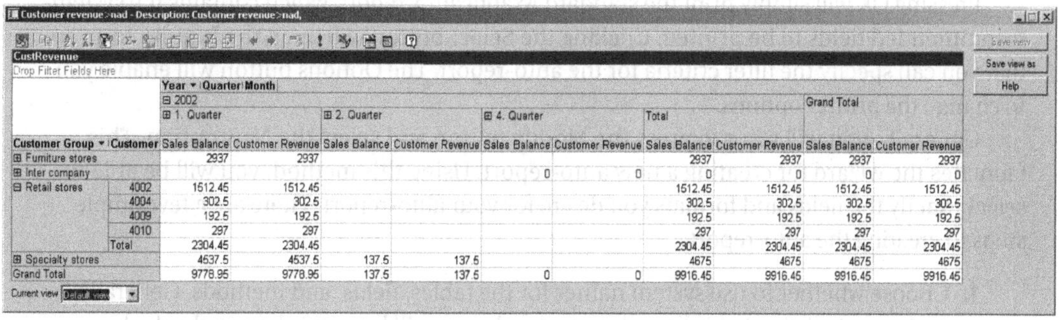

Customer Group	Customer	2002 / 1. Quarter Sales Balance	1. Quarter Customer Revenue	2. Quarter Sales Balance	2. Quarter Customer Revenue	4. Quarter Sales Balance	4. Quarter Customer Revenue	Total Sales Balance	Total Customer Revenue	Grand Total Sales Balance	Grand Total Customer Revenue
Furniture stores		2937	2937					2937	2937	2937	2937
Inter company						0	0	0	0	0	0
Retail stores	4002	1512.45	1512.45					1512.45	1512.45	1512.45	1512.45
	4004	302.5	302.5					302.5	302.5	302.5	302.5
	4009	192.5	192.5					192.5	192.5	192.5	192.5
	4010	297	297					297	297	297	297
	Total	2304.45	2304.45					2304.45	2304.45	2304.45	2304.45
Specialty stores		4537.5	4537.5	137.5	137.5			4675	4675	4675	4675
Grand Total		9778.95	9778.95	137.5	137.5	0	0	9916.45	9916.45	9916.45	9916.45

Figure 14-6. *The pivot table display of the Customer Revenue OLAP cube. Pressing the Excel icon will open Microsoft Excel with the same data displayed.*

Throughout Axapta there are links to cubes that might be helpful for business analysis purposes. It is also very common to have shortcuts created in convenient forms for cube viewing.

Pressing the Excel icon from the pivot table view will export the entire pivot table to Microsoft Excel for further manipulation. Alternatively, you can open cubes directly from Excel by setting Analysis Services as an external data type.

Auto-Report

Auto-report can be used to report on any data within Axapta that is presented in a form or via an on-screen inquiry. Whenever you see the printer icon on the Axapta tool bar, the auto-report functionality is available. For example, pressing the printer icon from the Items form will bring up the Auto-Report form shown in Figure 14-7. We recommend that before you try and create an auto-report, you determine the field names you wish to report on. In the following example we will create an auto-report to list item number, item name, module (price) type, and price.

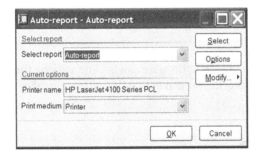

Figure 14-7. *The Auto-Report form opens when you press the printer icon.*

Pressing OK will simply print the standard Axapta auto-report, which contains the system-recommended fields to be printed. Clicking the Select button will open the Inquiry form so that you can specify the filter criteria for the auto-report. The Options button will enable you to change the printer options.

Generally, you will want to press the Modify button and select the New option. This launches the wizard for creating a new auto-report. Using this method, you will be able to select exactly the fields and formats you desire for your auto-report. There are a few simple steps to creating the auto-report:

1. Choose whether to use system names for the tables, fields, and methods. Generally, end users will check this box whereas developers will leave this box unchecked.

2. Name your new auto-report. Axapta will save the report so that you can access it using the Select Report drop-down menu next time you launch an auto-report from the same form.

3. Use the left and right arrow buttons to choose the fields you wish to be displayed in your auto-report. The available fields are on the left side, and the fields selected for your auto-report are on the right side, as in Figure 14-8. The standard auto-report fields are already selected; be sure to send any of the fields that you do not want to display back to the left.

4. If one or more of the fields selected are numeric fields (indicated by the small "1" on the field icon), the next step in the wizard will be to dictate any summation that is to occur on those fields.

5. Choose your report layout, orientation, and template, as Figure 14-9 shows.

6. Finally, press Finish to return to the Auto-Report form. Your named report will now be listed as the selected report. Pressing OK will print your report to your desired print medium; see Figure 14-10.

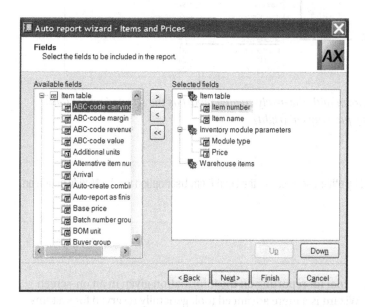

Figure 14-8. *The Auto Report Wizard form's Fields step. The fields in the left pane represent all of the ones available for your auto-report. The fields in the right pane represent the acutal fields to be reported on.*

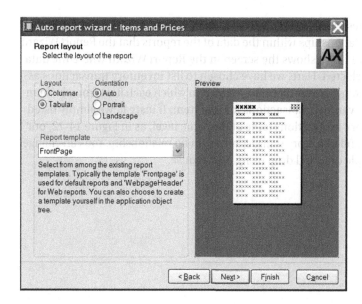

Figure 14-9. *The Auto Report Wizard form's Report Layout step. Choose the layout, orientation, and template. The default template is FrontPage.*

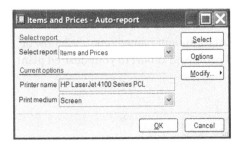

Figure 14-10. *The Auto-Report form with the newly created report as the selected report (left), and the report that is created by pressing OK (right).*

Tip To use auto-reports created by other users, select the Load From User option via the Modify button on the Auto-Report form.

Report Wizard

The auto-report is a very simple tool for reporting on the information given in an on-screen display or inquiry. The Report Wizard is a more advanced tool, generally reserved for systems administrators or developers. The steps for using this tool are very similar to those for using the Auto Report Wizard, and thus we won't go into great detail. The main difference is that with the Report Wizard the user has the ability to include any of the tables or fields from the Axapta database in the report. The Report Wizard is launched from Tools ➤ Development Tools ➤ Wizards ➤ Report Wizard.

The main feature that makes the Report Wizard much more advanced than the Auto-Report Wizard is its ability to create relationships within the data of the reports that the Report Wizard generates. For example, Figure 14-11 shows the screen in the Report Wizard where the data sources, or tables, are being selected. Here, we have chosen to list inventory transactions as children of the item table. By doing so, we will create a report in which each item from the item table is listed along with the inventory transactions for that item. If instead we simply listed the item table and the inventory transactions table at the same level, as in Figure 14-12, our end report would list all items and inventory transactions, with no relationship. You can change these relationships with a simple drag and drop using your mouse.

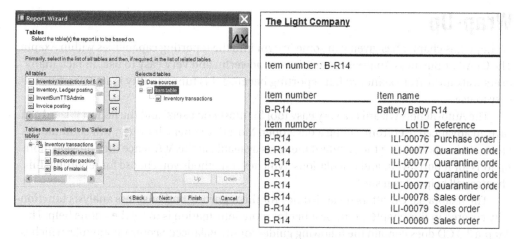

Figure 14-11. *A Report Wizard Tables selection in which inventory transactions will be displayed as the children of the items table (left). The report generated (right) displays each item from the item table, and all inventory transactions for the specific item.*

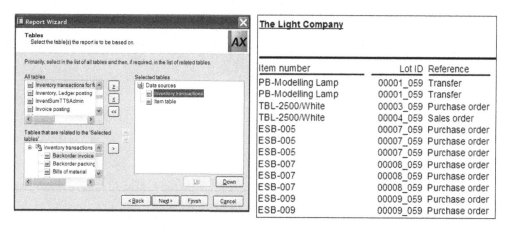

Figure 14-12. *A Report Wizard Tables selection in which inventory transactions and the item table are listed at the same level (left). The report generated (right) displays all item transactions followed by all items from the item table, with no relationship.*

The other features of the Report Wizard are generally straightforward; the wizard walks you through all of the steps and options. At the end of the wizard you will have the option to preview the report, further design the report (developers only), and save the report to the main menu. (If you do not save the report to the main menu it will be accessible only from the AOT. Also, note that once you have created a report using the Report Wizard, you can edit it only through the AOT; it is not possible to go back and edit the report using the Report Wizard.)

Wrap-Up

We hope this chapter has given you some insight into the reporting capabilities within Axapta. The OLAP or Business Analysis feature is very powerful and very easy to use. In fact, many users walk away from standard flat reporting because this functionality is so powerful and easy to use.

The Auto-Report Wizard is a very easy tool for most end users, and the Report Wizard can save an advanced user from calling a developer. Most developers, however, will continue to create their reports using the standard methods available in the AOT since they provide more options for report layout and calculations. Whichever methods you choose for reporting, this chapter will help get you started.

The Axapta 3.0 CD offers no assistance for the reporting and business analysis functionality covered in this chapter. Your best bet for more information is to try the online help. The Axapta 3.0 CD does contain the following guides for the Balanced Scorecard module, which is outside the scope of this book.

- *AX-300-USG-019-v01.00-ENUS.pdf*: Getting Started with Balanced Scorecard

- *AX-300-USG-015-v01.00-ENUS.pdf*: User's Guide for Balanced Scorecard

CHAPTER 15

■ ■ ■

Integration APIs

The objective of this chapter is not to turn you into an expert—some of the topics covered here are enough for a small book in their own right, as we are now probing into the more advanced features of Axapta. So what you can expect is a good overview of how Axapta can be integrated with other systems using the following technologies:

- Journals

- Module APIs

- Business Connector

- Microsoft .NET

- Commerce Gateway

With the exception of journals, all the other forms of integrating with Axapta are APIs in one form or another.

The technologies we will cover here are useful in real life. It's important to note that the different technologies serve different purposes. Some are ways to access external functionality from within Axapta, others are methods of accessing Axapta functionality from the outside, and some are a combination of the two. Let's look at them:

- Journals are simply tables in which you can post transactions to be performed within different modules, and offer by far the simplest form of integration from the viewpoint of the code that is using the journals, as these follow the same pattern for all modules.

- Module APIs are a set of classes within each module that you can program against to leverage the functionality in the respective modules. They're the way to go if you want to reuse existing functionality, and they offer an alternative to integrating via journals.

- The Business Connector is a COM object interface to Axapta and is the technological foundation of Commerce Gateway, as well the Web framework and Enterprise Portal, as well as the only external API into Axapta. It is used to access both Axapta functionality and data; you can execute Axapta logic from external applications and retrieve, read, write, and delete data.

- Microsoft .NET is not really supported in Axapta, but as the world is moving that way, I will tell you how to do anything you can do with Axapta through the Business Connector from a .NET assembly.

- Commerce Gateway is a data-exchange gateway to Microsoft BizTalk Server and, to an extent, is an XML-based remote procedure call (RPC) technology. It enables you to exchange data using documents that can be transformed to and from Axapta's format to any other using BizTalk. An interesting aspect is that it can actually be used to execute code.

Now that you know *what* you can do with the technology, let's look at *how* to do it.

Note Commerce Gateway, .NET, and Enterprise Portal all have the Business Connector as their technology in and out of Axapta. If any of these technologies or modules are relevant to you, make sure you read the "Business Connector" section of this chapter.

Journals

Out of the box, Axapta has a comprehensive set of journals for posting data to various modules such as General Ledger, Accounts Receivable, and Accounts Payable. It's a simple and powerful way for integrating Axapta applications by creating data and invoking the respective module to process it.

For example, if you develop a real-estate-management module, you would want to be able to post data to the standard modules referred to earlier. By using journals all you need to do is be acquainted with their data requirements, write the required data to them, and call their posting methods. You don't need to know the business logic behind how the module you are posting to processes the transaction—the developers of the module have taken care of that.

Note The concept of journals in Axapta is not what is usually understood as a journal (i.e., a regular recording of system events or activities), but rather is a system for invoking built-in processing of data programmatically. Using journals does, however, have the consequence of leaving a trail of data that has been posted around the system. You can think of the journal system as a worksheet where data can be created for a module, changed, reviewed, and approved before it's submitted by the module in question. After posting a journal to a module, the journal and its data as submitted can be preserved and can therefore be used for auditing purposes.

You perform four fundamental steps when working with journals:

1. Naming and registering your journals

2. Creating journals for posting

3. Creating data for the journals

4. Checking and posting the journals

■**Note** Microsoft documentation consistently states that there are three steps in working with journals because it groups together the last two steps. However, since creating data for journals does not automatically imply posting or checking it (you can leave it hanging there or delete it if you wish and actually post and check manually or programmatically also), we consider them distinct.

If you want to use journals to integrate with existing Axapta applications, the first step is to figure out which journals to post to—each application module documents its own.

■**Note** Unfortunately, documentation on each module's journaling abilities varies from nothing to close to nothing, so even though it's a great idea, using journals requires long hours of looking at existing examples, hacking, and debugging. We recommend getting started with the help of someone who already knows the ropes unless you really enjoy meaningless challenges.

You start by either creating a journal name in the respective module's Journal Names table or by getting hold of an existing one. Normally you will have created all your journal names manually using the main menu path of General Ledger ➤ Setup ➤ Journals ➤ Journal Names, but of course when you get that far you can also do it programmatically.

By convention, journal names carry the name of the module suffixed with "*JournalName*"; for example, the general ledger journal name table is called LedgerJournalName and contains all the names of all the postings that are made from around Axapta to the general ledger. Think of it as a register of all the different types of processes and transactions that post data to the general ledger. Assuming that this was a ledger posting that recurred daily and that you had created only a single journal name of that type for classifying this type of posting, the following code illustrates how to get a ledger journal name of the type Daily that you can then use to create a journal table entry:

Retrieve Journal Name

```
LedgerJournalName ledgerJournalName; // Declaration

select firstonly from ledgerJournalName
    where ledgerJournalName.JournalType == LedgerJournalType::Daily;
```

The next table that you have to deal with is the module's journal table—this is where you actually register postings to a journal. The naming convention for these tables is similar to the convention for journal names; i.e., the module name is suffixed with "*JournalTable*." For example, the general ledger table journals are in a table called LedgerJournalTable.

Continuing to use the general ledger as an example, you create a journal entry for processing by creating a record with any required fields then calling the Insert method. The code for the general ledger using the journal name we created previously looks like this:

Create Journal

```
LedgerJournalTable ledgerJournalTable; // Declaration

ledgerJournalTable.JournalName = ledgerJournalName.JournalName;
ledgerJournalTable.Name =  Daily Property Appreciation'
ledgerJournalTable.insert();
```

■**Note** While we suggest that you use the ledgerJournalName for identifying what you are posting to a module, its only purpose is the classification of journal postings, so you can use it in whatever manner you see fit—for example, to identify posts by different users, functions, periods, etc. For that matter, if you know the journal name you can just hard-code it—ledgerJournalTable.JournalName = _myJournalName— with the typical drawbacks that brings.

■**Note** In the preceding code there are only two mandatory fields in the ledger journal table, but you need to write other fields, depending on the journal and the process that you are posting from.

When you call the insert method, the journal table can calculate and create values that it needs, such as IDs. In the case of the ledger journal it creates a unique journal number.

With that done you then create journal lines—the actual data that is to be posted for the journal you have created. The table in which you create data for the journal follows the naming convention of the module name suffixed with "*JournalTrans*" (e.g., LedgerJournalTrans for the general ledger), and is generally called the JournalTrans table.

■**Note** Each journal entry in the *module*JournalTable is a journal posting, and it includes one or more records in the *module*JournalTrans that are part of the posting.

JournalTrans tables always have a field that associates each record to a journal in the corresponding JournalTable table—for example, the JournalNum field in LedgerJournalTrans is generated in LedgerJournalTable when you insert a journal record.

Summing it up, you get hold of the journal number, assign it to the journal number field for the line you create for the journal posting in the JournalTrans table, set values for all the fields required by the module you are posting to, and call the insert method of the table to persist it. Repeat as many times as necessary until all the records and lines to be processed for the journal posting are inserted. The code will resemble the following snippet, minus the specific fields required by LedgerJournalTrans:

Create Journal Line

```
LedgerJournalTrans ledgerJournalTrans; // Declaration
```

```
ledgerJournalTrans.JournalNum = ledgerJournalTable.JournalNum;
numberseq = NumberSeq::NewGetVoucherFromCode(ledgerJournalName.VoucherSeries);
ledgerJournalTrans.Voucher = numberseq.voucher();
ledgerJournalTrans.insert();
```

The last step is to check and process the journal and the associated data that you have created. The process varies from module to module, but each module provides the necessary classes to do it. The General Ledger module has a class called LedgerJournalCheckPost for the purpose. When posting a journal to the general ledger, you create an instance of the class by using its newLedgerJournalTable static method, and then run it. The following X++ code snippet shows you how:

Check and Post Journal

```
LedgerJournalCheckPost ledgerJournalCheckPost; // Declaration
ledgerJournalCheckPost =➡
    LedgerJournalCheckPost::newLedgerJournalTable(ledgerJournalTablet,NoYes::Yes,
    NoYes::No);
ledgerJournalCheckPost.run();
```

The static method takes the journal record that you want to post as its first argument, whether to post the journal after checking it as the second argument, and whether to transfer all data records with errors to another journal with the same name and description but a different journal number as the third.

■**Note** Checking validates the data in the records that you are submitting; records that are invalid can't be posted and will result in the post failing by default. By transferring invalid journal data lines/records, the ones that are valid can be processed.

As mentioned earlier in this chapter, you do not have to check or validate and post journals programmatically. Modules that use journals have a corresponding folder in the top level of their menu page in the main application menu. Look at one in the general ledger by opening the form at the main application menu path, General Ledger ➤ Journals ➤ General Journal. The form displays data from the LedgerJournalTable table. You can pull up the lines or records that are associated with the journal in the LedgerJournalTrans table, validate the journal, post it, approve it, and print it—most of these operations can also be applied to individual lines of the journal from the respective form.

■**Note** What you can do manually with a journal and its data record or lines varies from journal to journal, but generally you can view existing journals, their state, and the data that is associated with them, which is basically your audit trail.

Once you have been around the general ledger journal, check out a few other journals in some of the other modules.

Module APIs

The full application logic and everything Axapta does relies on the object types that you can see in the AOT, and in practice any public method of any object type contains functionality that you can use to interface with objects of that type—and getting to know them all is impossible. You must instead pick up the ones you need as you need them by looking at which object types the module at hand is using and how it is using them, by asking around, and by old-fashioned trial and error.

The somewhat good news is that generally only the class type objects are considered part of the API—but there are many of them, so it will take you a lifetime to learn what they are and how to use them. However, there is a small subset that you will need to integrate when you develop your own modules, and we cover that subset in this section. This set of APIs exposes the following areas of functionality:

- *General Ledger*: This is a core module used by almost all others.

- *Trade series*: This module includes Accounts Receivable and Accounts Payable, both of which follow the same general patterns in their API.

- *Warehouse Management*: This module has a lot of functionality; you can create, move, transfer, adjust, update, and reserve items, see on-hand items, and much more.

- *Production*: This module is primarily concerned with production orders.

- *Number Sequences*: This functional component is used throughout Axapta for obtaining number sequences.

Using the API is, however, more complex than using journals because the APIs don't follow a series of steps like the four specified for journals. Each module provides its own set of classes and methods, and you have to know which ones to use for each specific area of functionality—no easy task since it's basically undocumented outside the MBS training materials. Though we can't cover the API for each module in Axapta, let's look at a set of principles that you can use as guidelines as you investigate each module and figure out the API.

Note One way to figure out the APIs for the different modules is to look at a set of classes in the AOT whose names start with "Tutorial." These can be difficult to understand if you don't have some experience, as there is not a single comment in the code and there is no common pattern that can take you from one example to the next; however, keeping in mind what you've learned in this book and hacking a bit will help.

General Ledger

What you can do here is quite straightforward:

1. Create a LedgerVoucher using `LedgerVoucher = LedgerVoucher::newVoucher()`.

2. Create LedgerVoucherObjects using `LedgerVoucherObject = LedgerVoucherTransObject::newCreateTrans()`.

3. Register LedgerVoucherObjects with LedgerVoucher using `LedgerVoucher.AddVoucher(LedgerVoucherObject)`.

4. Create LedgerVoucherTransObjects using `LedgerVoucherObject = LedgerVoucherTransObject::newCreateTrans()`.

5. Register LedgerVoucherTransObjects with LedgerVoucher using `LedgerVoucher.AddTrans(LedgerVoucherTransObject)`.

6. Commit the LedgerVoucher using `LedgerVoucher.end()`.

Trade Series

This API allows you to do more than you will find in other modules, but the core steps in working with it are similar to posting to the general ledger except that you post to either the Accounts Receivable or Accounts Payable module—the steps are the same for both, but we show them only for accounts receivable:

1. Create a LedgerVoucher using `LedgerVoucher = LedgerVoucher::newVoucher()`.

2. Create LedgerVoucherObjects using `LedgerVoucherObject = LedgerVoucherTransObject::newCreateTrans()`.

3. Register LedgerVoucherObjects with LedgerVoucher using `LedgerVoucher.AddVoucher(LedgerVoucherObject)`.

4. Create a CustVoucher using `CustVoucher = CustVendVoucher::construct()`.

5. Create LedgerVoucherTransObjects using `LedgerVoucherObject = LedgerVoucherTransObject::newCreateTrans()`.

6. Register LedgerVoucherTransObjects with LedgerVoucher using `LedgerVoucher.AddTrans(LedgerVoucherTransObject)`.

7. Commit the LedgerVoucher using `LedgerVoucher.end()`.

You can also do the following with the existing API:

- Create new customers based on an existing customer that is used as a template. Call the static method `CustTable::createOneTimeAccount()` with either a SalesTable record or a CustInvoiceJournal record as an argument from which it obtains all the necessary data.

- Create new orders, which consists of constructing a PurchAutoCreate or a SalesAutoCreate using `PurchAutoCreate::construct()` or `SalesAutoCreate::construct()` and then actually creating a line using `purchAutoCreate.createPurchLine()` or `salesAutoCreate.createSalesLine()`.

- Invoice orders, which consists of constructing a PurchFormLetter or a SalesFormLetter using `PurchFormLetter::construct()` or `SalesFormLetter::construct()` and then calling `purchFormLetter.update()` or `salesFormLetter.update()` to post the invoice and possibly print it.

Warehouse Management

The Warehouse Management API works in a different way than the others you have seen; subclasses do most of the work. There are quite a few different types of inventory movements and Axapta comes with the necessary subclasses to handle them. Most of the classes and subclasses use the following naming pattern:

- *Base class*: Invent[Operation]; e.g. InventAdj and InventMovement.

- *Specialized class*: Invent[Operation]_[Dataset]. The operation is sometimes abbreviated; the data set indicates the type involved in performing the named operation—e.g., InventMov_Sales for performing an inventory-movement base on a sales order, InventUpd_Reservation for performing a movement of a reservation, etc.

If you keep this naming pattern in mind you can go into the AOT and easily identify the different API subgroups; however, using and learning them is tricky because they are inconsistent. Here's an example to get you started. The steps for inventory movements, assuming that you are changing the quantity in a sales order line, are as follows:

1. Create an InventMovement using `inventMovement = InventMovement::construct(sales)`, where the parameter is a sales table record.

2. Subtract "qty" from the quantity ordered with `inventMovement.setTransQty(qty)`.

3. Subtract "qty" from the sales quantity with `inventMovement.setTransQtyUnit(qty)`.

4. Finally, update inventory with `inventMovement.updateNow()`, using an optional Boolean parameter to specify if the reservation should be updated.

▪**Note** This API group contains a large set of classes that do not need to be specialized and that consequently are not subclassed.

▪**Note** Not all subclasses follow the pattern described here, and some follow the pattern but are not actually subclasses of what you would assume the superclass to be—for instance, InventCountCreate_Base extends JournalRunBaseBatch, and it's actually InventCountCreate that is a specialization.

Production

To some extent this API group resembles Inventory Management, using the same scheme by which subclasses actually perform the bulk of the work, and a set of classes that do not require specialization. But there's an odd twist: some of the classes in the group do not start with the prefix "Prod," but have totally unrelated names. Here is a list of the most interesting classes (all of which do follow the "Prod" rule):

- *ProdMulti*: For updating multiple production orders at the same time

- *ProdReport*: For getting information on product orders

- *ProdStatusType*: For moving production orders from one state or status to the next

- *ProdUpd*: For updating single production orders

- *ProdConsistencyCheck*: For checking the consistency of production data

Number Sequences

This API is quite important; it's the way to obtain and manage number sequences, whatever your need for them might be. Using your own scheme will invariably lead to trouble and force you to reinvent the wheel, so stick with this API.

Number sequences are normally created using the main menu path, Basic ➤ Setup ➤ Number Sequences ➤ Number Sequence. There is one fundamental class in this API group, and the core methods that you will need to know about are all static:

- *NewGetNum*: Creates a number-sequence object and generates a new number for the number sequence type specified as a parameter. You then can access it using the num() method, as shown here:

```
Num myNumNum;
NumberSeq numberSeq;
numberSeq =

NumberSeq::newGetNum(NumberSequenceReference:: ➥
find(extendedtypenum(InventJournalId)));
myNumNum = numberSeq.num();
```

- *NewGetVoucher*: Creates a new number-sequence object and generates a new voucher code that you can access using the voucher() method:

```
Num myNumNum;
NumberSeq numberSeq;
numberSeq = NumberSeq::newGetVoucher(NumberSequenceReference::➥
find(extendedtypenum(InventJournalVoucherId)));
myNumNum = numberSeq.voucher ();
```

- *NewGetNumAndVoucher:* Creates a number sequence object and generates a new number and voucher code that can be accessed using the num() and voucher() methods

- *NewReserveNum*: Creates a new number sequence object and reserves a new number or voucher that can be returned using the method release(), for example:

```
NumberSeq numberSeq;
numberSeq =    NumberSeq::newReserveNum(NumberSequenceReference::➡
    find(extendedtypenum(InventJournalVoucherId)));
NumberSeq::release(nsc, myNumNum);
```

Note A number sequence is consumed the first time you use the number-sequence object to retrieve it with the num() or voucher() methods, so if you do not want to consume it you must release it before you execute any of the getter methods.

Note The code here is generic and not enough for most real-world situations. The information in this section is worth the price of this book for most beginner to intermediate developers, but it's neither complete nor comprehensive. The point here is that you know that this stuff exists and have a general idea of how it works, but you will have to investigate on you own and work with different parts of Axapta to figure out what parameters to pass and what data to set. Knowing how this basic set of APIs works will help you figure out what to look for and what you can expect it to look like in code when you go through the tutorials or the multiple parts of the application that use these techniques.

Business Connector

During configuration and post-installation, we looked at registering the Business Connector and stopping it, so the first step now is to verify that all is as expected.

Log on to Axapta and fire up the Internet Parameters form (see Figure 15-1) using the main application menu path, Administration ➤ Setup ➤ Internet ➤ Parameters.

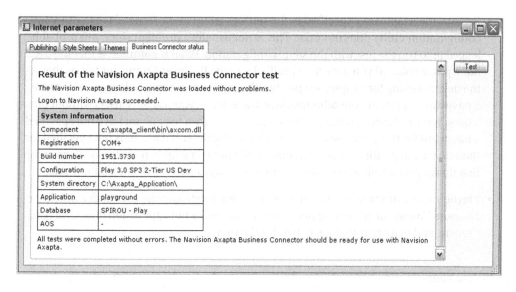

Figure 15-1. *The Internet Parameters form*

Go to the Business Connector Status tab and click on the Test button. After a few seconds you should see the connector test results, resembling Figure 15-1. If you don't see the results, Business Connector is not working and you need to troubleshoot it.

▓Note While you can register the Business Connector as a COM or DCOM object, it's best to register it as a COM+ object so that you can manage it with the Windows Component Services tool.

The most important thing to keep in mind if the test fails is that the error messages this form displays are notoriously misleading. Here are a few tips on debugging failed Business Connector tests:

- Is the COM object registered with the component services? Start the Windows component services manager, expand your way to the *COM+ Applications* folder—the path is Console Root ➤ Component Services ➤ Computers ➤ My Computer ➤ My Applications. It should resemble Figure 15-2, depending on what COM+ applications you have registered, and you should see an icon labeled Navision Axapta Business Connector. If you don't, start the Axapta Configuration Utility, go to the Business Connector tab and follow the instructions in Chapter 3 to register it.

- What is the identity of the user that the Business Connector runs under? You can check this by opening the Properties dialog of the COM object and going to the Identity tab—see Figure 15-3. Once you have selected the domain account to use, you need to make sure the account belongs to a database user with public and db_owner permissions on the database you have specified in the active Axapta configuration—remember that by default Axapta creates the user bmssa.

- Perhaps the password for the account under which the Business Connector is running is entered in the properties of the object. If the user password is changed or the user deleted or disabled it in the domain or the database, then it will fail to connect to the database.

- Perhaps the Axapta user specified in the settings group of the General tab in the Axapta configuration utility does not exist. This is not usually a problem since you probably logged in to run the test with the same configuration. What is common is that the user has a password, and you have not specified it in the Business Connector tab, as that is the default setting for Axapta. So specify either a user and password, or a user without a password—if you or your administrator are reckless, you will have users without passwords. You can be even more reckless and not specify a user if you have not specified a password for the admin Axapta user. It's used by default if a user is not specified for the active configuration—however, this should not come up in real life since one of the first things your administrator should do is to assign a password to the admin user.

- Maybe you are running in 2-tier or 3-tier fat client mode and the user under which the Business Connector is running does not have access to the application files. Give read, execute, and write permissions to files for the user.

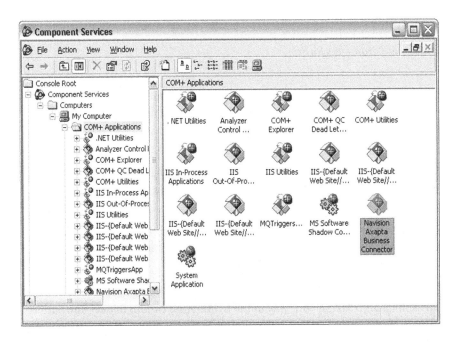

Figure 15-2. *The Component Services window*

Note Every time you change the settings of the Business Connector object, you need to stop it by using the Action menu on the menu bar or the pop-up menu that is displayed by right-clicking the icon, or use the appropriate button on the Axapta Configuration Utility in the respective tab. You can then start it manually if you wish, but that is not necessary; trying to access the COM object from Axapta will automatically start it for you.

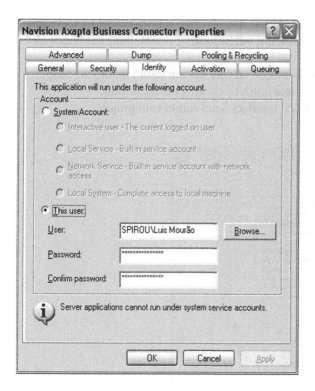

Figure 15-3. *The Business Connector Properties form*

Once you have the Business Connector up and running and connecting to Axapta, you can (as with any COM object) work with it in the same way whether it's from your own custom application code or from any application that can act as a COM client.

For example, you can write a Microsoft Excel Visual Basic script to populate cells in a spreadsheet, perform complex calculations and enter the results back into Axapta, create custom documents and correspondence from Microsoft Word documents, or generate dynamic content for ASP- and ASP.NET–based Web sites—that's how Enterprise Portal and Commerce Gateway work. The possibilities are limited only by your understanding of the mechanics of calling into Axapta using the Business Connector; once you have the hang of that, everything is possible. The following section provides an overview of how to use the Business Connector. The code for a stand-alone application can easily be converted to a Microsoft Excel or Word script.

Microsoft .NET

Great—so it's up and running; now we have an external application written in Visual Basic or C++ that needs to get hold of customer data in Axapta. How do we do this?

■ Note This section, while focusing on Microsoft .NET, applies equally to any COM client whether managed or unmanaged (i.e., whether it's a .NET assembly or a normal Windows application).

Start Visual Studio and create a new Visual Basic console project. Go to the Solution Explorer pane and add a reference. Go to the COM tab; you will be looking at something like Figure 15-4, give or take some components.

Browse down the list of components available on your system until you find the Axapta COM Connector 1.2 Type Library. Select it and finish by clicking the OK button.

You can now access Axapta's entire COM interface from within your project.

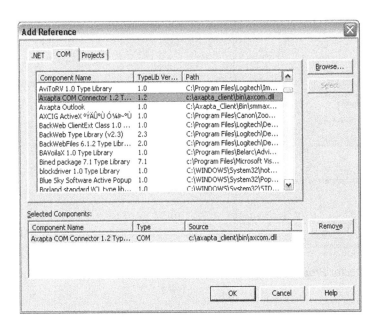

Figure 15-4. *The Add Reference dialog*

Code module AxCOM_Example_1 is a simple Visual Basic module that retrieves customer data and writes it to standard output; this illustrates the essentials of using the Business Connector. The code is comprehensively commented, so it doesn't require further explanation.

Code ModuleAxCOM_Example_1

```
Module AxCOM_Example_1

    Sub Main()
        Dim Axapta As AxaptaCOMConnector.Axapta2
        Dim AxaptaQuery As AxaptaCOMConnector.IAxaptaObject
        Dim AxaptaDataSource As AxaptaCOMConnector.IAxaptaObject
        Dim AxaptaQueryRun As AxaptaCOMConnector.IAxaptaObject
        Dim CustTableBuffer As AxaptaCOMConnector.IAxaptaRecord
        Dim CustTable
        Dim i
```

```
'Create an Axapta object reference.
Axapta = CreateObject("AxaptaCOMConnector.Axapta2")
'Log on to Axapta. Don't care about the user, password or company.
'Don't do this in real applications; authenticate properly.
Axapta.Logon2("", "", "", "")

'Table ID is an internal reference. In Axapta select the table, display the
'properties window and look it up in the ID field.
CustTable = 77

'Create an Axapta query object.
AxaptaQuery = Axapta.CreateObject("Query")
'Add a data source to the query.
AxaptaDataSource = AxaptaQuery.Call("AddDataSource", CustTable)
'Create a query runner.
AxaptaQueryRun = Axapta.CreateObject("QueryRun", AxaptaQuery)

i = 1
'Loop through the result set.
While (AxaptaQueryRun.Call("Next"))
    'Get the record.
    CustTableBuffer = AxaptaQueryRun.Call("GetNo", 1)
    'Write two fields to the console.
    Console.Write(CustTableBuffer.field("AccountNum") + " - ")
    Console.WriteLine(CustTableBuffer.field("Name"))
    i = i + 1
End While

'Always log off.
Axapta.Logoff()
'Free the instance for garbage collection.
Axapta = Nothing
End Sub

End Module
```

The essence of this simple application is to create an Axapta object reference, logging on, creating instances of exactly the same object that you would create in X++ if you were implementing the same functionality, executing the query, walking the result set, and writing data from each record to standard output. When you have finished, log out and free the Axapta object reference by setting it to null so that it can be garbage-collected. Compile it to see the results.

Note Just as you executed the next() method of the Axapta query runner—AxaptaQueryRun. Call("Next")—you could execute any other method on any object within Axapta. The trick is to create objects of the type you need, and the methods they support. The scheme is simple, and with that under control you can do whatever you want.

> ■**Note** If your target is a .NET assembly, Visual Studio will automatically generate a COM interop DLL for you, which serves as a bridge between your .NET managed code and the Business Connector, which is unmanaged.

Commerce Gateway

For the most part, Commerce Gateway is an advanced and complex module that uses the Business Connector to get in and out of Axapta. It is installed separately using the product CD—the last menu option in the menu bar of the Axapta installation portal. We haven't covered its installation in this book, but we'll provide a whirlwind tour of what it is, what it can do, and how you go about using it.

The module supports the electronic exchange of documents between systems using Microsoft BizTalk Server. Its value out of the box is pretty limited, as it provides support for only three document types:

- Purchase orders

- Sales orders

- Sales invoices

> ■**Note** Although the number of documents that Commerce Gateway supports out of the box is only three, Axapta allows you to add your own document types.

> ■**Note** In Axapta 3.0, Commerce Gateway supports only BizTalk Server 2002.

To use the module, you must have access to a BizTalk server, and within Axapta you must have the following licenses and modules:

- A license code for Commerce Gateway

- The Trade module

- The Accounts Receivable module

- The Accounts Payable module

Forms for setting up and managing the Commerce Gateway are grouped under the main application menu path, Basic ➤ Setup ➤ Gateway, and the Basic ➤ Gateway Queue form. The process is pretty complex and is documented (with limited success) in the file *AX-300-TIP-019-v01.00-ENUS.doc*, indicated in the "Wrap-Up" section of this chapter. If you need more than the standard documents, you will have to seek out other information.

Piecing together your own documents requires that you create and define the schemas of your documents (these are in XML and conform to xCBL specifications), make them available to BizTalk so that it can perform the necessary transformations between your Axapta documents and your partners, specify in Axapta where it can find the schema definitions, and finally specify how the code that supports the schemas interacts with them. This process is known as *schema mapping*.

Note You can import the standard schemas from a DAT file on the Axapta installation CD.

For each schema that you define and set up, you also need to define and implement Axapta classes and methods that know what to do when reading and/or writing to a document that conforms to the schema and the underlying data persistence layer. You do this in the Schemas form in the main menu path mentioned previously.

For each document you need to implement an xCBL class—it reads and writes the XML documents that are exchanged, which in turn maps through a linking class to an AxBC class, which reads and writes to Axapta tables. The following situations can occur:

- *Existing Axapta data is added to an XML document*: Requires that you modify the xCBL and linking class

- *New data is added to Axapta and a document*: Requires that you modify the xCBL and AxBC and linking class

- *You define a different schema for an existing document*: Requires you to create the corresponding schema class and modify the linking class

- *A new xCBL document is implemented*: Requires you to create new xCBL and AxBC classes and modify the linking class

That's as far as we go here, though this chapter gave you an idea of what you are up against and the level of expertise required for using Commerce Gateway.

Note We would like to leave you with a word on Commerce Gateway. We recommend that you seriously evaluate other solutions before you go with it. Naturally, because it uses BizTalk it can exchange data and documents with basically anything on this planet, and is extremely flexible and adaptable; however, there are solutions from two MBS partners, namely WM-data and Columbus IT Partner, that cover most needs. They are much more useful out of the box, and cost less—both up front and in terms of the learning curve and the know-how that you have to maintain in-house or buy from outside.

Wrap-Up

In this chapter we have covered the following:

- Integrating existing modules using the journal system

- Interacting with Axapta using COM

- Interacting with Axapta from .NET assemblies

- Exchanging documents with Axapta via BizTalk and Commerce Gateway

At this point you should have a good idea of what tools Axapta offers you for accessing its data and functionality from other systems and getting the technology up and running. And when the standard package falls short of your needs, you can hook into Axapta to do it your way.

You can read more about the topics in this chapter in the following document, available in the documentation folder of the product distribution package or CD:

- *AX-300-TIP-019-v01.00-ENUS.doc*: Commerce Gateway

CHAPTER 16

■ ■ ■

Enterprise Portal

Axapta not only comes with a native Windows client out of the box, but also with a Web framework and Enterprise Portal (EP), a Web application that allows users to interact with Axapta using a Web browser. Because EP is a Web application, you can ignore it if you like and develop your own Web application; however, because of the scope of EP, it's the best place to learn about the Web framework and what you can do with it. Generally, EP is taken to be both the Enterprise Portal and Content Management modules.

Because these modules are so closely integrated, we have gathered them here so that you don't have to jump around from chapter to chapter to understand how they fit together.

EP relies on the Web framework, and the Content Management System in turn depends on EP, both in terms of licensing and installation. But it's actually a module in itself that you can use in your own Web applications.

At the bottom of the technology stack is the Business Connector—also knows as the COM Connector, which wraps up Axapta as a COM object with a very basic and cryptic interface. Leveraging the COM interface is really for hackers or developers who like a challenge; however, MBS's Web framework and the aforementioned modules go a long way toward covering the needs that you are most likely to run into in the field.

■**Note** Although the modules and technologies covered in this chapter are a step in the right direction, using Axapta as a back end for a Web application or portal is difficult business. So even though you should expect to be able to breeze through this chapter, we recommend that you brace yourself for some head-scratching in the real world if you get a setup detail wrong. Figuring out what is wrong with EP is notoriously hard. The good news is that MBS is working on changing this.

In short, this chapter will cover the EP and Content Management modules, with an emphasis on Enterprise Portal. This should give you an idea of what you can do with the Web framework, as well as EP and the Content Management System.

Basics

To use the modules, you will need to have the Business Connector and Microsoft Internet Information Services (IIS) up and running to create Web users (who are not the same as normal Axapta users). Finally, you will need to create Web sites to deliver the functionality of your Web applications. That is the essence of what this section is about.

■**Note** Because of the difference between version 3.0 and previous versions of Axapta, you can't use an upgraded Web application as the base for a Web site, but you can reuse custom-made elements to put a new site together. Web applications are developed using MorphX, the standard Axapta development environment. You'll use different structure and classes when developing a Web application instead of a standard application, but for the most part the process and techniques are the same—more about this in Chapter 18.

The following sections will teach you what you need to have running before you can make practical use of Axapta's end-user functionality.

■**Note** The Business Connector is covered in Chapter 15. We suggest that you read it and verify that the Business Connector is in good health before proceeding with this chapter.

Internet Information Services

You must have IIS installed and running before you can make any real use of EP, Content Management, and Commerce Gateway.

■**Note** In Windows 2003, a bug in the IIS COM calling interface causes calls to the Business Connector to fail. A patch is available and it should be included in Windows 2003 SP2 by the time you read this. If not, you can get the patch from your local Microsoft sales rep, or from this URL: http://support.microsoft.com/default.aspx?scid=kb;en-us;839003.

Test that IIS is running by starting up your browser (go to http://localhost). This will display a page confirming that all is well. If the server is not running, get it running before you continue.

■**Note** Axapta portals use Active Server Pages (ASP) technology, and therefore ASP support must be installed—it's not installed by default in Windows 2003—and any Web portals you create must allow scripting.

For our purposes you can run IIS on the server where you installed the application component of Axapta. However, we recommend you install IIS on a dedicated system. We also highly recommend that you install the Axapta client component on the same system as IIS to install the Business Connector automatically. You can then use the Configuration Utility to specify an application and a database on another system. Remember that the Business Connector is an Axapta client without a user interface and a COM interface bolted on.

Web Users

In Axapta you can use normal user accounts to access business logic and data through the Business Connector. You can develop you own COM client in C# or VB, for example; however, normal users can't log on to a Web portal. Instead, you have to create special Web users who are associated with special internal or external Web user types and mapped against a normal Axapta user.

The process is painless; use the main application menu path Administration ➤ Setup ➤ Internet ➤ Web Users. This displays the dialog in Figure 16-1.

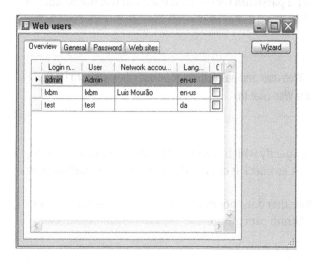

Figure 16-1. *The Web Users form*

You have the option of using a wizard by clicking on the corresponding button or by using the keyboard shortcut Ctrl+N. Using the wizard requires that you have set up and created base data in one of the application modules, depending on the type of user that you want to create. Table 16-1 shows the user types and the corresponding modules.

Table 16-1. *User Types and Corresponding Modules*

User Type	Module
Employee	HR
Customer	Accounts Receivable
Vendor	Accounts Payable
Network	HR

In the Overview tab, map the Web user to a real user by selecting one in the User field. Provide the network account name (the user's domain name) in the respective field, then indicate the language to use. The last field with a check box is used to mark the user as a campaign target. For the purpose of this book, create a user with whatever login name you like, and map him to the standard admin account or to a user that belongs to the Admin user group.

Note If you have not done so previously, create a standard Axapta user that does not belong to the Admin user group.

The General tab is where the user is mapped against one of the user types in Table 16-1, and you can leave it empty if you have not set up base data in the respective modules, but eventually you can use it to map your Web users to real employees, customers, vendors, or contacts.

In the Password tab you must specify a password for the Web user. You will not be able to save the Web user until you have done this.

Note This password is associated with the Web user and has nothing to do with the password for the standard Axapta user that you have mapped the Web user to.

The last tab, Web Sites, is where you specify which Web sites the Web user has access to. At this point we have not created any sites, so check it out but don't add any—we will do that when we create our Web sites.

Save the Web user, and create another that does not map to the standard Axapta admin account or to a user that belongs to the Admin user group.

Tip Now that you have at least a couple of Web users, you are ready to forge ahead, but make sure you control what Web users can and can't do by managing the permissions of the standard users that they are mapped to.

Web Sites

The last step before you have something to show for all your time is to create a Web site, and Axapta makes this a snap. You use the form at the main application menu path, Administration ➤ Setup ➤ Internet ➤ Web Sites, to display the form shown in Figure 16-2.

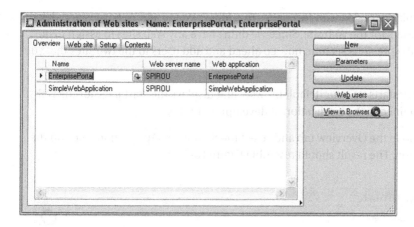

Figure 16-2. *The Web Sites form*

The first step is to create a site by using the New button or the standard keyboard short-cut. This brings up the Web site creation wizard, which is for the most part intuitive. The parts that require explanation are as follows:

- On the Web Application page of the wizard you need to select an existing Web application. The Shared/Private toggle button tells Axapta whether the application has been created as a private or a shared project—projects are explained in Chapter 18. Axapta comes out of the box with two shared Web applications. Create two sites and select the Enterprise Portal and SimpleWebApplication respectively for each.

- The language specified for the Web site is overridden by the language specified for the Web user, and used for users for whom no language has been specified.

- Specify development mode on systems where you might change the Web site or the underlying Web application. It flushes caches when the Web site is launched, ensuring that you have the latest code and data rather than something stale in a cache.

- Until you have played enough with Axapta Web sites to feel that you are an expert, accept the default values proposed by the wizard; there is not much to gain from fiddling with them during creation of the site and before you have tested that it runs as expected with the default settings. Once you have verified that your Web site is functioning as expected, you can use the Web Sites form to make any changes you want.

Let's take a close look at the buttons on this form:

- *New* fires up the wizard for creating new Web sites, as you have already seen.

- *Parameters* allows you to specify just that for Enterprise Portal—more about that in the "Enterprise Portal" section of this chapter.

- *Update* is extremely important; you must use it to push any changes you make to your Web application or Web site to IIS. Always do an update when you make changes to a Web site or underlying Web application.

- *Web Users* displays a dialog with two panes that allows you to add Web users and delete existing Web users for the Web site. Since we didn't have any Web sites to assign to our Web users in the previous section, now go ahead and add users to the two sites that you have created.

- *View in Browser* starts up your default browser and displays the start page for the Web site—this is defined in the application at development time.

Let's try it out. Go to the Overview tab and select the SimpleWebApplication, click on the View in Browser button. The result should resemble Figure 16-3.

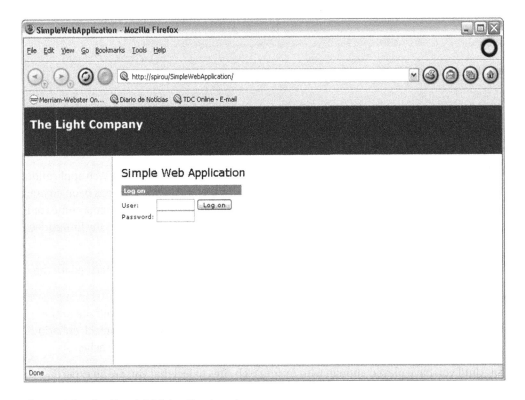

Figure 16-3. *The SimpleWebApplication site*

Now try logging in as one of the users that you have assigned to the site. The application behind this site doesn't include a lot of functionality, so it's a good one to use for checking if all the pieces that go into creating an Axapta Web site are up and working well.

Now select Enterprise Portal, fire it up, and log in. Bingo!—the full functionality of EP is in front of you.

Note You can develop your own sites from scratch or use one of the ones included with Axapta and customize it. Many people use EP as the base for their own custom solutions. However, you can (and in most cases *should*) build your solution from scratch, and include only what you need instead of all the stuff in EP. If you don't want to start from scratch, the SimpleWebApplication is a wise starting point.

To conclude this section we would like to encourage you to read the following section, "Enterprise Portal," even if you don't plan to use it. It contains some important details that will improve your understanding of things by providing some context.

Enterprise Portal

Axapta Enterprise Portal is a very extensive and sophisticated (but kind of ugly) role-based Web application. It exposes functionality and data through a Web site (i.e., the client is a Web browser instead of the Windows client provided with the product), and it requires a dedicated license code that also enables the employee role—licenses for other roles need to be purchased as extras.

Setup

The first step is to set up EP, and you have already seen how you can get it up and running using the EP setup wizard. The truth is that you don't need to use the wizard, and that you can simply map the Web users to normal users and manage what they can and can't do by managing the respective user-group permissions. This is the way to do it if you are going to build your own Web portal or customize EP and you don't really care about roles or about paying for the MBS EP role licenses.

Axapta includes seven predefined Web user groups that correspond to the roles currently available for EP, plus administrator and guest roles. These determine what functionality is available to a given user—more on roles in the "Roles" section.

If you want to set up EP via the setup wizard, use the main application menu path (Administration ➤ Setup ➤ Internet ➤ Enterprise Portal ➤ Setup Wizard)—this is the way to do it if you want to use EP as is. Here is what the wizard does for you:

- Imports some data before it even displays the welcome page; when the welcome page appears, click Next to go to the User Groups page. Here you can see all the user groups available and the roles they map to.

- Displays the Web panels that are available with EP—the Wizard page explains them.

- Displays the Web parts available with EP—conceptually similar to Microsoft Sharepoint Web parts.

- Displays the mapping between Axapta document types and EP document categories— if you run the wizard, at this point there will not be any types or categories.

- Displays the document categories per functional area—you can add and remove document categories if you wish.

- Allows you to specify the number of days that documents are shown in the news section of EP—the default is 7.

- Allows you to specify whether to count categories or not. Checking the Count Records check box instructs EP to hide menu items for document categories for which there are no documents—this feature impacts performance negatively, so we don't advise using it.

- Displays the categories available to the article system—a part of the integrated Content Management module that can be used to group and categorize articles. You can add and delete categories if you wish.

- Sets up the data crawler—a poor man's search engine for EP. The page allows you to specify which tables are to be indexed, and consequently which tables can be searched. This is a really ugly thing, since the data dictionary is not documented and generally no one except experienced developers and consultants has any idea which tables and fields are enabled for searching; often they are not the ones users would expect. Last but not least, you can always change the settings of the data crawler by using the main application menu Basic ➤ Setup ➤ Data Crawler ➤ Table Setup and Basic ➤ Setup ➤ Data Crawler ➤ Data Crawler respectively.

- Asks how often you want to run the data crawler and whether to start it when the wizard exits. The frequency with which the data crawler is run and the performance of your site impact when new data will be searchable.

- Asks when to run the transaction summary process. This process is run as a batch job and aggregates information on usage of EP on a customer basis.

- Informs you about additional setup steps that you have to perform when the wizard is finished.

- Displays a summary of the choices and selections you have made (which is of doubtful value). Press the Finish button to have the wizard persist your choices.

▓**Note** If you need a search engine, consider a commercial product that you can integrate with your database and Web portals. It's possible, however, to employ a trickery to actually provide good performance and search scope, but you'll need to refer to a book on advanced administration.

▓**Note** Tables that are indexed to use in searching are not automatically connected to an area of functionality—but they are associated with specific user roles. You can see the tables and add or delete them at the main application menu path Basic ➤ Setup ➤ Data Crawler ➤ Table Setup, and you need to use the Search tab in the Parameters form at the main application menu path Administration ➤ Setup ➤ Internet ➤ Enterprise Portal ➤ Parameters to add them to the different activity centers explicitly.

You can manage the base data for the wizard by using the forms at the following main application menu paths:

- Administration ➤ Setup ➤ Internet ➤ Web Panels

- Administration ➤ Setup ➤ Internet ➤ Web Parts

- Administration ➤ Setup ➤ Internet ➤ Enterprise Portal ➤ Parameters

Have a look around these forms to get an idea of what they are, but keep in mind that the wizard is the only way to associate all the different types of objects with EP roles.

■Tip If you are using single sign-on, as explained in Chapter 5, you need to use the Internet Information Services Manager to disable anonymous access to the Web site. Remember that the standard Axapta user that you are mapping Web users to must have a network account name.

Last but not least, the functionality that EP exposes relies on the existence of data such as product data. What you will be able to make practical use of depends on the data you have created as you've gone through the application chapters. Assuming that you imported the demo data in Chapter 3, you have enough data to be able to play around with EP.

Roles

The functionality available to a user after he has logged on to EP is determined by the user's role. A user can be assigned more then one role in which case he has access to the combined functionality of the assigned roles. The existing role definitions are based on typical job functions found in most modern business organizations.

The roles offered by Microsoft as of this writing provide the following functionality:

- *Customer*: Also covers what Microsoft designates as a guest (i.e., a potential customer). Guests can view the product catalog and register to become customers, while customers can browse the product catalog and purchase products.

- *Vendor*: Can maintain their account data, maintain price and discount data, view purchase orders, history and item data, and supplier data.

- *Employee*: A very limited role that can only look up contact information about other employees.

- *Sales*: Can issue, accept, and process quotations, sales orders, credit, contacts, pricing and product information, and request a variety of sales reports.

- *Consultant*: Can register time usage on projects, and view invoicing and time-usage data.

■Note New roles can be created if necessary, but it's no walk in the park. We understand the rationale of roles as a way of grouping functionality and access to the functionality; however, Axapta already has companies, user groups, and users, which serve the same purpose. Therefore, we fail to see any real purpose for EP roles other than as a sales gimmick that makes managing access to the system unnecessarily complicated and expensive. However, for now you are stuck with them.

■Note As you experiment with the EP Web site, you will notice that a series of questionnaires are available. These are created and maintained in the respective application modules and therefore we won't cover them here.

Content Management

The Content Management System (CMS) is not a content-management system in the terms we normally think of, such as Microsoft's own CMS, Vignette, and Stellent. It's a simple system for publishing articles, running discussion forums, and conducting online polls within a Web site.

In practice, the Axapta CMS is part of EP and requires that you have an EP license code. Additionally, it's setup automatically when you use the EP setup wizard. You can, however, use it independently of EP in your own Web applications and sites.

Parameters

Setting up the Axapta CMS starts with defining a few simple parameters using the form at the main application menu path Administration ➤ Setup ➤ Internet ➤ Content Management ➤ Parameters. Here you can specify the e-mail messages to use for notifying article proofreaders and approvers—you can select from the standard list created by the administrator or define your own.

■**Note** Remember that you can create needed data in lookup fields by clicking on the field with the right mouse button and selecting the Go to the Main Table menu item. In the case of the CMS parameters e-mail messages, you can use the main application menu path Basic ➤ Setup ➤ E-mail Messages.

Finally, you can specify a document type to use when users attach a document to an article. If you don't specify one, then users can't attach documents to articles.

Categories

The next step is to define the categories of articles that users can see and subscribe to using the form at Administration ➤ Setup ➤ Internet ➤ Content Management ➤ Categories, which resembles Figure 16-4.

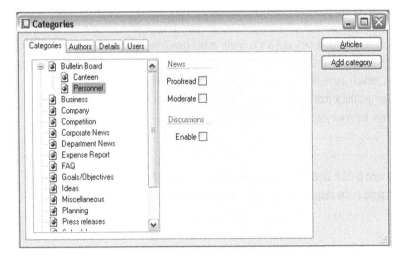

Figure 16-4. *The Article Categories form*

The Categories tab displays a tree of all the existing categories to the left of the tab page. To the right of the tab page you can mark the selected category as requiring proofreading and having a moderator as well as a discussion forum by checking the respective boxes. You can use the right mouse button and the pop-up menu or the Add Category button to create a category under the one selected, and the Articles button to associate and create articles associated with the category.

■**Note** One small catch is that there is no way to create a root category from here. A root category is always selected and therefore any new categories you create will always be subnodes of whichever category is selected. Settings are not inherited by child nodes for either the Categories tab or the Authors tab.

The Authors tab is where you specify which users can do what to documents within the selected category. If you have checked the Proofread and Moderator check boxes on the Categories tab, you will also be able to specify these functions for each user that you add, as well as make the user an author and/or administrator of the category.

The Details tab allows you to change the name of the selected category and to specify whether Web users can decide for themselves if they want to see articles for the category.

The Users tab allows you to specify and see which users are subscribed to the selected article category.

News Articles

The next step is to create articles designated as news articles. You can do this directly from the Web site for the categories for which you are configured as an author—log in first. Alternatively, you can use the main application menu form at Administration ➤ Setup ➤ Internet ➤ Content Management ➤ Categories, which will display a form resembling Figure 16-5.

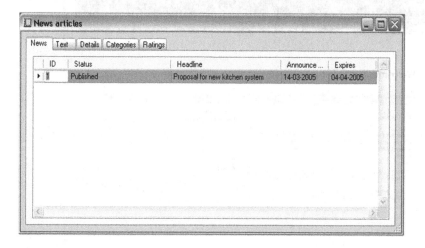

Figure 16-5. *The News Articles form*

This is where you create and manage news articles to be displayed at your site using the Axapta Windows client.

On the News tab you create articles, provide a unique ID, and assign a status—it's then changed as the article is processed by the proofreader, the author, and the administrator. The headline is useful when the article is to be made visible to subscribers, and the Announce and Expires settings determine when the article will debut on the site and be removed from it.

The Text and Details tabs are pretty straightforward; the text tab is where you enter the short text of the article and the body. Details is where you add a field to specify the author of the article.

Note The author doesn't default to the logged-on user; though this seems like an oversight, you may want to specify an author other than the current user to create articles on behalf of others or to use a pseudonym for articles that may be controversial.

The Categories tab is where you can specify under which categories the article is to be displayed—you can select as many as you like. Subcategories do not inherit from parents.

The last tab, Ratings, shows information about how Web users rate the article—here you can also change the ratings if you don't like them.

That wraps it up, but before you continue we recommend that you try using the EP Web site to do what you have just learned. Once you have logged in as a user with author permission, you will be presented with the main page of the EP site, which will resemble Figure 16-6.

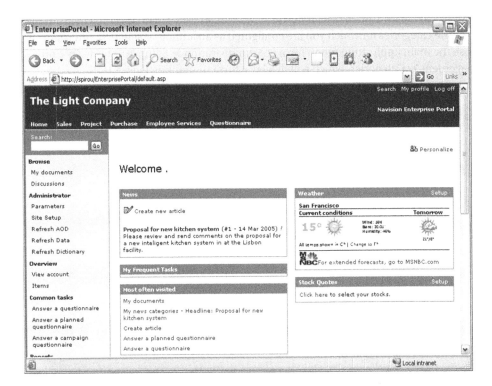

Figure 16-6. *The EnterprisePortal main page*

The left side of the page is the EP menu, which is how you navigate. Select My Documents and go to the corresponding page, where you can see the documents you have authored, edit them, and create new ones. It should resemble Figure 16-7, but contain the articles that you have created in the categories that the current user is subscribed to. What you can do here should be quite intuitive to you by now, so just experiment with it.

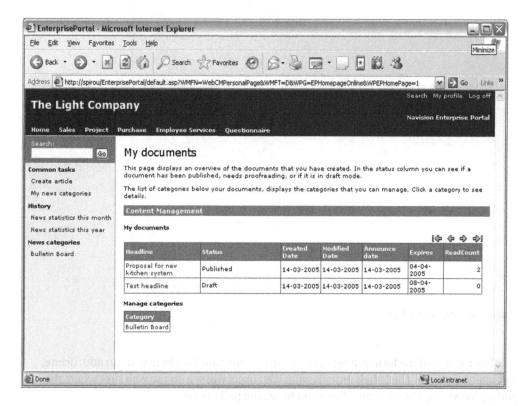

Figure 16-7. *The EnterprisePortal My Documents page*

Polls

The last feature of CMS is the ability to conduct online polls. Before you can use a poll, you need to create it using the main application menu form at path Administration ➤ Setup ➤ Internet ➤ Content Management ➤ Polls, as shown in Figure 16-8.

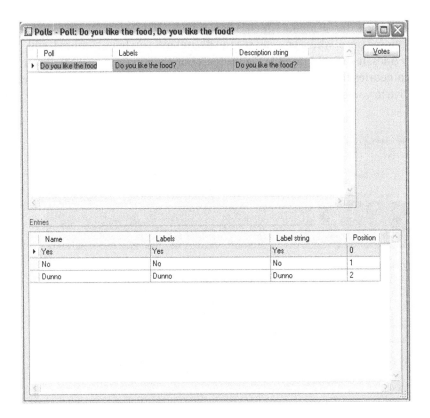

Figure 16-8. *The Polls form*

The top half of the form is a list of the existing polls, and it's where you can add, delete, and maintain them. The Labels entry is what Web users will see on the Web sites where the poll is placed. The Votes button allows you to see the poll results.

The bottom half of the form displays options that are available for the selected poll. As with the list of polls, you can add, delete, and maintain the options here. However; keep in mind that changing options—*entries* in Axapta-speak—is not a good idea once the poll has gone live.

The next step is to add the poll to a Web site. Open the Web Panels form at the main application menu path Administration ➤ Setup ➤ Internet ➤ Web Panels. In the Panel tab you can select a panel that is used at the site where you want to post the poll—select EPGenericHome for now. Go to the Content tab—this displays a list of the Weblets associated with the Web panel. Select the Poll Weblet and then click on the Properties button to see the properties panel shown in Figure 16-9.

Figure 16-9. *The Online Poll form*

In the WebPollId field, select the poll that you have just created.

Now open the Web Sites form from the main application menu path Administration ➤ Setup ➤ Internet ➤ Web Sites and go to the Setup tab. Click on the pencil icon to the right of the Web Application field. This displays the project structure in the Project Manager window. Find the Web Pages folder at the root and expand it and the Standard subfolder. Select the page where you want to include the poll—for now, select the EP home page, entitled EPHomePageOnline.

Double-click on the icon that represents the node, or right-click and select the Edit menu option. This opens the page in the Web application editor where you can define the content and layout of the page in question. It will resemble Figure 16-10, but without the poll Weblet and menu.

Now select the Insert ➤ Navision Axapta Element ➤ Weblet menu option. It opens the Weblets form, from which you can select the Weblet to add—select the Online Poll Weblet and double-click on it or press the OK button on the form. A large rectangular bitmap representing the Weblet is placed wherever your cursor is positioned on the Web application. This automatically displays the properties form for the Weblet (see Figure 16-9), where you have to select your poll in the WebPollId field. Then drag your poll to a position where it looks relatively attractive—below the Error Handler Weblet, for example.

■**Note** When you insert a Weblet, it's a good idea to place the cursor where you want to display the results at runtime, or it will be placed at the top automatically, and it's not easy to reposition it afterward.

■**Note** The Web application editor is not totally WYSIWYG when it comes to Weblets, so the page may look a bit different when it's displayed in a browser.

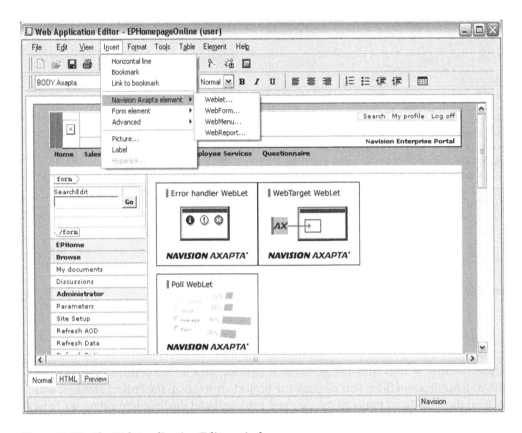

Figure 16-10. *The Web Application Editor window*

Save the changes you have made by using the keyboard shortcut Ctrl+S or by using the File menu on the menu bar.

That's it! Open the Web Sites form discussed in the "Web Sites" section of this chapter and use the Update button to push your changes out to the IIS, then relaunch the EP Web site by your preferred means, log in, and check it out.

■**Note** Each user can vote only once per poll, and what information the Weblet will display depends on the Online Poll properties for the poll and the Weblet—again, see Figure 16-9.

Wrap-Up

In this chapter we have covered the following:

- What you need to do to deliver Axapta functionality and data over the Web

- Getting Enterprise Portal up and running

- How to use the Content Management System, articles, discussion forums, and polls

At this point you should have a good idea of what Axapta offers for exchanging information with other systems, how it exposes itself over the Web, and what you need to get the features in the standard distribution up and running. Last but not least, you have learned how you can hook into Axapta to use it your own way when the standard package falls short of your needs.

We really recommend that you play with the modules, their settings, and different setup combinations, and test, test, test anything you do before you drop it in to a production system. Make sure your test environment is exactly the same as your production environment, down to all the operating system settings—these modules are quirky, and experience is the only thing that will save you some major headaches.

You can read more about the topics in this chapter in the following document, available in the documentation folder of the product distribution package or CD:

- *AX-300-USG-010-v01.00-ENUS.pdf*: Internet

CHAPTER 17

■ ■ ■

Architecture

This chapter discusses how Axapta is constructed and can be deployed—that is, the bits and pieces that make up the Axapta system and how you can use them. As with any complex system, Axapta's architecture can be viewed from different perspectives. It's important to understand how the different pieces of the system can be deployed across a network of computers and where to place code when developing and customizing the system.

Anyone can benefit from reading this chapter and understanding how Axapta is pieced together, but it's a must for developers and system administrators, and is highly recommended for consultants and anyone involved in managing, designing, and evaluating Axapta solutions.

Knowing how the different components of the system work together from the different viewpoints is fundamental to getting the most out of Axapta and addressing business requirements such as scalability, up-time, response time, system and data security, and geographical distribution. The locations and purposes of folders and files are important when adding your own code and metadata, when distributing it, when deciding what data to place and where to place it, when putting together a backup strategy, and when something goes wrong and you need those backups. The situations in which you will benefit from this chapter are too numerous to list here, but we recommend familiarizing yourself with the information here so you know where to find it when you need it.

Knowledge of the topics covered here is also important when you're ready to go beyond what we tell you in this book and what you will find in existing documentation. The chapter is comprehensive and detailed, so you can use it as reference when you need a refresher on what is located where and what it's used for.

The following topics are covered here:

- Applications, clients, and servers

- Folder and files

- Application layering

- System configurations

Axapta is designed to be very flexible, so we can't cover all the ways you can assemble it into a solution. Use what you pick up here as a base for your own system designs and configurations, keeping in mind the following:

- *Network bandwidth and latency*: How the different components communicate with each other

- *Hardware requirements, performance, and response times of the different components*: Where and what is executed, where data resides, and how it's read and written to persistent storage

- *How to secure your system and data*: A combination of the first set of points

Applications, Clients, and Servers

Axapta started as a client/server system, from which it evolved into a multitier system. This evolution was not achieved by redesigning the client/server architecture, but by creating a new multitier system that can coexist with the original client/server architecture.

This means that Axapta has two architectures. You can choose the one that best suits your needs, or you can leverage both simultaneously depending on what best fits the needs of specific user groups, functions, and geographical locations within your organization.

When Axapta was installed, only the application and the client components were required. These are the components necessary for deploying Axapta in the simplest mode—that is, in a client/server setup—commonly designated as 2-tier. At the same time, the Axapta Object Server (AOS) 3-tier mode also was installed. Axapta was started in 2-tier mode to set it up, and after this initial setup we switched to 3-tier mode.

■**Caution** It's very important to remember the peculiarity of Axapta's mixing of architectures. You must always set up and start Axapta in 2-tier mode the first time after you have installed it, even if you do not plan to deploy it in 2-tier mode.

2-Tier Setup

The Axapta 2-tier setup includes the following components:

- *Application*: This is where all the business logic and metadata definitions reside—form, report, menu definitions, etc.

- *Client*: This is where the application is executed and the interaction with the end user is handled.

- *Database*: This is where all business and system data is persisted.

As you can see, you are now looking at three components. What about the 2-tier mode? In practice and from a runtime viewpoint, the client reads the application definitions from the files typically placed on a dedicated Application File Server and handles user interaction (the presentation logic) and executes the application code in its memory space (the business logic layer). The combination of the two makes up a tier. The database executes in another memory space and constitutes the second tier. Notice that the client interacts directly with the database tier. This deployment configuration is commonly known as a client/server architecture, which is shown in Figure 17-1.

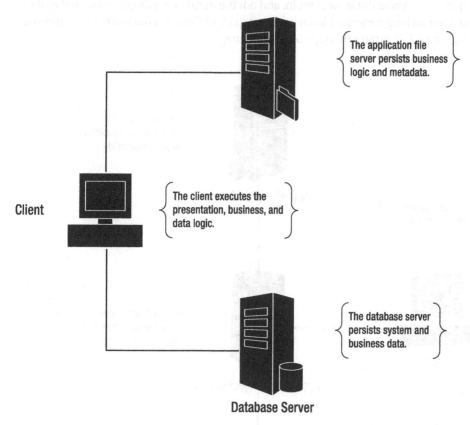

Figure 17-1. *2-tier setup*

■Note Clients in 2-tier setups are generally designated as "fat" clients, meaning that they handle both the presentation and the business logic.

3-Tier Setup

3-tier setups are somewhat more complex and come with some interesting twists, so let's look at what they are made of:

- *Application*: This is where all the business logic and metadata definitions reside—form, report, menu definitions, etc.

- *Application Object Server*: This is where the application is executed and data access is performed in "thin" mode.

- *Client*: This is where interaction with the end user is handled and data access is performed in "fat" mode.

- *Database*: This is where all business and system data is persisted.

We have already determined that the number of tiers has to do with how many independent memory spaces the whole thing executes in, and not the number of components. That is, the application layer no longer executes in the memory space of the client but of a new component, the AOS. Figure 17-2 illustrates this type of architecture.

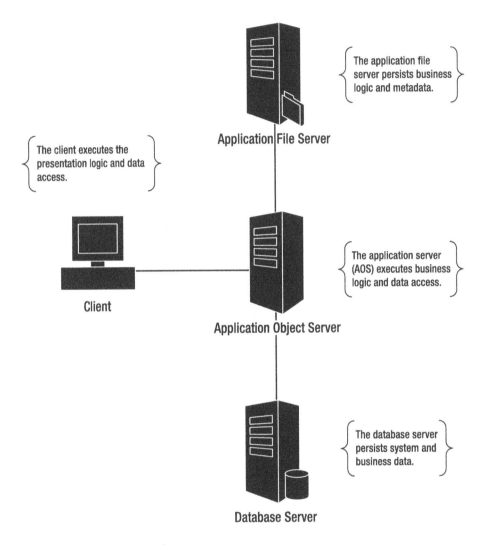

The application file server persists business logic and metadata.

Application File Server

The client executes the presentation logic and data access.

Client

The application server (AOS) executes business logic and data access.

Application Object Server

The database server persists system and business data.

Database Server

Figure 17-2. *3-tier thin mode setup*

Note In a 3-tier fat-mode setup, the client would communicate directly with the database server instead of using the AOS.

What makes 3-tier setups interesting in Axapta is the fact that the clients can be of two types:

- *Fat client*: The AOS executes the application on behalf of the client; however, the client directly accesses the database.

- *Thin client*: The AOS executes the application on behalf of the client and also brokers all access to the database for clients.

In practice, 3-tier mode is either real 3-tier mode or a 2.5-tier mode, depending on the type of client you select. The latter (or 2.5-tier fat client) theory is that allowing the client to access the database directly off-loads processing to clients instead of hammering your servers, and consequently improves system performance. See Figure 17-3.

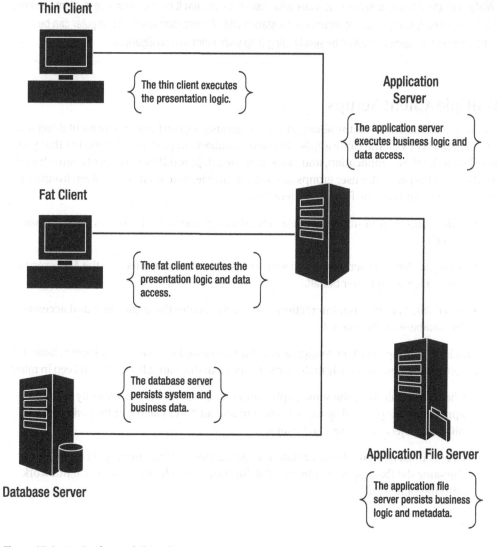

Figure 17-3. *3-tier fat and thin client setup*

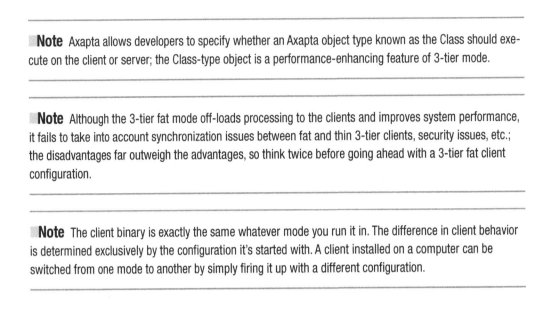

■**Note** Axapta allows developers to specify whether an Axapta object type known as the Class should execute on the client or server; the Class-type object is a performance-enhancing feature of 3-tier mode.

■**Note** Although the 3-tier fat mode off-loads processing to the clients and improves system performance, it fails to take into account synchronization issues between fat and thin 3-tier clients, security issues, etc.; the disadvantages far outweigh the advantages, so think twice before going ahead with a 3-tier fat client configuration.

■**Note** The client binary is exactly the same whatever mode you run it in. The difference in client behavior is determined exclusively by the configuration it's started with. A client installed on a computer can be switched from one mode to another by simply firing it up with a different configuration.

Multiple-Client Setups

The Axapta architecture has the ability to simultaneously support combinations of 2-tier and 3-tier client setups on the same application and database. In practice, this means that you install your database, application, and AOSs, and then deploy different types of clients based on what best fits particular user groups and the requirements of their physical environment. You can deploy and mix the following client setups:

- *2-tier*: Handles user interaction, executes the application, and accesses the database directly.

- *3-tier fat*: Handles user interaction and accesses the database directly—the AOS executes the application on their behalf.

- 3-*tier thin*: Handles user interaction—the AOS executes the application and accesses the database on their behalf.

This is done using the client configuration utility discussed in Chapter 2. All these clients can work together and simultaneously in the same system, but there are a few things to keep in mind:

- Clients must all share the same application (i.e., 2-tier clients must specify the same application as specified by the AOS for thin and fat 3-tier clients, or they will execute different object definitions and code).

- Clients must all share the same database (i.e., 2-tier and fat 3-tier clients must specify the same database specified by the AOS for thin 3-tier clients, or they will not work with the same data).

- Mixing clients that directly access the database with clients that use the AOS for data access can result in synchronization delays between data cached in the AOS and the database; that is, changes to data in 3-tier thin clients are not persisted immediately, creating a delay in availability to clients that access the database directly.

- Using multiple AOSs is equally problematic, even if they use the same database. If you need to have multiple AOSs to support larger user loads, the solution is to configure them as part of an AOS cluster so they will synchronize.

Reasons for using the different types of clients with a common database and application are as follows:

- Reduce load on AOSs by off-loading processing of business logic to 2-tier clients.

- Reduce load on AOSs by off-loading data access to 2-tier and 3-tier fat clients.

- Support low-end clients by centralizing processing of business logic on AOSs.

- Support low-end clients by centralizing data access on AOSs.

- Enforce centralized access control of users with 3-tier thin clients.

- Hide the physical location of the application from 3-tier fat and thin clients.

- Hide the physical location of the database from 3-tier thin clients.

Multiple-AOS Setups

In Axapta, you can run multiple instances of the AOS on the same server computer independently of each other, or run multiple instances as part of an AOS cluster on the same server computer or distributed over multiple server computers.

This ability to run multiple AOSs simultaneously can be viewed from two different perspectives:

- *Running several AOSs in a cluster*: Allows you to scale up your system to follow increases in demand for server performance and provides a round-robin form of load balancing for the servers and system resilience.

- *Running several AOSs separately*: Allows you to share the same hardware for different installations.

Let's look at what's in it for you and how you can deploy an AOS cluster:

- You achieve resilience by configuring an AOS cluster on different server computers or multiple AOS instances on the same computer. If one AOS dies then the other AOSs will continue to serve your users—running multiple AOS instances on different server computers provides a higher degree of resilience than running multiple instances on the same computer.

- You achieve scalability by running multiple AOS instances on different computers and being able to add new server computers and AOS instances to increase the overall performance of the system.

■**Note** In a 3-tier configuration, the AOS management service connects a client to a server and does load balancing. However, once the AOS management service has assigned a server to a client, the client works with that server for the remainder of its session (i.e., until it logs off). This means that load balancing distributes users evenly among the nodes in an AOS cluster; it does not ensure a balanced load on the nodes that participate in a cluster.

Figure 17-4 illustrates this at a glance.

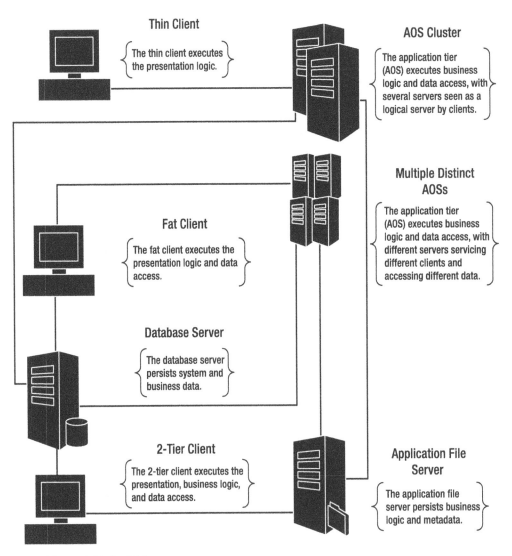

Figure 17-4. *Multiple-AOS setup*

> ■**Note** An AOS cluster appears to clients as one single logical system, so if one goes down, the server manager stops assigning it to client requests. However, because a client is actually assigned to a specific AOS for the length of its session, if the AOS crashes the session is lost.

Multiple-Application Setups

When you create an Axapta configuration using the client or AOS configuration utilities, you specify which application and database to use for the configuration. Here are some typical applications for this feature:

- As a developer, you develop and maintain several different customized applications, one for customer A and another for customer B. By creating a configuration that uses the same client and AOS but different applications and databases, you can start up both applications on your workstation or on a development server when you need them, and you don't need separate physical environments. You can run the two applications simultaneously, each in its own memory space. The code base and data will be different even though the Axapta client and AOS are on the same physical hardware.

- As an administrator, you can centralize and consolidate your infrastructure by setting up different databases on the same database server for development, test, and production systems, and then make a configuration that points to the application where development takes place, another for the application where you test, and one for your production application. When developers are finished with a feature they copy it to the test application, and when testers are happy they copy it to the production application. Everyone can share the same AOS server machine application disk server, and database server while actually working on different versions of the application without interfering with each other.

- In a geographically distributed organization, different branch offices can have local copies of the client application and AOS but share a database. In this way, you minimize traffic to data flowing back and forth between the branches and your central database. However, any changes to your production application must be applied to all the branches where there is a local copy. You also can have local databases that replicate to a central database, enabling the branches to operate even if there is no access to the central system where all data is consolidated.

Figure 17-5 illustrates this.

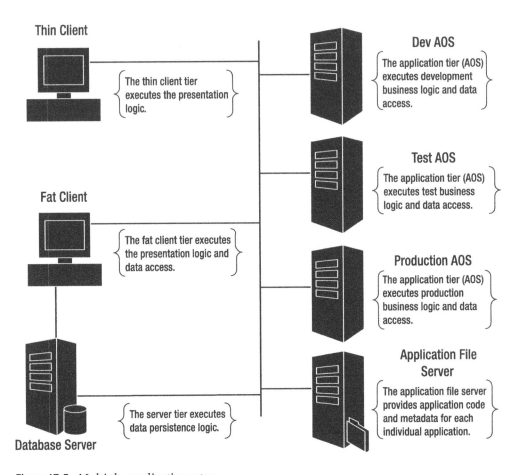

Figure 17-5. *Multiple-application setup*

That's it in a nutshell; in the next section you'll see the components' physical makeup.

Folders and Files

When you installed Axapta, three folder structures were created, and if you followed our naming recommendations you have them on the selected disk as *Axapta_Application*, *Axapta_Client*, and *Axapta_Server*.

■**Note** You must always install the client and application components and the corresponding files. The server component is installed only if you decide to have a 3-tier configuration, and consequently the AOS files will be there or not depending on your decision.

Each of the components we have looked at in the previous section is made up of a series of files that are grouped together in corresponding folder structures. Knowing these is particularly important for development and backup purposes.

As a developer, knowing where the different objects in Axapta are gives you an understanding of how the system physically functions and what goes on as you customize it and add your own code and metadata. As a system administrator, you need to know what to back up and restore, and when to do so.

The following sections provide a detailed description of the folder structures and files that make up the Axapta system by component.

Application

The application component is the X++ code and metadata representing the business applications, such as forms, reports, and tables. The root of this group is the *Axapta_Application* folder (or whatever you decided to call the folder at installation). In Figure 17-6, you can see the folder structure as it looks in Windows Explorer.

Figure 17-6. *Application folder tree*

■**Note** Notice that we have a Playground application—this is the application we use for experimenting. We also have preserved the standard application in case we need to get back to a clean start.

The application has the most complex structure of all the Axapta components. Table 17-1 lists and describes the full folder structure, its contents, and the purpose of each file.

Table 17-1. *Axapta_Application Folder Contents*

Folder Name	File	Description
Appl		This is the root folder for all applications. You can have several applications. By cre-ating different configurations using the tools provided with the client and server com-ponents, you can connect specific groups of users with specific applications or you can switch between different customized applications that have been installed.
		If you have more than one application, you need to place them here. For example, you could have a sub-folder called "Development" for a development environment and a sub-folder called "Test" for a test environment. In a production environment, you will typically only have one application that by default is named "Standard". Developers will, however, typically have an application for each project they are working on, as will testers. You can select a configuration that points to application A, B, or C (depending on which customer project you want to work on) and run Axapta with the corresponding application.
		Another common use of this ability is to have a development application that developers use to customize Axapta, a test system where consultants and users can validate stable features delivered from the development system, and a production system for business users where features are made available once they have been validated on the test system. In this way, whatever one group is doing does not interfere with the other groups even though they may all be working on the same physical system using the same client and AOS.
	axappl.ico	Axapta standard icon—it's used by the WebDeploy utility.
Appl\Standard		This is the standard application from MBS that is installed when you install the application component. We recommend that you do not use this application. Instead, make a copy that you can work with and set your configurations to point to it—call the copy "folder work," for example. That way if you blow up your appli-cation or it's too much work to recover it to a previous state after you have hacked away at it, you can simply make a new copy of the standard application and you have a clean application to work with. See Chapter 19 for details on how to do this with the standard database.

Folder Name	File	Description
	axsys.aod	The Axapta Object Data file for the SYS application layer. This file contains the application code and metadata that make up the application. Each layer has an AOD file. The naming pattern is *ax[layername].aod*. This applies to normal application layers as well as to patch layers—you can read about layers later in this chapter.
	axapd.aoi	The Axapta Object Index file for the whole application. This file contains an index of the contents of all the AOD files to make it easier and faster for Axapta to find the code it needs when it needs it.
	Axsysen-us.ahd	The Axapta Application Help Documentation for US English for the system layer. Each application layer language that has application documentation has an AHD file. The naming pattern is *ax[layer][languagecode].ahd*, where DA is Danish, EN-US is US English, etc., and the layers are SYS to USR. This documentation is displayed in the AOT beneath the Application Documentation node, and/or when the user presses F1.
	Axapden-us.ahi	The Axapta Application Help Index for US English for all layers. Each language that has application documentation has an AHI file. The naming pattern is *axapd[languagecode].ahi*, where DA is Danish, EN-US is US English, etc.
	axsysen-us.add	The Axapta Application Developer Documentation for US English for the system layer. Each application layer that has application documentation has an ADD file but only US English exists. The naming pattern is *ax[layer][languagecode].add*. This documentation is available in the AOT beneath the Application Developer Documentation node.
	axpden-us.adi	The Axapta Application Developer Documentation Index for US English, for all layers. Each language that has application developer documentation has an AHI file. The naming pattern is *axapd[languagecode].adi*, where DA is Danish, EN-US is US English, etc.
	axsysen-us.khd	The Axapta Kernel Help for US English for the system layer. Each application layer language that has application documentation has a KHD file. The naming pattern is *ax[layer][languagecode].khd*. This documentation is available in the AOT beneath the System Documentation node, and is available only in US English.

(Continued)

Table 17-1. *Continued*

Folder Name	File	Description
	axpden-us.khi	The Axapta System Documentation Index for Danish, for all layers. Each language that has system documentation has a KHI file. The naming pattern is *axapd[languagecode].khi*.
	axapden-us.alt	The Axapta Label Temporary Store for US English. It is used by Axapta to save newly created labels until it flushes them to permanent storage. Each language that has labels has an ALT file. The naming pattern is *axapd[languagecode].alt*, where DA is Danish, EN-US is US English, etc.
	axsysen-us.ald	The Axapta Label Data for US English. It is used by Axapta to save labels when flushing the ALT file. Each language that has labels has an ALT file. The naming pattern is *ax[layer][languagecode].ald*, where DA is Danish, EN-US is US English, etc.
	axsysen-us.ali	The Axapta Label Index for US English. Each language has labels has an ALT file. The naming pattern is *ax[layer][languagecode].ali*.
	axsysen-us.alc	The Axapta Application Label Comments file. Each language that has labels has an ALT file. The naming pattern is *ax[layer][languagecode].alc*, where DA is Danish, EN-US is US English, etc.
	axdat.udb	Persisted information about user sessions such as login time. The file is created the first time a user logs in.
Bin		Contains a license in plain text and RTF formats and a Readme file.
Log		Contains log files. This is the default placing of all log files related to the applications placed under the Appl folder.
Share		Contains a variety of files that are used if the application is run in shared mode. If the application is not run in shared mode, then the corresponding files in the client installation folder are used.
Share\Config		Initially empty. Suggested by Axapta when you export and/or save application configuration data, such as your configuration key setup.
Share\Include		Contains icons, graphics, and AVI files used when rendering the user interface.
Share\Include\Web		Contains three subfolders and no files. Contains ASP examples of using the Business Connector and graphics used in Web applications.

Folder Name	File	Description
Share\Include\Web\Apps		Contains folders representing Web applications.
Share\Include\Web\Apps\ EmployeeSelfService		This folder is used for option pack provider files.
Share\Include\Web\Apps\ PeformanceManagement		This folder is used for option pack provider files.
Share\Include\Web\Images		This folder is used for option pack provider files.
Share\Include\smm		This folder is used for option pack provider files.
Std		Label and help files are backed up to this folder during installation. The files are copied to the *Shared* and *Application* folders if the application is to be run in non-shared mode.

■**Note** ALD files are updated in 3-tier mode only when the AOS is shut down, and when the client shuts down in 2-tier mode. That means that if your system does not shut down properly (it crashes), then you will lose any created labels because they will not be flushed to the ALD file. The good news is that they will still be in the ALT file and a crafty Axapta developer can recover them.

Client

The client component is the Windows 32 executable and end-user interface to the system. The root of this group is the *Axapta_Client* folder or whatever you decided to name the folder during installation. Figure 17-7 gives a quick visual presentation of the folder structure as it looks in Windows Explorer.

Figure 17-70. *Client folder tree*

For the most part, the folder structure of the client component is the same as for the application, but several folders are empty. Table 17-2 lists and describes what you will find in it.

Table 17-2. *Axpata_Client Folder Contents*

Folder Name	Files	Description
Appl		Contains some of the same folders that you will find in the application folder structure but there are no files other than *axappl.ico*.
Bin		Contains the client executables, Help files, and Kernel Translation files.
	ax32.exe	The Axapta Windows client executable.
	AxConfig.exe	The Axapta client configuration utility.
	AxDebug.exe	The Axapta debugger.
	[name].chm	Help files.
	Axsysen-us.ktd	US English kernel translation data file for the SYS layer. This file is where Axapta persists kernel messages for the SYS layer. Each application layer language that has kernel data has a KTD file. The naming pattern is *ax[layer][languagecode].ktd*, where DA is Danish, EN-US is US English, etc.
	Sxsysen-us.kti	US English kernel translation data index for the SYS layer. This file indexes the objects in the KTD file for faster access. Each application layer language that has kernel translation data has a KTI file. The naming pattern *isax[layer][languagecode].kti*, where DA is Danish, EN-US is US English, etc.
	[name].dll [name].ocx	Dynamic link libraries and ActiveX controls used by the client component.
Log		Contains log files. Log file placement defaults to the corresponding folder under the application installation folder, but it can be useful to specify in your client configurations to place them under the client, particularly if you are running different client configurations and don't want to mix up the log files.
Share		Contains a variety of files that the client uses if the application is not run in shared mode.
Share\Config		Initially empty. Suggested by Axapta when you export and/or save client configurations. If they are specific to a client, then this is as good a place as any. However, if the same configurations are used by other clients, then placing them in the corresponding folder under the application installation folder is probably a better idea because it's shared.

Folder Name	Files	Description
Share\Include		Contains the same as the corresponding application folder.
Share\Include\Web		Contains the same as the corresponding application folder.
Share\Include\Web\Apps		Contains the same as the corresponding application folder.
Share\Include\Web\Apps\ EmployeeSelfService		Contains the same as the corresponding application folder.
Share\Include\Web\Apps\ PeformanceManagement		Contains the same as the corresponding application folder.
Share\Include\Web\Images		Contains the same as the corresponding application folder.
Share\Include\smm		Contains the same as the corresponding application folder.
Std		Label and help files are backed up to this folder during installation. The files are copied to the *Shared* and *Application* folders if the application is to be run in non-shared mode.

■**Note** The DLLs and OCXs needed by a client must be present on all systems on which clients are installed when running in 2-tier mode or in 3-tier mode if the code executes on the client. This applies to any DLLs or OCXs needed by any custom code that you add to Axapta. For example, if you write a statistics library in C++, pack it in a DLL, and use it in your application code, then you must remember to make it available to all the clients installed around the organization.

Server

The server component (also called AOS) is the Windows 32 executable application server. The root of this group is the *Axapta_Server* folder or whatever you decided to name the folder during installation. Even though the server has a very simple folder structure for the sake of consistency, Figure 17-8 gives a visual representation of the folder structure as it looks in Windows Explorer.

Figure 17-8. *Server folder tree*

Let's look at the files, listed and described in Table 17-3.

Table 17-3. *Axpata_Server Folder Contents*

Folder Name	Files	Description
Bin		Contains the server executables, Help files, and Kernel Translation files.
	ax32serv.exe	The Axapta server executable.
	Ax32Mgr.exe	The Axapta server manager utility. This is a Windows service.
	AxAdSetup.exe	The Axapta Active Directory setup wizard.
	AxCtrl.exe	The Axapta server configuration utility.
	[name].chm	Help files.
	Axsysen-us.ktd	US English kernel data file for the SYS layer. This file is where Axapta persists metadata (definitions for menus, forms, etc.). Each application-layer language that has kernel data has a KTD file. The naming pattern is *ax[layer][languagecode].ktd*, where DA is Danish, EN-US is US English, etc.
	Sxsysen-us.kti	US English kernel data index for the SYS layer. This file indexes the objects in the KTD file for faster access. Each application-layer language that has kernel data has a KTI file. The naming pattern is *ax[layer][languagecode].kti*, where DA is Danish, EN-US is US English, etc.
	[name].dll *[name].ocx*	Dynamic link libraries and ActiveX controls used by the client component.

■ **Note** As with the client, DLLs and OCXs needed by the server must be present on all systems on which servers are installed. This applies to any DLLs or OCXs needed by any custom code that you add to Axapta and that executes on the server. In 3-tier mode, if you keep code in such customizations to execute on the server side, you have to deploy only your DLLs and OCXs to the servers.

Log Files

Because log files can be very important for managing your system and for debugging purposes, we decided to give them a section of their own. Several log files may be present in the log directory of the application or client, depending on your logging options. Table 17-4 lists them.

Table 17-4. *Log Files*

File	Content
TrcAxaptaSync.log	Log of all synchronization events performed, showing all changes done to the schema (i.e., tables).
TrcAxaptaError.log	Log of all SQL errors, showing the error code and text generated.
TrcSQL-[UsrName].log	Logs all SQL statements executed by the named user. It is generated only when SQL tracing is enabled in the user options and the Write to File check box of the Multiple SQL Statements field group is checked.

File	Content
TrcLongQuery-[UserName].log	Logs all SQL statements executed by the named user exceeding the time limit specified in the Threshold field of the Long Queries field group of the user options. It is generated only when SQL tracing is enabled in the user options and the Write to File check box of the Long Queries field group is checked.
TrcWarning-[UserName].log	Logs all SQL warnings for statements executed by the named user. It is generated only when SQL tracing is enabled in the user options and the Write to File check box of the Warnings field group is checked.
TrcDeadlocks-[UserName].log	Logs all database deadlocks for statements executed by the named user. It is generated only when SQL tracing is enabled in the user options and the Write to File check box of the Deadlocks field group is checked.
[ClassName]Comp.log *[ClassName]prco.log*	Logs information about the compilation of a class, including actions and errors.
[MethodName]Comp.log *[MethodName]prco.log*	Logs information about the compilation of a class method, including actions and errors.
[NodeName]exp.log	Logs information about the AOT exported node. The node name is truncated to five characters.
[NodeName]imp.log	Logs information about the AOT imported node. The node name is truncated to five characters. Imported objects are compiled, and will generally be accompanied by class and method log files.

■**Note** Compilation and AOT export and import log files are by default placed in the operating system default path for your documents (e.g., C:\Documents and Settings\[UserName]\My Documents in Windows XP). We suggest that you specify an alternative in the client configuration. For these logs to be generated, compile logging needs to be activated by checking the AOT Log check box on the Compiler Setup tab page in the user options.

■**Note** Enabling compilation logging generates a file per class and one per method in each class compiled. It can result in a lot of files being generated, so consider compiling only the files that you need as opposed to recompiling the whole system. Unfortunately, the compile output window is not a lot of use if you compile a large group of classes—its buffer is small and the compile results will scroll off the buffer of the compile window, which is by default 1,000 lines but can be changed in the Development tab page's Message Limit control or the User Options form.

The same idea applies to imports and exports. They output any errors that occur to the Axapta info log where you can see them. Printing them to file is useful only if you need to keep the log.

This is the most comprehensive description of files in the Axapta system that exists, so you now know at least as much about them as the most seasoned developers. Keep this section handy until you know them off the top of your head.

Application Layers

The Axapta application component consists of metadata definitions for objects like forms and reports, and code written in the X++ language. All of these exist technically in the same flat name space. However, Axapta implements a layering system that provides a hierarchy of levels in the application source code where definitions and code in the higher levels supersede definitions and code in the lower levels. The best way to visualize this is as an inheritance hierarchy.

When you log in to Axapta, you work in the layer specified by your login parameters and you can customize any object that exists in the layers below your work layer. When you save your changes to an objects definition or code and save it, Axapta actually creates a new object definition with a new ID and saves it in your working layer, where it overrides the underlying definition.

■**Note** What Axapta actually saves when you customize an object is a delta—the changes you have made in your working layer—and the rest is inherited from the layers below.

At runtime, Axapta walks through its application layers, top-down—from USR to SYS—until it finds the first definition of the object it's looking for. If, for example, a user has customized the Sales Order form while working in the USR layer, then Axapta will have two definitions of the Sales Order form, one in the SYS layer and one in the USR layer, each with a unique ID. When you try to run the sales form, Axapta determines from its ID that your custom definition is in a higher layer than the standard Sales Order form and uses it instead of the standard definition in the SYS layer.

■**Note** Table 17-5 lists ID ranges for each application layer. Because Axapta object definitions and code exist in a flat name space, Axapta assigns an ID number to every object definition it creates. At execution, it can determine the layer a specific object belongs to from its ID range.

Because any changes you make to the system exist only in the layer you are working on and do not change the definitions in the layers below, if you regret any customization you have made, simply delete it—the definition from the lower layers will return. Of course, if you customize an object's definition that exists in your working layer and you delete it, you have deleted not only your changes but the original definition, too.

■**Note** If you delete your custom definition of the sales order from, then the next time you run the form, the first definition of the form it finds will be in the SYS layer (the standard form) and that's the one that it will use.

Access to the different Axapta layers is determined by the layer codes provided by MBS when you purchase a license, and which you specify in your login parameters—the only exception is the USR layer that is always accessible to all users.

In practical terms, the layering system ensures that you can make modifications and additions to the system without interfering with the application objects on the levels below your working layer. When you make an object modification in one level, the modified object overshadows the object on a lower level.

The layers are designed with different classes of Axapta developers in mind, and MBS provides codes to access the different layers based on which group you belong to. Developers fall into three classes:

- MBS application developers who create the standard applications

- Business partner developers who customize the standard application from MBS or create add-on solutions

- Axapta end-user developers who customize the standard system from MBS and/or add-on solutions provided by partners

---

■**Note** What is commonly called a layer is actually a set of layers making up a layer category: the application category, where the standard released application code and objects reside, and the patch category, where patches can be applied between releases.

The application-layer hierarchy actually consists of 16 layers, divided into 8 layer categories, each consisting of 2 layers. All application layers are accessible by all the tools available in the Axapta MorphX development suite, as well as all by object types (e.g., tables, classes, macros, extended data types, forms, reports, online help, and label system).

Each layer is maintained/persisted in a corresponding file following the naming pattern *ax[layer].aod*, for example—axsys.aod for the SYS layer, axdis.aod for the DIS layer, etc.

■**Note** The .aod file type is an acronym for Application Object Data.

The files are stored in the *Standard* folder of the application installation path. Table 17-5 lists and describes all the Axapta layers.

Table 17-5. *Axpata Layers*

Name	Description
System (SYS layer)	This is the innermost layer where the standard Axapta application is implemented. The layer is controlled and maintained solely by Microsoft Business Solutions. The application objects in the standard application can never be deleted. ID range: 1-8000
Global Solutions (GLS layer)	Microsoft Business Solutions has an option of certifying and distributing strategic global solutions that have not been developed in-house. These solutions are delivered as a standard part of the Axapta product. The solutions have been created with the same development standards as the standard application, and qualified as such. Solution examples: Shop Floor Control, Human Resource Management. ID range: 8001-16000
Distributor (DIS layer)	The local Microsoft Business Solutions offices are provided with a DIS layer to include country-specific functionality developed locally in between releases. Local developments are automatically included in the following global release. The local offices maintain this layer locally. ID range: 16001-18000
Local Solution (LOS layer)	The local Microsoft Business Solutions offices are given the same opportunity to certify and distribute strategic local solutions that have not been developed in-house. Solutions in the LOS layer are protected by the license code framework that the standard application utilizes. Solution examples: Payroll, EDI ID range: 18001-20000
Business Solution (BUS layer)	Business partners are given the opportunity to develop and distribute vertical and horizontal solutions to other partners and customers using the BUS layer. Solutions in the BUS layer are protected by the same license code framework that the standard application utilizes. Note that the BUS layer is reserved for the Add-on Solution program and requires a signed agreement to utilize for development and distribution. ID range: 20001-30000
Value Added Reseller (VAR layer)	Business partners are provided with a separate layer that they can use without any business-related restrictions. This means that any developments the partner would like to do for their customers can be added to this layer. The business partner must keep a catalogue of what application functionality and what VAR/BUS configurations customers have been able to correctly update to their installation. ID range: 30001-40000

Name	Description
Customer (CUS layer)	Corporate enterprises, as well as business partners, can modify their installations. If a corporate enterprise has an internal IT department with Axapta programming skills, this would be the layer to add generic enterprise modifications. The Customer and User layers are included to support enterprises and individual companies in their need for in-house development, without jeopardizing the modifications made by the business partner. This means that application code made in the VAR layer will not be changeable. ID range: 40001-50000
User (USR layer)	Individual companies or companies within an enterprise can utilize this layer to make customizations that are unique to the customers' installation, including reports via the report wizard. The USR layer, in combination with the CUS layer, can be used if the customer develops an enterprise-specific vertical. However, to comply with local market needs, additional requirements need to be implemented. This setup requires more than one installation as changes made in the USR layer and any other layer will be available to all company accounts within the same installation. ID range: 50001-60000

Patch Layers

Each application layer category has an additional application layer for handling patches, minor updates, service packs, hot fixes, and additional functionality. These layers are additions to the previously-described application layers and are situated between them. They can be distinguished from the application layers by the use of the letter *P* in the end of the layer name. The layers are SYP, GLP, DIP, LIP, BUP, VAP, CUP, and USP.

According to MBS, there are no predefined rules for what you can use the patch layers for, and they can therefore be used to support the customers/business partners in any way you like. However, MBS uses the patch layers for sending out service packs, and we suggest you do the same.

The patch layers provide a mechanism for sending out corrections without interfering with definitions and code in existing layers. When the next version of Axapta is developed, the fixes in the patch layers are merged into the corresponding application layer, and the patch layers are deleted. This procedure can be used for all layers in Axapta, and enables the implementation and distribution of corrections without needing to perform a full upgrade.

You should use patch layers only to provide bug fixes, not for new functionality. Do not make changes to the data dictionary under any circumstances—it requires a data upgrade. Adding functionality is not a problem, but it makes no sense to use a patch layer for it, and deleting or modifying existing functionality is a guaranteed way of breaking whatever system the patch layer is applied to.

Other than the brief notes in this section on the usage of patch layers, they are technically exactly the same as the corresponding application layers and exist in the same ID ranges.

Working Environment

You can mix the different components—client, server, and application—in different configurations depending on what you need. Exactly how these are combined depends largely on the specific needs of your organization, which are generally determined by the requirements for the following environment types:

- Development environment

- Test environment

- Production environment

Although you can just have one environment on which you develop, test fixes and new functionality, and make these available to end users, that is not recommended and we can almost guarantee that you will regret a decision of that kind a million times. Instead, we recommend that you have separate environments for each of the uses indicated for Axapta.

Having separate development, test, and production environments does not mean that your hardware requirements explode. You must logically separate the environments, but you can share the physical infrastructure. Exactly what to share and how depends on the requirements that you have for these environments and understanding the benefits and downsides of your options.

In the following sections, we'll go through the issues involved for these environments and typical setups being used in the field.

Development

This is an environment that is typically unstable and CPU-bound; most of the time the code and metadata are broken one place or another because of unfinished fixes or new functionality, and the users of this environment often compile and recompile parts of the system, placing high demand on CPU power. Data sets for this environment tend to be the minimum necessary for developers to validate their work as they progress, and place low requirements on the database. It's also an environment that needs to be flexible and easy to change so developers can quickly switch applications, data sets, and startup configurations.

Development environments tend to have a stable usage pattern within professional software development organizations and cyclical usage in end-user organizations. A dedicated infrastructure is a good idea in the first case but not in the second. Keep this in mind when determining your setup.

The ideal setup for this environment type consists of 2-tier clients and a common server hosting the database and the application files, as illustrated in Figure 17-9. This setup allows developers to work simultaneously on the same shared applications and data sets on the file and database server, while giving them dedicated CPU power and independence to do what they like in their working environments without disrupting other developers or Axapta users in your organization.

■**Note** 2-tier setups pose security issues and are not recommended in production systems, particularly if you allow access to the database and application servers from outside your firewall.

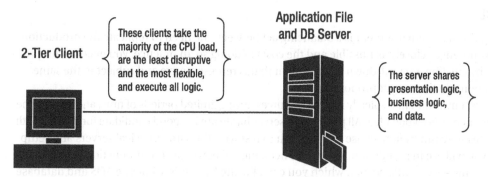

Figure 17-9. *A high-performance development environment*

Here are some points to keep in mind:

- *Few well-known users*: You normally know how many users your development environment has. Because their numbers are generally quite low, scalability is not an issue.

- *High CPU load*: Distribute CPU load by installing clients on development workstations; having a shared environment using a terminal server type of setup will result in your developers grinding to a halt every time one of them performs a compilation. In a 3-tier setup, keep in mind that the AOS will suffer from this too.

- *Unstable system*: A development environment is much more likely to need to be taken off-line, require a reboot or the killing of running processes, and then a test or production environment. Therefore, you should minimize sharing so developers do not disrupt each other.

- *Need for flexibility*: Developers need to experiment and work on different applications and data sets. In a 3-tier setup developers share AOSs and therefore can't just kill and reconfigure them when they need to—assuming that having one AOS per developer is senseless, share as little as possible.

Tip For greater flexibility, create a set of configurations—one for each application hosted on the file server—and provide it to your developers. Let each developer maintain and modify his own on his workstation according to his needs.

Tip If you want to use the same server hardware setup to host a production environment, then using a 2-tier setup for the development environment gives you the best combination of stable servers with low CPU load. Because production systems typically have higher up-time and resilience requirements than development and test environments, you should have separate physical servers for the database and the application server in a production system.

Test

Designing a test environment is a balancing act between the need to replicate the production environment as closely as possible and the costs of doing so. In practice, you need to compromise by creating a scaled-down environment that is representative and subject to the same constraints in the correct proportions.

Test environments typically require resources during limited periods of time, and sharing the infrastructure is a good idea. All production server hardware is a good candidate for sharing with your test environment because it allows you to test with the same physical servers and setup that you will use in production. You do not need the full power of your production environment for testing—just a little corner, which you can allocate by configuring one AOS and database cluster node for test, and leaving the rest exclusively for your production environment, as shown in Figure 17-10.

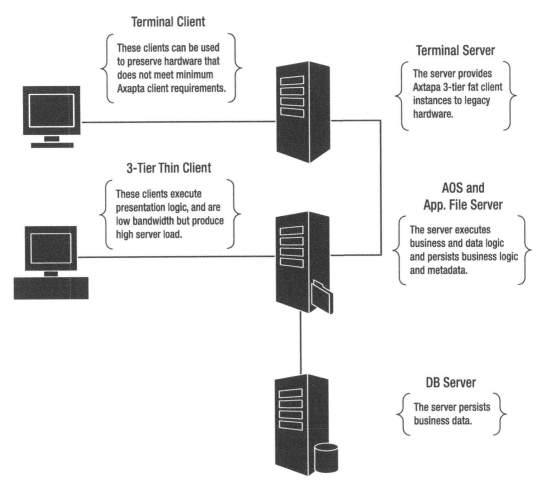

Terminal Client

These clients can be used to preserve hardware that does not meet minimum Axapta client requirements.

Terminal Server

The server provides Axtapa 3-tier fat client instances to legacy hardware.

3-Tier Thin Client

These clients execute presentation logic, and are low bandwidth but produce high server load.

AOS and App. File Server

The server executes business and data logic and persists business logic and metadata.

DB Server

The server persists business data.

Figure 17-10. *A scaled-down test environment*

Production

This type of environment is generally business-critical, and there are three very important factors to work with when designing one:

- *Stability*: The system must provide high up-time and resilience to failure.

- *Performance*: Includes CPU power and communication bandwidth.

- *Scalability*: The ability to expand the system with increases in usage and load.

Production environments are typically dimensioned to handle peak demand and failure gracefully, and the environment tends to be quite static, with changes planned and managed strictly. The ideal setup that will save you headaches should focus on providing the following:

- *Redundancy at the physical and logical level*: Ensure stability by gracefully degrading in the event of failure.

- *Processing power*: Ensure acceptable response times for CPU-bound tasks.

- *Bandwidth and throughput*: Ensure acceptable response times for I/O-bound tasks.

- *Ability to add processing power and disk space transparently*: Enable the system to rapidly scale up to follow demand and load as needed.

- *Support of legacy client hardware*: Make effective use of existing investments in infrastructure.

Physically, this type of environment will resemble the test environment, with the following differences:

- Database and file server with fast RAID or SAN to protect against disk failure, provide easy scaling of disk storage, and provide fast throughput for I/O-bound tasks

- Database cluster for protection against database process failure

- AOS cluster to protect against AOS failure and provide easy scaling of processing performance for CPU-bound tasks

- Terminal server pool to provide good levels of CPU power and memory to legacy client hardware

- High-speed data network to provide high throughput to I/O-bound tasks

Beyond the items listed here, production systems require significantly more attention to security and centralized administration if you want to maintain your sanity with the number of users in any medium-sized installation. We recommend that you stick with 3-tier thin clients, whether they are hosted on their own workstations or on terminal servers, and consider a centrally managed software distribution/management system such as Microsoft SMS to deploy and update client systems. If Axapta is all you care about, Axapta offers a Web-deployment tool that you also can use with a little work.

Runtime and Development Codes

The standard Axapta distribution includes all the functionality that is available from MBS and its solution partners. As you might remember from Chapter 5, the functionality you have access to is determined by the license codes you have received from MBS and entered in Axapta.

If you are a VAR or business partner, you will have received license codes with names matching some of the layers that we covered in this chapter, typically VAR and BUS. These codes—unlike the ones you can enter in the configuration utility when building Axapta configurations—provide runtime access to the respective layers(that is, they allow you to use the development tools to make changes to the layers).

■**Note** The codes you enter in the Axapta configuration provide access to the respective layers so you can customize the layers. A CUS layer code in the configuration you use to start Axapta with means you can change objects in that layer. If you later start Axapta in the USR layer and make changes to the same objects, then any properties or methods that changed in the USR layer will override those in the CUS layer.

Out of the box, Axapta provides runtime access to the SYS, GLS, DIS, LOS, and the corresponding patch layers. That is, you can execute code in these layers—not change it. For example, business logic can be executed in the VAR layer if the VAR layer runtime license code is purchased, and code can be changed in the VAR layer if the development code is purchased.

You don't have to concern yourself with the runtime codes for the first four layers, as they are part of the base package and are always and transparently there. The VAR and BUS layers require runtime codes. The CUS and USR layers don't require codes as they are part of the X++ source code and are always and transparently there.

Development codes in Axapta are divided into two categories:

- Development codes for using the development tools in Axapta's MorphX development suite, consisting of the following:

  - Windows MorphX Development Suite

  - Web MorphX Development Suite

  - X++ source code

- Development codes for accessing the application layers

The X++ development code also includes access to the BUS/BUP, VAR/VAP, CUS/CUP, and USR/USP layers' runtime, and makes the application layers CUS/CUP and USR/USP accessible for application development.

■**Note** Having development codes allowing you to customize a layer does not give you access to the development tools. The codes for the tools are purchased separately.

Internationalization

Axapta has claimed to be an international product from the start; however, the definition is not what many people would assume it to be. In practice, the internationalization features of Axapta consist of the following:

- Country-specific functionality

- Customized units of measurement and currency

- Multilanguage user interface

Out of the box, Axapta offers country-specific functionality for 15 countries. This support is mostly for compliance with local legal accounting requirements. You can enable and disable the country-specific features you want using the Axapta main application menu path Administration ➤ Setup ➤ System ➤ Configuration, expand the Country-Specific Features configuration key, and check those you need, as shown in Figure 17-11.

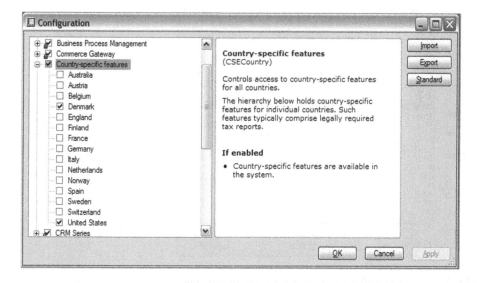

Figure 17-11. *The Configuration form*

The user interface provides support for different languages that can be configured at runtime using the configuration utility shown in Figure 17-12. The exceptions are:

- License codes

- Configuration keys

- Security keys

- AOT tool

- Project tool

- Recycle Bin tool

- Debugger

These elements exist only in English and can't be changed at the application level.

Axapta is oblivious to the standard measurement units for any given culture. You set them up yourself, so it's not a problem. The only exception is that by default you have no control over which system of measurement you use when entering data. For example, if you have defined pound and kilogram as units of weight acceptable for a particular field, then they can be used by anyone whether or not they're valid in their culture.

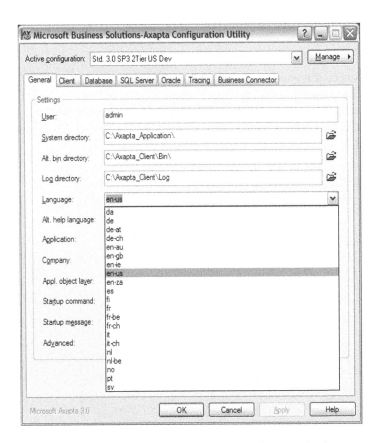

Figure 17-12. *The Axapta Configuration Utility's General tab page*

Looking at the language options in the configuration utility (see Figure 17-12), you would assume that Axapta is culture-sensitive, but in fact it's not. The available languages can be called anything, and you can define your own language if you like, using the Label File Wizard Main Menu bar path Tools ➤ Development Tools ➤ Label ➤ Label File Wizard. Check the Create New Label File ID and Label Language check boxes on the first page of the wizard, then click on Next. The following page of the wizard will help you create a unique label file ID to use in identifying your user interface labels.

The next step of the wizard looks like Figure 17-13. Here you can select the languages to create label files with the specified ID, and even create your own languages if you want. This is a really cool feature, allowing you to add support for any language that is not supported by MBS or a partner. Once you have generated the label files, you can simply select an existing language file (EN-US, for example), open it in your favorite text editor, and translate the labels to your own. Save yours, specify it in the configuration, and—bingo!—Axapta user interface in Martian!

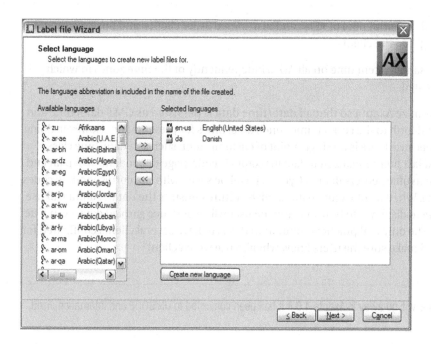

Figure 17-13. *The Label File Wizard*

▉**Note** A label file ID allows you to add your own labels to the system, independent of the existing ones. This feature is particularly useful when you develop your own solution because all you need to distribute is your label files. Alternatively, you would need permission from MBS to redistribute theirs with your labels in them.

▉**Note** Creating a language generates label files for the language for all existing layers, while creating a label ID creates label files with the given ID for all languages installed.

It's also worth noting the following internationalization features that are limited in or absent from Axapta:

- Date and time functionality supports only the Gregorian calendar.

- Axapta has no time zone awareness.

- Axapta is DBCS (Double Byte Character Code)-based.

The first item means that you have to roll up your own calendars and date/time functionality if you need to work with calendar systems other than the Gregorian.

The second is far more serious because it's not evident that Axapta has no knowledge of the time zones where its clients and servers are located; therefore, timestamps have been and continue to be a problem. For example, two orders created at exactly the same time will be registered with different times if the code creating them is executed on two different clients in two different time zones. This issue can create a whole array of problems. There's a couple of possible solutions:

- Sticking with a central pool of AOSs and distributed 3-tier clients, and not executing business logic on the clients

- Having the same system time on all AOSs independently of the time zones in which they are located

You can customize Axapta so that all date/time data is persisted as GMT date/time and converted back and forth to the correct time zone's date/times for presentation. However, doing so is impractical because there is no single point of customization such as a date/time class.

The third and last point means that data in Axapta is code-page dependent. When an end user in your Russian office enters data in Cyrillic, it will be saved with the corresponding codes for that code page. When a colleague in an English culture consults the data, Axapta will use another code page to display it to him/her, and the user will experience garbled data, even if he can read Cyrillic. The only real practical solution to this is to have several clients configured for each language and make sure the users know when to use which client.

■**Note** These issues will go away in Axapta 4.0 if it has been converted to UNICODE and internationalized, as is expected.

Caching

Axapta has several caches in what amounts technically to a sophisticated caching architecture that is not always easy to figure out and use effectively. Let's go through them so that you know when and how to employ them.

Record Caching

The record cache is used for full key lookups. On clients, it contains the 100 most recent records retrieved per table, and on AOSs it has the 2,000 most recent. It comes in several flavors and the type is specified on a per-table basis using the CacheLookUp property of table objects. There are three flavors:

- *NotInTTS*: Always read from the database when inside a transaction block.

- *Found*: The cache does not keep track of statements that do not return a result set and the key used. If new records are subsequently added, they will be retrieved in subsequent queries with the same key.

- *FoundAndEmpty*: The cache keeps track of statements that do not return result sets for a given key. Subsequent statements using the same key will be ignored even if new records have been inserted that satisfy the key.

Both clients and AOSs have record caches, so in a 3-tier environment there are actually two levels of record caching. The client record cache is private, but all its clients share the AOS record cache.

It's flushed automatically when the clients and AOSs exit, and automatically at midnight on AOSs.

Full Table Caching

This cache exists on AOSs, 3-tier fat clients, and 2-tier clients. 3-tier thin clients rely on the table cache on the AOS that services them. It caches only simple data sets. That is, it does not cache the results of joins and is per-company-based. As with the record cache, it's specified using the CacheLookUp property of table objects; there is only one flavor:

- *EntireTable*: Caches the entire table when it's selected within a simple statement

The table cache is implemented using Axapta temporary tables—also known as maps. Therefore, you should specify table caching only for tables that you do not expect to significantly exceed 1,000 records, because temporary tables are inefficient with larger data sets.

AOSs share their caches with all the clients they service, and they flush their caches automatically at midnight. Flushing is also performed by clients and AOSs on exit.

To ensure that clients and AOSs in a system have the same view of the systems business data, the table cache is synchronized every 60 seconds by default—you can specify a different value if you wish as a startup parameter using the Max. Cache Sync. Time field of the configuration tool, as shown in Figure 17-14.

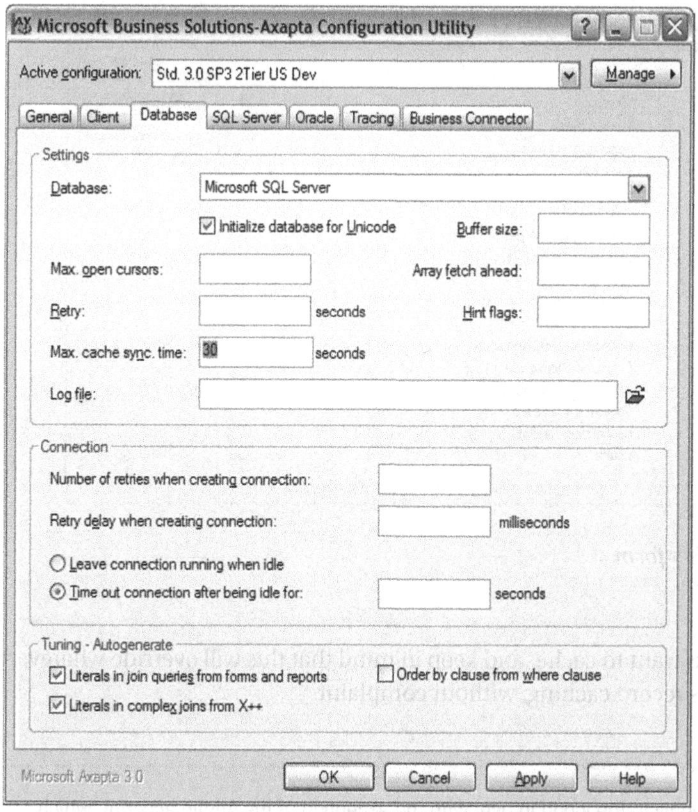

Figure 17-14. *The Axapta Configuration Utility's Database tab page*

■Caution Setting the sync time too low will result in the cache update restarting before it's finished. The consequence is that the synchronization never completes and the cache is never refreshed.

The performance of the table caching mechanism can be monitored to identify tables whose caching negatively affects system performance. You do this by setting threshold values for the number of records cached and the time taken to populate the cache. Any table exceeding the specified thresholds will produce warnings that can be saved to a log file by checking the respective check box on the same tab page.

You can define the tables to cache using the Preload tab page on the Options form at the Axapta main application menu path Administration ➤ Users. On the User form, click on the User Options button to the right of the form to display the Options form shown in Figure 17-15.

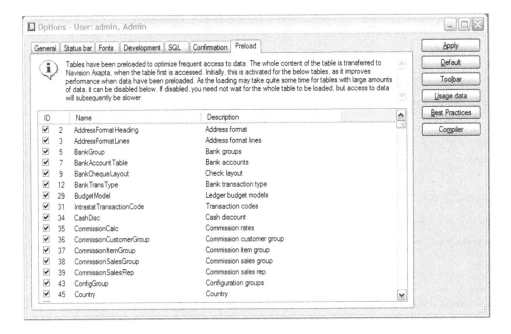

Figure 17-15. *The Options - User form*

Check the tables that you want to cache, and keep in mind that this will override whatever settings the table has, such as record caching, without complaint.

■Note The preloaded settings apply to the logon in use, with the exception of the Admin account, which overwrites the settings for all users.

Record View Caching

This cache type provides a temporary result set that can be activated and deactivated only from X++ code, and is of interest only for advanced developers. However, they'll need to research the API on their own or wait for our advanced development title in this series.

Read-Ahead Caching

This form of caching is used to improve performance when populating forms. It's automatic and always on, and basically consists of fetching 100 records or as many records as will fit in 24 Kb at the time so that a round-trip to the database is not required every time you scroll a record in the data set.

Wrap-Up

This chapter gave you a good idea of the different aspects and views of Axapta that affect the way you customize and deploy it. We've seen how these features are important when sizing a system, pinning down hardware requirements and network configurations, managing security, moving a system to a new platform or expanding capacity, designing solutions and coding them, and undertaking daily operations and management. Specifically, we've discussed the following:

- The different pieces of software that make up the system

- Where to find the different pieces

- How the different pieces work together as a system

- Layering of the application code and metadata

- Data caching and performance

There is not much documentation on the product CD that specifically covers Axapta architecture, although it's implicit in several of the documents indicated in other chapters. The exceptions are available in the technical information folder of the base documentation folder of the product distribution package or CD:

- *AX-300-TIP-046-v01.00-ENUS.doc*: Utilizing Axapta Application Layers

- *AX-300-TIP-059-v01.00-ENUS.doc*: Country-Specific Configuration

Before you move on, configure your system with a combination of all the possible deployment architectures (2- and 3-tier setups), and play around with them for a few days.

CHAPTER 18

■■■

Development

This chapter covers the Axapta development environment and related tools, and how to apply them to customize Axapta, and for that matter how to develop your own applications and add-ons to the standard functionality delivered out of the box. Although this chapter is directed at developers, we recommend that everyone read the section entitled "IntelliMorph"; and we recommend that consultants also read the whole chapter in order to get a good idea of what it takes to develop in Axapta, what kind of ideas and solutions are technically natural, and which ones can prove challenging even for the most seasoned developers.

By now, you are well aware that Axapta has an integrated development environment, alias IDE. However, Axapta goes beyond that. It is a fully integrated environment, and you develop in exactly the same environment as your users work in. In practice, the only real differences between the environment you develop in and a production system are as follows:

- You do not develop in a production system, but you make a copy that you work on to avoid clobbering your production environment as you code, make mistakes, and debug your customizations. Also, since changes are available right away, whatever you are working on will not be stable until you are finished, and you don't want anyone suddenly evoking your code.

- You don't install licenses for the development tools, alias MorphX and X++, in production, to avoid changes that could introduce bugs or functionality being accidentally introduced.

Note Even without development tools and the ability to code, you can still customize Axapta using IntelliMorph.

The great thing about this is that you don't have to develop in one environment, compile, deploy, and run the resulting application to see what your users will finally see, go back to your development environment to fix this or that, and repeat the process to see the results. While IDEs certainly have come a long way in making this process easier, Axapta goes beyond anything else. You log in to Axapta, pull up the tools you need to make any required customizations, and as you go and save these customizations, they are automatically compiled and ready to be run right then and there.

The development environment can be divided into six major areas:

- *IntelliMorph*: For designing, editing, and building user interface elements

- *MorphX*: For developing business logic and editing the Data Dictionary

- *Web MorphX*: For developing Web-based applications

- *X++*: For getting around the programming environment and coding

- *Debugging*: For figuring out what you did wrong or could have done better

- *Best practices*: For making sure that you make life easy for everybody and less dangerous for yourself

What you can or can't do in terms of development depends on which license codes you have purchased:

- *Base Package*: Everyone has this one, and you can't do anything without it. It enables you to create, delete, and modify the following object types:

    - Reports

    - Menus

    - Queries

    - Jobs

- *MorphX Development Suite*: This enables you to work with, create, modify, and delete the following object types:

    - Data Dictionary object types

    - Forms

    - Macros

- *Web MorphX Development Suite*: This enables you to create, modify, and delete the following object types:

    - Web object types

    - Style sheet editor

- *X++ Source Code*: This gives you the following capabilities:

    - Creation, modification, and deletion of all the remaining object types

    - Posting to journals

    - Access to the development code for the CUS layer, so if you are an end-user organization you can place your modifications in it to protect them from changes in the USR layer

    - Access to execution of the BUS and VAR layers so you don't need the respective runtime license codes

■Note Before discussing the different topics of this section, we would like to call your attention to the fact that only the AOS that your changes pass through, that is, that the AOS your client is connected to, is updated when developing in a 3-tier environment. Do not set up a development environment with multiple AOSs—all the clients should pass through the same AOS, and do not mix 2-tier and 3-tier clients. When you save a change, only the AOS you are connected to will have it; clients connecting to other AOSs will not, and neither will 2-tier clients, as they do not know that they need to reread the application.

IntelliMorph

IntelliMorph is a user interface engine that enables you to define user interface elements, save them as metadata, and finally use them to render the user interface. It makes it easy to customize Axapta by rearranging user interface elements in forms and reports, hiding them, and changing labels. It automatically takes care of resizing the elements where appropriate and ensures that your user interface always has the same look and feel.

Another of IntelliMorph's tasks is to figure out what functionality is installed and which user interface elements to make available to users. It does this by using the configuration key system and only loading definitions for objects that are associated with active configuration keys.

■Note All data and menu object definitions in Axapta have a `ConfigurationKey` property that specifies which configuration key they depend on. If the key is disabled, then the object is not loaded and made available by IntelliMorph, which reduces memory usage and in-memory management overhead.

In practice, there are two aspects to IntelliMorph. The first is what is commonly known as the *user setup tool*, which is available to all users and that, as you will see in a moment, allows them to change the layout of forms and even add or hide data fields without any programming. The real cool thing about this part of IntelliMorph is that the changes are on a per-user basis, so every user can have it his way without imposing himself on others.

■Note The idea of letting every user customize the user interface to his heart's content is something you probably should establish clear rules about, because it can make life difficult for support engineers who don't necessarily know what customizations users have done when they submit a support request.

The second aspect of IntelliMorph is that it automatically takes care of arranging the layout of your user interface at runtime. This is a fantastic feature because developing a form in English might look great, but what happens if you have non-English speaking users? For example, Finnish words and consequently labels are a lot longer than their English counterparts. The answer, of course, is that either the labels would resize and push the controls to the right in left-to-right locales or not, and they would simply be gobbled up after exceeding whatever number of characters you had left space for at development time. Whereas IntelliMorph takes your user interface object definitions and rearranges the controls on them at runtime so that your Finnish users have just as nice a user interface as their English colleagues.

▓**Note** You can, to a limited extent, actually hinder IntelliMorph in its mission to make Axapta look good, by hard coding the positioning properties of controls when you develop. So unless you have a good reason to do so, then accept the default of automatically positioning them.

Having fun with IntelliMorph and the user setup tool is very simple, so let's see what it's all about. Open up any form, for example Administration ➤ Users, click in the grid control of the Overview tab, and you will see the pop-up menu shown in Figure 18-1.

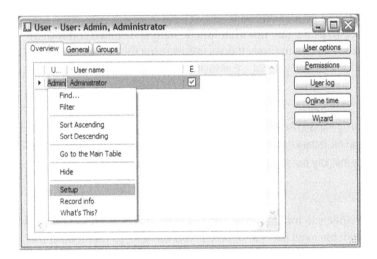

Figure 18-1. *The Setup menu option*

Select the Setup menu option to display the User Setup form shown in Figure 18-2, where you can customize the User form.

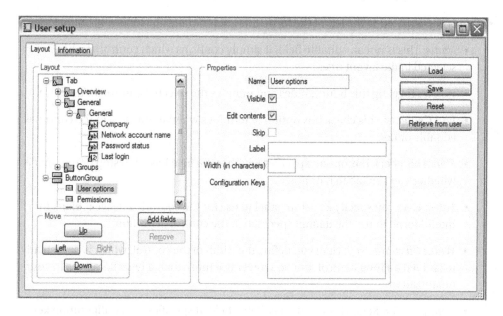

Figure 18-2. *The User Setup form*

■**Note** The pop-up menu is different when the content of the tab page is not filled with a grid control, as is the case with the General and Groups tab pages; however, the Setup menu option is there in all of them.

■**Note** To display the pop-up menu, you must right-click inside the client area of a tab page or one of the buttons—in the lighter colored inner margin, not on the area outside the tab control, by default gray in Axapta.

This form is made up of two tab pages, the first allowing you to manipulate the layout, and the second providing a variety of information about the form you are working with.

The Layout tab page is made up of two control groups:

- *Layout*: Situated to the right of the form, this area contains the following items:

    - A tree of all the controls on the form that you can expand and collapse to navigate to the exact control that you wish to change

    - Two buttons that allow you to remove or add data fields to the form

    - The Move subgroup, with four buttons that move the selected control to a different relative position

- *Properties*: Situated to the left of the form, this area contains the following options:

  - *Name*: This is not an editable field; it simply confirms which control you have selected in the layout tree.

  - *Visible*: Toggling this button hides and unhides the selected control on the form.

  - *Edit Contents*: This check box option determines whether the data in the control is editable or not.

  - *Skip*: This check box option specifies whether the field has a tab stop or not, that is, whether you can tab to it or not.

  - *Label*: Here you specify a custom label to use for the control, or leave it blank for IntelliMorph to use the default specified in the control definition.

  - *Width (in characters)*: Here you define the width of the control, which is particularly useful if it's a long control, but you never use more than a few characters in your organization.

  - *Configuration Keys*: This is not an editable field; it specifies the configuration key that the control depends on.

Note If the cursor is placed inside a control when you bring up the pop-up menu and select the Setup menu option, then the control tree in the layout group of the User Setup form is automatically expanded as needed and the corresponding control is selected.

Note When you make a change to the layout of a form, it is automatically reflected in the respective form, so if you have the form open, you can immediately see the results.

The form buttons on the right side work as follows:

- *Load*: Retrieves a form layout that was previously saved

- *Save*: Saves a form layout with a name that you specify and, in conjunction with the Load button, allows you to have different definitions that you can use as you like

- *Reset*: Restores the form to the default layout

- *Retrieve from user*: Loads the currently active form layout of the specified user

The layout control group requires a little more explaining, specifically the control tree, and the Add Fields and Remove buttons. As you may have noticed in Figure 18-2, some of the controls in the control tree are overlaid with small yellow locks, which means that there are restrictions in the customizations that you may make to the controls. The locks may also appear in red, which means that you can't customize them at all. The level of customization allowed is determined by the AllowUserSetup property setting for the Axapta Object Tree (AOT) control that contains the control in question or for a parent control.

Note Some controls marked as restricted actually have the `AllowUserSetup` property set to `Yes`. The reason for this is that the property is either set to `Restricted` in application code at runtime, or in some cases by kernel code that only MBS developers have access to. You cannot decrease the restriction level, only increase it from `Restricted` to `No`, in which case the control will display a red lock instead of yellow.

Table 18-1 presents a set of rules for what you may and may not customize in the layout using the user setup tool.

Table 18-1. *User Setup Limitations*

Control Type	Rules
Form	Everything can be moved in, out, and about in a form except tab pages.
Tab	The only customization possible here is moving tab pages within the tab.
Tab page	Everything can be moved in, out, and about in a tab page except tab pages.
Group	Everything can be moved in, out, and about in a group except tab pages.
Button group	Buttons of all types can be moved in, out, and about, but that is it.
Grid	Only data controls can be moved in, out, and about in a table.
Table	Only data controls can be moved in, out, and about in a table.
Menu button	Buttons, command buttons, menu item buttons, and separators can be moved in, out, and about in menu buttons.

The Information tab page is for the most part pretty straightforward, but there are three fields and buttons worth having a quick look at:

- *Form Name*: Specifies the name of the form that you are running the user setup on

- *Caller*: Specifies the object that invokes the form you are running the user setup on

- *Menu Item*: Defines the name of the menu item that displays the form

What is most interesting about these is that they all have a corresponding Edit button. If you click it, the corresponding object definition is retrieved in an AOT window so that you can work with it. This is really a great feature, particularly for support engineers who often have forms as the start reference for bug reports. It makes it easy to go to the definition of the form as well as to the object definitions of its callers.

MorphX

MorphX is a set of tools for developing the user interface, business logic, and underlying data model of Axapta's applications and requires a corresponding license code. Without MorphX, you can only create, edit, and delete reports and menus with the Application Object Tree (AOT) tool. You can create new reports using the Report Wizard and place them in the AOT tool. With the MorphX license, you can also create, edit, and delete any object type in the AOT with the exception of classes, for example, forms and tables that require an X++ source code license.

MorphX consists of a series of individual tools and utility groups:

- *Project tool*: Tool for grouping collections of object definitions that you work on within a specific task.

- *Application Object Tree*: Tool for navigating and managing the object definitions in the system and from which to launch other tools.

- *Visual MorphXplorer*: Tool for drawing Entity Relationship Diagrams.

- *Code Profiler*: Exactly what you would expect, a tool for profiling X++ code.

- *Benchmark tool*: This is a sophisticated tool for benchmarking Axapta. It's actually not part of the MorphX license code, but part of the X++ Source Code license code, and we look at it in Chapter 21.

- *Code Explorer*: Tool for browsing Axapta's object definitions and code in a Web browser.

- *Help Text tool*: This is really just a form where you can edit and preview the contents of the AOT's documentation folders.

- *Web Development*: This a group of utilities for developing and working with Web portals.

- *Version Update*: This is a group of utilities for helping you track and fix object definitions after an upgrade.

- *Wizards*: This is a group of utilities that guides you through the creation of several types of Axapta object types, such as label files and reports.

- *Label*: This a group of utilities for managing and working with labels.

Tip The different tools in the suite add specialized buttons to the main tool bar, and provide their own tool bars, pop-up menus, and even menu bars. We cover using their pop-up menus and occasionally keyboard shortcuts; however, we encourage you to check the tool bar for the buttons that are added when the focus is on a specific tool window and to explore them.

Generally, you access these tools by selecting Tools ➤ Development Tools; however, not all the tools there are part of the MorphX suite, and the debugger is conspicuously missing. Also, because of Axapta's tight integration, it's not always easy to figure how to classify a piece of functionality, whether it's a tool, a utility, or just an application. To make matters worse, various pieces of functionality are available in different contexts.

We provide you here with in-depth coverage of the most important tools and an overview of the more advanced and less used ones, so you have the essence of what you need to know to get around productively in the development environment. We have, however, given the debugger its own section on par with the X++ language, because it's actually an external Windows 32 program that is invoked by the interpreter if and when there are break points in the code being executed or if an exception is thrown and the debug mode is set to Always.

Let's then get down to what really matters and look at the different tools that make up the MorphX environment, what you can use them for, and how.

Labels

The label subsystem enables you to decouple the strings in your user interface elements by providing the ability to insert label references in your object definitions and code that are resolved at runtime to the appropriate label resources for the language selected by the end user.

The way labels work is as follows:

- Data and UI object definitions include a label property, such as a table field or a button where you can specify a label reference. You can, of course, just type in the textual value you want displayed, but this is not language independent.

- At runtime, the label reference is resolved to a string of the appropriate language when an object of the type is instantiated.

- In code, you can't rely on a property, but what you do is provide the label reference anywhere you want the string to appear.

Label strings are not stored in the metadata definitions of your applications, but in external files, one set per language (you have already seen what these files are in Chapter 17). Axapta is delivered with an extensive package of label files, so it's important to understand the process for dealing with label references in your object definitions and X++ code.

In object definitions, all object types that have labels have a corresponding label or caption property, as you can see in the Object Properties window in Figure 18-3.

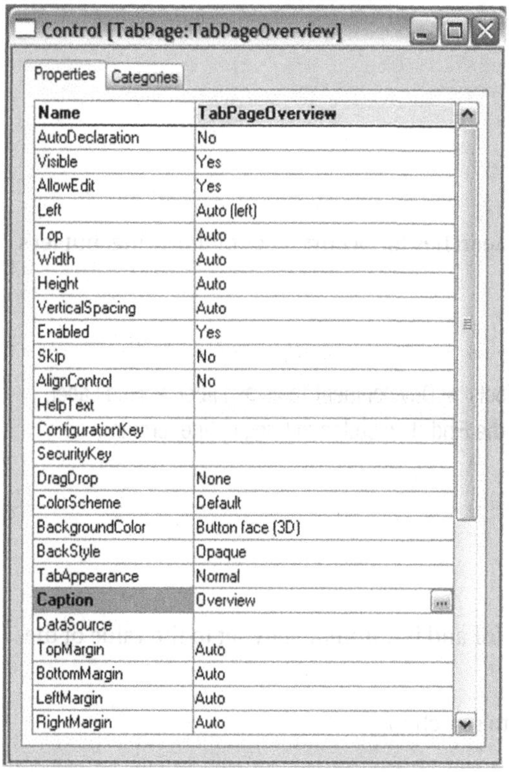

Figure 18-3. *The Object Properties window*

For the purposes of illustrating how it works, we have a string literal in the caption of the tab page we're working with. This is, of course, not what you should do because it will always display the string literal, whatever language your users may select to use. The correct way to go about it is to click the button with an ellipsis to the right side of the field. This will bring up the Find Label Form, shown in Figure 18-4, where you can find the ID for the string that you want to use as the caption. If the string is not defined for your working language, then no results will be displayed in the bottom half results grid. The property will be blank when you invoke it, and the grid will not be displayed.

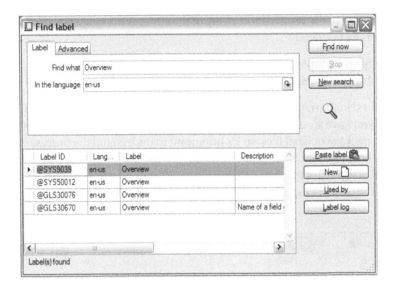

Figure 18-4. *The Find Label form*

When the form is opened, it automatically searches for occurrences of the string, but let's quickly go through it.

■**Note** You can also bring up this form by selecting Tools ➤ Development Tools ➤ Label ➤ Find Label, entering **Overview** in the Find What field, and clicking the Find Now button to bring up the form in Figure 18-4.

The Label tab on the form works like this:

- *Find What*: Specifies the string to search for and is automatically set to the value of the property from which it was invoked

- *In the Language*: Specifies the language to search in

- *Find Now button*: Starts searching

- *Stop button*: Exits the search

- *New Search button*: Clears your current search settings

- *Paste Label button*: Inserts the reference selected in the results grid into the property from which the form was invoked and closes the form

- *New button*: Lets you create a new label literal and a corresponding ID that you can use in your object definitions and code

- *Used By*: Provides a list of all the object definitions in which it's used

- *Label Log button*: Displays a log of changes to the label

Note The Used By button only finds and lists places in object definitions and in X++ code where the label is used if they are cross-referenced object definitions.

Note On development environments, you will have performed a full cross-reference when you stepped through the installation checklist in Chapter 3, but in other environments you probably will not since it's time consuming and adds a lot of data to your database that is not really relevant to people other than developers. Last but not least, as you customize Axapta, it's a good idea to update the cross-reference when you are out to lunch or leave it running when you go home in the evening by either updating specific elements or the whole system. Do this by selecting an AOT node, right-clicking to display the pop-up menu, and selecting Add-Ins ➤ Cross-Reference ➤ Update or, from the menu bar, selecting Tools ➤ Development Tools ➤ Cross-Reference ➤ Periodic ➤ Update, respectively.

The Advanced tab has the following settings:

- *Label File ID*: Allows you to select label files that you may have created yourself as shown in Chapter 17. This is empty if you don't have any label files.

- *Auto Search*: Automatically searches for the text in the Find What field when the form is opened; otherwise you must do it explicitly by using the Search button.

- *Select Languages*: Checks the languages that you want to see the label value for. What you will see depends on whether the string for the label ID is translated or not; if you select any language here, then a new results grid is appended to the bottom of the one for the selected language, where translations of the selected label for the selected languages are shown.

The grid in the lower half of the form is placed directly in the form, visible independently of the selected tab page, and displays all occurrences of the string found. Notice the ID, that is, the left-most column.

When you create a new label reference, it is automatically added to the file for the currently selected language with its string literal value. A reference is also created for each of the installed languages in the respective files. You can then open the Axapta Label Data (ALD) files. For all the languages for which you need translations, find the appropriate reference and provide the translated string. The ALD files are plain text files that you can edit in any plain text editor.

Open the file, find the line with the ID that was generated for you, and write the translated string, remembering to leave a blank space between the ID and the string. Repeat the process for all the languages you want to support.

An important aspect of the label system is that you can't add labels to the standard label files supplied with Axapta. You need to use the label wizard described in Chapter 17 to create your own label file set. Then make sure that you select the correct one in the label file ID combo box in the Advanced tab page.

■**Note** When you distribute your customizations, remember to provide all of the label files that you have created.

Label IDs are a string built by appending several elements according to the following formula:

- The at symbol (@)

- A three-letter label file ID that is specified when you create the label file set

- A sequence number

The ID is the same for all available languages. It's only the string literal that changes.

To give you a short recap: the label files are named following the pattern *ax[file_ID] [language].[file_type]*, for example, the US English ALD file for the SYS layer is *axSysEn-Us.ald*. If you had created your own label file set with the ID ABC, then Axapta would have generated a US English ALD file named *axABCEn-Us.ald*. Following this last example of a label file name, the first label you create, for the word "Google" for example, would be @ABC21 and would exist in the files *axABCEn-Us.ald*, *axABCEn-Ie.ald*, *axABCDa.ald*, and so on, for all languages.

■**Note** Curiously, Axapta starts numbering labels at number 21. The other numbers are reserved, and if you look in custom ALD files, you will notice that the first one from the first 20 is assigned the creation date and author, and that several of them are defined without an assigned value. Looking at the standard label ALDs, you will see that not all are defined.

And that wraps it up for labels.

The Project Tool

The purpose of this utility is to allow you to group objects that you customize as part of a logical task or assignment so that you can easily keep track of which objects were involved. The objects in question reside in the AOT, and a project only holds references to the objects that you place in it. Projects can also be selected and exported, which makes it easy to provide your customizations to other people and even manually feed them into a source code version control system.

■**Note** From Axapta 3.0 onwards, project definitions are saved per user so that each user working on a project only sees the objects that are relevant to himself in that context.

■**Note** MBS has been working on an interface to its own commercial version control software package, that is, SourceSafe; however, even when that is released, if you are using another package like CVS, you can export your projects to XPO-type files and then use the package's own user interface to place and retrieve them from the respective repositories. Since XPO files are text only, only deltas between versions are saved, and your repository will not rapidly fill up, as would be the case if you were dealing with binary files.

■**Note** While Axapta only supports three types of project types, you can actually create your own by extending the class projectNode.

The Project tool shown in Figure 18-5 consists of a window with a tool bar at the top and pane with a tree control that has two root node alias folders, where you can add projects and expand and collapse the view:

- *Private*: All projects created under this node are only visible to the creator.
- *Shared*: All projects created under this node are visible to all users.

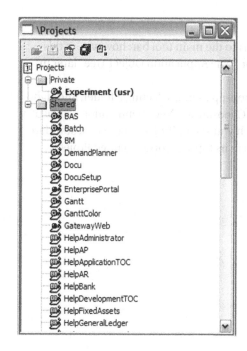

Figure 18-5. *The Project tool window*

The tool bar consists of five icon buttons from left to right that are enabled or not depending on the type of node in the tree that is selected. These buttons do the following:

- *Open*: Opens a project in its own window

- *Compile*: Compiles all objects in the selected project

- *Properties*: Displays the Properties window shown in Figure 18-3

- *Save All*: Saves all changes made to the objects contained in the project

- *Import*: Enables you to import object definitions into the project from a previous export

---

■**Note** Importing object definitions from a previous export can also be done from a corresponding menu option in the main menu tool bar's Command menu. You will also find the Export command in this menu.

■**Note** All the tool bar commands have shortcut key combinations that you can see by positioning the cursor over them, with the exception of Import.

■**Note** All objects that you change are marked with a red vertical bar to the right of their icon in the tree—jobs actually display a red ball; when you save them, the red bar or ball disappears, and the name of the object is displayed in bold font. This applies equally to the AOT.

Opening the Project tool adds a block of buttons to the main tool bar; however, at this point, we will defer discussing them until the section "The Application Object Tree" later in this chapter, because they apply to the AOT also.

You create projects in the folders by using the pop-up menu, selecting a folder, and right-clicking it. This will display the menu in Figure 18-6. Choosing the New menu option will display the submenu shown in the same figure, from which you select Project to create a standard project—represented by an icon with a yellow circle in its top-left corner, named Project1.

Figure 18-6. *The Project pop-up menu*

Briefly, here is what the menu commands in Figure 18-6 do:

- *New*: Shows a submenu with these commands:

  - *Project*: Creates a new project definition

  - *Web Project*: Creates a new Web portal project, which is distinguished from a standard project by a blue circle at the top-left corner of its icon

  - *Help Book*: Creates a project where you can group various types of online help information and that is distinguished from the other types by an open book in the top-left corner of its icon

- *Open New Window*: Opens the folder in a new project window

- *Properties*: Displays the Properties window

■**Note** You probably noticed we did not include the Add-Ins command in this list. We will look at the Add-Ins submenu in the section "The Application Object Tree" later in this chapter. There are fewer options for this command here in the Project tool, so we encourage you to explore it now in order to get a feeling for what it can and cannot do.

Select a project within one of the root folders and bring up its pop-up menu. The most interesting menu options are listed here:

- *Rename*: Enables you to rename your project. You will find yourself using this regularly so that you can give your projects a meaningful name.

- *Open*: Displays the tree of objects contained by the project in question in its own window.

- *Restore*: Rolls back any changes you have done to the project, that is, added or removed objects, as long as you have not saved them.

- *Lock and Unlock*: Has no effect whatsoever on projects.

■**Caution** The Restore menu option of the project pop-up menu only rolls back unsaved changes to the project; it does not roll back changes to the objects in the project, and it can't roll back beyond the last save point.

■**Note** The easiest way to open a project is to simply double-click its node.

Opening a project displays it in its own project window, which looks like the main Project tool window but adds one button to the tool bar—specifically, the Filter Records button, which allows you to specify criteria for objects to include in the project, as is commonly used to add objects following a specific pattern. An example is to group all the objects changed in the last calendar week. The Filter Records button brings up a project filter form in which you can specify how the objects are to be added to the project and how they are to be grouped. Most important, this form, shown in Figure 18-7, presents a Select button that allows you to build a query for selecting all the objects you want. In Figure 18-7, we are appending all forms modified on March 12, 2005—the date is in US format MM/DD/YYYY.

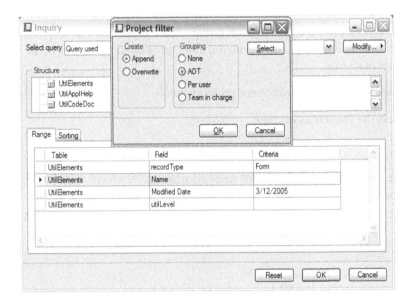

Figure 18-7. *The Project Filter form*

▨Note When you open the Inquiry form, it will not match what you see in Figure 18-7. Select the Field column in a row that has no value, select an option from the provided drop-down list, and then use the criteria to enter or select a value for the field. You can also change the Table field and add more rows as with any normal grid by using the keyboard shortcut Ctrl+N.

The rest of the project window is an object tree that resembles the AOT, with the difference being that you can create and place any object that you want in the root. While we regularly see objects like forms and reports being placed directly in the root of project folders, and there is nothing technically wrong with this, it's a good practice to follow the same pattern as in the AOT: create the appropriate object groups in the root and then place the objects that you want in the respective groups. The results should resemble the example shown in Figure 18-8 of our Experiment project.

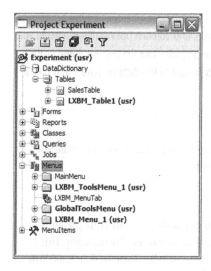

Figure 18-8. *The Project Experiment window*

Note When you create new objects, Axapta puts them at the top of the tree in the node where you create them, and if you want to preserve the same order as in the AOT, start with the last group first. Alternatively, you can move them about afterwards by dragging them with the mouse—this is not a straightforward thing, but we will leave it up to you as an exercise.

All nodes in a project have a corresponding pop-up menu. For the most part, the options are self-explanatory, but here are the ones that are less intuitive:

- *New*: Creates an object definition or a group. Object definitions are also created in the AOT, as the project only has a reference, and we recommend that you create groups of the different object types and then create objects of the corresponding type.

- *Find*: Evokes the Find utility that you can use to search for objects that match a given criteria.

- *Delete*: Deletes the object definition from the AOT, so as a precaution it always displays a dialog box to ask you to confirm that is what you want, or whether you just want to remove the object from the project. Contrast this to the Remove menu option given next.

- *Remove*: Removes the reference of the selected object from the project.

- *Lock and Unlock*: Locks and unlocks objects, respectively, in the selected node and all subnodes. It's a good idea to use these when you need to change an object to prevent developers from overwriting each others' customizations. Locked objects have their icon overlaid with a lock on the lower-right corner and can't be changed by other users.

Note While groups are created in a project with an undefined type, and you can put whatever objects you want in them, it's a good idea to go to the Properties window for the project—use the pop-up menu or the keyboard shortcut Alt+Enter, set the `ProjectGroupType` property to one of the defined types, and name your groups accordingly.

Note When locking, you should lock only the object you really need; don't select the project node and lock it, as that will lock every object that the project has a reference to.

Oddly missing is an evident way of placing existing object definitions in your projects when you need to change existing ones as opposed to creating new ones. Fortunately, this is very simple and is one of those few things in Axapta that can only be done in one way. You select the objects you want in the AOT, drag them over to the project window, and drop them in the appropriate group.

Note that when you drag an object from the AOT to the project tool, you do not chage anything in the AOT, you simply create a reference to it in your project.

In this discussion of the Project tool, we have gone on about the AOT, so it's about time we gave you a closer look at it.

The Application Object Tree

The Application Object tree, or AOT as it's commonly known, is where all development starts and ends. The AOT tool, shown in Figure 18-9, consists of a window with a tool bar at the top and a pane with a tree control that has 14 root nodes, which group each type of object. We have intentionally expanded the Data Dictionary and Web groups because these actually contain subgroups that in turn contain objects of specific types. In the following sections, we will look at each object type and how to use it.

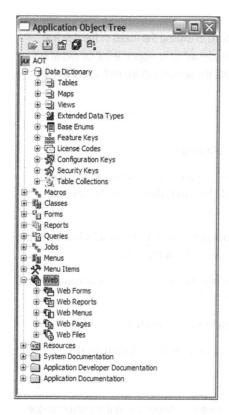

Figure 18-9. *The Application Object Tree window*

Before we go ahead and look at the object types, let's first walk through what you can do in the AOT window. The tool bar has the following five buttons, from left to right:

- *Open*: Executes the selected object type if the object type supports being executed

- *Compile*: Compiles the selected object or all objects in the selected group

- *Properties*: Displays the Properties window for the selected object or subnode

- *Save All*: Saves all changes made to the selected object or objects within the selected group

- *Import*: Allows you to import previously exported objects as already described in the section "The Project Tool"

Opening the AOT also adds the block of buttons shown in Figure 18-10 to the main tool bar, as we mentioned previously.

Figure 18-10. *The AOT tool bar*

> ▓**Note** You can navigate the AOT by using the mouse or keyboard to expand the nodes of the tree and descend the tree; however, a smart trick is that you can position yourself in an object definition within any group, and as you type at the keyboard, it will automatically move the selection to the first object whose name matches the pattern you have entered.

Following are descriptions of the functions for these buttons:

- *AOT Recycle Bin*: This button brings up a feature similar to the Windows Recycle Bin. When you delete an object, it is kept in the recycle bin until the end of the session, where you can recover it.

- *Next Error*: This steps you through the list of errors generated by a compilation, opening up the appropriate editor and placing you at the location of the error.

- *Filter Records*: This is equivalent to the same function found on the project window tool bar, as previously described and shown in Figure 18-7.

- *Import*: This lets you import object definitions previously exported.

- *Compile*: This compiles the selected object or all objects in the selected group.

> ▓**Note** Opening objects directly from the AOT can result in an exception being thrown if the object in question was designed to be called from another object that passes it parameters.

> ▓**Note** Stepping though your errors using the Next Error button on the tool bar places you in the appropriate editor, and consequently the AOT tool bar goes out of context and is hidden. You need to go back to the AOT to make it visible so you can use it again to step to the next error. The editors are typically the Properties window for errors in object definitions and the X++ code editor for coding errors.

With some variations, all nodes in the AOT have a pop-up menu resembling the one shown in Figure 18-11.

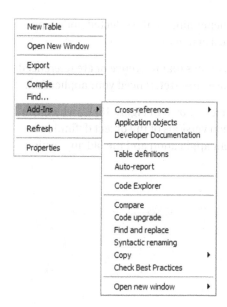

Figure 18-11. *The AOT pop-up menu*

Many of the menu options you will find are already known to you or are self-descriptive; however, there are a few worth mentioning here:

- *New*: Creates a new object definition of the selected type and usually displays the name of the type in the menu option, for example Table or Form, depending on the node group type selected. When you select the Extended Data Types group node, the New menu option displays a submenu from which you can specify a subtype.

- *Synchronize*: Only displayed for the Data Dictionary and table definition nodes. This forces a synchronization of your definitions in the Data Dictionary with the database and is useful if you make changes to objects of this group to make sure that your application and database are in sync.

- *Open New Window*: Opens the selected node in its own AOT window.

- *Layers*: Available on most object types. This displays all the existing definitions, one per layer. So if you changed the definition of the Address table while working in the USR layer, the AOT would display two Address table nodes, since Axapta comes out of the box with a definition in the SYS layer that you override when you change it.

- *Restore*: Restores the state of an object that you have made changes to back to the last save point, but once you save a change, you can no longer restore anything.

- *Add-ins*: Presents a group of utilities that varies depending on the selected node type. The most interesting of the submenu options are listed here:

    - *Cross-Reference*: Allows you to look up object types that reference or are referenced by the one selected and requires that you have cross-referenced your application.

    - *Compare*: Brings up the Comparison tool that is shown in Figure 18-12, which you can use to investigate the differences between versions of the object definition in different layers and even between the current application and the old application that has been upgraded.

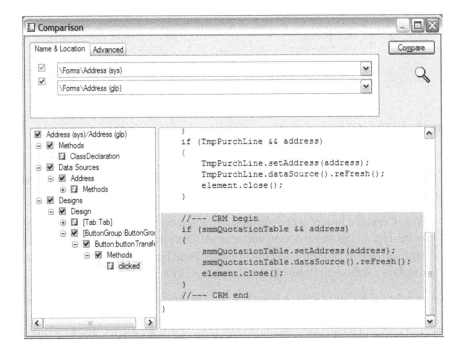

Figure 18-12. *The Comparison tool*

- *Table Browser*: Applies only to tables. This displays raw data from the selected table that makes it easy to check your data if you suspect that the data displayed by another object type is mangled by the definition or a coding error.

- *Code Upgrade*: Shown in Figure 18-13, this is similar to the Comparison tool, but focuses on X++ and displays the object type tree from where you can select individual methods. It then displays all existing versions in a tabbed workspace where you edit the code.

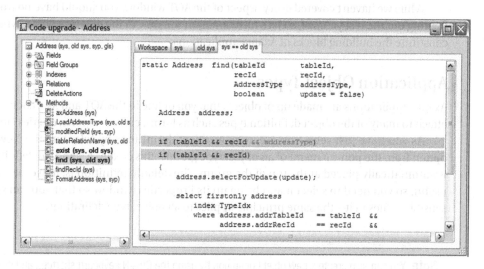

Figure 18-13. *The Code Upgrade tool*

- *Find and Replace*: Allows you to search for a given string and replace it.

- *Check Best Practices*: This is a very useful tool for developers with bad coding habits as well as new Axapta developers who can use it to make sure that their objects and code comply with the Axapta best practice guidelines. Running this tool displays the compiler output window in the Best Practices tab page as shown in Figure 18-14. This lets you see what you have done wrong (we discuss more about the Compiler Output window in the section "The Compiler" later in this chapter).

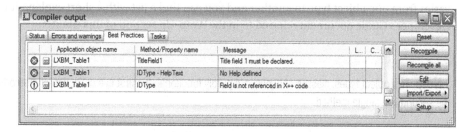

Figure 18-14. *The Best Practices tab page of the Compiler Output window*

■**Caution** The Find and Replace operation actually requires you to define a query and is very powerful, as it will walk the whole AOT, so be careful with this utility. A few other utilities in the Add-Ins submenu work in the same way, and as a general rule be careful with any tool or utility that allows you to define a query, as the whole AOT is at its mercy.

While we haven't covered every aspect of the AOT window, you should have no trouble figuring out the rest yourself, so let's turn our attention now to the different object types that constitute the building blocks of Axapta applications.

Application Object Types

Axapta applications are made up of objects that you define in the AOT and X++ code and can attach to many of the object definition types such as forms, classes, reports, queries, and tables.

As you have just seen, you create new object definitions by selecting the New menu option from the pop-up menu of an object type group—this creates a standard definition that is automatically placed at the top of the group. The default definition is, however, not very useful, so you need to select it and bring up its Properties window so that you can set some sensible values in it—the same principle applies to all object type definitions.

Note You can also create a new object definition by using the Ctrl+N keyboard shortcut, and pressing Alt+Enter to display the Properties window.

Note Most top-level object types contain other objects whose groups are automatically created under the new object when you create a new definition, and it's your responsibility to create whatever you need to support your application. For example, tables have fields, field groups, indexes, relations, delete actions, and methods.

The properties of your objects make up the static view of your applications, and most object types also include a methods group where you attach code in order to add functionality (that is, the dynamic side of your applications). The total set of properties is very large and varies from one object type to another and you can find a list with a short explanation in the Developer's Guide document referred to in the Wrap-Up section of this chapter.

Note Two object types, classes and jobs, are purely functional; the first is a collection of methods, and the second is a single method.

Note To find the list of object properties in the document indicated, type the keyword **ActiveBackColor** in the Index tab page.

Before we dive in, here are the essential steps for developing an application in the most natural sequence—whenever possible reuse and/or extend existing object definitions or functionality:

1. Obtain all the license codes that you need and install them.

2. Create all the configuration and security keys that you need.

3. Create all the extended data types that you need.

4. Create all base enumerators that you need.

5. Create all the tables that you need.

6. Create all the forms and reports that you need.

7. Create classes as needed to encapsulate functionality that is independent of the data or presentation layers of your application.

8. Create resources as needed.

9. Create queries as needed.

10. Create documentation as you go.

11. Create menus and menu items to allow users to invoke your forms, reports, and jobs, and execute processes represented by classes.

Depending on your development process (Waterfall, for example), you might create all the needed extended data types before you create your tables, create all your tables before you create your forms, etc. If, instead, you have a prototype approach, you might only create the extended data types you need to create the fields for a table, create the table or tables you need for a form, and then repeat the pattern.

Note With informal development processes often driven by the user interface, there is a tendency for developers to start hacking away at forms, menus, and other user interfacing elements first. It's really up to you, but that kind of approach invariably leads to going back and forth from your user interface to other objects that you implement as you realize you need to support your user interface. The result is software that is patched together, and lacks design and an underlying architecture. add sentence after this one: The previous approach is a good compromise where you first define your data model, then your user interface and your buisness logic as needed.

Data Dictionary

The purpose of the Data Dictionary is to group all the object types that represent data in one way or another. The basic process of creating a new data type definition consists of the following:

1. Select the node under the Data Dictionary that represents the object type you want to create.

2. Create a new definition of the data type and set its properties.

3. Create subtypes and set their properties.

4. Add functionality by creating new methods in the respective group and/or modifying behavior by overriding existing methods.

Each Axapta data type has its own twists in how you go about this. Each contains different subtypes. As a rule, all data types are created with a default name that you need to change in the corresponding property to something meaningful. You should also provide a label using the label system, which is a string that is commonly displayed to designate the table in the user interface. Some controls also have a help text property where you can provide a short text description that is displayed in the status bar when the control is selected—these are really labels and work exactly the same way. Because these are general properties and their use is straightforward, you now know everything there is to know about them, and we will not mention them further.

Note It's a good idea to establish a naming pattern for the data types people in your organization create and even for naming properties, so that you can easily identify and distinguish the ones you have created and/or changed from the rest. A common practice is to prefix them with the organization's acronym; for example, if you work for a commercial organization named ABC, then you might use ABCPhoneNumbers for a table and ABCGetAddressFromPhoneNumber for a method to retrieve an address from a telephone number.

Last but not least, remember to do a synchronization after you have made changes to object types in the Data Dictionary group, to make sure that any changes that may result to your tables are pushed to the database.

Tables

Tables are objects that represent the data that is persisted to the database of your choice. They are a little different from other object types in that you can't extend them, and their properties or variables are public. The most important properties to provide when creating a table are as follows:

- *TitleField1 and TitleField2*: Specify fields that are displayed in the active title bar of forms

- *ConfigurationKey and SecurityKey*: Specify that only users authorized to access the data can do so. We strongly recommend setting these options.

- *CacheLookup*: Specifies how the table is to be cached to optimize data access. Caching is a complex subject with a discussion of its own in Chapter 17.

- *CreateRecIdIndex*: Allows you to create a RECID index. Axapta automatically adds a RECID to every table when its created, so that you can use it as an index; however, if you have a well-designed data model, then that should not be necessary.

- *PrimaryIndex and ClusterIndex*: Specifies which field is your primary and clustered index, which requires that you have created the respective fields beforehand.

Note Axapta not only automatically adds a RECID field to every table but also a DATAAREAID. The first is a sequence number, and the second is the ID of the current working company. The RECID is guaranteed to be unique for a company, that is, together these IDs make up a unique key.

Defining tables consists of creating the table itself and the following subtypes:

- *Fields*: Dictates where your data is actually placed, and when you create these you specify the base data type each holds. However, you should as a rule set the ExtendedDataType (EDT) property to an existing one so that the definition is maintained centrally for ease of reuse and maintenance.

- *Field groups*: Allows you to group fields that are normally used together, such as name and surname, so that you can reference them as a block when you need to use them.

■**Note** Axapta automatically creates two field groups; AutoReport and AutoLookup, that it uses to generate standard reports and lookups on the table. You can create your own as needed.

■**Note** You can create table fields by dragging EDTs to the field groups of the table.

- *Indexes*: Defines indexes that you need to optimize data access to your table.

- *Relations*: Defines relations between the table and others for enforcing relational constraints.

- *DeleteActions*: Specifies what to do with related tables when you delete a record; you specify a table that is the subject of the action and the action that has possible values:

  - *None*: Disables the delete action

  - *Cascade*: Deletes related records

  - *Restricted*: Prohibits deletion if related records exist

  - *Cascade+Restricted*: Behaves like the Restricted value if you delete a record directly in the table, but cascades if the record is deleted as the result of a cascading delete on a table higher on the cascade chain

---

■**Note** The purpose of Cascade+Restricted is somewhat mystifying, and it's not easy to really grasp its rationale or application.

Maps

The main reason maps exist is to overcome the limitations of Axapta tables, specifically the fact that tables can't extend each other. They resemble a table, but are actually just a collection of methods that can be shared by tables. They have no properties that deserve a special mention here, but some of the object types they contain do:

- *Fields*: These are fields that your map provides shared functionality for.

- *Field groups*: These are the same as for tables and rarely used.

- *Mappings*: This is where you specify which tables the map provides functionality for, and these will typically contain one or more of the fields you created.

- *Methods*: This is where you add the functionality that you want to share across the mapped tables for the fields you created.

Views

Views are a form of transient tables that are populated at runtime using their definition and code. There is not much to say here about their properties except for the following:

- *TitleField1 and TitleField2*: As with tables, these specify fields that are displayed in the active title bar of forms.

They do, however, have some subtypes that are worth a word or two:

- *Metadata*: A container of data sources that are references to the tables from which the view is populated.

- *Fields*: The fields that the view populates from the specified data sources.

- *Field groups*: The same as in tables.

- *Methods*: As usual, this is where you can add functionality, for example, X++ code, by creating methods.

Typically, you would use a view to represent a subset of a table or a joined set of two or more tables.

Extended Data Types

Extended Data Types, or EDTs, allow you to define your own data types by building on the basic data types like Real, Integer, String, etc. Because these are actually object definitions, they have properties that allow you to control how they are displayed and formatted. They can also extend other EDTs so that you can create a specialization hierarchy.

Since EDTs can be of any base data type, their properties vary accordingly, and there are none that deserve any special remarks here; but as with most other object types, they do have interesting subtypes, specifically the following:

- *Array elements*: These enable you to define an array of relations such that each array element specifies a relationship constraint that has to be met when validating data input to any fields that use the EDT.

- *Relations*: These specify a table and a field that the EDT is related to such that any table fields created using the EDT automatically inherit the relationship; these come in different flavors, and you can read more about them in the documentation indicated in the "Wrap-Up" section.

By using EDTs as properties of your object types instead of base data types, you not only provide a much richer data type, but also, if you reuse it consistently, have the ability to change it in one place and have it automatically changed everywhere where it is used.

To give you a practical example, assume that you had decided that names were limited to ten characters (the default for String EDTs) and that some of your users got back to you and said customers or suppliers in some of the countries they work with typically have names that are more than ten characters long. If you had defined name fields in several tables, such as customer, employee, supplier, as a String with a `StringSize` property of 10, then you would have to find them all and correct them. If instead you had used an EDT, you would change the EDT, and the fields would all be automatically changed for you.

Base Enums

Base Enums are enumerator objects that you can define yourself, have a specific base data type, and contain elements of the type in question that have a name and a value. The advantage of Base Enums is that they are objects and more or less work along the same lines as EDTs.

Feature Keys

These correspond to configuration keys and are present in Axapta 3.0 for backward compatibility.

License Codes

License codes represent the functionality in the system that is turned on or off, depending on the codes supplied to you by MBS and entered in the license information form using the main application menu path Administration ➤ Setup ➤ System ➤ License Information.

Configuration Keys

Configuration keys depend on license codes or other configuration keys. They are features that you can turn on or off in the system using the main menu path Administration ➤ Setup ➤ System ➤ Configuration Form.

■**Note** When you turn off a configuration key, all tables that are associated with it are dropped from the database and other object types are hidden.

Security Keys

Security keys depend on license codes, configuration keys, or other security keys. They represent features, and you can use them to control the level of access granted to user groups, and consequently the access users have to different areas of functionality in Axapta. You do this using the Permissions tab page on the User Group Permissions form, which you access by selecting Administration ➤ Setup ➤ Security ➤ User Group Permissions. The levels of access that you can assign a user group per security key are defined here:

- *No access*: Users belonging to the selected user group cannot access any object types that are associated with the key.

- *View*: Access to the object types associated with the key is limited to viewing them and their properties.

- *Edit*: Members of the selected user group can view and make changes to objects of the type associated with this key.

- *Create*: Access to the objects associated with the key by members of the selected user group is limited to viewing and creating objects of the specified type.

- *Full control*: There are no limits to what the users in the selected user group can do with object types associated with the key—have fun!

Note The Admin user group has full control over all security keys, and you can't change this.

Table Collections

A table collection is a grouping of tables that is required by virtual companies. Basically, you create collections of logically related tables, and then you can associate them with a virtual company. That way, all the companies that are associated with the virtual company in question share the tables and their data.

Macros

When your code is compiled to intermediate binary form for persistence, the X++ preprocessor expands all macros. They come in different flavors, and you can see more on this in Chapter 20. The type found in the AOT is a macro library; that is, it's a collection of macro statements typically related in one way or another, for example, math macros that you can use anywhere by declaring the library and then using the macros you need through their specific notation.

Macros have no interesting properties or subtypes.

Classes

Throughout this chapter, we have intentionally used the term *object types* instead of classes to distinguish other object types—often called classes in Axapta, from a specific type of Axapta object, the Class. Objects of this type exist in the AOT under the Classes node in the root, and they are purely functional objects. They have one property worth singling out here: RunOn. In 3-tier setups, classes have the option of being run on the server, the client, or from where they are called, offering the possibility of placing the execution of business logic close to where it's used from to improve performance.

Otherwise, they contain only methods, and their purpose is to encapsulate generic functionality written in X++; you can read more about them in Chapter 20, but here is a set of particular methods that are important enough for you to be aware of at this point:

- All classes are created automatically with a Class declaration, alias the classDeclaration method, and serve the following purpose:

  - It specifies the scope and name of the class.

  - It can specify that it extends another class.

  - You can use it to declare class variables but not initialize them.

- New is the default constructor of the class where you can perform whatever initialization is required.

- Finalize is the destructor and is not invoked automatically, that is, you must explicitly invoke it on the class when you want to clean up.

- Your own methods fall into two categories:

  - *Object methods*: Each instance of this object type has the method and they are invoked using the pattern *myClass.myObjMethod()*.

  - *Class methods*: These are declared with the static keyword, and there is only one instance of such methods. They are called using a different notation from object methods, that is, *myClass::myClassMethod()*.

- If you define a Main method, you can call it from a menu item, and it is the only class or object method that can be called from a menu item.

Note that if you have a 3-tier setup, then you should set classes to execute on the server as much as possible, as it's very costly for the AOS to retrieve them from the AOD and pass them to the client for execution.

Forms

Forms are the core of the user interface and are primarily used to create, delete, edit, view, and process data in real time. They do not have any properties worth going through here, but they have three subtypes of objects, namely the following:

- *Methods*: This is where you add code that adds functionality at the form level.

- *Data sources*: These specify which tables you create, delete, edit, view, and process data for and include methods so you can provide processing that is specific to the usage of the underlying tables; they would not apply to uses of the same tables by other forms or object types such as reports.

- *Designs*: This is the actual presentation of the form as well as the corresponding presentation logic and can be quite a wide and/or deep tree, so we need to explore it a little further by itself.

The Designs subtype of a form is actually just a group that contains one single Design node, that is, the definition of the presentation of the form. There are two approaches for working with form designs:

- *The visual representation of the form*: Click the right mouse button on the Design node to display its pop-up menu and select the Edit menu option. This displays the form in design mode, and you can navigate it using the mouse to select controls you want to work with.

- *The container tree*: Use the AOT, expand the Design node and navigate the tree to the controls you wish to work with.

Visually working with a form can be practical, because it provides immediate recognition of any changes you make. You cannot use this approach to add new controls to the form, so it's limited to modifications. The tree is, however, the common way of working with forms. By selecting any control at any level and displaying its pop-up menu, you can create nested controls. Axapta makes sure that you can only create nested controls that make sense; for example, you can only create tab pages within a tab control.

The general pattern when creating a form is as follows:

1. Create the form.

2. Specify its data sources.

3. Implement any form-wide methods.

4. If all the controls that you need can be displayed in a window with a maximum resolution of 640×480 pixels and make up a logical group, then do not create a tab control or tab pages; otherwise do the following:

   1. Create a tab control.

   2. Create all the tab pages you need to group your data into logical sets—a standard pattern here is for the first tab page to be called Overview and have a grid control that displays the core data from your data sources, and a second tab page called General that displays more or less the same data in groups of fields.

5. Create groups to hold logically related subsets of the data for your form.

6. Create the control that you need to work with your data in their respective groups.

7. At the same level as the tab control, add form-wide buttons.

A typical form tree resembles the expanded tree of the Address form shown in Figure 18-15. Something that is missing from the preceding list of steps for creating forms is that many of the controls have method groups that you can use to add functionality as you create the respective controls.

The most interesting properties of forms and the container controls they can contain are the following:

- *DataSource*: Specifies the primary data source for the form, which is inherited by all subcontrols.

- *Columns*: Indicates the number of columns over which to lay out the form. IntelliMorph uses this information to distribute the controls you place on the form evenly.

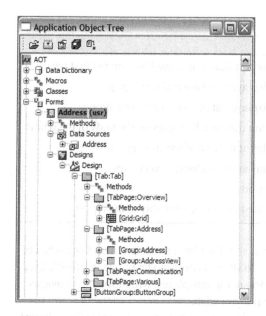

Figure 18-15. *The Address form tree*

Data controls add the following field worth remembering from the start:

- *DataField*: The data field from the specified data source to bind to the control

Reports

Reports to some extent resemble forms in that they contain methods, data sources, and a design—actually a report design. However, unlike forms, reports are not used to work with data but rather to output data in hardcopy. Normally, reports are also intended for summarizing or aggregating data for supporting business decisions and analysis.

■**Note** Actually, there is a little twist with the data sources of a report, and that is it actually contains a single query that is used to retrieve the data with which to populate the report.

When you select the ReportDesign node of a report, you don't create a new control, but instead generate a new design, of which there can be only one per report.

■**Note** When you create a report, it automatically generates a default design called AutoDesignSpecs, used in the absence of a design generated by you, that is literally called Generated Design.

Creating the report is pretty straightforward. Within the generated design, you can create different sections, and each is typically associated with a particular usage and placement in the final layout, as you can see in Table 18-2.

Table 18-2. *Report Sections*

Block Type	Description
Prologue	Introduction to the report that is displayed only on the first page
Page header	Information to be displayed at the top of every page
Header	Information to be displayed at the top of a section group
Section group	A group of information that usually makes up the body of the report
Footer	Information to display at the end of a section group
Page footer	Information to display at the bottom of every page
Epilogue	Conclusion of the report
Programmable selection	A block that can be used to add functionality to the report

Another important aspect about reports is that you don't have to design them from scratch. In the real world, it's usual for a variety of reports to share a common layout even though they may contain different data. In Axapta, this is done using templates, which Axapta provides a good set of, and to which you can add your own if you wish.

Last but not least, you can design your reports from scratch, but Axapta provides a Report Wizard, which you can invoke from the menu bar path Tools ➤ Development Tools ➤ Wizards ➤ Report Wizard. This wizard walks you through the creation of a report, after which you can then modify the report if the wizard doesn't give you exactly what you want.

The properties to single out in reports are for data fields:

- *Table*: The table the control is bound to

- *DataField*: The field in the table to bind the control to

- *DataMethod*: A method that can be used to populate the field

Like forms, you can also work with reports visually by selecting the generated design and the respective pop-up menu option Edit, or you can use the container tree in the AOT.

Queries

Queries are prebuilt definitions of data retrieval statements that you can easily adapt at runtime using their properties. A query consists of one or more data sources and methods that are executed when the query is run. The aspects of queries worth looking into here are the controls or object subtypes contained by the data properties:

- *Table*: Represents a property of each data source that designates the primary source of data for the query

- *Fields*: Defines the fields from the specified table to retrieve from the data source table

- *Sorting*: Allows you to specify how to sort the results of the query

- *Ranges*: Allows you to specify a range of values to limit the result set to

- *Relations*: Enables you to create joined queries; you define joined data sources within the master data source node.

Queries are typically used in reports and in X++ code and occasionally in forms, where they can actually be created fully in code.

Jobs

Jobs resemble classes with a single static main method. They are purely code and have no properties of major interest. They are used typically for administrative purposes and quick-and-dirty prototyping.

Menus

Menus are the folders you see in the application menu window, and their function is to navigate the functionality of Axapta and group like menu items, which in turn are used to invoke executable object types and code.

Menu Items

Menu items are contained in menus and are used to invoke executable object types and code.

Web

This group contains the object types used for Web-based user interfaces; the definitions are for the most part used to generate ASP pages that are placed in a Microsoft Information Server Web site when you use the Web management tools to save or update a site definition. For the most part, working with these object types is similar to working with the corresponding user interface object types used to create applications for the standard Windows client.

The object types available for developing Web applications are as follows:

- *Web Forms*: Dynamic Web pages

- *Web Reports*: Reports that can be output to a Web page

- *Web Menus*: Links that are used to navigate Web pages and sites

- *Web Pages*: Static Web pages

- *Web Files*: Static Web site files, typically ASP and HTML files

Resources

This represents external files such as images, animations, etc. that, once defined, can be used in Axapta as any other object type.

Documentation

There are actually three documentation nodes:

- System Documentation

- Application Developer Documentation

- Application Documentation

These are where documentation produced in the corresponding tab pages of the help text tools is stored in the AOT.

You access the tool by selecting Tools ➤ Development Tools ➤ Help Texts, which brings up the form shown in Figure 18-16.

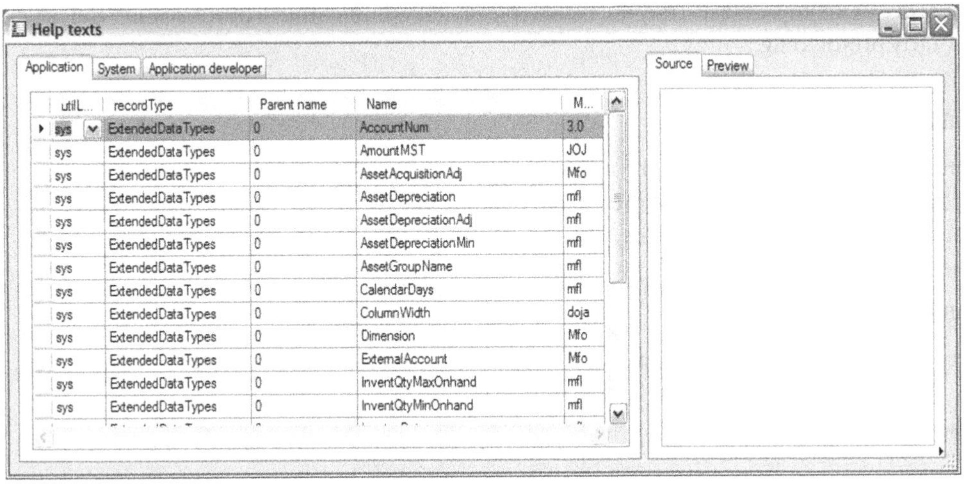

Figure 18-16. *The Help Text tool*

The fundamental aspects of creating these types of documentation are as follows: the documentation will be in HTML format; you need to decide who your target audience is and then use the appropriate tab page to either create a new record in the respective grid and enter the source documentation in the memo control to the right of the form, or modify or delete existing documentation. As you see in Figure 18-16, you can immediately preview your documentation in the corresponding tab page.

The documentation is classified using the fields you can see in the grid:

- *utilLevel*: The application layer in which the documented object type is located

- *recordType*: The object type

- *Parent name*: The object type that the current one extends

- *Name*: The name by which the object current type is known in the AOT

- *Modified By*: The user who last modified the documentation for the current object type

Help System

Axapta has a fully integrated help system in HTML format that allows you to modify the contents by using a built-in HTML editor. You can modify help text by selecting any control and clicking F1 to bring the help text for that control up in a Web browser window, which should resemble what you see in Figure 18-17.

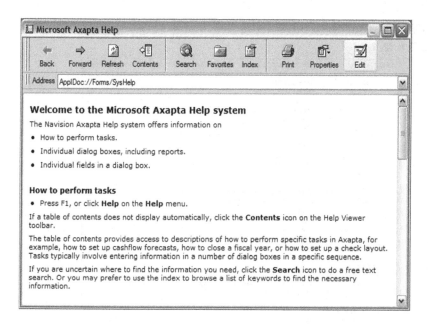

Figure 18-17. *The Help text browser*

Click the Edit button to the left of the tool bar, and the HTML editor will be called so you can make any modifications you wish.

■**Note** Here you can modify the help texts delivered by Microsoft Business Solutions, as well as your own, if you prefer, instead of using the help text tool when you create them, as this is a much better editor.

X++

In spite of the power of IntelliMorph and MorphX, the fact is that there is only so far you can go without coding. X++ is the built-in Axapta programming language that enables you to overcome the limits that you get from the product out of the box.

The X++ Editor

Axapta includes its own integrated code editor for working with X++. It's quite a simple editor, without bells and whistles; however, it provides everything you need to program in X++, and its simplicity keeps you focused on what's important.

To start coding, you either select the Methods node of an object type or a specific method that it contains and double-click it. From the node's pop-up menu that appears, select the Edit menu option. The result resembles Figure 18-18.

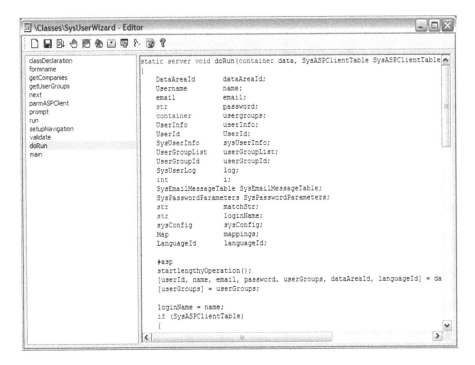

Figure 18-18. *The X++ code editor*

Note The easiest way to find out which application objects have methods and that you can therefore add code to is to expand the respective node in the AOT and see if it has a methods subnode. The two exceptions to this rule are jobs, which basically are a static method, and classes that are a class declaration and a set of methods; these you double-click directly on the main node or on a method so as to open them in the code editor.

The editor consists of a tool bar: the left pane displays a list of all open methods, and the right pane is where you work with the code. If you click a Methods node, then all the methods in it are opened and you will see them on the open methods pane. If you open several methods in the same Methods node, then they will be added to the list of open methods; however, Axapta will open a new editor window for each object type; if you open methods on two different forms, then you will have two editor windows. Clicking a method in the left pane of the editor will automatically place the code for the method in the right pane for you to work with.

The tool bar provides shortcuts to the most commonly used functionality, specifically from left to right:

- *New*: Creates a new method in the current object type and/or Methods node. The new method is named method1 and has a void return type. Change the name and the interface as needed and save it to rename it.

- *Save*: Saves the content of the edit window, which automatically compiles the method.

- *Go*: Executes the method, but notice that most methods are not designed to be executed directly with the exception of jobs or the main method of classes, so using this will probably cause errors or do nothing.

- *Toggle Breakpoint*: Sets or removes a breakpoint for the debugger on the line where the cursor is positioned.

- *Enable/Disable Breakpoint*: Activates or deactivates an existing breakpoint so that you don't have to delete breakpoints when you don't need them and then re-create them when you do.

- *Remove All Breakpoints*: Really removes all breakpoints including those in other methods that have nothing to do with the ones you are working on. It's practical if you have been setting breakpoints around the application and can't remember where.

- *Compile*: Compiles and saves the current method and is equivalent to saving.

- *Lookup Label/Text*: Looks up the selected string or label identifier in the label system.

- *Lookup Properties/Methods*: Displays a list box with the methods and properties of the given object type that you have access to if you have selected or placed your cursor on an object instance. This is equivalent to typing the method and property operators for object types or instances, that is, double colons (::) or periods (.). Double-clicking a node inserts these as you will see in the next bulleted list.

- *Script*: Displays a pop-up menu from which you can select a code template that inserts a piece of code at the cursor position, for example, an empty while statement. This is especially practical as you can add your own pieces of code and save yourself the trouble of having to constantly retype statements or constructs that you use frequently.

The number of commands supported by the editor is quite extensive, and you can look them up in Appendix D, whereas the X++ programming language is covered in Chapter 20.

As we already mentioned, the editor is quite simple, but it provides all the important features you need to code, and you can easily pick it up in a few minutes on your own. A few very useful features of the editor that we haven't told you about are as follows:

- Besides options for creating new methods, pasting deleted code, and saving the current method, the pop-up menu displayed if you click anywhere in the edit pane has a series of list menu options that display a list box with all objects in the system of the current selected type. It also contains a series of lookup menu options that provide the same functionality as we have already seen on the tool bar.

- Whatever you select from the lists mentioned in the preceding bullet point, you can expand the nodes to drill down into them, and double-clicking a node inserts it at the cursor position. For example, if you list classes and select SysUsersOnline, expand it, select the isUserOnline static method, and double-click, then SysUsersOnline::isUserOnline(will be inserted, and you can then just finish this off by entering whatever arguments the method requires—the user ID in this case.

- The editor provides real-time lookup and completion of statements, meaning that whenever you enter the double colon (::) or period operators following an object type name or instance, then the editor automatically displays a list of available methods and properties.

- Methods that do not compile successfully are marked with a red dot on the AOT or with a red wavy line in the methods list pane of the editor.

- Methods with errors that have been corrected but not saved are marked by an asterisk (*) at the end in the methods pane of the editor.

- Statements that have generated compile errors are underlined with a red wavy line in the code editor pane.

The Compiler

Before any object definition or code you create or modify can kick in, it needs to be compiled. You can do this explicitly using the Compile menu option on most object types' pop-up menus. In the case of code, it happens automatically when you save it.

What is really important for you as an application developer is that the compiler reports errors, warnings, and best-practice deviations in your code when it tries to compile it. When you compile, a Compiler Output window resembling what you see in Figure 18-19 is displayed.

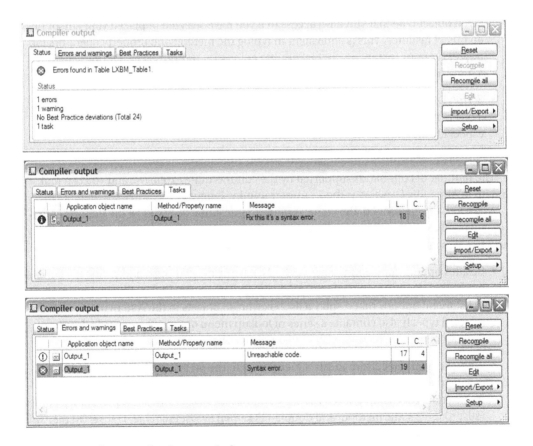

Figure 18-19. *The Compiler Output window*

The Compiler Output window consists of four tab pages:

- *Status*: This tab page displays a running status of the compilation, where you can see the counts of what the compiler has found.

- *Errors and warnings*: This tab page provides a list of all statements that have either generated an error or a warning with all the information you need to find the code that is causing it.

- *Best practices*: You have seen this tab page earlier on in this chapter. It is equivalent to the Errors and Warnings tab page, but lists best practice violations instead.

- *Tasks*: This tab page lists all occurrences in the code of // TODO: statements. This is a very useful feature when for some reason you lack the information or decisions to enable you to finish off a piece of code. You can insert a comment literally as quoted starting with the TODO: keyword and whatever text you want to follow; the compiler will then list all of your TODOs so you can easily find them again.

There isn't much more to know about the compiler, but as a matter of curiosity the compiler does not produce binary machine code that can be executed directly. Instead, it produces an intermediate binary form that is then compiled to the target machine binary form by the runtime engine.

Debugging

A very important aspect of any development environment is a solid debugger to help you step through the code and see what's really going on when it executes.

The Axapta debugger is one of the few tools that is not fully integrated with the Axapta environment—it's an external binary that executes outside the Axapta environment. You set the debug mode for each user through the Development tab page of the Options form that you can access by selecting Tools ➤ Options. It's important to understand how these settings determine what you can and can't do, so let's look at them:

- *No*: The debugger does not start when you execute your code, but as soon as you set a breakpoint in the code editor, the setting is changed automatically to When Breakpoint.

- *When Breakpoint*: The debugger is started if there are breakpoints in the code.

- *Always*: The debugger is always started, so if an error occurs, even if you have no breakpoints, you are thrown to the debugger and placed at the point in the code the error occurred.

The first step in debugging is either to have the debugger always running and wait for an error to occur, or more commonly to place breakpoints in a piece of code from within the code editor and then execute it through a menu, tool bar button, menu button, or programmatically. When you reach the point in the code where the breakpoint is located, Axapta brings up the debugger window and marks the breakpoint line with a red ball superimposed with a yellow right arrow, as you can see in Figure 18-20.

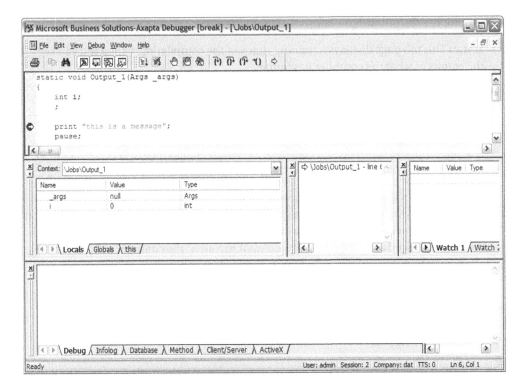

Figure 18-20. *The debugger*

The debugger is pretty straightforward to use for any developer, and the only remarks worth making here are that the keyboard shortcuts are not the same as in other debuggers. But you can see what they are from the menu and tool bars, so check them out. Last but not least, the trace pane at the bottom of the window differentiates different types of Axapta-specific events that you don't find in other debuggers and is therefore very helpful.

While not strictly part of debugging, Axapta has a very rich set of tools to help find bugs, discover performance bottlenecks, and in general improve your code, and we would like to leave you with them so that you know what tools you can rely on if and when the situation calls for it:

- *SQL Tracing*: This tool allows you to log a variety of event types that generally indicate opportunities for improvement. These can all be set in the SQL tab page of the Users Options form, accessed by selecting Tools ➤ Options from the menu bar.

  - *Multiple SQL Statements*: Logs all statements issued to the database

  - *Long Queries*: Logs statements exceeding a threshold that you specify

  - *Warnings*: Logs warnings produced when generating and executing SQL statements

  - *Deadlocks*: Logs deadlock situations and helps you identify concurrency problems

  - *General*: Logs the query plans for SQL statements so that you can see the steps required to perform a given statement

- *Error Message*: This a fixed feature of Axapta. All SQL error messages are written to the Infolog (discussed in more detail in a moment) and to a log file in the log directory specified in the client configuration. There is quite a lot of information in these logs, and they are very helpful in identifying database problems.

- *System-wide Tracing*: The client configuration utility has a Tracing tab page where you can set up logging for all users as opposed to the per-user tracing of the Options form:

  - *Trace All SQL Warnings to File*: Does exactly that to a file in the log folder specified for the respective configuration.

  - *Trace All SQL Statements to File*: Does exactly that to a file in the log folder specified for the respective configuration.

  - *Query Time Limit*: Queries exceeding the specified threshold are logged.

  - *Number of Records Preloaded*: If the quantity of data in a preloaded table is too high, then that may be a performance problem, and you can see here which tables are causing it.

  - *Time Used for Preloading*: Axapta allows you to specify tables to preload so that you pay an upfront penalty the first time you access them, but subsequently they are present in the data cache, reducing access time to data. Here you can see those that exceed a certain threshold.

A nice debugging feature of Axapta is the Infolog, shown in Figure 18-21. This feature is automatically displayed when anything is posted to it. As a general rule, all errors and warnings are posted to it, and you can obtain more information on a specific error or warning by double-clicking the respective line in the Infolog tree.

Figure 18-21. *The Infolog window*

The last tool that we need to make you aware of is the Code Profiler that comes with Axapta. This is a very powerful and advanced tool that you can use to profile your application and find out where time is being used. You can access it from the menu bar by selecting Tools ➤ Development Tools ➤ Code Profiler. Using it is pretty simple:

1. From the form that is displayed, click the Start button, and if you want to limit the calling depth that you want to profile, then specify it.

2. Run the functionality that you want to profile.

3. Go back to the code profile form and stop the profiler.

4. Finally, use the Profiler Runs button to see the profiler results in the respective form.

Analyzing the data collected by the profiles is pretty straightforward for anyone with experience using code profiles. The only suggestion we have is to profile small pieces of functionality and clean up the data that is saved, because the quantities of data that it generates are very large, and you will quickly get bogged down in them if you don't.

Web Applications

Developing Web applications follows the same principles as developing applications for the Windows client supplied with Axapta; however, the user interface is a browser, which places a series of constraints on what is technically possible.

As you have seen, the AOT Web group contains a series of object types that are specific to Web applications, and that you should use instead of the normal object types, but otherwise the big difference is this: the user interface of your application must somehow be made available to a Web server that can then service Web browsers functioning as clients.

Best Practices

As with any language, there is a right way to design and write code, and there is a wrong way. Axapta helps you stay on the right path by providing a Best Practices tool that you can extend with your own rules. It is called automatically by the compiler, or you can execute it on any object definition in the AOT to get a list of deviations from recommend best practices.

Unfortunately, this tool doesn't tell you what you are doing right. To find out, you need to read the documentation indicated in the "Wrap-Up" section of this chapter.

If you explicitly invoke the Best Practices tool using the pop-up menu of a specific object definition, it automatically opens the Compiler Output window, as shown previously in Figure 18-13, and places you in the correct tab page through which you can see what it has found and where. As with the other tab pages in the Compiler Output window, you can use the buttons located at the left side of the window to go to and edit the properties or code where the violation has occurred and export or import the results of the run to or from a file.

The only functionality provided that is specific to best practices is the Setup menu button. Through this button, you can use the Best Practices menu option to display the form shown in Figure 18-22, where you can specify the warning level and the types of checks to perform.

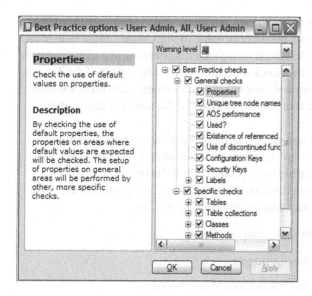

Figure 18-22. *The Best Practices Setup form*

The Best Practices tool is also invoked automatically by the compiler every time you compile an object definition; the only difference here is that you are not automatically placed in the Best Practices tab page and that you must explicitly select it to see the details of the violations encountered, if the information in the Status tab page indicates that there are any.

Even after reading the documentation provided in the product CD forwards and backwards and working with Axapta for a while, it's extremely unlikely that you will remember every rule and the do's and don'ts, so we suggest that you keep the default setup, which is to check for everything and always correct any violations right away as you do with errors. If you don't, the quantity will grow out of hand, and you will never have the time to go back and fix them all.

Wrap-Up

You should now be comfortable with the tools and techniques used to customize Axapta, so let's recap what you have seen in this chapter:

- User-level customization with IntelliMorph

- Customizing for developers with MorphX

- Writing your own code in X++

- Debugging, profiling, and analyzing your code

- Developing Web portals and customizing Enterprise Portal

- Following established coding practices

What you have picked up here has given you a very wide and comprehensive grasp of the Axapta development environment and what you can use it for, so start cracking. As you use the tools and technologies we have walked you through, you will discover the myriad possibilities, become acquainted with the different twists of the environment, and even develop your own techniques and tools. But before you do so, please notice that in this chapter, more than most others, we have focused on making sure that you have a good understanding of Axapta's richness and scope at the cost of details that require a book unto themselves. The details of the Axapta development environment are reasonably well covered in the documentation included with the product CD, and it is very important that you read further on the topics in this chapter before proceeding.

Developing in Axapta is a lot of fun and gives you the opportunity to exercise both technological and business expertise, and the greatest benefit, especially for software engineers, seeing your work being put to use solving business problems and challenges.

You can read more about the topics in this chapter in the following documents available in the documentation folder of the product distribution package or CD:

- *AX-300-DVG-002-v01.00-ENUS.chm*: Developers Guide

- *AX-300-DVG-007-v01.00-ENUS.chm*: Debugger

- *AX-300-DVG-003-v01.00-ENUS.chm*: Development Best Practices

- *AX-300-DVG-001-v01.00-ENUS.chm*: User Assistance Best Practices

CHAPTER 19
■ ■ ■

Data and Databases

Data persistence in Axapta is a complex issue, and in practice—as you have surely noticed by now, Axapta stores data in different formats in flat files as well as in a relational database, and provides different techniques and tools for exchanging data with other systems.

In this chapter we'll look at the following:

- What data is stored in flat files

- How Axapta works with its supported relational database management systems

- Managing the database layer

- Differences between Microsoft SQL Server and Oracle

- Limitations Axapta imposes when working with the supported databases

- Exchanging data with other systems

Since for the most part we have used Microsoft SQL Server as our reference database in this book, in this chapter we will present the important differences between SQL Server and Oracle to help you if you are using Oracle.

We would like to call your attention to the importance of knowing your database system well and, in particular for developers, the importance of good database design. Bad database design is the cause of many performance problems with Axapta, and combined with bad coding it will run any system into the ground. However, much of the database design and code we all have has been produced by others and it would be impractical to rewrite it; but by knowing your database system well, you can often improve performance by tweaking it.

Flat Files

You have already encountered numerous situations in which Axapta uses flat files to store data. Axapta uses files to store system data such as definitions for forms, reports, and basically all the objects you can see in the AOT. The same applies to labels, help information, and the X++ code.

Furthermore, Axapta allows you to save and read different types of information such as configuration-key setups, startup configuration settings, and logs in files. These vary in format but for the most part are plain text, so you can open them with a text editor. The formats vary, but Axapta provides all the necessary tools to read, write, and manipulate them.

Because Chapter 17 provides a description of all the files that make up the Axapta system, for the most part this chapter will focus on the data that Axapta stores in the database system of your choice—i.e., the business data that is persisted to Microsoft SQL Server or Oracle. The only exceptions here are the tools used for exchanging business data with external systems that rely on files. They are covered in the "Import and Export" section of this chapter.

It's important to know that the data that is stored in external files is system data, data that has been exported, or data that is available to import into Axapta. The most important of these that are not covered in Chapter 17 are as follows:

- *XPO files* used for the following:

    - Saving definitions of objects or object branches from the AOT

    - Exporting configurations made with the client and server configuration utilities

- *CFG files* used for exporting configuration key setups

- *AXC files* used for saving configurations made with the client and server utilities that can be used as shortcuts for starting Axapta with the configuration data they contain

- *TXT files* used for license codes

- *DAT and DEF files* used for Axapta business data; typically used for exchanging data between systems

- *XLS files* used for saving Microsoft Excel templates containing definitions of Axapta tables that can be used to import data from other systems

That's it in a nutshell.

Data Dictionary

Axapta is designed to be database-independent, and therefore it relies as little as possible on the database layer. In practice, the only database objects that Axapta uses are tables and indexes, so for the most part Axapta hides the database from you and whatever you can do with one database you can with the other. But nothing is perfect, and even relying so little on the data layer, you should be aware of some differences. This chapter provides you with a walk-through of the database-related features and includes subsections that describe the limitations Axapta imposes on the data layer, as well as noteworthy differences between using Axapta with Microsoft SQL Server and Oracle.

The Axapta schema master is not in the database, but in Axapta, i.e., the table and index definitions are stored as metadata in AOD files, and any changes you make directly to the database are not reflected in the Axapta meta definition; they may be lost if the meta definition is changed and subsequently pushed to the database by a process called *synchronization*.

Consider two important aspects concerning the database:

- Configuration keys determine whether a table object is defined in the database—if the configuration key is not enabled, the tables that support the respective functionality are not created in the database even though their definitions exist in the AOT.

- Temporary tables (tables whose Temporary property is set to Yes) are not created in the database; their data is transient.

Furthermore, even though a table may be persisted, not all fields or indexes are persisted automatically; it depends on their settings and on other objects on which they depend being enabled.

A field is persisted if the following terms are met:

- The table in which it is defined is persisted

- The extended data type the field is derived from is enabled

- The configuration key for the extended data type they derive from is enabled

- The SaveContents property of the field is set to Yes

An index is pushed to the database in the following circumstances:

- The table and fields that it depends on are persisted

- The configuration key on which they depend is enabled

- The Enabled property of the index is set to Yes

Naming Conventions

Tables and indexes in Axapta have the following naming conventions in the underlying database system, and knowing them is a great help when you have to look under the hood.

- *Tables* are given the same name as in the AOT, but if the name is a reserved word in the database system, then the name is delimited by the values given in system variables QUOTEPRE and QUOTEPOST.

- *Fields* are given the same name as in the AOT, but if the name is a reserved word in the database system, then like table names it is delimited by the values given in system variables QUOTEPRE and QUOTEPOST. If a field is derived from an extended data type that has array elements, a field is created in the table for each respective array entry following this pattern:

    - [FieldName] for the first array; e.g., *PhoneNum*

    - [FieldNameN_]]for all but the first array, where *N* starts at 2; e.g., *PhoneNum2_*, *PhoneNum3_*

- *Indexes* follow the pattern [I_][TableId][NameOfIndex]—TableId is a generated number that is assigned to a table when it's created.

System Fields

For internal reasons, Axapta automatically adds two fields to the tables it creates in the database, and it creates an index automatically on all tables that do not have an index defined in the AOT. The two fields are DataAreaId and RecId:

- *DataAreaId* is a unique identifier per company that can be up to three characters long and specifies which company the data in the record belongs to.

  - When a new record is inserted, Axapta inserts the current company ID in this field automatically.

  - When selecting records from a table with the SaveDataPerCompany property enabled, DataAreaId = [Current Company] is added to the where clause automatically so only records for the current company are selected.

  - When dealing with a company that is part of a virtual company setup, the DataAreaId of the virtual company is used for the tables that are shared.

- *RecId* is always added to tables, and is an 8-bit signed integer that is unique for every record in a company.

Note System variables for the data layer are set in the class SqlDatabaseInit that Axapta executes automatically at startup. The class contains a method for initializing each of the supported databases.

Note An unsupported feature introduced in Axapta version 3.0 allows you to configure Axapta to generate unique RecIds per company/table pair, which allows you to significantly increase the number of records you can have per company. You do this by setting the system variable INDEX to 64—system variables are explained later in this chapter. It's very important to notice that this feature must be turned on from the start, or not turned on at all. Turning it on on an existing system will result in mixing two different numbering systems, but Axapta will process all data using the currently specified system only, causing havoc.

Note RecIds are drawn in sets of 25, and numbers from drawn sets are lost if not used, but Axapta has a utility called Check Record IDs that can reclaim unused IDs. However, it's unlikely that this will help except temporarily—it will not likely yield a significant pool of RecIds once you hit the limit of 4,294,967,296 imposed by the biggest number that can be represented by a 32-bit integer.

Virtual Fields

Virtual fields, also know as *virtual columns* in Axapta, are fields that can be referenced in tables but are not defined by default in the database. Table 19-1 lists them. Most virtual fields can be changed into real fields by setting a property on the table; only the TableId and SequenceNum fields cannot be changed from virtual to real.

Table 19-1. *Virtual Fields*

Field	Description
ModifiedDate	Date the record was last modified
ModifiedTime	Time the record was last modified, in seconds since midnight
ModifiedBy	Axapta user who made the last modification
ModifiedTransactionID	Transaction ID of the transaction that made the last modification
CreatedDate	Date the record was created
CreatedTime	Time of creation of the record, in seconds since midnight
CreatedBy	Axapta user who created the record
CreatedTransactionID	Transaction ID of the transaction that created the record
TableId	ID of the table
SequenceNum	The same value as in RecId

Data Types

All database field data types correspond to one of the following Axapta system variables:

- Str

- Int

- Real

- Date

- Enum

- Blob

- Text

Table 19-2 shows the mappings to both Microsoft SQL Server and Oracle, as well as the default values.

Table 19-2. *Data Type Mappings to MS SQL Server and Oracle*

Axapta	MS SQL Server	Oracle	Default Value
Str(n)	Varchar	Varchar2(n)	MS SQL Server '' or Oracle ASCII(2)
Str memo	Text	Clob	NULL
Int	Int	Number(10)	0
Real	Numeric(28,12)	Number(32,16)	0
Enum	Int	Number(3)	0
Date	DateTime	Date	1900-01-01 00:00:00
Time	Int	Number(10)	0
Container	Image	Blob	NULL

Referential Integrity

To stay database-independent, Axapta does not implement referential integrity at the data model layer, but instead provides support for relational integrity directly within the business logic through relations, delete actions, and table methods.

Relations

You can specify *relations* between tables in the following ways:

- Directly in the table definitions by adding a relation to the parent or child table.

- By specifying a relation for an extended data type that a field in the table uses; this automatically creates the relationship specified for any table that uses the extended data type and centralizes the definition.

Relations in Axapta fall within the following categories:

- *Normal*: Based on the fields in the related tables

- *Fixed field*: Based on a value in the field of the referencing table

- *Related fixed field*: Based on a value in the field of the referenced table

Relations are checked if the relationship is defined in an extended data type or if the Validate property is set to Yes; otherwise they are not checked.

Delete Actions

Delete actions are equivalent to a limited form of what is known in most database systems as *referential constraints*, and they are specified directly in the tables of the Axapta data dictionary. Unlike database triggers, they are used only for ensuring relational integrity. They come in the following flavors:

- *None*: Disables the delete action and only the rows of the table containing it are affected.

- *Cascade*: Deletes records in the specified related table whose related fields fulfill the conditions specified by existing relations.

- *Restricted*: Does not delete records in the table for which there are related records in the related table.

- *Cascade+Restricted*: Works like cascade, but the table method validateDelete will return true or false depending on whether the related table has related records.

Note Cascade+Restricted will prevent deletion of records from the tables involved only if the delete is done from a form; if you are calling it from your own X++ code, you have to check the return value and decide what to do yourself.

Note Delete actions are relevant only within the context of related tables.

Table Methods

The last type of referential integrity toy in Axapta is *table methods*. These are methods like any others in X++ and you can use them to execute any form of logic you want; however, you should not use them for purposes other than to operate on the data set represented by the table and to implement triggerlike functionality directly in Axapta.

Synchronization

The master definition for the Axapta data dictionary is maintained in Axapta itself and pushed to the database from there. The essence of the process is that when certain events occur Axapta checks its definition against those of the database. If it finds differences, it pushes its internal definition to the database. The same applies to indexes.

■**Note** Where technically possible, Axapta preserves data during synchronization by using the ALTER TABLE SQL statement; otherwise the table is dropped and re-created. If an alter table can't handle the existing differences, Axapta will perform a more-complex operation that creates a new table and copies existing data to it.

■**Note** We'll say once again since this is very important that changes to the definition of the data dictionary directly in your database system are not reflected in the Axapta internal definition, and will be lost the first time the tables are synchronized.

Synchronization is performed when the following events occur:

- The first time Axapta connects to a schema.

- The first time Axapta connects to a schema after an application upgrade has been performed.

- When changes made to the Axapta data dictionary definition correspond to elements of the database definition. However, changes not directly related to these will not automatically fire a synchronization that you will have to perform manually. For example, when you enable or disable configuration keys, the affected tables are not automatically created or deleted.

- When you start synchronization manually.

Database Connections

Axapta connects to MS SQL Server through ODBC, and to Oracle through OCI (Oracle Call Interface). In the first case (and as you have seen previously), you can specify an ODBC data source in the Axapta configuration. If you omit it, Axapta creates one automatically for you. Understanding this topic is very important, particularly if you are interested in performance-related issues.

Each 2-tier session in Axapta has at least three connections:

- *Session connection*: Primarily for system-management tasks

- *Application connection*: For executing business logic

- *Read-only connection*: For business logic that does not perform data manipulation

Beyond this, you can create your own user connections in X++ by using the classes `Connection`, `UserConnection`, and `OdbcConnection`.

- The `Connection` class provides a handle into the current open connection (which is typically the application connection), which you can then use programmatically.

- The `UserConnection` provides a new database connection with the same properties as the application connection but in its own transaction space.

- The `OdbcConnection` allows developers to access ODBC data sources.

Because logging in to the database is a relatively heavy process, Axapta implements connection pooling in the AOS, which allocates unused but open connections when they are needed if available and opens new ones when it runs out of free open connections. The connection pool mechanism times out connections that are not used after a specified interval, thereby freeing them.

Note You can set the timeout interval in the Axapta configuration utilities, but keep in mind that while you minimize the overhead of having to open new connections by increasing the timeout value, you increase the number of open connections and the overhead of managing more connections.

Note Because opening Microsoft SQL Server connections is relatively light and opening Oracle is much heavier, the default timeout values for database connections are 60 seconds and 30 minutes respectively.

Administration

While Axapta hides the underlying database for developers and users alike, as an administrator you need to be able to access it.

The first step for any administrator that needs to find his way around the setup and configuration of the Axapta database is to get hold of the Database Information form from the main application menu path at Administration ➤ Inquiries ➤ Database ➤ Database Information; that will bring up the form in Figure 19-1.

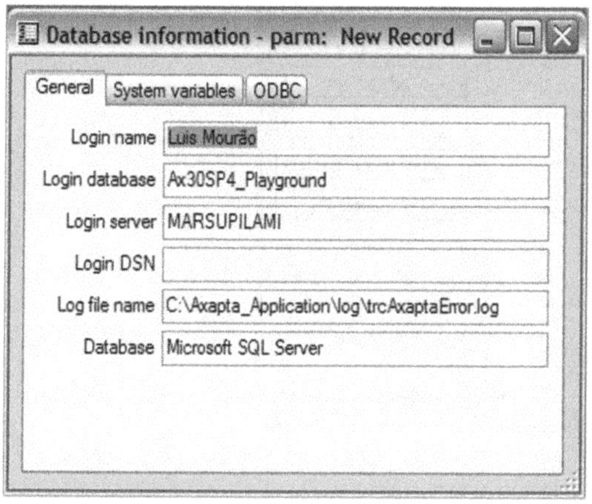

Figure 19-1. *The Database Information form's General tab page*

The General tab provides basic information about what database you are connected to and the login you're connected with; the fields are self-explanatory. The System Variables tab page, shown in Figure 19-2, is a lot more interesting and enables you to view all the Axapta settings for the database.

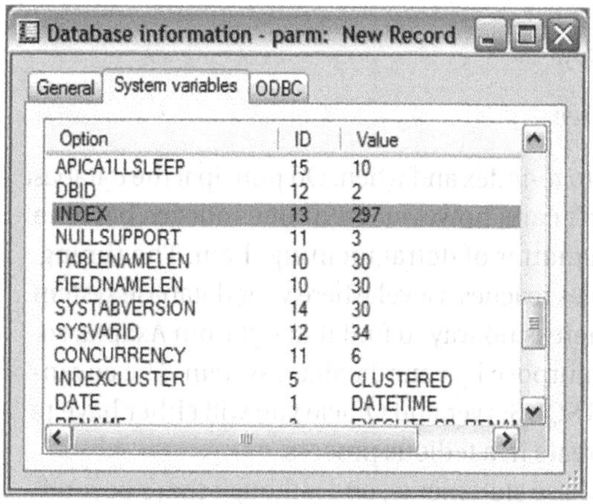

Figure 19-2. *The Database Information form's System Variables tab page*

Finally, the ODBC tab exists only if you are using Microsoft SQL Server. It displays information about the ODBC data source that is equivalent to what you can see on the System Variables tab page.

You can also obtain a report of all the information contained in the Database Information form via the main application menu path of Administration ➤ Reports ➤ Database Information.

Another important tool for database administrators is the SQL Administration tool shown in Figure 19-3. You can find it at the application main menu path Administration ➤ Periodic ➤ SQL Administration.

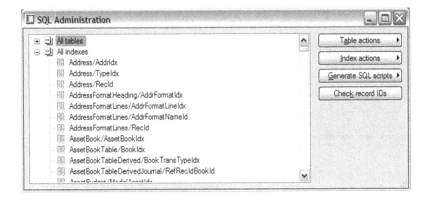

Figure 19-3. *The SQL Adminstration form*

You have seen this form elsewhere in this book, but now we will look at one element in more detail. The form's importance for DBAs is that it enables them to re-index the database. You do this by selecting the All Indexes top-level node of the tree panel in the form, or by expanding it, selecting a particular index, and clicking on the Index Actions menu button on the right side of the form. That displays a single menu option very appropriately called Re-Index.

The criteria for what to re-index is basically the following:

- Indexes on large transactional tables

- Indexes with a monotonous increasing key

- Indexes with many levels in their index tree

The really critical aspect is figuring out why to re-index and when. On principal the database takes care of indexes for you and you shouldn't care; however, with time indexes become fragmented and lose efficiency, so it's really a matter of defragmenting them. The timing depends on when the fragmentation of your tables reaches a level where your database system recommends defragmenting them; however, there is no way to find that out from Axapta, so you will have to use the tools provided for that purpose by your database system. The advantage of having Axapta do it for you is that in MS SQL Server and Oracle you will either have to script it or manually drop every index and re-create it, a tedious process.

Axapta offers great utilities for tracing database statements, and although that's beyond the scope of this book, we would like to call the attention of all DBAs and developers to their importance in debugging database errors and in performance tuning. The heart of this functionality is the Options form (see Figure 19-4), which you can access from the menu bar path of Tools ➤ Options.

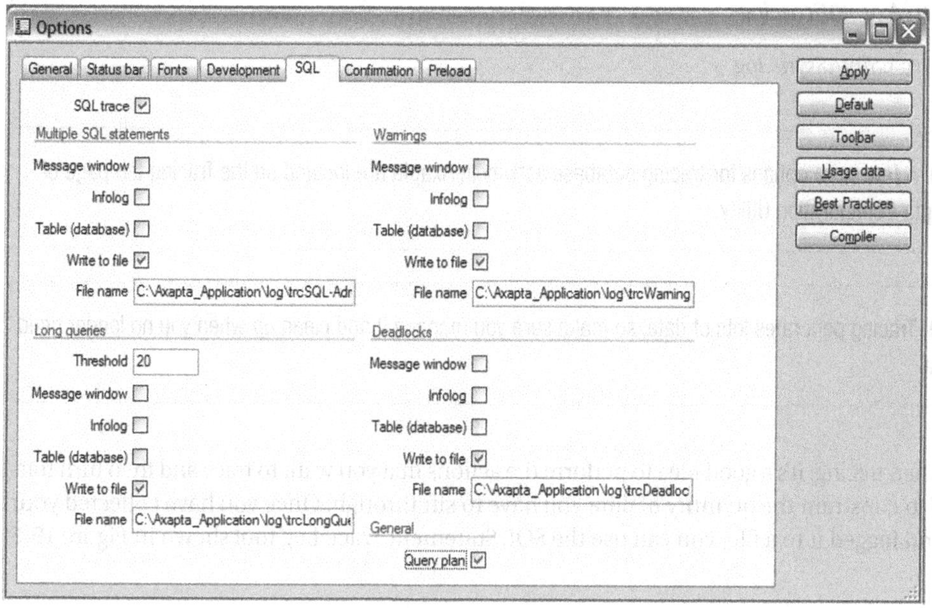

Figure 19-4. *The Options form's SQL tab page*

In the SQL tab page you can select a variety of information that you want to trace, as well as where to display and/or persist it. The most practical is to log the information to a file that is suggested automatically when you check the File Name check boxes in the different control groups—we recommend you accept the default, as it gives you the ability to use the SQL Statement Trace Log tool, including the visual query plan analyzer and access to the calling function in X++. It also allows you to import it into another system for analysis, and it doesn't fill your database with data, but you will have to import the file before using it. Alternatively, you can save the traces to the database and then export them if necessary—just remember to clear the log when you are finished.

As you can see from Figure 19-4, Axapta can give you an enormous wealth of information.

While the Development tab page is mostly concerned with stuff that is not related to the database layer, the Trace control group is relevant and worth investigating. It allows you to request tracing of the following:

- Database calls

- Method calls

- Client/server interaction

- ActiveX calls

The first and third items are particularly important in the context of Axapta's data layer.

Once you have turned on tracing for any of the event types in the list, you can inspect the logs files to figure out whatever you are looking for.

While it's not specifically a database-related log, an error log in Axapta is always enabled; it lets you find, among other things, errors related to the database layer. More interesting here is the synchronization log that is also always enabled, where you can see information on the operations performed during synchronizations. These files are placed in the default log directory specified in the configuration you are running. They are respectively named:

- *trcAxaptaError.log*

- *trcAxaptaSsync.log*

Note A few more options for tracing database activity in Axapta are located on the Tracing tab page of the Axapta Configuration Utility.

Note Tracing generates lots of data, so make sure you manage it and clean up when you no longer need the data.

When tracing, it's a good idea to perform the actions that you want to trace and then turn tracing off to constrain the quantity of data you have to sift through. Once you have collected your data and logged it to a file, you can use the SQL Statement Trace Log tool shown in Figure 19-5.

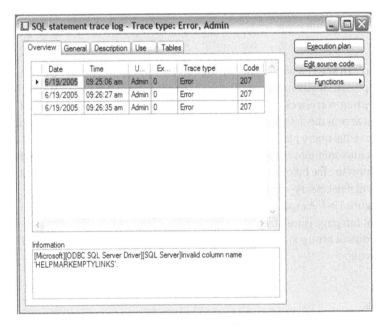

Figure 19-5. *The SQL Statement Trace Log form*

This form presents all the collected information in a way that is easy to understand and navigate, and it adds powerful functionality to help you work with it.

The tabs on this form display the following information:

- *Overview*: Displays core information about each collected record that you can quickly scroll through to get to the particular trace logs that you are interested in

- *General*: Expands on the Overview tab and provides details about the statement traced and the connection

- *Description*: Displays the SQL statement, the error text, and details (if available)

- *Use*: Displays the call stack leading to the traced statement

- *Tables*: Displays the tables involved in the statement

The buttons on the form are quite powerful and useful in working with the traces:

- *Execution Plan*: Displays the statement, the selected traced statement, and its execution plan in a tree; you can then calculate the cost of the plan, edit it, and recalculate the cost of executing the new plan.

- *Edit Source Code*: Places you in the X++ editor at the point in the code where the statement is executed.

- *Functions*: Has three suboptions:

    - *Import*: Allows you to import a log produced in another system for you to analyze

    - *Export*: Allows you to export a log so you can send it to another person for analysis

    - *Clear Log*: Deletes the records in the log

Last of all, the Axapta system monitor shown in Figure 19-6 is a great little tool for everyone interested in what their system is up to in real time. You can get hold of it by double-clicking on the disk icon on the right side of the Axapta status bar or via the path Tools ➤ Development Tools ➤ System Monitoring.

Figure 19-6. *The System Monitoring form*

This form displays system activity in real time and is good for a quick overview of what is going on if the system seems to be overloading or performing poorly. Of course, collecting the data in real time has a performance penalty that interferes with your system, so when you open the form, data collection is stopped and you must use the Continue button to restart it. You can then use the Pause button to pause and the Reset button to zero out the various counters in the two tab pages of the form.

You can find a few more tools under the main application menu path of Administration ➤ Inquiries ➤ Database and the menu bar path Tools ➤ Development Tools that are very helpful for developers, system administrators, in general, and DBAs in particular.

Programming

X++ has great support for data manipulation, providing a rich set of statements that makes it a snap to work with data. It's also very intuitive for anyone with database or SQL experience. Let's have a look at what Axapta has to offer.

Transactions

The X++ language supports three statements that you are probably well-acquainted with to support transactions when performing data manipulation in Axapta:

- `ttsBegin`: Starts a transaction block

- `ttsCommit`: Closes a transaction block and commits the data to the database

- `ttsAbort`: Closes a transaction and rolls back all data manipulation within the current transaction block

If data manipulation statements performing inserts, updates, or deletes are not enclosed in a transaction block, Axapta automatically commits with every insert, update, or delete statement.

If Axapta terminates abnormally or exits with open transactions, then all transactions not committed explicitly or implicitly are rolled back automatically.

It goes without saying that you should lock records that you select for updating by using the `forUpdate` keyword in X++ select statements.

Performance

How you code access to your data has a major impact on the performance of your code and system; here is a list of rules to go by:

- Unless you really need to and have tested the execution plan very well, don't use hints in database statements; the database optimizer will do a better job, and a bad hint can really hurt performance.

- Use table joins instead of using loops to walk through your data; this reduces the number of statements traveling around and the amount of data, plus it offloads processing of data to the database.

- Use aggregate functions where appropriate instead of aggregating in code.

- If you are deleting many rows that match specific criteria, use the `delete_from` statement instead of `delete`, as it performs better.

- If you are updating many rows that match specific criteria, use the `update_from` statement instead of the `update` statement, as it performs better.

- Think well about your indexes: lack of good indexes will lead to full table scans.

- Sort data using indexed fields and avoid conflicts between `where` and `order by` clauses.

- Write `where` clauses that select only the data you need.

- Minimize the time records are locked by not hanging on to data longer than necessary—i.e., don't select some data for update, do a bunch of other stuff, and then use it sometime later.

- Use recordset functions where possible, such as `array insert`, `insert recordset`, and `update recordset`.

System Variables

To support its database independence, Axapta stores information about its database characteristics in variables. These are delivered from MBS as part of the standard application in the class `SqlDatabaseInit`, which is used to initialize the SqlSystemVariables table as part of the process of initializing a new database.

On principle you should not change the system variables; however, if you need to you can do it directly in the database, via the Axapta table browser, or from within your own X++ code.

It's here that you will find variables such as those mentioned before: QUOTEPRE, QUOTEPOST, and INDEX.

The system variables are divided into nine groups:

- *Data-type mapping*: Maps Axapta data types to the database's base data types

- *SQL name mapping*: Keys for illegal SQL object names and for name mangling

- *SQL statement generation*: Maps keywords used for the current database when generating SQL statements

- *SQL statements*: Complete statements used for internal administrative purposes

- *Error code recognition*: Database error codes recognized by Axapta

- *Versioning*: Version information for setup and synchronization purposes

- *Database identification*: What database is being used

- *Concurrency issues*: How to handle concurrency issues

- *Data conversion, mapping, and retrieval*: Characteristics of the data for the current database

If you browse through the class or the corresponding table, the purposes of these will be evident for the most part.

Database Limitations

Axapta places some limitations on what you can do in the data layer beyond the limitations of the database base system you select to use:

- The maximum number of rows in one company is 4,294,967,296, as this is the highest record ID possible in Axapta.

- The maximum number of bind variables given in the where clause of a select statement is 200.

- The maximum number of tables per layer is 7999 in the GLS layer.

- The maximum number of tables per layer is 1999 in the DIS and LOS layers.

- The maximum number of tables per layer is 9999 in the BUS, VAR, CUS, and USR layers.

- The maximum number of user-defined fields in a table is 11439—notice that Oracle has a limit of 1000.

■**Note** The database you use will impose various other limits; for example, the size of fields of different data types will vary. To determine specific limitations, please check your database system documentation.

Database Differences

The most significant differences between Microsoft SQL Server and Oracle are outlined in Table 19-3

Table 19-3. *Database Differences*

SQL Server	Oracle
Readers can block for writers and vice versa	Readers don't block for writers and vice versa
Lock escalation—rows are locked up to a limit and then escalated to page and subsequently table locks, which increases the likelihood of contention	No lock escalation—all locks are row locks
Relatively CPU intensive	Relatively I/O intensive
Case-insensitive	Case-sensitive
Statistics are collected by default	Statistics are not collected by default
Single version of data—requires dealing with isolation levels and results in uncommitted data in forms	Several versions of data—provides read consistency so you can only see committed data in forms
Rough control over location of database objects and parameters	Location of database objects and parameters manageable by object
Generally possible to control isolation levels from queries	Not possible; isolation levels are controlled per session or transaction

SQL Server	Oracle
Index hints given for non-existent indexes produce database errors	Does not generate database errors and simply ignores the hints
Uses READ UNCOMMITED outside transaction blocks and READ COMMITED inside	Always uses the isolation level specified for the session or transaction

Naturally, there are far too many differences between SQL Server and Oracle to cover here, and because Axapta is tuned for the different databases it supports, you can take advantage of the finer-grained abilities of Oracle to control the schema and location of objects and to tweak many settings. However, SQL Server has the advantage of a higher level of administrative automation, so going with it means less control but also less administration.

Import and Export

Axapta needs to be able to exchange data with other systems and other instances of Axapta, and therefore it comes out of the box with two core techniques for exporting data:

- Importing and exporting data in Axapta format using pairs of DAT and DEF files—data and data definition files respectively

- Importing data from other systems using Excel spreadsheets

Of course Axapta offers many different interfaces, such as access to ODBC, the Windows API, XML, COM, and ActiveX support, and you can easily roll up your own interface, but the points here cover the core needs of most users.

The data import and export tools can be found under the main application menu path of Administration ➤ Periodic ➤ Data Export/Import shown in Figure 19-7.

Figure 19-7. *A data export/import menu*

Definition groups are used to create templates for exporting and importing data; you can specify which tables and fields to use and the format of the data, as well as add code to filter data and preprocess it during the actual import or export. Axapta supports three formats:

- *Standard*: Can be used for both exporting and importing and only allows you to specify the tables to be included

- *Custom*: Allows data to be imported only, but has all the bells and whistles

- *Excel*: Like custom, but specific to importing data from Excel spreadsheets

When importing from an Excel spreadsheet, you can use the utility at the main application menu path Administration ➤ Periodic ➤ Data Export/Import ➤ Excel Spreadsheet ➤ Template Wizard to create an Excel template of the tables and fields to be imported. You can then use them with the system that is exporting data.

In Figure 19-7 you can see that there is a *Default Data* folder in the *Data Export/Import* folder; if you expand it in the main menu, you will see that it contains two wizards: Export and Import.

The Import Wizard is used to import a default data set provided with the distribution CD that contains common generic data such as countries of the world, currencies, zip codes, and parameters for tax, general ledger, etc. They are supplied for the following locales:

- DE-AT: Austria

- DE-DE: Germany

- EN-GB: Great Britain

- EN-US: United States

- FR-BE: French Belgium

- NL-BE: Dutch Belgium (actually Flemish)

- NL-NL: Netherlands

- NO-NO: Norway

- SV-SV: Sweden

The default data doesn't normally fit your requirements perfectly, but most of it will work and will save you a lot of time compared to having to enter it manually. Once you have set up your system it can be useful to save the default data so you can reuse it if you have to repeat your installation in a branch office, for example. You can do that using the Export menu item.

Wrap-Up

In this chapter we have walked you through the following fundamental aspects of dealing with data in Axapta:

- How Axapta works with data and the different database technologies it uses

- Managing your data

- How Microsoft SQL Server and Oracle differ from each other

- What limits Axapta imposes

- Importing and exporting data

You can read more about the topics in this chapter in the following documents available in the documentation folder of the product distribution package or CD:

- *AX-300-DVG-006-v01.00-ENUS.chm*: Database Wizard

- *AX-300-TIP-021-v01.00-ENUS.doc*: Axapta on Oracle 9iRAC

- *AX-300-TIP-030-v01.00-ENUS.doc*: Oracle Company Partitioning

You now have a good understanding of the Axapta data layer and a strong basis for managing it and leveraging it in your development efforts. However, a good understanding of your RDBMS is very important in getting the most out of Axapta, especially in terms of performance. We encourage you to invest in them to sharpen your skills in Axapta.

CHAPTER 20

■■■

X++

As you have already seen, you can get pretty far with Axapta just dragging-and-dropping stuff like menus, reports, and even sophisticated forms to capture and display data. However, implementing business logic requires programming, and Axapta offers its own object-oriented language that is specially designed for developing business software and leveraging all the great tools that come with Axapta.

In this chapter we will look at the following:

- Elements and syntax of the X++ language

- Application objects

- Development best practices

- Documenting your work

The X++ language is an interpreted language similar to Java in that it's actually compiled at development time to an intermediary binary format that is then compiled to the target machine code at runtime. This model has advantages and disadvantages:

- Code is available to the system as soon as you compile it without the need to go through a compile-deploy cycle.

- Automatic memory management takes care of allocating and freeing memory as necessary.

- Performance is affected negatively by the need to compile to the target machine instruction set at runtime.

Note Although the interpreted nature of X++ impacts performance, you shouldn't be concerned—in practice it's not a bottleneck in Axapta.

Because X++ was designed specifically for Axapta and developing business software, it has a wide variety of great features that make customizing, extending, and even developing Axapta basic functionality highly productive. The features are as follows:

- Object-oriented design so code is well encapsulated, easily reusable, and modular

- A data-oriented instruction set that makes it easy and intuitive to work with data

- Excellent compile-time checking supplemented by second-level runtime checking

- Extensive class library covering almost anything you can think of

A very interesting feature of Axapta is that class definitions are not persisted or manipulated as code, but as metadata that is stored in AOD files. A good example is a form and all its controls, such as tab pages, input controls, buttons, etc. These are simply persisted by Axapta as an XML-like hierarchy of definitions, and then you manipulate them in the AOT tree, so you don't have to deal with code except to add processing logic to your objects either by adding your own methods or by overwriting existing methods when you need to override standard functionality.

■**Note** If you select an object of any kind and export it, and then open the resulting XPO file in your favorite editor—Notepad for example—you can read the definition of the object, including all the code in its methods.

X++ is one of the best-documented areas in Axapta, so we are giving you only a crash course here; make sure you read the documentation indicated in the "Wrap-Up" section for all the details—figuring out how to use huge amounts of existing functionality that Axapta places in your hands (i.e., the API) is, however, a different story and is basically undocumented.

Elements of X++

As with all languages, X++ has a specific syntax and semantics that you need to learn to use it. By most standards X++ is an easy language, and if you are a developer this chapter will have you programming in no time.

In this section we look at the following:

- Data types

- Operators and expressions

- Methods and variables

- Classes and objects

- Language constructs

- Macros

Data Types

Data types in Axapta come in three forms: primitive, composite, and extended. Axapta defines the first two and you will recognize them right away, but read their definitions; they are not exactly what you know from other languages. Tables 20-1 and 20-2 list them respectively.

The third type is the kind you can define yourself in the AOT, and is derived from the Extended Data Type class. Because these are not implemented directly in X++, we will look at them only in the section on Axapta classes and objects.

Table 20-1. *Primitive Data Types*

Data Type	Description
Integer	A numerical value without decimals. Defined internally as a long integer. Automatically initialized to 0.
Real	A numerical value with decimals. Defined internally as a Binary Coded Decimal. Automatically initialized to 0.0.
Date	A representation of day, month, and year. Represented internally as a date. Automatically initialized to null. Math can be performed with integers such as Date = Date + 10, which will increase the data by 10 days.
TimeOfDay	A representation of hours, minutes, and seconds. Represented internally as a short integer. Automatically initialized to 0.
String	A character string that can be of variable or fixed length and left- or right-aligned. Represented internally as string. Automatically initialized to an empty string.
Boolean	0=false, 1=true; all other values are undefined and you can use the predefined X++ enums false and true Defined internally as a short integer. Automatically initialized to 0 (or false).

■**Note** The documentation from MBS indicates that enums are a primitive data type, but this is not correct; you can't, for example, declare Enum myEnum.

Table 20-2. *Composite Data Types*

Data Type	Description
Arrays	A collection of variables of a given data type. Initialized automatically to an empty array. Cannot contain classes or tables.
Containers	A collection of variables of any data type. Automatically initialized to an empty collection. Cannot contain classes or tables.
Classes	A definition for an object. Initialized to null.
Tables	A definition of a record of the table class and equivalent to class variable. All fields are automatically initialized to the default for their respective data types.

Note MBS documentation does not clearly define composite data types, and can be a little misleading. The best way to get a grip on how they work and what they are is to write a job that will let you experiment with them.

The basic principles of conversion between data types in Axapta are as follows:

- Integers are converted to dates in expressions.

- Primitive data types are implicitly converted upward.

- Axapta includes built-in conversion functions for explicit conversion between primitive data types.

- There is no implicit or explicit conversion between composite data types.

- Classes are implicitly converted to their superclass or explicitly by casting.

- Tables are automatically converted to a special table class called common.

Operators

X++ supports the operators listed in Table 20-3 in order of precedence, which you will easily recognize.

Table 20-3. *Operators*

Type	Operators
Postfix	[], (params), expression++, expression--
Unary	++expression, --expression, +expression, -expression, !, ~
Instantiation	new, (type) expression
Multiplication and division	*, /, %, DIV, MOD
Addition	*, /, %
Shift	<<, >>
Relational	<, >, <=, >=
Equality	==, !=
Bitwise	&, ^,	
Logical	&&, ||
Ternary	?, :
Assignment	=, +=, -=

Expressions

Expressions are the building blocks of statements, and they represent a value—i.e., their resolution returns a value, and should present no challenge to you if you are a developer. If you really need the details of valid X++ expressions, the MBS documentation includes a complete EBNF (Extended Backus-Naur Form) specification of the X++ grammar.

Variables

Variables in X++ are identified by a name consisting of any combination of alphanumeric characters from the ANSI character set—a minimum of one—and the underscore character (_).

All variables must be declared before they are used, just as in C (i.e., all declarations must be made before any programming statements). In the same manner, you can initialize variables when declaring them by using expressions. There is no difference between declaring a simple variable or an object variable, and they can be declared in three ways:

- *Simple*: int i = 1;

- *Initialization*: int i = 5;

- *Multiple*: int i = 1, j = 2;

An important thing to note with variables in X++ is that Axapta will sometimes choke on a method if the variable declaration section is followed directly by statements. The solution to this is to always insert an empty statement at the end of the variable declarations—i.e., a line with a semicolon (;). Here is what it should look like:

```
public myMethod(str _aString)
{
    // Vars.
    int i;
    str anotherString;
    ; // Var section terminator!

    ... ; // Statements.
    ...;
}
```

Note You actually can't always intialize a variable in its declaration; specifically, you can't do that in class declarations.

Classes

Classes are created using the AOT by selecting a Class group node, right-clicking on it, and selecting the New and Class menu options, respectively. Axapta automatically generates a class named Class1 that contains a class declaration method named Class1 too. The resulting code looks like this:

```
public class Class1
{
    int i;
    str myStrring;
}
```

You can open the code editor by double-clicking on the Class node. This shows all the methods in the class on the left panel of the code editor, or on the method itself from the AOT after you have expanded the class you want to work with.

Unlike other AOT objects, you can't change the name of a class in the AOT. You can, however, change the name of the class in the declaration in the code editor:

```
public class Cookie
{
    int i;
    str myStrring;
}
```

The class is automatically renamed to Cookie in the AOT as soon as you save the changes. A class declaration consists of the following elements:

- *Modifier* is one of the following:

    - *Abstract*: The class is declared but not implemented; implementation is left up to subclasses

    - *Final*: Specifies that the class can't be extended

- *Visibility*: Public or private; if omitted, a class is private

- *Class keyword*: Required

- *Class name*: Same rules as for variables and methods; required

- *Superclass*: The keyword extends followed by the name of the superclass; e.g., public class myClass extends mySuperClass{}

Naturally, the class declarations are exactly that, so you can't assign values to the variables you declare, but you can define class macros, as shown here:

```
public class Cookie
{
    // Macros
    #define.myName('Luis')

    // Vars.
    int i;
    str myStrring;
}
```

Beyond this, the most important aspects of classes are as follows:

- All classes have a constructor method called new that you can override to do your own initialization.

- All classes have a destructor method called finalize that you can override to do your own finalization—finalizers are not called automatically in Axapta, so you have to do it explicitly in your code—something like myClass.finalize();.

- Classes are blueprints that you use for instantiating objects of the class type using the new constructor—something like MyClass myObject = new MyClass();.

- Objects of a class always have a reference to themselves named this that you can use to refer to itself, as when you need to call one method from another in the same class—e.g., this.myMethod(). You can also use it to pass a reference to the object or to make a reference to a variable that exists both locally and in the class with this.myVar = _string value_; that unambiguously refers to the class variable as opposed to a local variable with the same name declared in the method.

- Axapta classes have single inheritance; that is, they can extend only one class and the subclass inherits all methods and variables from the superclass.

Axapta foundation classes fall a bit out of the class concept that we have been discussing. These overcome some of the limitations of the X++ collection classes and are implemented in the kernel in C++. Table 20-4 explains them.

Table 20-4. *Foundation Classess*

Type	Operators

List	Can be of any X++ type; all elements must be of the same type specified when the list is created and may be traversed using an iterator. Creating a list of integers and adding a few elements looks like this:
	list li = new list(types::int);
	li.addStart(1);
	li.addEnd(10);.

Map	Consists of two values—a key and a value for the key; these may be of any X++ data type that is specified when the map is created; multiple keys can point to the same value but each key can point to only one value, so adding a key that already exists will change the value referenced to the new one given for that key, and they may be traversed using an iterator. Creating a map and adding a few elements looks like this:
	map myMap = new map(type::integer, types::string);
	myMap.insert(40,_Milou_);
	myMap.insert(39,_Nestor_);.

Set	Elements can be of any X++ data type and all values must be of the same type; if you add a value that already exists it will be ignored and it can be traversed using an iterator. Creating a set and adding a few elements looks like this:
	set mySet = new set(types::string);
	mySet.add(_Tintin_);
	mySet.add(_Haddock_);.

Array	Consists of an indexed set of elements of any data type, including classes and tables (which X++ arrays can't include). The elements can be accessed directly by their index. Creating and adding a few elements looks like this: array myArray = new array(types::class) myArray.value(1, aObject); myArray.value(2, anotherObject);.
Struct (a.k.a. structures)	Consists of a set of any X++ data type; each element (also called a field) can have a name through which it can be accessed, or alternatively it can be accessed through the index of the element. Creating a struct and adding a few elements looks like this: struct myStruct = new struct(types::string, _fname_, types::string, _lname_);

```
myStruct.value(_fname_, _Tryphon_);
mystrcut.value(2, _Tournesol_);.
```

Methods

The same naming conventions apply to methods as to variables; however, to make it easy for different developers to understand each other's code, Axapta has various recommendations for how to go about naming them. These are described in the Development Best Practices Guide indicated in the "Wrap-Up" section of this chapter, and apply equally to method parameters.

All methods exist within a class—i.e., they are class methods and you create them using the AOT by selecting a class and then selecting to create a new method. Axapta will automatically generate a default method declaration named method1 and generate code looking like this:

```
void method1()
{
}
```

As with the class name, you need to change the name in the code editor to something meaningful.

A method implementation consists of the following elements:

- Modifiers: Specified in the next bulleted list

- Return data type: Void if there is no return value

- Method identifier: The method name

- Method parameters: A comma-separated list consisting of the data type and an identifier

- Method body: Enclosed in curly braces—{}

The most important things to know about methods include the following:

- Methods are polymorphic, so the same method name can provide multiple interfaces. However, this is awkward when using the AOT because it displays the method names in a class only when you expand it. The trick is to place the cursor over the methods; Axapta will then display the interface in the tooltip.

- You can change methods in superclasses by simply by using the Class node pop-up menu, selecting the menu option Override Method, and selecting the superclass method you wish to override.

Tip Generally when overriding a method, you should remember to call the superclass somewhere in your method to make sure any logic the superclass provides is executed—unless the reason for overriding is to prevent the superclass code from executing. Do any preprocessing before calling super(), and do any post-processing afterward.

- Method visibility is determined by the following access modifiers:

  - *public*: Visible to any caller with an instance of the class the method belongs to, and can be overridden.

  - *protected*: The method can be called only from methods in subclasses, and can be overridden.

  - *private*: Can be called only from other methods in the class where the method is declared, and can't be overridden.

- Methods can also have the following type modifiers:

  - *abstract*: The method is declared but not implemented and subclasses must define it; by default the method is concrete and implemented.

  - *display*: The method returns a value used by a field in a form or report and can't be changed.

  - *edit*: The method returns a value used by a field in a form.

  - *final*: The method can't be overridden by subclasses; this modifier can't be used with constructors and destructors.

  - *static*: The method is a class method and is invoked using the "::" notation on the class instead of on an object instance using the "." notation.

- Method parameters can have default values that are assigned directly in the declaration, like this:

```
public void myOverideMethod(str _myString=_Hello_ )
{
}
```

If a value for the parameter is not specified, it's automatically assigned the default value specified in the declaration.

You can provide pre- and postprocessing for an existing class by overriding the appropriate methods and adding your code before or after invoking execution of the superclass with something like the following:

```
public void myOverideMethod(str _myString)
{
    Str newString;
    ;
    // Preprocessing deletes trailing blanks
    newString = strRTrim(myString);
    super(newString);
    // Postprocessing appends my name
    newString=newString+_Luis_;
}
```

Last but not least, a particular curiosity of X++ is that methods can contain functions. These have the method as their scope and are coded like this:

```
public void method myMethod(int _myInt)
{
    Boolean b;

    boolean myFunction()
    {
        Return(true);
    }
    // A bunch of code...
    // Call the function.
    B = myFunction();
}
```

Variables within a function have function-only scope and visibility.

Statements

A statement is a logically grouped set of expressions and operators that you terminate with a semicolon (;)—with the exception of the compound statement.

Axapta supports nine types of statements. Each type is detailed on the following pages.

- *Declarations*: Applies to classes, variables, and methods; there are three declaration types.

- *Compound*: A sequence of statements that is grouped

- *Comments*: Code documentation

- *Assignments*: Used to set the values of variables

- *Branching control*: Used to conditionally control the flow of execution

- *Loop control*: Used to repeat statements

- *Data*: SQL-like data access statements

- *Transaction*: Used to group data statements into logical units to succeed or fail as a group, and to ensure data consistency

- *Exception*: Used for handling unexpected errors

Declarations

Declarations take the following forms (all described earlier in this chapter):

- *Class*: A description of a class

- *Method*: A description of a method and its interface

- *Variable*: A description of a variable, which can include its initialization

Compound Statements

A compound statement is a collection of logically grouped statements enclosed in curly braces. It looks like this:

```
public void method myMethod(int _myInt)
{
    int i, j;
    ;

    // Start compound statement.
    {
        i = _myInt MOD 5;
        j = _myInt - I;
    }
    // End compound statement.
}
```

Comments

Comments in Axapta can be a single line and are indicated by starting the line with a double forward slash (//); multiline comments open with a forward slash and an asterisk (/*), and close with an asterisk and a forward slash (*/). In code it looks like this:

```
public void method myMethod(int _myInt)
{
    /* This is a multiline
    Comment. */
    int i, j;
    // This is a single-line comment.
    i = _myInt MOD 5;
}
```

Assignments

You have already seen assignments on several occasions in this chapter; they consist of an assignment operator and two operands, with the left side being assigned *to* and the right assigned *from*. Typically the first operand is a variable and the right one is an expression. The fourth statement of the preceding code snippet is an example of an assignment.

Branching Control Statements

Branching or conditional statements in X++ are as follows:

- if: Evaluates an expression and executes a single or compound statement depending on the logical result of the expression—i.e., it executes it if the expression is true, and doesn't if it's false. It looks like this:

```
public void method myMethod(int _myInt)
{
    int i, j;

    if(_myInt == 0)
        i = _myInt MOD 5;

    if(_myInt == 0)
    {
        i = _myInt MOD 5;
        i++;
    }
}
```

- switch: A multibranch construct that executes the branch whose expression evaluates
  to true. Each branch is identified by the case keyword, with the default keyword specifying
  the branch to execute if all others evaluate to false. If you do not provide a default branch
  and all others evaluate to false, then no branch will execute. As with most languages,
  once a branch is entered, all code from there onward will be executed unless the switch
  is exited with a break statement. It looks like this in code:

```
public void method myMethod(int _myInt)
{
    int i, j;

    switch(_myInt)
    {
        case 1, 10, 100:
        {
            i = _myInt;
            j = _myInt / 100;
            break;
        }
        default:
        {
            i = _myInt;
            break;
        }
    }
}
```

- Terniary: Executes one of two statements based on the true or false result of evaluating
  an expression. We can assign a value of 0 or 1 to a variable depending on the value of
  another variable being bigger or smaller than 100; see the following code:

```
public void method myMethod(int _myInt)
{
    int i;
```

```
    i = _myIn > 100 ? 0 : 1;
}
```

The break statement can be used in conjunction with the if and switch statements to break out of the compound statement being executed.

Loop Control Statements

There are three loop control statements; outlined here:

- while: Repeats a statement or compound statement while its test expression evaluates to true; in code it looks like this:

```
public void method myMethod(int _myInt)
{
    int i;

    while(i < 10)
    {
        print(num2str(i,10,2,1,1));
        i = i ++;
    }
}
```

- do while: Similar to the while statement, but here the expression is evaluated only at the end of the statement or compound statement that is executed. This means that the statement is always executed at least once. In code it looks like this:

```
public void method myMethod(int _myInt)
{
    int i;

    do
    {
        print(num2str(i,10,2,1,1));
        i = i ++;
    }
    while(i < 10);
}
```

- for: The for loop statement enables you to initialize and change—typically increment or decrement—the values of the variables to be used in the test expression, and it executes a statement or compound statement repeatedly as long as the test expression evaluates to true. In code it looks like this:

```
public void method myMethod(int _myInt)
{
    int i;

    for(i = 1; i < 10; i++)
```

```
            {
                print(num2str(i,10,2,1,1));
            }
        }
```

The break and continue statements can be used in conjunction with loop control statements to either break out of the compound statement being executed or to ignore the rest of
the statements in it and go to the test statement.

Data Statements

Functionally, data statements are roughly equivalent to their SQL counterparts, but you need
to read the MBS documentation before you start firing away; there are fundamental syntactic
differences. There are four types of single-line data statements (meaning they operate on only
one record at a time):

- *Select*: Used for retrieving data from the database; in code it looks like this:

```
public void method myMethod()
{
    CustTable custTable;

    custTable.reread();
    select AccountNum, AccountName from custTable
        where custTable.AccountNum "1";
}
```

- *Insert*: Used for creating new records in a table; in code it looks like this:

```
public void method myMethod()
{
    CustTable custTable;

    custTable.AccountNum = _1_;
    custTable.Name = 'Name_' + _Spirou_;
    custTable.insert();
}
```

- *Update*: Used for updating records in a table; in code it looks like this:

```
public void method myMethod()
{
    CustTable custTable;

    ttsbegin;
        delete_from custTable
            where custTable.Name like 'Name_*';
    ttscommit;
}
```

- *Delete*: Used for deleting records in a table; in code it looks like this:

```
public void method myMethod()
{
    CustTable custTable;

    ttsbegin;
        delete_from custTable
            where custTable.Name like 'Name_*';
    ttscommit;
}
```

These statements are very powerful and fast. However, they have a drawback: They do not pass through the application logic in Axapta and directly manipulate the data in the database that you are using, so make sure you really know what you are doing before you use them.

The preceding statements are single-row statements, but Axapta 3.0 introduced equivalent record-set statements that are much more efficient because they operate on an entire set of records at a time. These are:

- UPDATE_RECORDSET

- INSERT_RECORDSET

- ARRAY INSERT

We highly recommend using record-set statements when manipulating data with data statements.

Transactions

Transactions allow you to explicitly group a set of data statements into a logical block that either succeeds or fails as a whole. If a data statement in a transaction block fails, then all changes to the data are rolled back; if all statements succeed, then all changes are committed. Here are the transaction types:

- ttsbegin: Starts a transaction block

- ttscommit: Ends a transaction block and commits all data changes to the database

- ttsabort: Discards all changes to the data so the database is rolled back and its state restored to the state at entrance to the transaction block

---

Note Transaction blocks may be nested within each other.

In code, transactions look something like this:

```
public boolean myMethod()
{
    try
```

```
    {
        ttsBegin;
            select forUpdate * from myTable;
            myTable.fname = _Dupont_;
            myTable.update();
        ttsCommit;
    }
    catch(exception::Error)
    {
        ttsabort;
        return(false);
    }
}

    return(true);
}
```

If you do not explicitly close the transaction block, your changes are never committed and are instead discarded when the block goes out of scope. Therefore, in the preceding code you do not need to have a ttsabort in the catch clause of the try statement, but you could explicitly force the discard of your update by inserting it.

Exception Statements

This statement type consists of two statements: try-catch and throw.

The try-catch statement consists of a try block enclosed in curly braces, followed by a catch block enclosed in curly braces too. Any exception that is thrown within the try block causes execution to jump to the catch block, where you can look at the exception and handle it gracefully. You saw the try-catch statement in the previous code sample.

The throw statement enables you to do exactly that—throw exceptions that can then be caught by a try-catch. In code it looks like this:

```
public boolean myMethod()
{
    int i = 99;

    if(i == 99)
    {
        throw::error;
    }
}
```

Thrown exceptions are passed up until they are either caught by application code in the execution chain or they reach the standard exception handler.

Macros

Macros are a contentious subject in object-oriented languages. They cloud the readability and purpose of the code, introduce their own syntax, are not objects, and can't be debugged. However, they do have their uses.

Macros can contain any X++ set of statements, and are an easy way to provide reusable code snippets. But you can and usually should consider creating a class to encapsulate whatever functionality you want to implement.

You can define macros in the AOT by creating a macro—however, this creates a macro library where you have to define your macros by clicking on the macro object to open the X++ code editor. You can use these macros anywhere in your code by declaring the macro library.

Alternatively, you can define macros anywhere in your code where you can define variables—i.e., in class definitions or in the variables section of your methods—but these have only class or method visibility, depending on where you define them by using the keyword #define followed by the name of the macro, and the value in round parentheses. It looks like this in code:

```
#define.FName(_Dupond_)
```

There's no need for a semicolon (;). Yes, that's right—no semicolon for macro definitions. You use the macro by preceding the name of the macro with the hash character (#), which in code looks like this:

```
public void myMethod()
{
    #define.FName("Luis")

    print(#FName);
    pause;
}
```

In reality, macros are a much more complex subject then what you have seen here, but the MBS documentation says everything that needs to be said about them. Now you know they exist and what you can use them for, as well as the basic macro how-tos.

Wrap-Up

We have been through the essentials of the X++ language. As with any programming language, practice makes perfection—so get cracking. The language is easy and powerful; you can code, compile, run, and debug your stuff in an exact copy of the Axapta environment your end users work with. You see what they see and do what they do, and you can immediately see the results as they will once they apply your customizations to a production environment.

Axapta's greatest weakness is its lack of good documentation for the thousands of classes that it comes with. But because all the application source code is available to you, you can not only change Axapta to fit your specific needs, but you also have the best possible documentation any developer can wish for—over 800,000 lines of source code where you can see how others have done something similar to what you need. Couple this with the great development tools that Axapta provides, and you have an ERP system that comes with comprehensive functionality out of the box, and is a snap to modify to fit your needs.

> **Tip** The lack of comprehensive API documentation is a significant drawback, as the code generally has no comments and can be very difficult to understand. Often you will not realize that the functionality you need is already there. Therefore, it's a good idea to ask around and share what you know with others; in turn you'll learn from others.

After reading this chapter, you should now be comfortable with the following topics:

- The X++ language and the fundamental aspects of writing code in X++

- The different kinds of objects you can program and what their applications are

- Writing good code and placing it in the right kind of objects

- Documenting your code and objects

You can read more about the topics in this chapter in the following documents available in the documentation folder of the product distribution package or CD:

- *AX-300-DVG-002-v01.00-ENUS.chm*: Developers Guide

- *AX-300-DVG-003-v01.00-ENUS.chm*: Development Best Practices Guide

There is also some pretty good training material produced on Axapta programming and X++, so we recommend you attend some courses or get hold of some of the classroom materials to advance to the next level.

CHAPTER 21

■■■

Deployment

While many of the readers of this book may not be developers, they will, as consultants, project managers, administrators, operations managers, etc., still be involved in the process of determining the infrastructure that needs to be put in place to support an Axapta installation.

Typically Axapta consultancy and development companies will be involved in putting together offers to their customers and will need to design and propose hardware and software architectures, as well as deliver required customizations and generally even install them. End users may even sometimes cooperate with external consultants in several of the activities typically performed by the consultants and, depending on the sophistication of the organization, may actually do their own in-house customizing and deployment.

This chapter presents the process, techniques, and tools we recommend, and consists of the following main steps:

- Determine the infrastructure you need

- Define your system architecture

- Measure your system performance

- Define a software deployment/distribution strategy

Once you have read this chapter, you will be able to determine what you need to get started with Axapta. But, most important, you will be able to determine and plan your infrastructure needs as your system and user base evolves over time, making sure that it's always sized correctly to respond to its load.

Sizing

An extremely important step when you have decided to go with Axapta is to figure out the size and power of the infrastructure needed to match the number of users and the load you expect the system will have to handle. Sizing a system consists of the following basic steps:

- *Identify the types of users the system will support*: This is where you assess what functionality users will need; for example, sales or purchase orders in the logistics module.

- *Identify the average number of transactions per hour performed per user type*: For example, how many sales-order lines does each person who uses that functionality create per hour?

- *Identify the number of users for each function*: For instance, how many users of the sales-order functionality do you have?

The last two tasks are practically impossible if you have to do them for each piece of functionality that you plan to use, but fortunately MBS has defined a series of reference processes and weights that you can work with to correctly size your system—Table 21-1 lists them. In the "Wrap-Up" section of this chapter, we provide references to a set of spreadsheets that MBS uses for this purpose.

Table 21-1. *Sizing References*

Module	User Function	Axapta Function	Transactions per Hour	ASU Load
Financials	Analyst	Major reports	4	2
	Operator	Ledger journal lines	50	0.5
Trade and Logistic	Sales order	Sales-order lines	50	1
	Purchase	Purchase lines	50	1
Production	Manager	Major reports	1	0.3
	Planner	Productions	100	6
	Foreman	Productions	20	0.8
	Operator	Productions	5	0.1
Warehouse Management	Receiver	Goods	200	1.5
	Operator	Goods	50	0.2
Human Resources	Personnel	Work hour lines	200	3
	Individual	Hour lines	8	0.1
CRM	Analyst	Major queries	10	2
EP	CSS Frequent user	Shopping basket lines	10	0.1
Project	ESS Frequent user	Work hour lines	10	0.1
Questionnaire	KM Questionnaire planner	Questionnaire creation	1	2
	Business process management	Actions	10	1
	Balanced scorecard planner	Performance indicators	1	6

Module	User Function	Axapta Function	Transactions per Hour	ASU Load
Shop Floor Control	Shop floor Employee	Shop/BOM journals lines	50	0.5
	Payroll employee	Payroll transactions	35	0.5
	Shop floor foreman	Time results	20	1

■**Note** ASU is a metric created by the Axapta development team; its reference is 50 sales-order lines per hour, representing 1 ASU (Axapta Standard User). Once you know how many ASUs your system will have to support, you can use the benchmarking tool to determine how many ASUs a specific platform can support and therefore determine your choice of platform, network topology, number, and type of servers.

Using Table 21-1 is pretty straightforward. Multiply the number of users by the number of transactions per hour of each given type, divide the result by the number of transactions per hour in the table, then multiply by the ASU load in the table.

For example, consider three users of the sales order functionality creating and average of 100 order lines per hour each:

- 3 × 100 = 300 sales-order-line transactions per hour

- 300 / 50 = 6 ASU absolute value

- 6 × 1 = 6 ASU weighed value

Now consider four financial analysts running an average of six major reports per hour each:

- 4 × 6 = 24 major financial reports per hour

- 24 / 4 = 6 ASU absolute value

- 6 × 2 = 12 ASU weighed value

Add up all the weighed values, and you will have the total number of ASUs your system needs to support. Armed with this, you then need to put together some tentative system designs that you can benchmark to determine their ability to support your requirements, and from which you can select the one that best meets your needs.

System Design

At this point you know the load expected for your system and you must now work out an infrastructure to support Axapta. The load results you have obtained by performing the sizing exercise are very important, but they're not the only factor. You have to consider several other aspects that impact performance, availability, security, and even costs. The main points to consider are the following:

- *Network bandwidth*: The number of bits per second that can be transferred over your network

- *Network latency*: The time it takes for a request from a client to a server to perform a round-trip over your network

- *Axapta workstation capabilities*: Determines if you can execute Axapta Windows clients on your workstations, the specific types of clients you can execute, and whether you need to evaluate a terminal server solution

- *Up-time*: Determines the level of resilience you need in the event of a server process going down or a hardware failure

- *Axapta network topology*: Determines where your users need to access your system from—i.e., your internal network, VPN, or Internet

In Chapter 17 we looked at the Axapta architecture, and you now know how to mix and match the different Axapta components, so let's look at how the points just mentioned impact your system and affect your choice of architecture.

Bandwidth

Table 21-2 shows the bandwidth requirements.

Table 21-2. *Bandwidth Requirements*

From	To	Bandwidth
2-tier client	Database	10–100 Mbps
3-tier fat client	AOS	10–100 Mbps
3-tier fat client	Database	10–100 Mbps
3-tier thin client	AOS	6.4 Kbps per user
AOS	Database	100 Mbps–1Gbps

Note While 6.4 Kbps is the minimum recommended bandwidth availability by MBS for the connection from a 3-tier thin client to an AOS server, it's highly unlikely that this will deliver acceptable response times. We do not recommend anything below a basic rate interface ISDN connection per client—i.e., 128 Kbps.

Latency

Table 21-3 shows the latency requirements.

Table 21-3. *Latency Requirements*

From	To	Latency
2-tier client	Database	< 5 msec
3-tier fat client	AOS	< 5 msec
3-tier fat client	Database	< 5 msec
3-tier thin client	AOS	< 100 msec
AOS	Database	< 5 msec

■**Note** Axapta will generally survive the latency values indicated with the exception of the one indicated for the 3-tier thin client connection to an AOS. The value of < 100 msec indicated by MBS is at the upper limit of what you want to play with, and values above that are quite likely to result in time-outs and disruption of sessions. We recommend a latency < 50 msec.

Your system administrator should be able to provide you with the information you need, but Axapta can also help you if you set up combinations of the client/AOS/databases in Tables 22-2 and 22-3 by using the Axapta performance testing module as described in the "Performance" section of this chapter.

Here are our recommendations for when to use what:

- *2-tier*: Avoid it if you can; bandwidth consumption is quite significant and will eat away at your network. We usually keep one around so that we can access Axapta and fix anything that might be causing our AOSs to not start or to die, as using a 3-tier client is impossible.

- *3-tier fat client*: MBS suggests the use of this for clients located inside the corporate network and capable of delivering the performance necessary to execute application logic. What that performance is specifically is unclear, but you can generally consider this on any CPU above an Intel Pentium III with 256 MB RAM as a way of offloading processing from the AOSs to the clients.

- *3-tier thin client*: This is real 3-tier computing. It loads the AOSs automatically, and will work on almost any hardware in existence today. It's definitely the way to go for clients with low-bandwidth connectivity. Stick with this solution whenever you can, if only for security reasons.

- *Terminal server*: Though not really an element of the Axapta architecture, you can use the different client types in combination with a terminal server if you need to support very low-performance and low-bandwidth clients. However, it's important to keep in mind that each Axapta client on the terminal server is an independent process, and to consider the requirements this puts on the processing and memory capacity of the system.

Caution All client configurations except 3-tier thin execute business logic on the client where authentication and authorization are performed. This makes subverting security much easier than it would be if the application logic were to reside in a central server under your control.

Caution 2-tier and 3-tier fat clients know the names and paths to the application and/or database used by their configurations, basically exposing information that can be exploited to subvert security.

We don't cover deployment of the Microsoft SQL Server or Oracle databases—we recommend you utilize the rich and extensive library of excellent documentation and books on this topic for both database systems.

Last but not least, we suggest you consider installing a batch server to offload the processing of heavy reports or calculations (such as invoicing and financial closings or inventory adjustments) so they do not bog down normal work for the users requesting them.

Note A batch server is just a client that is dedicated to running batch jobs. By dedicating a workstation to this, you avoid disrupting other operations and, where possible, you can schedule such jobs to run at off-peak hours to avoid impacting your system as a whole. A batch server is a good candidate for a 3-tier fat client so as to offload processing from your AOSs to the dedicated batch server.

Note When any end user from his Axapta client submits a batch job, it will automatically be picked up by a batch server according to the setup of the batch servers and the batch group to which the submitted batch job belongs.

Benchmarking

Once you have determined the load your system will handle, you need to choose the hardware that can deliver the required performance.

MBS has, in cooperation with Compaq, IBM, and Fujitsu-Siemens, developed a Web-based tool where you can enter a variety of information from which the performance requirements would be calculated and the proposed hardware from the respective manufacturer presented. Unfortunately, the Compaq and IBM pages have now vanished—and in reality, though the tool provided an indication of what you needed, you can do much better by working with an experienced Axapta system designer. Making you into one is what this section is about.

Axapta has an excellent benchmarking tool that you can use to determine the performance not only of any single piece of hardware, but also of any combination of clients and servers. Of course, in real life most people don't have the time to test every available piece of hardware and configuration to discover exactly what to get for their system. Consider the following points to limit the scope of your effort:

- Assume that you will never have any real control over the types of clients that will access your Axapta system, and benchmark using whatever is most common in your organization.

- Until you know otherwise, assume that your network topology and existing investments in hardware are to be preserved.

- Focus on benchmarking whatever server brands are mandated at your organization, and forget the clients.

- Benchmark by starting at the lowest-performing hardware available to you; you can safely work with anything that delivers 200 ASU.

■**Caution** The factors affecting performance are too numerous and their interplay too complex for anyone to be able to accurately determine the load of a system by any process other than direct observation. This means that using a system that benchmarks at 200 ASU for a sizing of 200 ASU is suicide—even if the system is initially capable of performing at acceptable levels, your users will quickly find other ways to exploit it and you will hit a wall.

Axapta benchmarking is divided into two distinct activities:

- Creating a data set to use in benchmarking

- Running benchmarks

Let's look at them.

Creating Data

Before going any further, you need to make sure the configuration key for the benchmark tool is on. You do this by using the Configuration form at the main application menu path Administration ➤ Setup ➤ System ➤ Configuration, as shown in Figure 21-1.

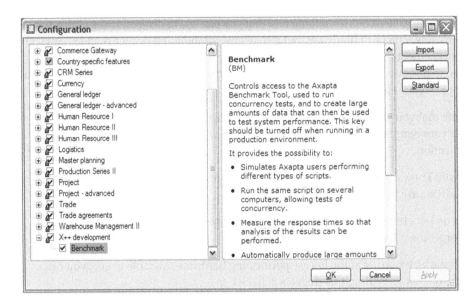

Fugure 21-1. *The Configuration keys form*

The next step is to create a company and data for the company so you have a valid data set to run the benchmarks against. By creating a company for this purpose, you ensure that you have exactly the same data to benchmark against on all systems. Start the benchmarking wizard from the tool bar menu path Tools ➤ Development Tools ➤ Benchmark.

Note As you can clearly see in figure 21-1, the benchmark key should be turned off in production systems because it allows the execution of benchmark runs that will significantly impact system performance and create large amounts of non-business-related data in the database. (Actually, *having* the key does nothing, but you should not create a company and large amounts of test data on a production system.)

Whatever company you are logged on to, a dialog box will inform you that you can't use it for benchmarking unless it's a company created previously for that purpose. It will also say that Axapta always names the new company account BMD, as you can see in Figure 21-2. Go ahead now and create a benchmark company. Unless you have a particular dislike for the suggested company ID, accept it and go ahead.

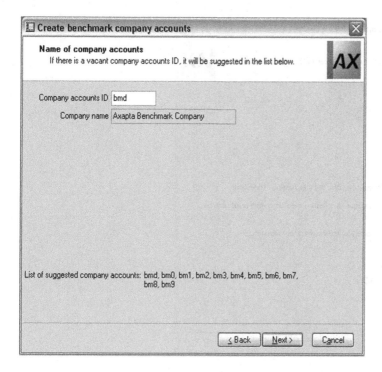

Figure 21-2. *The company creation page*

The page that follows allows you to initialize the benchmark company account using data that you have created and exported yourself. You can use it to benchmark the different systems that you are assessing.

■**Note** Using a data set that you have created previously is especially useful when you want to benchmark an existing system with large quantities of data, because Axapta performance does not deteriorate gracefully with increases in data, due to a poor data-model design. However, making sure that you have data for all the different tests available with the benchmark tool out of the box is impractical, so focus on testing specific functionality whose data models you know well.

The wizard then asks you to create a laboratory that allows you to group the tests you run for comparison with the results run on other systems, or for that matter with other test groups (or *lab*s, in Axapta speak). Figure 21-3 shows the wizard page for this.

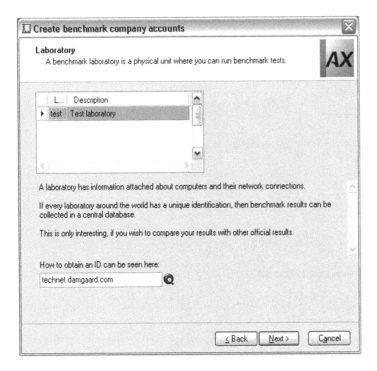

Figure 21-3. *The Laboratory page*

The next page allows you to create a series that corresponds to a test run. In other words, you can have several labs—all the test data for a specific system—which in turn contain test series, with each series containing a set of benchmarking tests and benchmarking test results.

The wizard will display a summary of what you have specified. Click on the Finish button to proceed and go to the Data Creation form shown in Figure 21-4, where you will see a standard benchmark definition for the data to be created for your lab.

The benchmark building block corresponds to the Axapta modules for which a data set will be generated. The check-box field indicates that benchmarking data should be generated for the corresponding module, and the Scaling field specifies how much data to generate for the module, proportionally to the others (i.e., how much it should weigh in the data set for the lab).

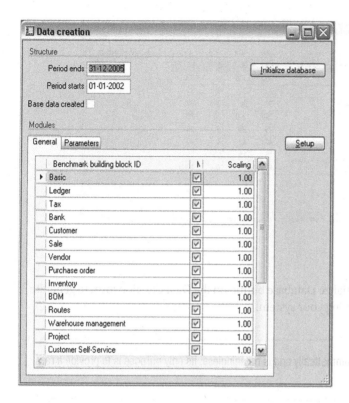

Figure 21-4. *The Data Creation form*

Note Unless you really know what you are doing and you're creating a lab to test a specific module or modules with well-known relative weights, just keep the standard definition. What's important is that you always use the same data set so you can compare labs.

On the form shown in Figure 21-4, there is a very interesting button called Setup. It opens the Base Data form shown in Figure 21-5, where you can see which tables in the selected module data will be created.

Note Do not alter the scaling factors for the different modules or building blocks within them— just stick to using the default values.

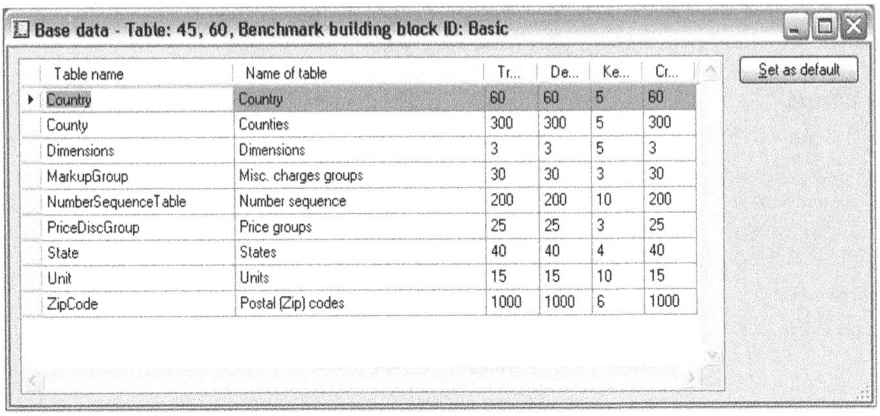

Table name	Name of table	Tr...	De...	Ke...	Cr...
▶ Country	Country	60	60	5	60
County	Counties	300	300	5	300
Dimensions	Dimensions	3	3	5	3
MarkupGroup	Misc. charges groups	30	30	3	30
NumberSequenceTable	Number sequence	200	200	10	200
PriceDiscGroup	Price groups	25	25	3	25
State	States	40	40	4	40
Unit	Units	15	15	10	15
ZipCode	Postal (Zip) codes	1000	1000	6	1000

Base data - Table: 45, 60, Benchmark building block ID: Basic — Set as default

Figure 21-5. *Building-block data*

At this point, click on the Initialize Database button on the Data Creation form to generate the data you need for benchmarking your system.

■**Note** The data is generated programmatically and is meaningless; its only purpose is to provide a raw data set.

Running Benchmarks

Selecting the tool bar menu path Tools ➤ Development Tools ➤ Benchmark does not start the Data Creation Wizard, but instead displays the application menu designed specifically for the benchmark module, shown in Figure 21-6.

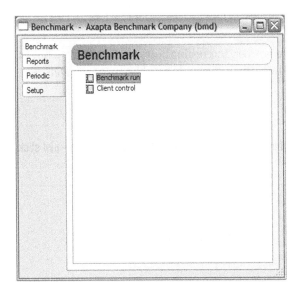

Figure 21-6. *The Benchmark application menu*

Running a benchmark consists of the following:

- Creating the run itself using the corresponding menu option on the Benchmark tab of the application menu

- Starting client emulators using the Client Control menu option

- Starting the benchmark cockpit, from where you can control the execution of the selected run

- Actually running and stopping the benchmark run from the cockpit

Let's start with creating the run by using the benchmark application menu. Benchmark ➤ Benchmark Run brings up the Benchmark Runs form shown in Figure 21-7.

Note Always make sure you have selected the benchmark company when performing these steps.

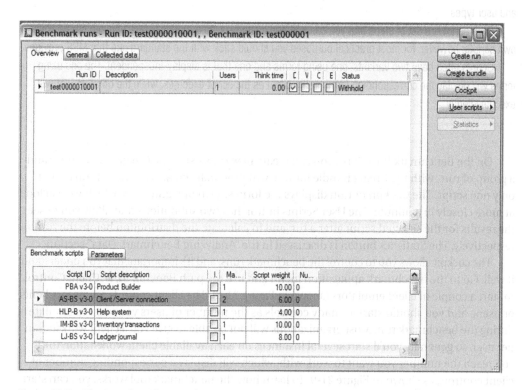

Figure 21-7. *The Benchnark Runs form*

Describing the benchmarking tool in fine detail is beyond the scope of this book, but here is a summary that will get you going and from which you can investigate further:

The top pane lists existing runs and run information, and the bottom pane provides information on the benchmark scripts executed during the run, with the check-box column indicating whether the script is actually executed. Main Loops indicates the number of times the script is executed, and Script Weight tells you how much relative load each creates. Finally, Number of Scripts is the number of times to execute the respective script.

▪**Note** The online help (accessed via F1) is not very informative, but it does provide some extra information that you might find useful when you're using this form.

▪**Note** By default the scripts for a run are all unselected. Select the ones that you expect will be run on your system and set the Script Weight field to the number of users that you expect to have using it. By doing this, you should end up with a benchmarking run that is representative of your system load in terms of processes and user types.

Each script is a set of steps that you can edit and customize. As a matter of fact, you can create your own scripts; however, for most practical purposes you should stick with the standard one that MBS provides.

Scripts often have two variants, one using forms and one that is display-independent. The one using forms will display the corresponding forms in the client as the script executes, while the other variant will execute silently.

On the Benchmark Runs form you can create new runs using the Create Run button, and a group of runs with the Create Bundle button, which actually creates a series of runs using only one script. The Cockpit button displays the form shown in Figure 21-8, which we will look at more closely in a minute. The User Scripts button has two suboptions that allow you to see the results for the selected script after a run and to calculate the distribution before the run, respectively. The Statistics button is discussed in the "Analyzing Benchmark Data" section.

The cockpit allows you to control the benchmark runs, and it's important that you understand it well. Go to the benchmark application menu and use the path Benchmark ➤ Client Control to start a couple of client emulators (shown in Figure 21-9). The client controls represent clients or users, and you should start as many controls as the number of users you want to emulate during the benchmark run. Most organizations will not be able to give you a client workstation per user, so generally you'll start several instances on each available client workstation until you reach the number you want to work with, which will display a corresponding number of client controls, as shown in Figure 21-9. To learn how the benchmark tool works, you can start just a couple on the system that hosts the cockpit.

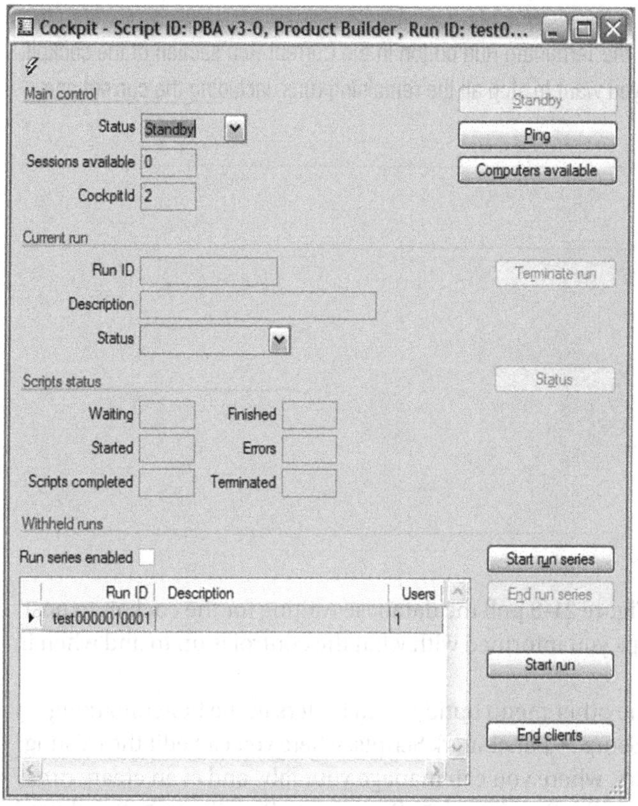

Figure 21-8. *The Benchmark cockpit*

Most of what you can see in the cockpit is self-evident; however, here is a brief explanation of the core elements. By default the cockpit is in standby mode, so the Status pull-down option is grayed. You can check if all the client controls you have running are communicating with the cockpit by using the Ping button and then checking if the balance field in the client controls reflects the fact that they are being pinged. The Computers Available button allows you to verify what computers your cockpit knows it can use in the run.

The Current Run section of the cockpit displays information about the run in progress and allows you to terminate a run and check on the current status in the Status Run form. The Scripts Status section provides a summary of the runs executed in the current session.

The most interesting section is Withheld Runs, where you can see a list of the pending runs in your lab. The Start Run Series button starts up the runs in the sequence in which they are listed, and the End Run Series button will end the whole series. Start Run executes only the run selected in the list, and finally, the End Clients button closes down the Axapta clients that you are using, not just the client control.

Tip When running a series, if you use the Terminate Run button in the Current Run section of the cockpit, only that specific run will be stopped. If you want to stop all the remaining runs, including the current one, you must use the End Run Series button.

Figure 21-9. *Client controls*

The client controls shown in Figure 21-9 poll the database waiting for the cockpit to post instructions. The Balance field keeps you informed with what the control is up to and when in a run it displays the respective ID.

We encourage you to look at the other menu options and folders in the benchmarking application menu—particularly in Setup ➤ Benchmark Scripts, where you can edit the existing scripts; Setup ➤ Laboratory Registry, where you can manage your labs and even create runs and execute them as an alternative to the Benchmark ➤ Benchmark Run, Setup ➤ Benchmark Parameters, where you can set up defaults for labs and runs. Finally, check out Setup ➤ Company Accounts, from where you can create benchmark companies and data.

Analyzing Benchmark Data

After all the work of creating benchmark data, companies, and labs and setting up and executing runs, you need to analyze the results. Here are the highlights.

You can view data on the environment and timing totals for each run by selecting a finished run in the Overview tab and then going to the Collected Data tab of the Benchmark Runs form (Figure 21-7).

Note Completed runs are easily identifiable because their rows are colored.

Once you have looked at the data collected on the environment, it's time to look at the statistics for the run by using the Statistics button on the Benchmark Runs form. The Statistics button has the following suboptions:

- *Calculate*: If there are any errors the corresponding statistics are not calculated automatically, so you select this option to do it explicitly.

- *Show*: Displays the form in Figure 21-10, which provides a wealth of information about the execution of the run.

- *Batch details*: Provides information about runs executed as batch processes.

- *Computers*: Displays environment data on the individual workstations and servers participating in the run.

- *Report*: Provides a summary hard copy of the statistics for the run.

The Show option of the Statistics button is the most interesting—let's take a closer look.

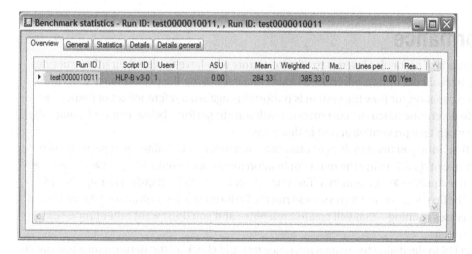

Figure 21-10. *The Benchmark Statistics form*

The Benchmark Statistics form has five tabs. The first three provide data about the run; the Details tab displays the steps of the scripts executed, and the Details General tab provides information about the step selected in the Details tab.

Unfortunately, the Axapta benchmark tool does not provide you with a performance measure of your system in ASU. As a matter of fact, the ASU field in the Statistics form does not appear to be used for anything. The good news is that you can calculate it yourself once you have benchmarked a system and with the help of Table 21-1.

In practice, since the ASU reference metric is 50 sales-order lines per hour, you can run the sales-order line script 50 times (i.e., 50 main loops) to produce 50 sales-order lines. You can then divide the time your run took by the number of runs to determine the number of sales-order lines per second. The formula in the following example will reveal the ASU value for your systems.

For example, if your run took 10 seconds like mine, your system is capable of executing 0.2 sales order lines per second (10 / 50 = 0.2). 3600 / 0.2 = 18000 sales-order lines per hour, meaning that the system has a performance of 360 ASU (18000 / 50 = 360).

So if your sizing table indicates that your expected load is less than that, then one server will do; otherwise, you will have to add servers of the benchmarked type until you reach the required total ASU level.

■**Note** MBS's weighing of the different Axapta processes and the ASU metric does not appear to be supported by any empirical or theoretical model or documented research, so don't trust it blindly—make sure you give yourself some elbow room when designing a system for deploying Axapta.

Also, be aware that the benchmark module is not as stable as you might wish it to be, and it takes time to get to know it and learn to live with its idiosyncrasies and the occasional waste of time because of unexpected errors that force you to start over, etc.

Performance

Performance is of particular interest to administrators who have to plan their infrastructure upgrades to avoid disruption of service as loads increase. Using the performance tools in Axapta you can monitor how the system is performing against a reference set of points and use that to determine when the current setup will start to perform below required standards, so that you can take preventive action in due time.

The first thing you need to do is to establish a reference or baseline set of performance metrics. You can do this using the main application menu path Administration ➤ Periodic ➤ Performance Analysis ➤ Performance Test Wizard, and you will be required to establish the baseline. The first time you use it you should run the Performance Test Wizard with the minimum set of processes running—that will create a reference and you don't want other processes to interfere with it.

Select OK in the dialog to create a reference test and check all the performance tests available, as shown in Figure 21-11.

The reference test run gives you a basis for comparison for when you run a test or set of tests again. By comparing the results of the different tests you get a picture of how performance is evolving over time on your system, and you can extrapolate that to calculate when you will need to intervene.

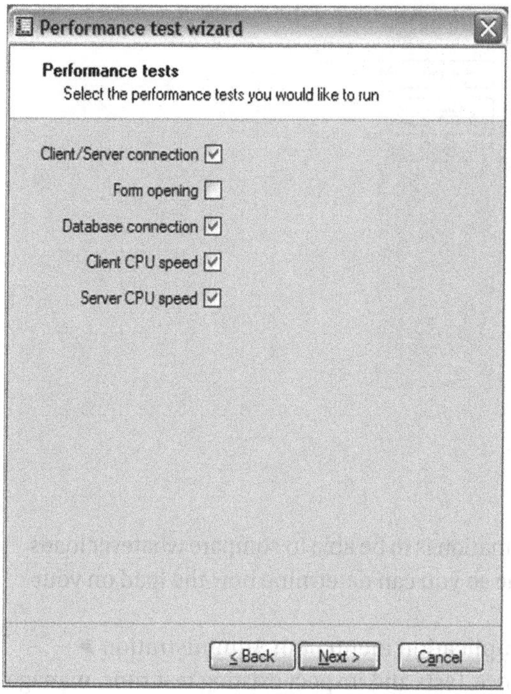

Figure 21-11. *The Performance Test Wizard*

Using the form at Administration ➤ Inquiries ➤ Performance Analysis ➤ Load Overview (shown in Figure 21-12), you can see your system's current load and how close to or far from disaster you are. (Actually, it would be more correct to view the load as how fast your system is responding.)

■**Note** In practice, the load overview can be quite misleading; the current load doesn't really tell you if it's good or bad, even though you can assume that loads above 80% mean trouble is coming your way.

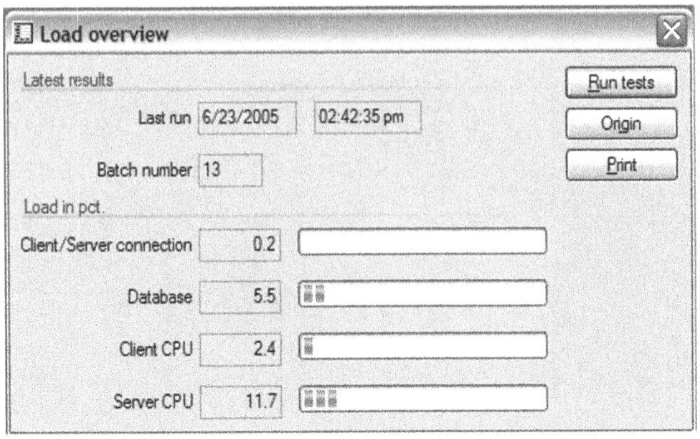

Figure 21-12. *The Load Overview dialog*

The really important usage of the load information is to be able to compare whatever loads your latest tests generated against your baseline so you can determine how the load on your system is evolving.

With that done, you can go to the main application menu path Administration ➤ Inquiries ➤ Performance Analysis ➤ Performance Tests and inspect existing test runs, manage them, and rerun them to compare performance levels. The form for this is shown in Figure 21-13.

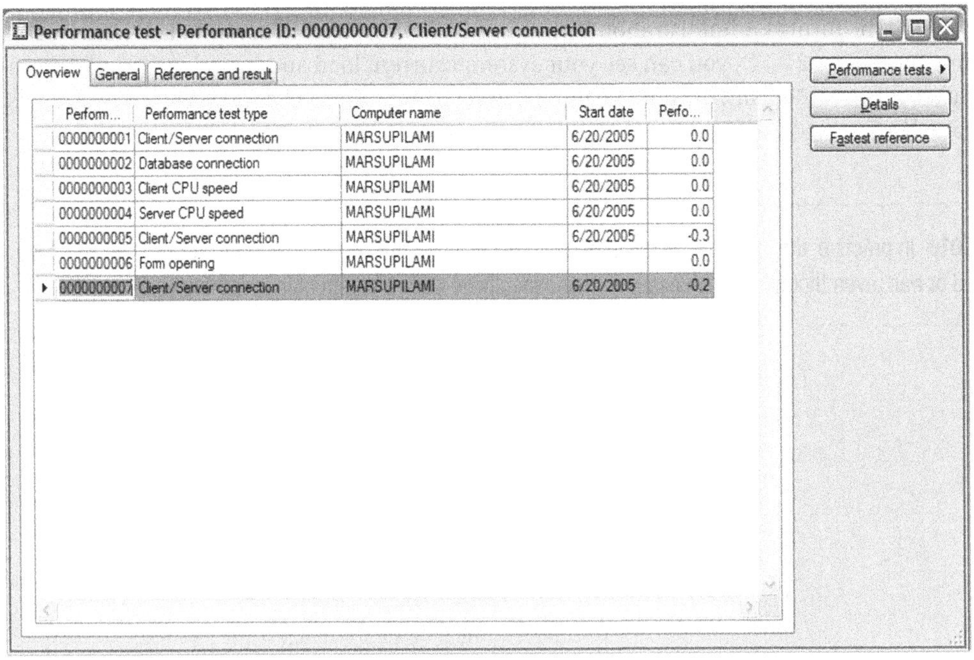

Figure 21-13. *The Performance Test form*

As you can see, we have not run any form-opening test, and we have repeated the client/server connection three times. The first, with an index of 0, is our reference run; the second and third, interestingly, were faster than the reference, as you can see by the negative index value.

Note You can use the Fastest Reference button to make the selected test your new baseline. Axapta then recalculates all existing indexes for the test based on the new reference.

The General tab displays details for the selected record, similar to the timing and environment data collected by the benchmarking tool. The most interesting tab is Reference and Result, which provides a comparison between the result for the run and your current baseline, as well as a standard set of references provided by MBS—in the case of the client/server connection you will see the latency. By comparing your test result to the references from MBS, you can easily see if your performance is acceptable, good, or bad. By comparing to your own reference, you can see if performance is improving or deteriorating.

Figure 21-14 shows the results of a run we made on the client/server connection; the latency was higher than in the fastest test—the baseline—but much lower than the acceptable value provided by MBS, so performance on the client/server connection is excellent but lower than when I established my reference. This means it could be better under other operating circumstances.

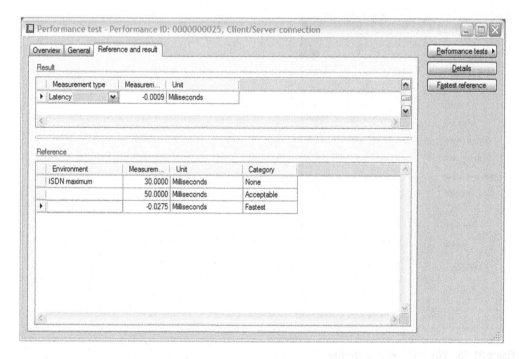

Figure 21-14. *Reference and result*

■**Note** The None category of network latency does not mean that it's good or bad, just the best you can expect with an ISDN connection.

The Performance Tests button at the right of the form displays a pull-down menu that allows you to select and rerun any of the existing tests to do a performance check on a specific element, such as the Client/Server connection or Database connection tests.

The Details button lets you see that the selected test actually consists of groups of operations, what those groups are, as well as individual performance results—typically each operation is repeated ten times. The performance varies for each loop of the test, and the index is actually a statistical basis.

As an alternative to running individual tests from the Performance Test form in Figures 21-13 and 21-14, you can use the Performance Test Wizard and select only the ones you want to run, or select Administration ➤ Periodic ➤ Performance Analysis ➤ Periodic Performance Test, which provides access to the exact same list of performance tests. If you follow that path, though, you can't specify the length of time to run each test.

Last but not least, the performance module includes the Open Menu Forms test at Administration ➤ Periodic ➤ Performance Analysis ➤ Open Menu Forms, which can transverse all forms and exercise them (assuming that there is data in all tables). It can also exercise all reports if you select the Run Reports radio button instead of Open Up Forms (see Figure 21-15).

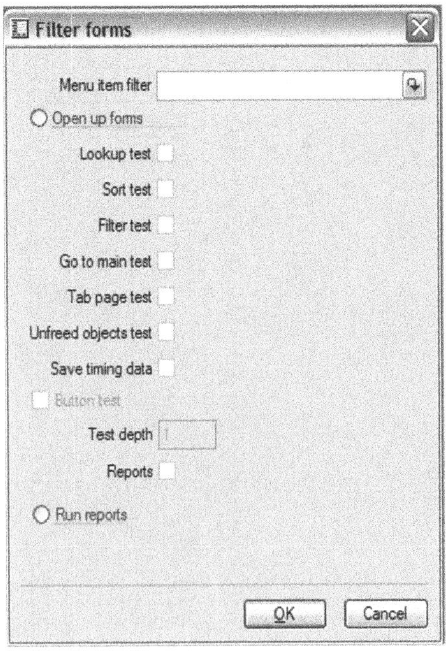

Figure 21-15. *The Filter Forms dialog*

Selecting the different controls does the following:

- *Menu Item Filter*: Tests only forms whose names match the filter criteria

- *Open Up Forms*: Traverses all forms in the AOT instead of reports

    - *Lookup Test*: Looks up data for lookup fields in forms

    - *Sort Test*: Re-sorts all grid columns in the inverse of the default order

    - *Filter Test*: Sets a filter on each grid column

    - *Go to Main Test*: Displays the main form of lookup fields

    - *Tab Page Test*: Activates and traverses all tab pages in a form

    - *Unfreed Objects Test*: Dumps active objects when finished traversing a top-level form

    - *Save Timing Data*: Saves the time taken to open the form and perform field lookups

- *Button Test*: Presses buttons on forms and navigates down the call hierarchy

- *Test Depth*: Specifies how many levels to go down the call hierarchy

- *Reports*: Traverses reports called by buttons

- *Run Reports*: Traverses the reports in the AOT instead of the forms

If you save timing data, then you can use the Performance Test form to see the results. Selecting a test and looking up the details will, among other things, show you the call tree that the test walked. Other than that, this test creates a log file named according to the pattern *BMInfo_UserID_SessionID.log* (if you're logged in as Admin BMInfo_Admin_2.log) and located in your system *My Documents* folder. If the test crashes, the last line in the log will tell you how far the text got and where you should look for a problem with your forms.

■**Note** We recommend you delete any test runs that you no longer need so you don't get lost in them. You can print the test results if you prefer by using the report provided in the *Reports* folder of the Administration menu (Administration ➤ Reports ➤ Performance Results).

Distribution

Distribution consists of two subtopics:

- Installing and updating clients at end-user workstations

- Making application changes available to test and production

Traditionally, both elements of distribution have represented a challenge to system administrators, but Axapta offers a series of alternatives that make the process unusually easy and painless for an ERP system.

The traditional means of installing and updating clients at end-user entails going to every client system and installing and configuring the software, using a software distribution tool to push the software and update out, and convincing users to download, install, and configure the software.

This works, of course, but Axapta makes the tasks a lot easier by letting users simply go to a Web page and clicking on an ActiveX control. The rest is taken care of for them—it's called the Web Deployment Client, and we will look at it in a minute.

The other aspect of distributing Axapta is concerned with getting new code and application objects from development to testers and end users. The traditional way has been to compile all your stuff, package it with an installer, and then ship it. Axapta offers you two easy ways to do this, each with advantages and drawbacks, which we will cover here.

The Web Deployment Client

The Web Deployment Client tool—generally called NAWDC (Navision Axapta Web Deployment Client)—is a simple and easy way of deploying the Axapta client across an organization and making sure that everyone has the latest version installed. It's an ActiveX control that can be embedded in a Web page where you can run it. When it's run, it checks the user's workstation for the presence of an Axapta client, and makes sure it's the correct version.

If the result is negative, the current client version or the latest service pack is loaded from the Web server and installed on the end user's workstation. If the result is positive and/or after the end-user's workstation has been updated, the Axapta client is run using a configuration file on the Web site you created. You get three things with the NAWDC:

- Easy and automated Axapta client deployment

- Easy and automated Axapta client patching

- Central management of configurations

Here are the steps involved in deploying Axapta clients using the NAWDC:

1. Your system administrator (SA) installs the NAWDC in a Web site.

2. The SA creates a Web page where the NAWDC is embedded.

3. The SA places the Web client files where the Web site can access them.

4. The SA gives out the URL to the Web page.

5. Users go to the URL provided and run the NAWDC.

6. The NAWDC makes sure that the client binaries installed on the end users' workstations are the latest specified by the server.

7. The NAWDC starts the client with a configuration stored on the server.

Note Providing users with different configurations they can start is simply a matter of providing a page with multiple references to the NAWDC—or different pages on the Web site, each pointing to a different configuration on the server.

Getting the whole thing up and running can be a little tricky, so let's step through it—we are assuming that you have a Microsoft IIS Web server where you can do this:

1. Create a Web site by creating a virtual directory under the Web server you want to use and set it to the local path of C:\Inetpub\wwwroot\AxWebDeploy, for example.

2. Go to the respective section of the Axapta install portal or the product CD folder *Setup\Web Deployment* and copy the *AxWebDeploy.cab* file to the local path you have just created.

3. Extract the DLL file in the CAB file by using the expand command-line utility or any other CAB extractor of your preference.

   a. Start a command-prompt window and go to the folder where you saved the *AxWebDeploy.cab*.

   b. Create a subfolder to extract it to—e.g., *AxWebDep*.

   c. Extract it with the command-line expand AxWebDeploy.cab /f:AxWebDeploy.dll AxWebDep.

4. Go to the extraction folder.

5. Register the NAWDC on your system with the command line regsvr32 AxWebDeploy.dll.

6. Copy the folder *Setup\Client30* from the distribution CD to the local path.

7. Copy the folder *Setup\Client* from the latest service pack to the local path; name it *Client30_SP4*, for example.

All that remains is for you to create a page that your users can navigate to and where you embed a link or button to run the NAWDC. The following HTML snippet is a quick and dirty example you can use as a base. We'll also use it to walk through setting up the NAWDC's properties.

```
<HTML>
<HEAD>
<TITLE></TITLE>
</HEAD>
<BODY>

<P>Click on the button to start Axapta</P>
<P>
<OBJECT id=AxWeb codeBase=➡
http:\\marsupilami\AxWebDeploy\axwebdeploy.cab#version=3,0,0,1
        classid=clsid:B6905E70-4B33-11D3-A498-0008C7DB06E6>
    <PARAM NAME="_cx" VALUE="2328">
    <PARAM NAME="_cy" VALUE="503">
    <PARAM NAME="AutoSize" VALUE="-1">
    <PARAM NAME="Enabled" VALUE="-1">
    <PARAM NAME="ServerSetup" VALUE="http:\\marsupilami\AxWebDeploy\Client30">
    <PARAM NAME="ServerServicePack" VALUE=➡
```

```
        "http:\\marsupilami\AxWebDeploy\Client30_SP3">
    <PARAM NAME="AutoStart" VALUE="0">
    <PARAM NAME="Configuration" VALUE=➡
        "http:\\marsupilami\AxWebDeploy\Ax30sp3.axc">
    <PARAM NAME="Version" VALUE="3,0,1951,3730">
    <PARAM NAME="TempDirectory" VALUE="">
    <PARAM NAME="AxaptaLanguage" VALUE="">
    <PARAM NAME="Database" VALUE="">
    <PARAM NAME="DatabaseParm" VALUE="">
    <PARAM NAME="CopyFiles" VALUE="-1">
    <PARAM NAME="WarnDownload" VALUE="-1">
    <PARAM NAME="CommandLineSetup" VALUE="">
    <PARAM NAME="CommandLineServicePack" VALUE="">
</OBJECT>
</P>

</BODY>
</HTML>
```

The snippet includes only a minimal set of parameters that you need to make things work; however, an extensive set is well-documented in the Axapta Web Deployment Client document referred in the "Wrap-Up" section of this chapter.

Note Values of -1 are equivalent to false; 0 is equivalent to true.

Let's take a quick look at the absolute must-have parameters in our HTML snippet—the first five are standard for ActiveX controls and are not explained in the aforementioned documentation:

- *_cx*: The horizontal positioning coordinate for the ActiveX control icon.

- *_cy*: The vertical positioning coordinate for the ActiveX control icon.

- *AutoSize*: Specifies whether the browser can size the ActiveX control as it likes.

- *Enabled*: Specifies that the ActiveX control is active.

- *ServerSetup*: The folder that contains the client software to be installed.

- *ServerServicePack*: The folder that contains the service pack to be installed.

- *AutoStart*: By default it's false (i.e., -1); if it's true the ActiveX control will be downloaded and installed to the client as soon as the page is loaded. Otherwise this will happen only when the user runs it by clicking on the control.

- *Configuration*: A mandatory parameter that points to the Axapta configuration file to use when starting the client.

- *Version*: A mandatory parameter that indicates the version number of the Axapta client that is wanted on the client workstations using the Web Deploy page, and that you can see by inspecting the Version tab of the Properties page for the Axapta client executable (*ax32.exe*); it resembles Figure 21-1.

- *CopyFiles*: This is an optional parameter that specifies whether the files should be copied to the client; default is true.

- *Warnownload*: This is an optional parameter that specifies whether the user should be prompted for acceptance of the download; default is true.

We intentionally left the OBJECT tag for last; however, without it you are nowhere—so let's look at its properties:

- *id*: Any unique identifier you wish to use.

- *codebase*: The CAB file containing the ActiveX control suffixed with the # character and version number of the CAB file, which you can find by looking at the file version field on the Version tab of the corresponding DLL, as shown in Figure 21-16—but notice that the separators in the properties in the dialog are "." while in the codebase they are ","—so always remember to use "," as the separator, not ".". Finally, the classid consists of the keyword clsid: plus the ActiveX class ID that you can find in the registry under the key HKEY_CLASSES_ROOT\CLSID\ by doing a search for *axwebdeploy.dll*.

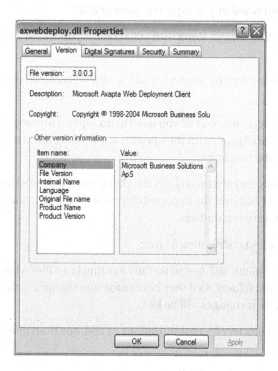

Figure 21-16. *AxWebDeploy.dll file version*

Check your work by going to a workstation that does not have an Axapta client installed, navigating to the Web site and page that you have just created, and clicking on the button.

Watch as the NAWDC does its thing and an Axapta Windows client starts up. Log in; if all is well, send your users instructions for navigating to the Web page.

Naturally, as you go, copy new releases of the NAWDCs and Axapta client and service packs in the same manner to the local path and change the properties of the Web page to point to the correct directories. That done, the next time a user starts Axapta using your Web deployment page, his workstation will be updated automatically without your having to lift a finger.

Distributing Customizations

There are two approaches to distributing customizations and add-on solutions—in other words, your code and Axapta objects such as forms and reports.

- *Ship an application layer*: This is a set of files that contains, among other things, all the code and metadata that you have customized and added, and requires that you also ship any label files that you have created. The pattern for the files is *axLayer.FileType*; for example, the application file for the VAR layer is *axVAR.aod* and *axVARen-us.add* is the US English application developer documentation file.

- *Export the code, metadata, and label files that you want to distribute, and ship*: This creates an XPO file with whatever name you decide on when doing the export.

  - Provide recipients with instructions on whether to import labels, and/or provide them with IDs (depending on whether you exported them or not).

  - Include the documentation files that go along with your code as you would when distributing a layer.

Both of the distribution techniques require the person installing your customizations to perform certain tasks:

- *Ship an application layer*: On the receiving end all you need to do is place the layer files in your application folder, then start Axapta with the updated application; it will rebuild the application and incorporate the new layer.

- *Export*: Import the XPO file, making sure that you check the check boxes indicated by the distributor of the customizations or add-ons; the imported objects and code are compiled during the import and your application is updated.

Keep the following issues in mind when distributing a layer:

- When you ship a layer file, the recipients will overwrite their existing layer files when they copy yours to their application folders, so if they have made any changes to theirs that you have not incorporated, their changes will be lost.

- The same will occur if your recipients receive customizations or add-ons from different parties using the same layer.

You must also bear in mind some issues when distributing an export:

- If you do not select to export and import with IDs, all your objects will be assigned IDs when they are imported. If you later provide an update, you must not export with IDs, as the objects will exist at the destination systems with other IDs. So leave it to Axapta to figure it out.

- If you export with IDs, always do so and instruct your recipients to import with IDs or they will end up with different IDs than yours, which will cause conflicts the next time you provide a fix or update.

- When exporting with IDs, the import must be made to the same layer as the export because each layer has its own ID range; therefore IDs from one layer can't be allocated to another.

That's it in a nutshell. Distributing your materials with Axapta is a breeze. Whether you choose to provide a layer or an export, just follow some simple rules and the tips presented here, and you will have no problems.

Wrap-Up

This chapter has walked you through what you need to know to figure out what sort of infrastructure you need to support Axapta within your organization. Specifically, we've covered the following:

- What load you should expect to handle

- Considerations when putting together a system solution

- Determining the servers and quantity you need

- Monitoring your system's performance

- How to get the base software to its users

- How to distribute your customizations to testers and users

Unfortunately, there is not much documentation on the product CD that addresses these issues specifically. The exception is available in the Technical Information folder in the base documentation folder of the product distribution package or CD:

- *AX-300-TIP-027-v01.00-ENUS.doc*: Axapta Web Deployment Client

Two very useful documents are the sizing spreadsheets that you will need to obtain from MBS or a partner:

- *Single-site questionnaire version 2.5.xls*: Axapta sizing spreadsheet for single-site installations

- *Multi-site questionnaire version 2.5.xls*: Axapta sizing spreadsheet for multisite installations

As you venture out on your own, keep in mind that sizing and the tools available in Axapta will get you started safely, but you can't really know what it takes to deliver the performance your users expect until the system is in use—monitor it and plan ahead.

APPENDIX A

■■■

Documentation

Learning Axapta is not a walk in the park and you will need all the documentation you can find. This appendix will help you track down existing documentation, whether it's on the product distribution CD, an MBS Web site, or one of the growing numbers of independent Axapta sites.

Although there is quite a lot of documentation around, it can be very time-consuming to find the stuff you need, so it's very important that you are clear about what you are looking for and have a strategy for hunting down the documents and information you need so you don't waste time browsing through hundreds of pages that get you nowhere. Consider the following:

- What type of information or documentation are you looking for?

    - *Target*: user, administrator, developer

    - *Subject*: financials, logistics, debugger, etc.

- The materials of any training sessions you have attended are generally the most comprehensive and authoritative documents you will find; check them first.

- All the documentation on the product CD is accessible from the Installation Portal, which you should use as your portal to the documentation. The file names on CD are generally meaningless; the portal is the only way to know what's in them without opening and reading each one.

- For easy access to the Installation Portal, we suggest you copy the *Documentation* folder from the CD to your local hard drive so you can easily read the documents when you need them. You'll need various software to read the documentation, which comes in the following formats:

    - Windows Help

    - Adobe Acrobat

    - Microsoft Word

    - Plain Text

    - Microsoft Wave

    - HTML

- To use the Installation Portal, you need to copy the *\Setup.htm* file and the *\Autorun* folder as well as the *\Documentation* folder, and maintain the structure so that the links on the Web pages that make up the portal can be resolved.

- The documentation on the product CD provides a comprehensive walk-through of Axapta from installation to application modules and country-specific features. It does not, however, give you much of a clue as to how things fit together, and is often hard to read and understand, so we suggest waiting to read it until you have finished this book—it will make it easier to understand and it will provide much more value.

- MBS's online eAcademy courses are the best place to get started; they provide a quick overview of the product, administration, and development topics, and information on using the application modules.

It goes without saying that information available at Web sites or news groups comes and goes, so download anything you find useful and keep it within easy reach.

Tip There is a significant degree of crossover in the existing product documentation, so if you don't find what you are looking for in the documentation types that fit your search topic, look at other related types. For example, if you are looking for administration of Web users, you will find that information on the Users Guide for Internet, *AX-300-USG-010-v01.00-ENUS.pdf* on the product CD even though you might be inclined to look at the main administrative guide *AX-300-USG-009-v01.00-ENUS.pdf*. That document covers setting up other types of users, but not Web users.

Caution The comprehensiveness and authoritativeness of training materials varies; the MBS documentation consists of supporting material that will not get you very far without an instructor or course notes.

Note The majority of the Microsoft eLearning courses (also known as eAcademy courses) have been suspended, and it's anyone's guess if and when they will be updated and reintroduced, but even the small number of courses remaining are well worth the time.

Tables A-1 through A-4 provide a quick overview of what documentation you can find where, broken down by repository type.

Table A-1. *Installation Portal or Product CD*

Location	Topic	Comments
Product CD *\readme.txt*	Last-minute information that didn't make the product documentation	Includes issues with the installation, so make sure you always read it.
Installation Portal *\Documentation\Readme* or the product CD at *\Autorun\ Portal\DL-Readme.htm*	Generic info	Too general to be useful; it's there only because it's common practice.
Installation Portal menu *\Documentation\Prerequisites* or the product CD at *\Autorun\Portal\ DL-Prerequisites.htm*	Requirements for running Axapta	Covers preinstallation.
Installation Portal menu *\Documentation\Installation Guide* or the product CD at *\Autorun/Portal\ DL-Installation Guide.htm*	Installing Axapta	The steps for installing the binaries.
Installation Portal menu *\Documentation\What's New* or the product CD at *\Documentation\What's New*	Changes and new features in the release	Quite useful, particularly for IT professionals involved with different versions.
Installation Portal menu *\Documentation\Guides* or the product CD at *\Documentation\Guides*	Base documentation on application modules, administration, and development	A table with pointers and short explanations of the base document set.
Installation Portal menu *\Documentation\Technical Information* or the product CD at *\Documentation \Technical Information*	Includes additional documentation that complements the documents in the guides	Documents that address specific technical issues not covered in the base documentation.
Installation Portal menu *\Documentation\Guides* or the product CD at *\Documentation\eLearning*	An audio and video walk-through for installing Axapta	Start it manually from the product CD by running *autorun.exe.*
Installation Portal menu, menu bar items	Last-minute information that didn't make the product documentation for the respective section	All menu items in the menu bar of the portal open up in their respective subjects' Readme files.

■**Note** Much of the documentation on the product CD can also be found online at the MBS Axapta sites.

Table A-2. *News Groups*

Location	Topic	Comments
news.microsoft.com group microsoft.public.axapta	A mix of all things Axapta	This was the first news group created by Microsoft and was used for all purposes. You can also access this news group from your browser; see the Note.
news.microsoft.com group microsoft.public.axapta.application	Application layer news group	You can access this news group from your browser; see the Note.
news.microsoft.com group microsoft.public.axapta.database	Database layer news group	You can access this news group from your browser; see the Note.
news.microsoft.com group microsoft.public.axapta.localization	Localization news group	You can also access this news group from your browser; see the Note.
news.microsoft.com group microsoft.public.axapta.programming	Development news group	You can also access this news group from your browser; see the Note.

Note Most of the postings on the Microsoft Axapta news groups have been migrated from the defunct Technet, so they contain a lot of good stuff. You can read all the Microsoft news groups in your browser at www.microsoft.com/Businesssolutions/Community/Newsgroups/dgbrowser/en-us/default.mspx.

Table A-3. *Web Sites*

Location	Topic	Comments
www.microsoft.com/ BusinessSolutions	The Microsoft Business Solutions home page	Covers all MBS products and services.
www.microsoft.com/ BusinessSolutions/ partnersource.mspx	Microsoft Certified Partner portal for all things MBS	You must be a registered partner and have a login connected to a Microsoft Passport account.
www.microsoft.com/ BusinessSolutions/ customersource.mspx	Microsoft Business Solutions CustomerSource portal, for customers with a service plan	You must be a registered partner and have a login connected to a Microsoft Passport account.
www.partnerguide.com/	Localized Microsoft Certified Partner portal for all things MBS	For those of us not from North America.
www.axapta-links.com	A seemingly random collection of documents	Has quite a bit of useful information.
www.mbsgurus.com	Job site for people with MBS product skills, including Axapta skills	The best Axapta job resource on the Internet.

Location	Topic	Comments
`http://groups.yahoo.com/ group/development-axapta/`	Axapta mailing list	Courtesy of Thy Data Center, one of the leading Axapta development houses.
`https://mbselrn.partners. extranet.microsoft.com`	eLearning site	This is the best place to start for newcomers, but you will need an account login.

■**Note** We've listed only Web sites that have significant quantity and quality of content as this book is being written. However, the quantity of Axapta sites is growing, as is the quantity and quality of information they offer. For a more exhaustive list of sites, visit the MBS PartnerSource and CustomerSource sites.

■**Tip** Quite a few Axapta sites require that you be a registered user, so we assume that they intend to exploit your information commercially. Think carefully before you sign up; it can be quite difficult to find out how to remove yourself from their mailing lists or terminate your membership.

Table A-4. *Books*

Title	Topic	Comments
Managing your Supply Chain Using Microsoft Axapta by Scott Hamilton (McGraw-Hill)	A good walk-through of the supply chain business processes and how to use Axapta to manage them	Even more important than the Axapta aspect of the book is the coverage of the SCM topic.

Command-Line Parameters

The configuration utilities provided with Axapta allow you to specify the most important parameters to control Windows clients and Axapta Object Servers using different Windows controls; however, Axapta provides a large set of parameters for which there are no specific controls you can use to set them. You can specify other parameters in one of two ways: the Advanced text-entry field of the General tab page of the client and AOS configuration utilities, or in the target field of the Windows shortcuts you create to run your Axapta client.

Table B-1 is a full list of available command-line parameters for Axapta.

Table B-1. *Available Command-Line Parameters*

Parameter	Description
-allowunauth	When using Windows Authentication, this option enables users that do not pass the authentication process to be allowed to log in using a user name and password—the default Axapta logon method.
-aol=[layer]	"aol" is an acronym for Application Object Layer. Specify the layer to access upon successful login. Valid layers are sys, syp, gls, glp, dis, dip, los, lop, bus, bup, var, vap, cus, cup, usr, and usp.
-aolcode=[layer]	Access code for -aol. If you want to access a layer other than usr, use it to enter the code for the layer provided by MBS.
-aos=host:port	Connect to the AOS running at a given port number on the specified host. The host is either a DNS hostname (for example, axterix.comix.com) or an IP address (192.88.253.41, for instance). The port number is the number specified for the AOS instance that should be connected to. No instance name needs to be specified because only one instance can be running at a given port on a given machine. Using this option will connect the client directly to the AOS, bypassing the default initial search for the AOS. It thereby eliminates the need for networking that supports UDP traffic. This eases firewall configuration and network address translation (NAT) appliances.

(Continued)

Table B-1. *(Continued)*

Parameter	Description
-aos=instance@host	Connect to the specified AOS instance running at the specified host machine. Instance is the name (for example, "Axapta"), and host is the DNS name or IP address of the machine running the AOS. Specifying -aos=MyAOS@MyHost equals setting -servermask=MyAOS and -internet=MyHost (or specifying these in the corresponding fields on the Server tab of the Configuration Utility).
-aos=ad([adsn])	Use Active Directory integration. <adsn> is the Active Directory server name to search the Active Directory for. This is the same as By Name—Find a Specific AOS in the Axapta Configuration Utility.
-aos=adbrowse	Use Active Directory integration. Search the Active Directory for Active Directory server names in User objects and organizations units. This is the same as By Organization—Browse for Per-User or Per-Organizational Specific AOS in the Axapta Configuration Utility.
-aos=ad	Use Active Directory integration—search the Active Directory for any AOS. This is the same as Simple—Find Any AOS in the Axapta Configuration Utility.
-applexclusive	The application files are opened in exclusive mode. Note: You cannot give both applexclusive and -applshare. If you do give both, the one given last on the command line will take effect. You will not get any error messages.
-application=[application]	Specify the name of the Axapta application. The default is Standard.
-applshare	The application files are opened in shared mode by default. Note: You cannot give both applexclusive and -applshare. If you do give both, the one given last on the command line will take effect. You will not get any error messages.
-broadcast= xx.xx.xx.xx	Specify a broadcast address to be used in -client mode. A request is sent to all the broadcast addresses to obtain identification of the available application servers. The address consists of four decimal values between 0 and 255, separated by dots.
-bwsim=[speed]:[latency]	Speed is the bandwidth simulated in bytes per second. Latency is the number of milliseconds spent for a communication round-trip—the fixed overhead time the network applies for sending a package to the server and for receiving one back.
-client	Connect to an AOS and run as a three-tier thin client. Use -aos= to specify which AOS.
-client = thin	Like -client; connect to an AOS and run as a three-tier thin client. Use -aos= to specify which AOS.
-client = fat	Connect to an AOS and run as a three-tier fat client. Use -aos= to specify which AOS.
-company=[company]	Specifies the company to activate upon successful login. The default is dat.

Parameter	Description
-connectionidletimeout= [seconds]	Set the time in seconds to leave an idle database connection open before closing it. Shorter idle time will decrease database server and Axapta memory usage, but will potentially cause time-consuming re-logins on the fly. The default is 60 seconds for Microsoft SQL Server, 30 minutes for Oracle.
-createdsn=microsoftsqlserver or -createdsn=oracle	Have the data source created automatically in the ODBC manager.
-createdsn_tcpipport=[integer]	TCP/IP port number required for Oracle. This parameter is relevant only when -createdsn=oracle is given. The parameter is ignored if given with -createdsn= microsoftsqlserver.
-database=[database]	The database to use when connecting to the database server. The default is to use the database set in the ODBC driver.
-dbcli= [ODBC]|[OCI]	Runs Axapta in either ODBC or OCI mode. -DBCLI=ODBC is the default.
-dbserver=[server]	The server to log into. The default option is to use the server set in the ODBC driver.
-dbunicodeenabled=0 | 1	Initialize the database for Unicode.
-directory=[directory]	Specify the Axapta root directory.
-doclanguage=[language]	Use this option if you would like to have the documentation in a different language than the one used in menus and dialogs. For example, -doclanguage=de will give you the documentation in German. The default documentation language is the language used in the system, which is set via the -language option.
-dsn=[dsn]	The ODBC driver data source to use. The default is BMSDSN.
-featurekeysystem	The 3.0 security system is on by default. Use this parameter to enable the old feature key system.
-fetchahead=[records]	The maximum number of records retrieved from the database at a time. The default is 100.
-hint=[hint]	Apply database-dependent SQL hints.
-internal=relaxedsyntax	The 3.0 kernel defaults to strict X++ syntax checking. For relaxed syntax checking, use this parameter to ease restrictions.
-internet=[address]	Specify an Internet address to be used in -client mode. A request is sent to all the Internet addresses to obtain identification of the available Axapta Object Servers.
-job=[job]	Run the specified external job prior to any other database-related action during startup.
-language=[language]	Specifies the language for the user interface. This is a required parameter.
-log=[logfile]	Specifies the SQL error log file path. The default is trcAxaptaError.log in the standard Axapta log directory.

(Continued)

Table B-1. *(Continued)*

Parameter	Description
-logdir=[directory]	Specifies an alternative directory for the log files generated when you compile, import, or export in Axapta. The default is the *log* folder.
-noauto	Use this parameter to bypass system-related application calls made by the Axapta kernel. This includes the ability to bypass startup code, and some timer-based calls. This parameter will allow you to start up Axapta to fix problems that were introduced in the application code. Normally these problems would prevent you from starting Axapta. For example, code may be introduced in the startup method that causes Axapta to go into infinite loop, and therefore it never finishes the startup procedure. To change this, start with the -noauto switch, correct the code and restart without the -noauto to have the startup code included again.
-opencursors=[number]	Specifies the maximum number of database cursors to keep open per connection for cursor reuse. The default is 90.
-port=[port]	Specifies the TCP port the AOS listens on for connections.
-preloadthresholdmsec=[milliseconds]	Specifies the time for preloading. For example, -preloadthresholdmsec=3000 results in the issue of a warning whenever preloading exceeds 3000 milliseconds. This value can not be specified per user in Tools ➤ Options ➤ SQL ➤ Warnings. This threshold is activated only when warnings are enabled.
-preloadthresholdrecords=[records]	Specifies the number of records to preload. For example, -preloadthresholdrecords=300 results in the issue of a warning whenever preloading exceeds 300 records. This value can not be specified per user in Tools ➤ Options ➤ SQL ➤ Warnings. This threshold is activated only when warnings are enabled.
-querytimelimit =[table:][milliseconds]	Specifies that queries running longer than the given number of milliseconds against the specified file should be logged to a file. If the value of querytimelimit is zero (0), which is the default, no queries are logged. This parameter supports directing output to a table, i.e., SysTraceTable (the default is disk-file). Use -querytimelimit=ms for tracing all SQL statements exceeding the milliseconds threshold and -querytimelimit=table:ms to do the same to the table.
-regconfig=[name]	Specifies that the named Windows registry configuration created using the Axapta Configuration Utility should be used to start up Axapta.
-regimport=[filename]	Writes the configuration in the specified file to the Windows registry. It is performed prior to the evaluation of any other options. This means that you can write a configuration using -regimport and then select it using -regconfig.

Parameter	Description
-repair	Any non-zero value will force a re-synchronization of SQL system tables during startup. The use of this command-line parameter is logged in the Event log. Use this option to handle situations when problems in SQL system tables prevent Axapta from starting (for example, missing indexes).
-retry=[seconds]	Specifies the delay in seconds before re-executing after a deadlock. The default is 5 seconds
-securityprovider=[securityprovider]	Selects the security provider to use with Windows Authentication and is relevant only for Object Server configurations. For AOS running on Windows NT the only valid option is NTLM, which provides authentication based on the NTLM security provider. For Windows 2000 systems, Kerberos is also a valid security provider. For Windows 2000 networks with solely Windows 2000 servers and clients, Negotiate is also an option. This will elect the best suitable security provider automatically.
-serveridletimeout=[seconds]	Specifies the number of seconds the AOS instance should be allowed to run without servicing clients. When this timeout expires without having clients connected, the instance will be shut down automatically. This option is well-suited to be combined with setting instance startup mode to OnDemand, making the server auto-start upon request from the client and shut down when no clients need service for a given amount of time.
-servermask=[mask]	Specifies the mask for selecting a subset of object servers when running in client mode. If this option is not specified and multiple object servers are found, all available object servers will be presented in a selection box.
-share	Share label and identifier files between several applications. If not specified, the files will not be shared.
-singleuser	Run the program in single-user mode.
-sqlbuffer=[bytes]	Specifies the upper limit in KB of the fixed internal data retrieval buffer. The default is 24 KB.
-sqlcomplexliterals=[0|1]	Setting sqlcomplexliterals to the value 1 enables this feature; the value 0 disables this feature.
-sqlformliterals=[0|1]	Setting sqlformliterals to the value 1 enables this feature; the value 0 disables this feature.
-sqloraclefirstrowsfix=[value]	Oracle versions 8.05, 8.06, and 8.15 occasionally select a poor query plan for queries using the Axapta keyword firstFast. The symptom is that an index matching the order by specification is preferred, even though another index is better when the number of rows returned is small. Axapta includes a workaround for this problem, which you should enable only if you have verified that the aforementioned problem is the cause of poor performance. The Axapta Query Analyzer can be used to detect this. A value of 1 enables this workaround; a value of 0 disables it.

(Continued)

Table B-1. *(Continued)*

Parameter	Description
-sqlparm=[parameters]	Add the specified parameters to the database login. The format follows the ODBC standard: key1=value1;key2=value2. For example, DIR=c:\db;ID=9.
-sqlpwd=[password]	Specifies the password to use for login to the database. The default is bmssa_pwd.
-sqltrace[=table]	Invoke a SQL statement tracing to a log file or table. Use -sqltrace for tracing all generated SQL statements to a file, and -sqltrace=table to generate them to a table. The default is no tracing.
-sqluser=[user]	Specifies the user name for login to the SQL database. The default is bmssa.
-startupmsg=[message]	A text message to be displayed during Axapta startup.
-startupcmd=MyCommand	A string that is passed to Axapta and can be used to have your own startup commands executed. The string is passed in the calls appl.startup(MyCommand) and info.startup(MyCommand). "appl" and "info" are instantiated objects of the application classes Application and Info, respectively. The application classes are inherited from the system classes xApplication and xInfo.
-useis	Use integrated security during SQL database login, thus disabling values set by using parameters -sqluser and -sqlpwd.
-user=[user]	Specifies the user to log onto Axapta as.
-useserverprinters	Have the client direct all printing to the printer connected to the server.
-warnings[=table]	Enable various runtime warnings that are logged to a file or table. Use -warnings to trace all developer warnings to file and -warnings=table to trace all warnings to a table. The default is no warnings.
-windowsauth=[0|1]	This option disables/enables Windows Authentication; when enabled, it provides single sign-on and authentication of client machine accounts and the user logging in.

APPENDIX C

■ ■ ■

Module Summaries

The functionality you need is contained in specific modules, and it's not always obvious what belongs where. Table C-1 lists and briefly describes the major areas of functionality that you will find in each module.

Table C-1. *Axapta 3.0 Module Summaries*

Module	Description
Financials I	This module includes basic functionality such as general ledger, bank management, accounts receivable, and accounts payable. The module is required by several other modules and includes the following: • General Ledger I • Bank Management • Accounts Receivable • Accounts Payable
Financials II	The module includes intercompany accounting, multiple-company consolidation, account allocations, cash-flow forecasting, and currency-requirement projections. It provides management of future cash requirements and definition of automatic allocations to dimensions based on predefined settings. It is a must for managing and consolidating organizations with independent business units and subsidiaries.
Electronic Banking	This is an add-on module for importing and exporting payment data to files for financial institutions in several countries. It draws from accounts receivable, accounts payable, and banking management, and requires the Financials I module.
Fixed Assets	Fixed Assets is for managing the entire life cycle of a business's fixed assets, from acquisition to resale or writing off. It uses assets budgeting and multiple depreciation models to track the status of fixed assets and integrates with other modules to enable ordering and receiving of fixed assets through purchase orders and inventory.
Sales Force Automation	Sales Force Automation registers prospect and customer information, and the details of each interaction between your sales staff and the outside world, and includes the following: • Contact Management • Sales Management

Continued

Table C-1. *(Continued)*

Module	Description
Sales Management	Sales Management lets you view the activities and performance of your sales staff, sales teams and the entire sales organization. You can drive your sales teams by managing and monitoring tasks, leads, and assignments via a workbook and task-oriented system for individuals and teams. • Sales Staff Budgeting • Statistics
Marketing Automation	The Marketing Automation module lets you divide your customers and prospects into groups, based on sales and demographic information from Microsoft Axapta Sales Force Automation. By grouping your customers and prospects, you can more easily identify likely customers or the most valuable customers so you can develop better, more tightly targeted marketing campaigns. This module can also be used to manage non-sales-related communications such as newsletters and membership drives. • Communications Management • Marketing Encyclopedia
Telemarketing	This module is designed for sales teams or telemarketing groups. It supports telephone-related customer support and marketing programs, including sales-lead generation, customer surveys, direct marketing campaigns, and customer support.
Trade	This module automates the sales and purchasing processes. It automatically checks credit limits, customer account information, and inventory levels, providing real-time information to you and your customers and suppliers. You can print, fax, e-mail, or publish order confirmations on the Web (requires Enterprise Portal). You can also offer your customers flexible invoicing options, keep track of back orders, and manage returned items.
Trade Agreements	The Trade Agreements module is for managing price agreements with your customers and suppliers, including customer, vendor, or item-specific pricing and discounts. You can also automatically retrieve prices and discounts when entering orders and assign validity dates to item prices as well as to customers.
Logistics	The Logistics module is one of the backbones of Axapta. It automates the management of the entire logistics process. It tracks inventory with item and storage dimensions, automates quality control by managing the quarantine of items for QA, provides bar-coding functionality to manage point-of-sale systems, and warehouses to track items and locations electronically. This module also contains a bill of materials designer (BOM).
Intercompany	Intercompany functionality enables business units, subsidiaries, and/or distribution centers to trade with each other internally within the same system, ensuring consolidated inventory and on-hand delivery-time information across the whole organization.

Module	Description
Master Planning	The Master Planning module uses information from across your company and supply chain to help you optimize production and materials planning and scheduling. Finite materials and capacity scheduling can be performed at the same time so that available capacity, inventory levels, and purchase lead times are taken into consideration in production planning. • Forecast Scheduling and Master Planning • Coverage Groups • Scheduling Methods • Messages • Order Promising
Warehouse Management I	The Warehouse Management I module provides inventory dimensions, which you can add to all your inventory items to track not only which warehouse they are in, but also precisely where they are stored in each warehouse.
Warehouse Management II	The Warehouse Management II module adds logic and rules to the placement of inventory across your warehouses. When you receive inventory items, this module suggests the optimal placement for storage in your warehouses, based on preset rules. When you receive an order, the functionality not only tells you where it is, but will generate an optimized picking route. • Placement and Storage • Zones and Locations • Shipment • Pallet Transport • Barcode
Resources	All the resources your company uses for production can be divided into four work centers: machinery, people, tools, and vendors. Microsoft Axapta Resources helps you register and organize all your production or project resources so you can use other tools such as Microsoft Axapta Production or Microsoft Axapta Project to get the maximum benefits from these resources.
Project I	Project I lets you track time and materials consumed and conduct follow-ups on the financial status of your projects. You can itemize time and materials for invoicing, while retaining sales prices and cost prices of items and man hours. • Data Entry • Invoicing • Project Management • Accounting • Inquiry and Reporting
Project II	The Project II module provides advanced financial management of projects, including work-in-progress analysis of more-complex Time & Material projects, internal projects, and fixed-price projects. • Contract Management • Work in Progress • Cost and Performance • Posting

Continued

Table C-1. *(Continued)*

Module	Description
Production I	The Production I module provides for the creation of production BOMs to track the raw materials that go into finished products, with raw material consumption and finished product information automatically posted to the General Ledger. • Production Orders • Production Bill of Materials • Scheduling • Production Consumption
Production II	Production II lets you plan and execute routes, operations and rough capacity to get accurate lead times. You can use finite or infinite scheduling, and you can track costs and calculate scrap, while posting all business information automatically to the General Ledger. • Route Complexity • Scheduling • Operation Components • Scrap Calculations • Cost Tracking
Production III	The Production III module provides a Gantt chart to give you a graphic overview of your production process. You can reschedule jobs simply by dragging and dropping jobs on the Gantt chart. The module also gives you detailed job management and production scheduling, including the ability to schedule jobs in each work center by the minute and second. • Gantt Chart • Task Group • Bottleneck Scheduling • Job Monitoring • Scheduling Properties
Product Builder I	Product Builder I allows you to manage configuration options for your products, and lets users customize products to their own preferences. It automatically generates bills of materials for existing product configurations as specified by the customers or users.
Product Builder II	Product Builder II is for creating validation rules for groups of variables and the complete product configuration to help ensure that customers don't choose a combination of product options that you will not be able to produce. Each variable is a product option that your customers can choose.
Product Builder III	Product Builder III lets you set up default routes through your production process. The module then automatically chooses the most efficient route for every order placed through the Microsoft Axapta Product Builder, based on the item configuration and quantity ordered by the customer.
Product Builder IV	Product Builder IV is for creating more-complex rules and formulas, using X++ code, which affects the options your customers and users can choose while configuring products.
Shop Floor Control I	The Shop Floor Control I module is designed to reduce manual data entry with automated collection of employee time and attendance. Set up profiles to track employee attendance, and capture actual attendance and absence time.

Module	Description
Shop Floor Control II	The Shop Floor Control II module registers time and resources used and the items created for each job on the shop floor to support the fulfillment of the order. The data can then be transferred to the Production or Project modules for analysis of actual costs of the items produced.
Shop Floor Control III	Shop Floor Control III uses the data collected in Shop Floor Control I and II to generate payroll data, complete with pay types and rates. For each employee, the module calculates the hourly wage as well as all types of bonuses and premiums. The payroll data generated by this module can be exported to an external payroll system for output.
Human Resource I	This module manages employee information and agreements, the reasons for a resignation and keeps track of transfers between departments. • Core HRM • Organization
Human Resource II	This module collects information regarding your company's recruitment process, including internal data like job profiles, and external-facing material like recruitment correspondence and media responses. The module also helps you track absences and understand trends in absenteeism. • Organization • Recruitment • Absence
Human Resource III	This module provides human-resource professionals with an overview of your resources and identifies potential skill gaps in your organization. Course administration tools help your human-resource staff administer training opportunities within your organization. • Employee Development • Skill Management • Course Administration
Business Process Management	The Business Process Management module enables you to analyze strengths, weaknesses, opportunities, and threats (called a SWOT analysis) and create a strategy that is linked to custom-designed KPIs. Best practices templates help you define actions and processes that are aligned with the overall strategy. • Strategic Planning • Action Management
Balanced Scorecard	The Balanced Scorecard module allows you to define KPIs as part of a business plan, and to track and measure a variety of aspects of your business. With KPIs, you can evaluate your overall business performance according to your business plan, track performance, and measure fulfillment of business goals. • Knowledge Account Plan • Metrics • Calculations • Periodic Metrics • Reporting and Statistics

Continued

Table C-1. *(Continued)*

Module	Description
Questionnaire I	Questionnaire I provides integration to sales and marketing functionality. You can design a questionnaire as part of their human resources procedure, to support CRM processes, to coach telemarketing personnel, or to send the questionnaire to a target group as part of a campaign and collect responses over the Web. • Design and Execution • Reports and Analysis
Questionnaire II	Questionnaire II gives you advanced distribution functionality that lets you select a specific group of respondents and e-mail them a link to a questionnaire that is tailored for them. The module also helps you carry out advanced statistical calculations and get an overview of your feedback by viewing survey results graphically. • Scheduling • Reports and Analysis
Cost Accounting I	Cost Accounting I provides the ability to import and use income statements from financial accounting to generate expense distribution sheets for different parts of your organization and to compare them by user-selected periods, and can be used to determine inventory valuation, profitability levels, direct and indirect costs, etc.
Cost Accounting II	Cost Accounting II provides the ability to group and categorize costs to measure consistency and compliance with costs-accounting standards.
Business Analysis	The Business Analysis module provides powerful functionality for visualizing, comparing, and analyzing your business data. • Core • Microsoft Analysis Server • Cube Generation • Security
CRM	The Customer Relationship Management group gathers and tracks all sales and marketing activities and keeps the information at your fingertips, giving sales and marketing professionals the insight to better segment leads, identify customer needs, and to make optimal sales and marketing decisions.

APPENDIX D

■ ■ ■

Keyboard Shortcuts

The table that follows provides a complete list of the shortcut key combinations available in Axapta and includes a short description of their purpose, the equivalent menu commands, and in which context the shortcuts are available.

Most people tend to progressively expand their usage of shortcuts with time, so we recommend keeping this reference handy. Come back to it now and again to pick up a few extra shortcuts. Use them until they stick to your fingertips, and then pick up a few more.

The entries in the Applicable column of the table are based on the type of tool for which the shortcut keys are active:

- General: The shortcut is generally available within the Axapta runtime and development environments.

- Editor: The shortcut is available in the different text editors and viewers, e.g. X++, HTML, and debugger.

- AOT: The shortcut is specific to the Axapta Object Tree.

- Forms: The shortcut is specific to forms.

- Debugger: The shortcut is specific to the debugger.

- Infolog: The shortcut is specific to the error-reporting tool.

- Report Viewer: The shortcut is specific to the report viewer.

Table D-1. *Shortcut Key Combinations in Axapta*

Shortcut	Description	Equivalent	Applicable
F1	Search for the selected object in the help system	Help	General
F3	Repeat the last find	Find Next	General
F10	Activate the menu bar	Menu Bar	General
Enter	Enter key	Enter	General
Tab	Tabulation key	Tab	General
Ins	Toggle between the insert and the overwrite settings	Insert	General
Up Arrow	Move the cursor one line up	Up	General
Down Arrow	Move the cursor one line down	Down	General
Left Arrow	Move the cursor one character to the left	Left	General
Right Arrow	Move the cursor one character to the right	Right	General
Ctrl-Space	Toggle between objects or editors	Toggle	General
Ctrl-Tab	Shift to the next tab page	Next Tab Page	General
Ctrl-C or Ctrl-Ins	Copy the selection and place it on the clipboard	Copy	General
Ctrl-F	Find the specified text	Find . . .	General
Ctrl-N	Creates a new object	New	General
Ctrl-O	Flush all cache contents	Free Cache	General
Ctrl-O	Execution	Open	General
Ctrl-P	Print the contents of the active editor buffer or definition of the active object, or bring up the auto-report form from within forms	Print . . .	General
Ctrl-Q	Cancel changes to the active editor buffer or object	Cancel	General
Ctrl-V or Shift-Ins	Insert the contents of the clipboard	Paste	General
Ctrl-X or Shift-Del	Cut the selection and place it in the clipboard	Cut	General
Ctrl-F4	Close the active window	Close	General
Ctrl-PgUp	Go to the start of the line	Start of Line	General
Ctrl-PgDn	Go to the end of the line	End of Line	General
Ctrl-Shift-PgUp	Go to the top of the page, and select	Shift Top	General
Ctrl-Shift-PgDn	Go to the bottom of the page, and select	Shift Bottom	General

Shortcut	Description	Equivalent	Applicable
Ctrl-Shift-Tab	Shift to the next tab page	Next Tab Page	General
Ctrl-Up Arrow	Ctrl key arrow up key	Ctrl Up	General
Ctrl-Down Arrow	Ctrl key arrow down key	Ctrl Down	General
Alt-F4	Exit Axapta	Exit	General
Alt-Down Arrow	Open the drop-down list for a combo box	Open Combo Box	General
Alt-Up Arrow	Close the drop-down list for a combo box	Close Combo Box	General
Shift-F1	Display the short description of the selected object	What's This	General
Shift-F10	Open the context menu	Context Menu	General
Shift-Tab	Backward tabulation	Backward Tab	General
Shift-Up Arrow	Move the cursor one line up and select	Shift Up	General
Shift-Down Arrow	Move the cursor one line down and select	Shift Down	General
Shift-Left Arrow	Move the cursor one character to the left and select	Shift Left	General
Shift-Right Arrow	Move the cursor one character to the right and select	Shift Right	General
F2	List all tables	List Tables	Editor
F4	List all Extended Data Types	List Types	Editor
F5	Execute the current job	Go	Editor
F6	Close the current tab, discarding all changes since last save	Abort Tab	Editor
F7	Compile the contents of the editing window	Compile	Editor
F8	Close, and save the current tab	Close Tab	Editor
F9	Set or delete a breakpoint	Toggle Breakpoint	Editor
F11	List all enums	List Enums	Editor
F12	List all classes	List Classes	Editor
Del	Delete the selection or the next character	Delete	Editor
PgUp	Go to the next page	Next Page	Editor
PgDn	Go to the previous page	Previous Page	Editor
Ctrl-G	Go to the specified page or line	Go To	Editor
Ctrl-L	Delete the line on which the cursor is positioned	Delete Line	Editor
Ctrl-R	Replace the specified text with new text	Replace . . .	Editor

(Continued)

Table D-1. *(Continued)*

Shortcut	Description	Equivalent	Applicable
Ctrl-Y	Redo the previous undone action or command	Redo	Editor
Ctrl-Shift-L	Delete from the cursor position to the end of the line	Delete to End of Line	Editor
Ctrl-Alt-H	Insert contents of a separate file at the cursor position	Insert File . . .	Editor
Ctrl-Home	Go to the top	Start	Editor
Ctrl-End	Go to the bottom	End	Editor
Ctrl-Left Arrow	Move the cursor one word to the left	Previous Word	Editor
Ctrl-Right Arrow	Move the cursor one word to the right	Next Word	Editor
Ctrl-Shift-Home	Go to the top and select all text from the current cursor position	Shift Start	Editor
Ctrl-Shift-End	Go to the bottom and select all text from the current cursor position	Shift End	Editor
Ctrl-Shift-Left Arrow	Move the cursor one word to the left and select all text from the current cursor position	Shift Previous Word	Editor
Ctrl-Shift-Right Arrow	Move the cursor one word to the right and select all text from the current cursor position	Shift Next Word	Editor
Ctrl-Backspace	Delete the word to the left	Ctrl BackSpace	Editor
Ctrl-Space	List properties and methods for the selected object	Look Up Properties/ Methods	Editor
Ctrl-Alt-Space	Look up a selected label or text	Look Up Label/ Text	Editor
Ctrl-Shift-Space	Go to the definition of the selected method	Look Up Definition	Editor
Alt-L	Select the current line	Select Lines	Editor
Alt-M	Show the Scripts pop-up menu	Script	Editor
Alt-S	Save the selected text to a separate file	Save Selected Text . . .	Editor
Alt-U	Cancel selection	Undo Selection	Editor
Alt-Down Arrow	Display optional values or the selected field	Field Help	Editor
Shift-F2	List Axapta language reserved words	List Reserved Words	Editor
Shift-F4	List Axapta's built-in functions	List Built-in Functions	Editor
Shift-F11	List Axapta application objects	List Application Objects	Editor

Shortcut	Description	Equivalent	Applicable
Shift-F9	View breakpoints	Breakpoints	Editor
Shift-PgUp	Go to the previous page, and block	Shift Previous Page	Editor
Shift-PgDn	Go to the next page, and block	Shift Next Page	Editor
Ctrl-N	Jump to the next error message	Next Error	Editor, Infolog
Ctrl-Z	Undo the previous action or command	Undo	Editor, Forms
Ctrl-A	Select the entire text buffer of the active editor	Select All	Editor, AOT
Ctrl-Alt-S	Save the state of an object or editor buffer with a new name	Save As . . .	Editor, AOT
Home	Go to the start of the line, page, or file	Home	Editor, Report Viewer
End	Go to the end of the line, page, or file	End	Editor, Report Viewer
Alt-F7	Display the previous page of records	Previous Page Records	Forms, Report Viewer
Alt-F8	Display the next page of records	Next Page Records	Forms, Report Viewer
Shift-Home	Go to the start of the line, page, or file, and block	Shift Home	Editor, Report Viewer
Shift-End	Go to the end of the line, page, or file, and block	Shift End	Editor, Report Viewer
F2	Edit the name of the application object	Rename	AOT
F7	Compile selected object and subnodes	Compile	AOT
Ctrl-D	Open the AOT	AOT	AOT
Ctrl-Shift-S	Save the state of all modified objects	Save All	AOT
Crtl-O	Run the object	Run	AOT
Alt-Enter	Display the Properties window	Properties	AOT
Alt-Left Arrow	Move the application object one level up	Move Out	AOT
Alt-Right Arrow	Move the application object one level down	Move In	AOT
Ctrl-Space	Extend or reduce the selection	Extend Selection	AOT
Esc	Close the form	Close	Forms
Ctrl-Alt-F4	Display the master table for a selected field	Go to Main Table	Forms
Ctrl-Shift-F3	Remove the setup filter	Remove Filter	Forms
Ctrl-Home	Go to the first record	First Record	Forms

(Continued)

Table D-1. *(Continued)*

Shortcut	Description	Equivalent	Applicable
PgUp	Display the previous page of records (effective only in scrolling screens)	Previous Page Records	Forms
PgDn	Show the next page of records (effective only in scrolling screens)	Next Page Records	Forms
Ctrl-End	Go to the last record	Last Record	Forms
F5	Restore the active record	Restore	Forms
Ctrl-K	Apply the value in the current input field as a filter for the current data source	Apply Filter	Forms
Ctrl-Shift-Home	Go to the first entry field in the form	First Field	Forms
Ctrl-PgUp	Go to the previous field group	Previous Field Group	Forms
Shift-Tab	Go to the next field	Next Field	Forms
Shift-Tab	Go to the previous field	Previous Field	Forms
Tab	Go to the next field	Next Field	Forms
Tab	Go to the previous field	Previous Field	Forms
Ctrl-PgDn	Go to the next field group	Next Field Group	Forms
Ctrl-Shift-End	Go to the last entry field in the form	Last Field	Forms
Alt-F9	Delete a record	Delete Record	Forms
Ctrl-F3	Filter the displayed records by keying in limits	Filter Records	Forms, AOT
Ctrl-Shift-F2	Open the node in viewer/edit mode	Edit	Forms, AOT
F8	Step into function calls	Step Into	Debugger
Shift-F8	Step over function calls	Step Over	Debugger
Ctrl-F8	Step out of the function	Step Return	Debugger
Shift-F9	View breakpoints	Breakpoints	Debugger
F9	Set or delete a breakpoint	Toggle breakpoint	Debugger
Alt-2	View variable	Variable	Debugger
F3	Toggle the exploded/unexploded source	Source	Debugger
F4	Toggle line-number format	Line Numbers	Debugger
Alt-4	Display the system status and the call stack	System Status	Debugger

Shortcut	Description	Equivalent	Applicable
Alt-3	Display the call stack	Call Stack	Debugger
Shift-PgUp	Go to the previous page	Previous Page	Report Viewer
Shift-PgDn	Go to the next page	Report Viewer	Report Viewer
Ctrl-PgUp	Go to the first page	Report Viewer	Report Viewer
Ctrl-PgDn	Go to the last page	Last Page	Report Viewer

APPENDIX E

■■■

License Codes

Axapta is delivered fully functional out of the box; however, what you can and can't do depends on the license codes you have purchased and installed. The process of activating a feature or area of functionality consists of entering the license code in the respective field of the License Information form in the main menu path, Administration ➤ Setup ➤ System ➤ License Information. You will then be prompted automatically to perform a synchronization, which creates any tables necessary to support the new features in the database. Deactivating a module is a simple matter of deleting the license code and performing a synchronization to delete any tables that are no longer necessary.

Table E-1 presents a list of available license codes in version 3.0, and what they provide.

■**Caution** Deleting a license code will delete tables that support the corresponding feature when you synchronize, and any data in such tables will be permanently deleted, so make sure you know what you are doing before deleting a license code—and always make a backup of your database before you do it.

■**Note** The functionality of the modules usually corresponds to the tabs in the top level of the main application menu. However, this is not always the case; for example, the Bank and General Ledger menus are all controlled by the Financials license codes. Going through each license key and associated configuration key is the only way to identify exactly what functionality is controlled by which license code.

■**Tip** You can see all the license codes and configuration keys in the system with the AOT, under the top-level data dictionary node. See the license code property of the configuration keys you are interested in to see which license codes control them.

Note Versions previous to Axapta 3.0 used feature keys, and these are still maintained for backward compatibility; however, there is no direct mapping between them and configuration keys.

Note The functionality of the modules is self-explanatory, so the Functionality column is blank for the modules in the following table.

Table E-1. *Axapta License Codes and Functionality*

Type	Designation	Functionality
System	Base Package	Underlying technology.
	Users	Max number of concurrent users.
	COM Clients	Max number of user connections allowed to the Business Connector.
	AOS Add-On Users	Max number of users allowed on the AOS; this license code is displayed in the License Information form, but it's no longer used.
	Axapta Object Servers	Max number of AOSs.
	Company Accounts	Max number of separate companies allowed.
	Domains	Groups of companies.
	Dimensions	Max number of dimensions available.
	Business Analysis	OLAP.
	Database Log	Logging of database activity.
	Record Level Security	Record-level user access control.
	Microsoft SQL Server Database	Access to MS SQL Server.
	Oracle Database	Access to Oracle RDBMS.
	Commerce Gateway	Commerce Gateway.
	Windows MorphX Development Suite	AOT.
	X++ Source Code	Access to X++ source code. Note that purchasing this license entitles you to the BUS and VAR Layer Runtime licenses as well.
	BUS Layer Runtime	Access to objects and code in the BUS layer, normally used by partners for customization.
	VAR Layer Runtime	Access to objects and code in the VAR layer, normally used by partners for customization.
Modules	Financials I and II	
	Electronic Banking	
	Fixed Assets	

Type	Designation	Functionality
Modules	Sales Force Automation	
	Sales Management	
	Marketing Automation	
	Telemarketing	
	Trade	
	Trade Agreements	
	Logistics	
	Intercompany	
	Master Planning	
	Warehouse Management I and II	
	Resources	
	Project I and II	
	Production I, II, and III	
	Product Builder I, II, III, IV	
	Shop Floor Control I, II, and III	
	Human Resources I, II, and III	
	Business Process Management	
	Balanced Scorecard	
	Questionnaire I and II	
	Cost Accounting I and II	
	ASP Management	
Web	Enterprise Portal Framework	EP and content management, including Web polls and news articles.
	Employee Role	Permission-based role.
	Sales Representative Role	Permission-based role.
	Consultant Role	Permission-based role.
	Customer Role	Permission-based role.
	Vendor Role	Permission-based role.
	Human Resources for EP	HR functionality for EP.
	CRM for EP	CRM functionality for EP.
	Product Builder for EP	Product Builder functionality for EP.
	Questionnaire for EP	Questionnaire functionality for EP.
	Performance Management for EP	Performance management for EP.
	Enterprise Portal Users	Max number of concurrent EP users.
	Web MorphX Development Suite	AOT for Web applications.

APPENDIX F

■ ■ ■

Codes and Mappings

License codes, configuration, security keys, system data, available functionality, and modules vary from one release of Axapta to another. Therefore, it's extremely important that you work with MBS and/or your partners to make sure you have the right codes and keys when going from one version to another. Use this appendix as a reference in determining what you need to deal with.

Caution Failing to have and enter the right codes and keys during an upgrade will very likely result in loss of data, so always make sure that you have a backup of your database before starting an upgrade and that you have identified and purchased the license codes you need, and you know which configuration keys you need.

Here we will look at the objects and code equivalencies between Axapta 2.5 and 3.0, as the focus of this book is Axapta 3.0; however, the same principles apply no matter which version you are upgrading from and to.

Note An important difference between Axapta 2.5 and 3.0 is that access to functionality is managed by feature keys in 2.5 and configuration keys in 3.0. Feature keys are still present in the 3.0 AOT for backward compatibility, however.

Table F-1 gives an overview of the code types and their purposes in versions 2.5 and 3.0 of Axapta. This is important when figuring your way around codes, keys, and authorization to access different types of functionality.

Table F-1. *Codes and Authorization*

Code Type	Axapta 2.5	Axapta 3.0
License codes	Used for enabling and disabling application modules and tools. Codes are provided by MBS and are defined in the kernel.	Used for enabling and disabling application modules and tools. Codes are provided by MBS and are defined in the AOT.
Feature keys	Controls the access rights for user groups to features, menus, and tables.	Exists for backward compatibility.
Configuration keys	Does not exist. The functionality is implemented using feature keys.	Used for enabling and disabling functionality for application modules and tools.
Security keys	Does not exist. The functionality is implemented using feature keys.	Used to control access to application objects by user groups.
Users	Used to identify individual users of the system. Access to functionality is controlled by user groups, and therefore a user that is not associated with a user group can do little or nothing besides log in.	No change.
User groups	Used to control access to functionality. A user group can belong to one or more domains where it can have different sets of permissions.	No change.
Companies	A company defines a business accounting entity.	No change.
Domains	A set of one or more company accounts that enables a single user group to have different levels of access to different sets of companies.	No change.
Record-level security	Does not exist.	Limits access by user groups to specific data sets on a per-company basis.
Form setup	Allows setup of the available controls on a form and is saved per user group by domain.	No longer exists. Form control access is set via the User Group Permissions form and is saved per user group by domain.
Table setup	A separate system to limit access to confidential tables and fields by overruling the feature keys.	No longer exists as a separate system. Security is managed by security keys.

The following tables list the license code names and their mappings from Axapta 2.5 to 3.0 for different functional groups:

- *System license codes*: See table F-1

- *Module license codes*: See table F-2

- *Web license codes*: See table F-3

- *Language license codes*: See table F-4

Partner modules are not indicated, as there are none in the standard package.

Note Which codes you can upgrade from and to and which codes require a new license is not static, so use this appendix as a reference but double-check with MBS on the policy for your region.

System license codes listed in Table F-2 enable and disable basic functionality, most of which is required to do anything in Axapta but is limited by the license type and number of licenses.

Table F-2. *System License Codes*

Axapta 2.5 Code	Axapta 3.0 Code
Version	Base Package
Users	Users
COM Users	COM Clients
AOS Users	AOS Add-On Users
Axapta Object Server(s)	Axapta Object Servers
Company Accounts	Company Accounts
Domain (Group of Companies)	Domains
Dimensions	Dimensions
OLAP	Business Analysis
	Database Log
	Record Level Security
	Microsoft SQL Server Database
	Oracle Database
Commerce Gateway	Commerce Gateway
MorphX Development Suite	Windows MorphX Development Suite
X++ Source Code	X++ Source Code
Runtime VAR	VAR Layer Runtime
Runtime BUS	BUS Layer Runtime

The module license codes listed in table F-3 control access to Axapta's core applications, and the functionality that most users experience as Axapta.

Note Several module license codes have been either split or merged from one version to the next.

Table F-3. *Module License Codes*

Axapta 2.5 Code	Axapta 3.0 Code	Comments
Financial series	Financials I	
Advanced Ledger	Financials II	
Electronic Banking	Electronic Banking	
Fixed Assets	Fixed Assets Sales Force Automation	
Sales Management	Sales Management	
Marketing Automation	Marketing Automation	
Telemarketing	Telemarketing	
Trade series	Trade	
Trade series	Trade Agreements	
Logistics series	Logistics Intercompany	
Master planning	Master Planning	
Warehouse Management	Warehouse Management I, Warehouse Management II	
Resources	Resources	
Project series	Project I, Project II	
Production series	Production I, Production II, Production III	
Product Builder	Product Builder I	
Routing Builder	Product Builder II	
Validation Types	Product Builder III	
Advanced Product Building	Product Builder IV	
Shop Floor Control	Shop Floor Control I	
Shop Floor Control, Job Registration	Shop Floor Control II	
Shop Floor Control, Pay Generation	Shop Floor Control III	
Human Resource	Human Resource I	HRM I in 3.0 requires a minimum of 100 employee records. The number of records available in 3.0 is the same as the number acquired in 2.5, up to 2500. Employee records for HRM in 2.5 can be acquired in packs. Above 2500 employee records in 3.0 requires an unlimited code.
Human Resource II	Human Resource II, Human Resource III	Enables 2500 to unlimited records

Axapta 2.5 Code	Axapta 3.0 Code	Comments
Business Process Management	Business Process Management	
Business Process Management II	Business Process Management	
Business Process Management III	Business Process Management	
Balanced Scorecard	Balanced Scorecard	
Balance Scorecard II	Balanced Scorecard	
Balanced Scorecard III	Balanced Scorecard	
Questionnaire	Questionnaire I	
Questionnaire Integration for Telemarketing	Questionnaire I	In 3.0, Questionnaire I includes questionnaire integration for tele-marketing.
Questionnaire II	No change	
Cost Accounting	Cost Accounting I, Cost Accounting II	
ASP Management	No change	

Web licenses didn't exist as a group in Axapta 2.5 and their codes are nowhere to be seen in the license form; however, most of the codes in 3.0 have equivalents in 2.5, and those are shown in Table F-4.

Table F-4. *Web License Codes*

Axapta 2.5 Code	Axapta 3.0 Code	Comments
Axapta Business Connector	Enterprise Portal Framework, Employee Role, Sales Representative Role	
ESS: Project WebApp	Consultant Role	If you have a 2.5 ESS Web App license, then you get an extra COM client.
CSS WebApp	Customer Role Vendor Role	If you have a 2.5 CSS Web App license, then you get an extra COM client.
ESS: Personnel Information WebApp	Human Resources for EP, CRM for EP	
Product Builder WebApp	Product Builder for EP	
Questionnaire WebApp	Questionnaire for EP, Performance Management for EP	
Axapta Business Connector Users	Enterprise Portal Users	If you have a 2.5 Business Connector Unlimited User license, you get an Enterprise Portal "WEB" Users: Pack of 250 with the 3.0 Web MorphX Development Suite.

In table F-5 we list only language codes that have changed between Axapta 2.5 and 3.0. All others exist in both versions.

Table F-5. *Language License Codes*

Axapta 2.5 Code	Axapta 3.0 Code	Comments
French (Luxembourg) (fr-lu)	French (Belgium) (fr-be)	2.5 language is deprecated
English (Canada) (en-ca)	English (en-us)	2.5 language is deprecated
English (New Zealand) (en-nz)	English (en-au)	2.5 language is deprecated

APPENDIX G

■ ■ ■

Database Compatibility

Axapta can work with Microsoft SQL Server or the Oracle RDBMS for persisting system and business data. However, you must have the right versions of Axapta and the database. This appendix tells you which versions of the respective databases MBS has certified for which version of Axapta from 3.0 and higher.

As a rule, all releases of a database higher then the one certified by MBS work with Axapta 3.0 and the available service packs; however, combinations that are not certified may introduce unknown bugs.

The Oracle compatibility list in Table G-1 is quite straightforward.

Table G-1. *Oracle Compatibility*

Axapta Version	Oracle Client/ODBC Version	Oracle Server Version
3.0	9.0.1 + Oracle Patch 9.0.1.3.1 Patch 5	9.0.1 + Oracle Patch 9.0.1.3.1 Patch 5
3.0 SP1	9.2.0.2	9.2.0.2

MBS has not issued statements of compatibility for Axapta 3.0 SP2 and SP3 with Oracle 9.0.1 + Oracle Patch 9.0.1.3.1 Patch 5 and higher 9i-series releases. However, the service packs are in use in production installations with no known new issues. Axapta 3.0 SP3 has also been tested and is in use at different sites with Oracle Database 10g without known new issues.

As with Oracle, the compatibility statements for Microsoft SQL Server are not very extensive, and likewise Axapta 3.0, SP1, SP2, and SP3 all work with SQL Server 2000 and all its service packs. Table G-2 sums it up.

Table G-2. *Microsoft SQL Server Compatibility*

Axapta Version	Microsoft SQL Server Version	Required ODBC Component Versions
3.0	SQL Server 2000 SP2	2000.80.194, 2000.80.528

■**Note** For security reasons it's important that you install the latest service pack for Microsoft SQL Server.

Generally it's recommended that you use an ODBC driver that corresponds to the SQL Server service pack installed. It will not start with an ODBC driver that's older than the one specified, and you should as a matter of principle use the latest one available; however, newer drivers are known to create issues that can be resolved by falling back to an older version that's certified by MBS.

Axapta functions with most SQL Server drivers, but compatibility issues exist with some ODBC/MDAC combinations. Table G-3 lists certified ODBC-to-MDAC combinations for Microsoft SQL Server 2000.

Table G-3. *MDAC-to-ODBC Compatability*

MDAC Version	ODBC Version
2.6	2000.80.194
2.6 SP1	2000.80.380
2.6 SP2	2000.80.528
2.7 (XP)	2000.81.7713.00
2.7 (.NET)	2000.81.8713.02
2.7 Refresh	2000.81.9001.0

Index

▮Symbols

/*...*/ (asterisk and forward slash), in comments, 385
// (forward slashes), in comments, 385
; (semicolon), 384

▮Numbers

2-tier clients, 28
2-tier mode, 5
 Axapta installation and, 16
 configuring, 34–52, 274
 system design and, 397
3-tier clients
 configuring, 66–68
 installing, 27
3-tier mode, 5, 274
 configuring, 63–68, 275–278
 system design and, 397
1099 functionality, 142

▮A

actions, Activities form (CRM) and, 214
Active Directory, integration with, 92
Active Server Pages (ASP), 256
Activities form (CRM main menu), 205, 214
 Workbook form and, 215
Adjust Global Types form, 58
Admin domain, 98
Admin user groups, 101
Admin users, 101
administration, 89–125, 362–368
administrative tools controls, for Business
 Connector, 51
ALD files (Axapta Label Data files), backups
 and, 120
Analysis Services (Microsoft SQL), 227–229,
 231
AOS (Axapta Object Server), 275, 289
 authenticating users and, 90–93
 installing, 26
 minimum requirements and, 14
 upgrading, 29
 using multiple, 279
AOT (Application Object Tree), 30, 314, 316,
 326–332
 keyboard shortcuts and, 441

APIs (Application Program Interfaces),
 integrating with Axapta, 237–254
application (of Axapta), 4, 11, 275
Application component, 283–287
 installing, 20–22
 upgrading, 29
application layers, 4, 292–295, 420
Application Object Tree. *See* AOT
application object types, 332–345
Application Program Interfaces (APIs),
 integrating with Axapta, 237–254
application server, 13
applications
 architecture and, 274–282
 multiple-application setups and, 281
 working environment and, 296–299
appointments, Activities form (CRM) and,
 214
architecture of Axapta, 4, 273–307
ASP (Active Server Pages), 256
assignments (X++), 385
asterisk and forward slash (/*...*/), in
 comments, 385
ASU load, 394
ASU values, 409
authentication, 44, 90–93
Authorization (general task), 62, 97–112
Auto-Report wizard, 232–234
auto-reports, 227, 232–234
Axapta
 administrative tasks in, 89–125, 362–368
 APIs, integrating with, 237–254
 architecture of, 4, 273–307
 configuring, 33–68
 command-line parameters for, 429–434
 customizing, tools for, 309–354
 deploying, 393–421
 exchanging data with other systems, 371
 hardware/software requirements for,
 11–15
 history of, 2–5
 installing, 11–31
 checklist for, 54, 62
 Microsoft-recommended setup and, 14
 step-by-step, for version 3.0, 18–28
 key strengths of, 1

license for, loading, 56
modifying, 28
multiple-client setups and, 278
post-installation phase for, 54–62
Service Pack 4 and, 162
system design for, 395–410
upgrading, 29, 453
versions of, 3
Web applications and, 8
X++ programming language for, 375–392
Axapta application, 11
Axapta client, 11
Axapta configuration utility (AxConfig.exe)
2-tier configuration mode and, 34–54
3-tier configuration mode and, 63, 66–68
Axapta debugger, 349–352
Axapta desktop, 71–78
Axapta Label Data files (ALD files), backups
and, 120
Axapta Object Server. *See* AOS
Axapta Object Tree. *See* AOT
Axapta server manager utility (AxCtrl.exe), 34

█ B

backups, 120–124
Balanced Scorecard module, 227, 236, 439
bandwidth, 396
Base Enums, 337
base package, 6
batch jobs, 116–118
batch numbering, 160
batch servers, 116
Benchmark tool, 316, 399
benchmarking, 398–410
analyzing data and, 408–410
running benchmarks and, 404–408
Best Practices tool, 352
bills of materials (BOMs), 183–185
BizTalk server (Microsoft), 8
Commerce Gateway and, 252
BOMs (bills of materials), 183–185
branching control statements (X++), 385–387
Business Analysis modules, 15, 227–235, 440
business applications, Application
component and, 283–287
Business Connector, 8, 237, 246–249, 255, 256
Commerce Gateway and, 252
Business Connector tab (Axapta
Configuration Utility), 49–52
business data, backups and, 120
business logic, 5
Business Process Management modules, 439
Business Relation form (CRM main menu),
205, 207–209

█ C

caching, 304–307
categories, 222, 264
category groups, 222
chart of accounts, 143
classes, 332, 338
classes (X++), 379–381
client (of Axapta), 275
Client component, 287–289
installing, 23–26
upgrading, 29
client hardware, minimum requirements
and, 13
Client tab (Axapta Configuration Utility), 38
clients
architecture and, 274–282
multiple-client setups and, 278
updating, 415–420
working environment and, 296–299
CMS (Content Management System), 255,
264–270
code
Best Practices tool and, 352
debugging, 93, 349–352, 441
performance and, 368
Code Explorer, 316
Code Profiler, 316, 352
COM clients, 249
COM Connector. *See* Business Connector
command-line parameters, 429–434
Command menu (Axapta desktop), 76
comments (X++), 385
Commerce Gateway, 8, 238, 252
company accounts, 99, 100
compiler (X++), 348
composite data types, 377
compound statements (X++), 385
Computer combo box (Server Manager), 63
conditional statements (X++), 385–387
Configuration form, 57, 96
configuration keys, 94, 96, 337, 356
Benchmark tool and, 399
configuration tools, 34
configuring
3-tier clients, 66–68
3-tier mode, 63–68
Axapta, 33–68
connection controls, for database
configuration, 41
consultant role, 263
Contact Persons form (CRM main menu),
205, 209–211
Content Management System (CMS), 255,
264–270

context menus, 80
Cost Accounting modules, 440
Cost Center dimension, 138
Cost Price – Hour form, 218
costs journal, 220
coverage groups, 194–195
CRM (Customer Relationship Management) modules, 205–216, 440
cross-references, updating, 60–62
Cube Definition Manager (Business Analysis module), 230
Cube Instances form (Business Analysis module), 230, 231
cubes (3-D views of data), 227–231
currencies, 141–143
customer groups, 147
customer records, 148
Customer Relationship Management (CRM) modules, 205–216, 440
customer role, 263
customer statistics, CRM modules and, 206
customers, quotations and, 211–213
customizations
    distributing, 415, 420
    service packs/hotfixes and, 31

■ **D**

Damgaard A/S, 2
data
    importing/exporting, 122–124, 371
    managing, 118–120
data dictionary, 333, 356–361
data layer, limitations and, 370
data sets (demonstration), 69
data statements (X++), 388
data types, 376–378
    adjusting, 58
    extended, 336
    mappings to SQL Server and Oracle, 359
data, in forms
    saving/restoring, 82
    searching/filtering, 85
DataAreaId field, 358
database compatibility, 31, 459
database field data types, 359
database logging, 114
database password controls
    for Oracle configuration, 47
    for SQL Server configuration, 44
database server, 13, 275
Database Setup page (Client Setup wizard), 24
Database tab (Axapta Configuration Utility), 39–42

Database wizard, 24
databases, 355–373
    connections to, 361
    limitations on, 370
    SQL Server vs. Oracle, 370
debugging, 349–352
    keyboard shortcuts and, 441
    option for, 93
declarations (X++), 384
definition groups, importing/exporting, 121
delete actions, 360
Department dimension, 138
dependencies
    Axapta 3.0 modules and, 7–8
    Web modules and, 8–9
deploying Axapta, 393–421
development codes, 300
development environment, 4, 296, 309–354
development server, minimum requirements and, 14
dialogs, 78, 82
dimensions, 138–140
discussion forums, 264, 265
distributions, 415–421
    customizations and, 415, 420
documentation, 343, 423–427
    accessing, 17, 31
documents
    exchanging between systems, 252
    handling, CRM modules and, 206
domains, 98
    logging, enabling for, 114

■ **E**

Edit menu (Axapta desktop), 75
EDT (Extended Data Types), 336
Electronic Banking module, 435
e-mail messages, 112–114
Employee form (Human Resources module), 128
Employee Option form (CRM modules), 207
employee role, 263
encryption, 66
Enterprise Portal (EP), 8, 255, 261–263
    logging in to, 266
    setting up, 261
error messages, 351
    startup database connection and, 44
events, Activities form (CRM) and, 214
Excel (Microsoft)
    importing/exporting data and, 124
    OLAP cubes and, 231
exception statements (X++), 390
exchange rates, 141

Export wizard, 372
exporting
    data, 122–124, 371
    definition groups, 121
expressions (X++), 378
Extended Data Types (EDT), 336

▮F

fat clients, 5, 27, 275, 277
    system design and, 397
feature keys, 337
features, disabling via license codes, 96
fields
    logging, enabling for, 114
    naming conventions and, 357
    pop-up menus and, 80
File menu (Axapta desktop), 73
files, within folder structures, 282–291
filtering data in forms, 85
Finance Management functional group, 6
Finance modules, 137–150, 435
    cautions for, 137, 149
financial dimensions, 138–140
financial periods, 140
Fixed Assets module, 435
Fixed-Price projects, 217
flat files, 355
folder structures, 282–291
forecast models, 197
forecast plans, 201
Forecast Scheduling, 193
    running the procedure, 203
forecasts, 199
form data, saving/restoring, 82
forms, 79–82, 332, 339–341
    keyboard shortcuts and, 441
forward slash and asterisk (/*...*/), in
        comments, 385
forward slashes (//), in comments, 385
foundation classes (X++), 381
FRx financial reporting software (Microsoft),
        138, 139
full table caching, 305

▮G

General Ledger, 137, 149, 239
    linking system accounts and, 146
    Module APIs and, 243
    processing journals and, 241
General tab (Axapta Configuration Utility),
        36

▮H

hardware/software requirements, 11–15
help system, 344
    initializing, 59

Help Text tool, 316
hotfixes, 30
hours journal, 220
Human Resources modules, 127–135, 439

▮I

IDE (integrated development environment),
        4
IIS (Internet Information Services), 256
Import wizard, 372
importing
    data, 122–124, 371
    definition groups, 121
indexes
    naming conventions and, 357
    re-indexing and, 364
Infolog, 351
    keyboard shortcuts and, 441
Inquiries function group (Main menu item),
        77
Insert method, 239
installation checklist, 54, 62
Installation Portal, 423–425
installing
    3-tier clients, 27
    Application component, 20–22
    Axapta, 11–31, 54–62
        installation checklist for, 54, 62
        Microsoft-recommended setup and, 14
        step-by-step, for version 3.0, 18–28
    Axapta Object Server (AOS), 26
    Client component, 23–26
    hotfixes/services packs, 30
integrated development environment (IDE),
        4
IntelliMorph, 310, 311–315
Intercompany module, 436
Internal projects, 217
internationalization, 2, 301–304, 458
Internet Information Services (IIS), 256
inventory dimensions, 138
Inventory Management modules, 151–163
    cautions for, 152, 163
    closing and adjustment processes in, 161
    journals and, 162
    Production API and, 245
item allocation, 197
item consumption journal, 220
item coverage, 195–197
Item form (Inventory Management
        modules), 152–158

▮J

jobs, 332, 343
journal lines, 240
journal tables, 239

journals, 144, 237, 238–242
    as understood in Axapta, 238
    for inventory management, 162
    naming, 239
    processing, 241
    Production modules and, 191
    Project module and, 220
Journals function group (Main menu item),
    77

■K

kernel (of Axapta), 4
key performance indicators (KPIs), 227
keyboard shortcuts, 441–447
keys, 337
KPIs (key performance indicators), 227

■L

labels, 316, 317–320
language license codes, 458
latency, 396
layered architecture, 4
Ledger Posting form (Project module), 222
ledger postings, 220–223
LedgerJournalCheckPost class, 241
license codes, 94–96, 300, 337, 453–458
    disabling features/modules via, 96
    list of, 449–451
    loading, 56
licenses
    Commerce Gateway and, 252
    development environment and, 310
Light Company data set, 69
Line Property form (Project module), 219
Loan Items form (Human Resources
    module), 132
Loan Types form (Human Resources
    module), 132
log files, 290
logging database changes, 114
Logistics module, 436
logon password controls, for Business
    Connector, 51
loop control statements (X++), 387

■M

macros, X++ and, 338, 390
Main menu (Axapta desktop), 77
maintenance tasks, 112–124
Manage menu (Axapta Configuration Utility),
    52–54
manufacturing, Master Planning module
    and, 193
    Manufacturing modules. *See* Production
modules
maps, 335

Marketing Automation module, 205, 436
Master Planning module, 193–204, 437
    complex processes and, 193, 204
    vs. Master Scheduling, 193
Master Plans form (Master Planning
    module), 201
Master Scheduling, 193
    running the procedure, 203
material requirements planning (MRP), 193
Menu bar (Axapta desktop), 73
menu items, 343
menus, 343
metadata, 4
    backups and, 120
methods (X++), 382–384
Microsoft
    BizTalk server, 8, 252
    Excel, 124, 231
    FRx software, 138, 139
    .NET, 238, 249–252
    OLAP cubes and, 231
    Outlook, CRM functionality and, 206, 214
    SQL Analysis Services, 227–229, 231
Microsoft SQL Server. *See* SQL Server
Microsoft SQL Server Desktop Engine
    (MSDE), 16
Module APIs, 237, 242–246
module license codes, 456
modules, 5–8, 435–440
    Business Analysis, 227–235
    Configuration form for, 57
    CRM (Customer Relationship
        Management), 205–216
    disabling via license codes, 96
    Finance, 137–150
    Human Resources, 127–135
    Inventory Management, 151–163
    journals and, 238–242
    Master Planning, 193–204
    Production, 183
    Project, 217–226
    Sales Management, 205
    Telemarketing, 205
MorphX, 4, 310, 315–345
MRP (material requirements planning), 193
MSDE (Microsoft SQL Server Desktop
    Engine), 16
multilingual support, 2, 301–304, 458

■N

naming conventions, 357
navigation, 71–87
Navision A/S, 3
NAWDC (Navision Axapta Web Deployment
    Client), 416–420
.NET, 238, 249–252

network bandwidth, 396
Network form (Human Resources module), 130
network latency, 396
newLedgerJournalTable static method, 241
news articles (Content Management System), 265
news groups, 426
next() method, 251
Number Sequences API, 245

O

Object Server. *See* AOS
Object Server controls (Server Manager), 64
OLAP (Online Analytical Processing), 227–231
OLAP cubes, 227–231
OLAP Databases form (Business Analysis module), 229
OLAP Parameters form (Business Analysis module), 229
OLAP Servers form (Business Analysis module), 228
Online Analytical Processing (OLAP), 227–231
online polls, 267–270
operating systems, minimum requirements and, 13
operation relations, 187
operations, 186–188
operators (X++), 378
Oracle, 15
    Axapta deployment and, 398
    configuring, 45–47
    data type mappings to, 359
    database compatibility and, 459
    vs. SQL Server, 370
Oracle tab (Axapta Configuration Utility), 45–47
Organization form (Human Resources module), 130
Outlook (Microsoft), CRM functionality and, 206, 214

P

passwords
    parameters for, 110
    troubleshooting, 44
performance
    code and, 368
    measuring, 410–415
    read-ahead caching and, 307
    table caching and, 306
    X++ and, 375
period allocation, 197
Periodic function group (Main menu item), 78

permissions, 97, 102–104
Pivot Table button (Cube Instances form), 231
Planned Orders form, 204
polls, 267–270
pop-up menus, 80
post-installation, 54–62
posting profiles, 148
preloading tables, 49
pricing, forms for, 218
primitive data types, 377
printer icon, accessing auto-report functionality via, 232
printers, allowing on AOS, 92
Product Builder modules, 438
Production API, 245
production environments, 299
Production modules, 183–191, 183, 438
production orders, 189–191
production scheduling, 200
project groups, 220–222
Project modules, 217–226, 437
    creating projects and, 224
Project tool, 316, 320–326
projects
    Project tool for, 316, 320–326
    types of, 217
PSA functional group, 6
purchase orders, 165, 173
    Commerce Gateway and, 252
Purpose dimension, 138

Q

queries, 332, 342
Query Definition forms, 84
Questionnaire modules, 440
questionnaires, CRM modules and, 206
Quotations form (CRM main menu), 205, 211–213

R

RecId field, 358
record-ahead caching, 307
record caching, 304
record-level security, 111
record view caching, 307
recruitment projects, 133–135
referential constraints, 360
referential integrity, 360
relations, 360
Report Viewer, keyboard shortcuts and, 441
Report wizard, 227, 234–235, 315
reporting, 227–235
reports, 78, 83–85, 332, 341
Reports folder (Business Analysis module), 227

Reports function group (Main menu item), 78
resources, 343
resources for further reading
    Active Directory integration, 124
    administration, 124
    Axapta, 7, 423–427
        architecture of, 307
        configuring, 69, 124
    Balanced Scorecard module, 236
    business process management, 135
    Commerce Gateway, 254
    CRM modules, 216
    data sets, 69
    Database wizard, 373
    debugging, 354
    development environment, 354
    finance, 150
    human resources management, 135
    Internet, 271
    inventory management, 163
    manufacturing, case studies of, 191
    Master Planning, 204
    navigation, 87
    Oracle, 124, 373
    projects, 226
    Server Manager, 69
    shop floor control, 191
    Web Deployment Client, 421
    X++, best practices and, 392
Resources module, 437
restoring form data, 82
revenue journal, 220
roles (user roles), 263
routes, 188
runtime codes, 300

S
safety stock journals, 193, 202
Sales Force Automation module, 205, 435
sales invoices, Commerce Gateway and, 252
Sales Management module, 205, 436
sales orders
    Commerce Gateway and, 252
    CRM modules and, 206
Sales Price – Costs form, 219
Sales Price – Hour form, 218
Sales Price – Revenue form, 219
sales role, 263
sales tax, 145
saving form data, 82
schema mapping, 253
SCM functional group, 6
searching data in forms, 85
security keys, 94, 97, 337
security, record-level, 111

semicolon (;), in X++ statements, 384
serial numbering, 160
Server Manager, 63–66
Server Manager controls, 63
Server tab (Axapta Configuration Utility), 65
Server/server component. *See* AOS (Axapta Object Server)
servers. *See also* Oracle; SQL Server (Microsoft)
    architecture and, 274–282
    testing, 14
    working environment and, 296–299
Service Pack 4, 162
service packs, 30
settings controls
    for 3-tier configuration, 66
    for Business Connector, 50
    for database configuration, 39
    for Oracle configuration, 46
    for SQL Server configuration, 43
    for tracing configuration, 48
Setup function group (Main menu item), 78
Shop Floor Control modules, 183, 438
shortcut keys, 86
Shutdown control group, for 3-tier configuration, 66
sizing, for Axapta deployment, 393–395
Skills form (Human Resources module), 131
Skills Types form (Human Resources module), 131
software requirements, 11–15
SQL Analysis Services (Microsoft), 227–229, 231
SQL Server (Microsoft), 15
    Axapta deployment and, 398
    data type mappings to, 359
    database compatibility and, 459
    vs. Oracle, 370
SQL Server tab (Axapta Configuration Utility), 42–45
statements (X++), 384–390
    compound, 385
    data, 388
    exception, 390
    loop control, 387
Status bar (Axapta desktop), 78
Summary projects, 217
Supply Chain Management, 6
synchronization, 356, 361
Synchronize item, 59
system accounts, 146
system design, 395–410
system fields, 357
system license codes, 455
system variables, 369

T

table collections, 99, 338
table methods, 361
tables, 332, 334
    logging, enabling for, 114
    naming conventions and, 357
    temporary, 356
TAPI (Telephone Application Programming
        Interface), linking CRM functionality
        to, 206
tasks, Activities form (CRM) and, 214
Telemarketing module, 205, 436
Telephone Application Programming
        Interface (TAPI), linking CRM
        functionality to, 206
temporary tables, 356
terminal server, system design and, 397
test environments, 298
testing server, minimum requirements and,
        14
thin clients, 5, 28, 277
    system design and, 397
Time & Material projects, 217
Title bar (Axapta desktop), 72
Toolbar (Axapta desktop), 76
tools. *See* utilities
Tools menu (Axapta desktop), 75
tracing database activity, 364–366
Tracing tab (Axapta Configuration Utility),
        47–49
Trade Agreements module, 436
Trade module, 436
    Module APIs and, 243
transactions (X++), 368, 389
troubleshooting
    authentication/passwords, 44
    Business Connector, 247
    tracing database activity, 364–366
Tuning - Autogenerate controls, for database
        configuration, 42
tuning control, for Oracle configuration,
        47

U

UNICODE support, Axapta 4.0 and, 304
Update Cross-Reference form, 60–62
Upgrade wizard, 29
upgrading Axapta, 29
    codes/keys, cautions and, 453
user groups, 97, 101–104
user roles, 263
user setup tool (IntelliMorph), 311, 315

users, 97, 104–110
    authenticating, 90–93
    authorization for, 97–112
    creating accounts for, 104
    Customer Relationship Management
        (CRM) modules and, 205–216
    logged-on, determining, 112
    Web, 257, 263
utilities
    Benchmark tool, 399
    configuration, 34
    for customizing Axapta, 309–354
    for development, 309–345
    Web Deployment Client, 416–420

V

variables (X++), 379
vendor groups, 147
vendor records, 148
vendor role, 263
Version Update, 316
views, 336
virtual company accounts, 99, 138
virtual fields/virtual columns, 358
Visual MorphXplorer, 316

W

Warehouse Management API, 244
Warehouse Management modules, 437
warehouses, 158–160
warning thresholds for preloading controls,
        49
Web applications, 8, 352
    Axapta versions and, 256
    Enterprise Portal and, 255
Web Deployment Client tool, 416–420
Web Development tools, 316
web journal, 220
Web license codes, 457
Web MorphX, 310
Web object types, 343
web sites
    Axapta, 7
    creating, 258–261
    for Axapta documentation, 426
    logging in to, 260, 266
Web users, 257, 263
wizards, 316
    Application Setup, 20–22
    Auto-Report, 232–234
    Client Setup, 23, 27
    Database, 24

Import/Export, 372
Program Maintenance, 28
Report, 227, 234–235, 315
Upgrade, 29
work centers/work center groups, 185
Workbook form (CRM main menu), 205,
    215

X

X++, 4, 310, 345–349, 368
    syntax of, 375–392
X++ editor, 345–348
XML documents, exchanging between
    systems, 252
XPO files, 30

Printed in the United States
By Bookmasters